**WORLD YEARBOOK
OF EDUCATION 1981**

World Yearbook of Education 1981
Education of Minorities

Edited by **Jacquetta Megarry** *(Series Editor)*
Stanley Nisbet *(Associate Editor)*
and **Eric Hoyle** *(Consultant Editor)*

Subject Adviser: **Ken Eltis** *Macquarie University*

**Kogan Page, London/Nichols Publishing
Company, New York**

Previous titles in this series:

World Yearbook of Education 1979
Recurrent Education and Lifelong Learning
Edited by Tom Schuller and Jacquetta Megarry
Consultant Editors: Gerry Fowler and Myron Atkin

World Yearbook of Education 1980
Professional Development of Teachers
Edited by Eric Hoyle and Jacquetta Megarry
US Consultant Editor: Myron Atkin

First published 1981 by Kogan Page Ltd,
120 Pentonville Road, London N1 9JN

British Library Cataloguing in Publication Data

World yearbook of education. — 1981
  1. Education — Yearbooks
  370'.5 L101

ISBN 0-85038-457-5
ISSN 0084-2508

First published in the USA 1981
by Nichols Publishing Company,
PO Box 96, New York, NY 10024

ISBN (US) 0-89397-105-7
Library of Congress Catalog Card No 32-18413

Printed in Great Britain by The Anchor Press Ltd
and bound by Wm Brendon and Son Ltd,
both of Tiptree, Essex

Contents

List of contributors

Anjali Purewal, Research Fellow, Department of Education,   *Chapter 20*
University of Keele
Bert-Olaf Rieck, Germanistisches Seminar der Universität   *Chapter 22*
Heidelberg
Catrin Roberts, Lecturer in Sociology, Education Department,   *Chapter 9*
Manchester University
Derrick Sharp, Senior Lecturer, Department of Education,   *Chapter 3*
University College of Swansea
Dr J J Smolicz, Reader in Education, Department of Education,   *Chapter 1*
University of Adelaide
Carew Treffgarne, Lecturer, Department of Education in Developing   *Chapter 12*
Countries, University of London Institute of Education
Dr Gajendra Verma, Senior Lecturer in the Psychology of Education,   *Chapter 15*
Postgraduate School of Studies in Research in Education,
University of Bradford
Dr Keith Watson, Lecturer in Comparative Education, Reading   *Chapter 6*
University
Doug White, Member of the Centre for the Study of Innovation,   *Chapter 19*
School of Education, La Trobe University, Melbourne
Dr Glyn Williams, Lecturer in Sociology, Department of Social   *Chapter 9*
Theory and Institutions, University College of North Wales,
Bangor

The affiliations given above do not imply identification wth the views expressed by the authors, who are writing as individuals.

Preface

The phrase 'education of minorities' raises a variety of questions. As a *World Yearbook* theme it demands clarification. We are using the word 'minority' to refer not to relative numbers but to 'the condition of being inferior or subordinate'. This could be taken to include students with a variety of handicaps — physical, intellectual, socioeconomic, cultural; pupils with low literacy or language problems; and victims of race or sex discrimination. However, we have concentrated in this book on the problems of students who are disadvantaged by differences of culture and language, especially ethnic minorities who do not possess the background, attributes and skills of the dominant group and are thus distanced from the sources of power and status in the country they inhabit.

In recent years, consciousness of ethnic identity and awareness of minority status have been growing rapidly all over the world. In places like Quebec, where both have been recurring and well-known themes, the problems have been underscored by politically vocal and even violent protests. In Britain, long-standing assumptions of ethnic homogeneity have been challenged by the growth of separatist political parties in Scotland and Wales, escalation of sectarian violence in Northern Ireland and the eruption of racial tension in Bristol and Brixton. Deeper and more wide-spread problems underlie these violent surface signs, and they recur in different forms all over the world. Given the essentially comparative nature of a *World Yearbook*, then, this choice of theme is easy to justify.

In our interpretation of the theme, we recognize that cultural, linguistic, psychological and sociological disadvantage are all closely connected, and all four strands run through this book. We make no apology for selecting the language and culture themes for strongest emphasis. Language is not only a clearly 'visible' identifier of many minority groups — more reliable, often, than physical characteristics. It is also the vehicle by which human beings persuade, manipulate and exercise power over each other — witness the way that a toddler's growing command of language enables him progressively to enchant and to tyrannize adults. Anyone who has been in the helpless position of a traveller far from home with no command of the language by which he is surrounded — lost, for example, on the Moscow underground — knows the need to regress to childlike techniques for soliciting help. The position of an immigrant child with no access to the language of the classroom is even more defenceless. Language, competence and power are intimately connected.

Another recurring theme is how far the language and cultural *differences* between minority and dominant groups should be viewed as *deficits*. Cultural relativists argue that one culture is not superior to another, nor one language richer, though a multilingual individual might be considered better equipped, and a multicultural individual better educated, for life in the modern world than a person who is limited to one language and culture. On this view, the problem is not merely how to educate minorities to know about and adapt to the world of the majority, but also how to educate the majority in minority ways, culture and language, not just so that they understand the problems of the 'under-dog', but because their education is otherwise incomplete. In other words, *all* ethnic groups — dominant or subordinate, indigenous or immigrant, privileged or under-privileged — should be educated for the multicultural society.

There are problems in this standpoint which will be discussed shortly. However, it should first be noted that it is a welcome corrective to the ethnocentrism of centuries. English has a long history as a language of dominance, even of oppression. The language of Shakespeare, Dickens and Tennyson has thus become associated with the experience of exploitation, colonialism and even racial persecution. Even today, the British abroad are partly insulated from the rude discovery that English is itself a 'foreign' language because so many 'foreigners' take the trouble to learn English and others already speak a variety of it (albeit 'mispronounced') because they are descended from early emigrants or live in a country where the English-speaking minority controls power and resources. The realization that it is just one language among many requires the same kind of Copernican shift in world-view that I remember experiencing in my early teens on picking up an atlas in the Soviet Union, only to find that Britain is not, after all, at the centre of the world. Over the last seven years, teaching university summer sessions in bilingual, multicultural Montreal (where this book was conceived) has driven home this lesson which could not be taught at school in England. However enlightened and well-informed teachers may be, however free of racial prejudice, however many second languages are on offer, however 'balanced' the syllabuses taught in geography, history, religious studies . . . it takes more than verbal learning to shake unthinking egocentrism and ethnocentrism. Direct experience of living and learning with other ethnic groups may be a short-cut to greater awareness of other cultures and races, but unless the dominant group is physically displaced from its home ground, its complacency is unlikely to be shaken.

Even the problem of deciding what language should be spoken and taught in school presents intractable difficulties. Let us look at a simplified numerical example. If an immigrant group is tiny (say 0.1 per cent of the population) educators should presumably provide immersion classes for the minority adults and children in the majority language, to assist their assimilation and to improve their educational opportunities and life chances; they are free to retain their own language and culture 'after hours'. If the proportion of immigrants were to rise to say, 10 per cent (and in practice this might be politically resisted) there would be arguments for providing appropriate texts, materials and teacher training for schooling in the minority language. The immigrant minority, becoming increasingly vocal, may itself press for native-language schooling. The dangers here are not only that separate schooling becomes inferior, but also that separate is visible, and perhaps provocative of backlash: 'Why don't they go home if they don't want to learn our language and ways?'

If the immigrant minority continues to grow, the problem changes in nature. To take an extreme case, if the proportion were to rise to 50 per cent, the question becomes whether native children should not be taught in the *'minority'* language as a matter of course; the textbooks and curriculum would certainly require major revisions as a result of the minority cultural heritage and presence. A bilingual nation with both cultural heritages enjoying equal status might be thought the ideal solution, though no country in the world has achieved it. Not only is bilingualism expensive to implement, but the likelihood is that natives will predominate in positions of power in the country, so that the 'majority' language will continue to enjoy higher status and 'majority' culture to be more prestigious than that of the 'minority' even if natives were to become numerically inferior.

In any event, nowhere are things so simple as this. Countries are never linguistically homogenous in the first place; ethnic minorities are indigenous as well as immigrant. In Britain there are not only several indigenous Gaelic languages (still spoken to the exclusion of English in places) but also a bewildering variety of dialects quite baffling to the speaker of Standard English, all with distinctive sentence structures as well as pronunciation and vocabularies. The social and political significance of Received Pronunciation and Standard English is still considerable, and in some cases it is taught almost as a quasi-foreign language to dialect-speakers. Moreover, the range of countries from which Britain receives immigrants would suggest that conceding non-English language state-supported schooling as a right to one immigrant group could set an expensive and perhaps unwise precedent for all the others. It also reminds us of the dangers of regarding 'minorities' as a homogenous group when they are often as different from each other as from the dominant group. Nevertheless, this hypothetical example does at least illustrate the way in which a *quantitative* change (increase in the size of the immigrant influx) demands a *qualitative* change in the educational response required. It also illustrates some of the genuine difficulties for well-intended politicians and educators to decide what policy is best, let alone how to implement it.

Part 1 of this volume consists of an examination of such concepts, issues and trends. Smolicz explores the subtle relationship between culture and ethnicity and provides a profound challenge to the simplistic assumption that assimilation (or 'dominant monism') is an inevitable or desirable fate for ethnic minorities. Indeed, his South-East Asian evidence that biculturalism can be the norm reminds us that the very *assumption* of monoculturalism may itself be culturally determined. Cultures should, he argues, accommodate to plurality rather than try to assimilate minorities into the dominant majority.

Edwards starts from the discontinuity which often exists between the culture of the pupils and that of the school, and asks how far pupils should be expected to respond to schools and how far schools should adapt to the backgrounds and equipment of their pupils. He points out that special intervention programmes and compensatory education generally often attract a stigma and that many ethnic minority leaders are opposed to cultural pluralism. Though his message is thus in tension with Smolicz', this is a product of his concentration on psychological and linguistic aspects of disadvantage, where Smolicz emphasizes cultural and ethnic plurality. Part 1 is concluded by Sharp's examination of current trends and future developments in education's response to the challenges of multi-cultural education. He gives examples of the kind of work in research, curriculum development and language policy which is just beginning.

Part 2 presents a range of national policies on minority group education for comparison and contrast. Grant discusses the relationships between language, educational level and economic development in the Soviet Union, the largest and most linguistically diverse state in the world. D'Anglejan surveys the scene in Canada, a country where the language issue has become publicly and politically identified with the Quebec separatist movement. She discusses provincial policies on the education of 'official' Anglophone and Francophone minorities, as well as of immigrant groups from other countries and native Inuit and Indians, and how they are influenced by federal policy on bilingualism and biculturalism.

Though smaller in land area than the Soviet Union, the People's Republic of China is the most *numerous* multi-ethnic country in the world; Watson shows how misleading is its reputation as ethnically homogeneous. The Han Chinese have been the dominant group but the presence of over 50 minority nationalities in the strategically important border regions has presented a strong incentive to successive governments to try to win and retain their allegiance. Watson illustrates how first the Nationalists and then the Communists have built up a network of schools for border nationalities and tried to achieve assimilation despite changing rhetoric about 'self-determination' for minority groups.

Greenland explores the inevitable tensions between on the one hand hard-headed administrative, political and economic demands and on the other hand the conventional values of 'curriculum development' as seen by educators in the context of Africa. The principles embodied in the Lagos Declaration pose the problem of how the school system can be flexible enough to equalize the access and achievement of various racial groups while at the same time remaining sufficiently uniform to contribute towards national unity and the fulfillment of manpower needs. Finally Little tries to identify the strategies for an acceptable national educational policy for the United Kingdom, which would help not only to combat the negative effects of racism, distortion and hatred but also to meet the special needs of ethnic groups in a positive way, while at the same time preparing all pupils for fuller life in a multiracial society.

Part 3 is specifically directed towards the problems of the relative status and currency of majority and minority languages in four parts of the world — Wales, Malaysia, America and parts of Africa. Williams and Roberts develop the notion of power relations, rather than numerical strength, as the key to the concept of majority or minority. They go on to give a penetrating and controversial analysis of the social and economic background against which the place of the Welsh language has become salient in recent decades, and raise questions about the implications for linguistic minorities elsewhere in the world. Platt traces the complex and interesting relationships between Chinese and other languages in Malaysia and illustrates how they are affected both by the growing sense of identity among the Chinese community there and by Malaysia's language policies.

It is difficult enough to generalize about contemporary American schools, but Cordasco and Bernstein manage to isolate common factors in their response to the needs of Puerto Rican children — namely the pressures towards assimilation, English language acquisition and Anglo-Saxon conformism. Finally Treffgarne provides welcome relief from preoccupation with the English language with an account of the implications of the use of Swahili in East Africa. The logistical problems of providing mother tongue education for everyone are overwhelming, and major African languages have to vie for status and currency with English, French and Portuguese which still enjoy government favour as official languages.

Part 4 shifts the balance of interest from the linguistic to the sociological by examining the distribution and determinants of educational opportunity for minority groups. Still drawing on African material, Dorsey looks at the past and future of educational opportunity in Zimbabwe, a country whose history demonstrates rigid social and economic divisions based on ascribed race. Bhatnagar and Hamalian examine how cultural minority immigrants in Canada lack power, status and access to opportunities. This provides a fresh perspective on the dilemma of whether attempts to preserve minority language and culture among ethnic minorities must end by being 'patronizing, condescending and dysfunctional' or whether they could be extended to the majority in a move towards the multicultural society.

The issue is taken up with a vocational emphasis by Verma and Ashworth, who look at the relationships between cultural conflict, self-esteem and the education system among South Asian adolescents in Britain. The concept of vocational choice presupposes both opportunity and aspiration, and they document how cultural, social and personality factors combine and conspire to limit both, even in the absence of overt or deliberate discrimination. An ethnic minority's estimation of its own worth not only influences its members' individual self-images, but also affects its valuation by the rest of the community in the job market and as citizens. Part 4 concludes with Poole's comprehensive account of

Australian research on educational opportunity for immigrant minority groups. She portrays disadvantage as primarily language-related, but connected with a lack of intellectual and economic resources and also with varying levels of commitment to schooling. Like Dorsey, she also notes the compound disadvantage of ethnic minority females, especially in respect of lower cultural expectations of their performance and aspirations; as with social class disadvantage in Britain, the effects of such compound disadvantages do not seem to add up, but multiply.

Part 5 consists of descriptions of individual innovations in minority group education, including the education of teachers. The first three chapters cover the education of indigenous minorities. Orvik covers recent approaches to cross-cultural education in Alaska, underlining just how different the 49th State is from the rest of the United States, with its huge size, sparse population, immense natural wealth and 20 distinct native languages. Elsewhere in the same continent, Eastman describes recent developments in the treatment of the American Indian. She traces the changes in US education policy toward Indian self-determination and the origins of the Indians' problems. New approaches include the schools contracted to Indian groups, who include Indian culture in the curriculum and take active steps to involve the community. From America to Australia, White shifts the discussion to materials and methods for teaching Aboriginal children. Here the argument for bilingualism is partly based on self-respect, ethnic identity and respect for the culture. White shows how identity ceases to be a problem when autonomy is asserted.

The next two chapters describe developments in in-service teacher education in England and Wales. Dunn, Eggleston and Purewal describe the trend away from narrow instructional courses on teaching English as a second language. A broader education of teachers about and for a multicultural society has manifested itself in a wide diversity of courses offered by a range of institutions. One such course at Bradford College is described by Chambers, its Vice-Principal, who sees this approach to teacher education as a consequence of the academic policy of the comprehensive community college ideal. Finally, Gutfleisch and Rieck describe recent teaching programmes for adult immigrant workers and their children in West Germany. These *Gastarbeiter* come from a variety of European countries, and they create a new social class below all previous social classes, both occupationally and socially. The philosophy behind the programme to meet their needs is clearly a deficit model in which it is assumed that the immigrants wish to be assimilated and imbued with the culture and language of the host country.

This 'benevolent paternalism' characterizes many countries' approaches to immigrant minorities and pervades our unconscious thinking, perhaps because we like to think that 'we were here first'. The challenge of cultural relativism is most sharply felt when we consider the treatment of indigenous minorities and ask ourselves who should learn from whom.

Jacquetta Megarry
Glasgow, May 1981

Part 1:
Concepts, issues and trends

1. Culture, ethnicity and education: multiculturalism in a plural society

J J Smolicz

Summary: The chapter defines ethnic or minority groups in cultural terms. A society that has more than one ethnic group may develop in a number of different ways. The ultimate outcome depends in large measure on the prevailing values adopted by the various cultural groups within society, especially the dominant group, while another factor is the relation between the core values of minority and majority groups.

The conceptual issues raised by cultural pluralism are also discussed. Two types of pluralism are distinguished, one of a separatist kind, which occurs at a communal level, and the second of a kind which takes place at the level of the individual. The latter type of pluralism can be encouraged in such a way that members of all ethnic groups are able to participate in economic and public life while still maintaining, developing and sharing their distinctive cultural traditions in other areas of life.

To develop cultural pluralism within individuals it is usually vital to maintain the ethnic language, which must be treated in a similar way to the language(s) of the dominant group(s), which all people share as a means of communication. We can distinguish between language-centred cultures, which decay on the loss of mother tongue, and those which can be maintained with the aid of other core values. Internalized cultural pluralism is only likely to be achieved if the state makes provision for the transmission of ethnic languages and cultures within the national education system, so that the culture of the home is maintained, all cultures can be shared, and the stability of society can be strengthened.

Ethnicity and culture

The possession of a distinct culture provides one of the most important identifying characteristics of an ethnic group (Smolicz, 1979). Culture is not peculiar to the individual, but depends on sharing, participation and transmission within a group. This does not mean that all members of the same ethnic group are completely identical in their ways of thinking and acting: social class, family and, above all, individual differences, always exist. Nevertheless, membership of an ethnic group implies sharing patterns of living with other participants. The actions and attitudes of individual members are therefore likely to bear a 'family' resemblance to one another.

In many ethnically plural societies, a further distinction needs to be made between the ethnic group that holds the dominant position through its numbers, early settlement or impact upon the main political and economic institutions, and minority or subordinate groups that have much less influence on policy-making, and limited access to resources.

In societies where there is one distinct majority group and a number of minority ethnic groups, there have been attempts to relegate ethnic cultures to sub-sets of the culture of the majority (Gollnick, 1980). It must be recognized, however, that ethnic minority cultures have their own independent historical continuity, and although they may interact with other cultures in a plural society, this does not make them a mere facet of the dominant group's tradition. The Greek language is not a derivative of English, even though spoken Greek in America or Australia may contain some words that are borrowed from English.

In this sense, ethnic cultures cannot be equated with working class sub-culture, teenage pop 'culture', or gay life-style — all of which may be regarded as variants on each of the majority and minority ethnic cultures in a society, since they relate only to a slice of the group's life. To use a musical metaphor, such slices or segments of culture represent variations upon a theme, while ethnic cultural pluralism refers to the different themes in a composition, rather than to variations upon any one of them. This is not to say that cultural analysis should be limited to the discussion of multiculturalism in relation to ethnic minority groups alone. An analysis of other cultural differentiation, especially in relation to class and other specialized styles of life, is also important, but this should be done in terms of sub-cultures which are but sub-sets of the parental cultural stock. By their relegation to the level of a sub-culture, ethnic minority cultures are implicitly made part of the dominant culture. Such cultural reductionism has not occurred in the plural societies of Asia, such as India, Malaysia or Singapore, where ethnic groups are often of a substantial size and have managed to preserve their cultural distinctiveness over many generations (Clammer, 1976, 1980).

Dominant monism

Once different ethnic groups have appeared within a given society, be it through conquest or other movements of population, the question arises as to their ultimate fate in relation to the majority group. Does government policy generally, and the education system in particular, work to eliminate, modify or encourage the cultural diversity they introduce? In some instances the ideal of a monocultural state has remained unquestioned and been enforced either by coercion or by the all-pervasive ideological orientation of assimilation, or *dominant monism*. In America and Australia, for example, this was manifested in the prevailing social pressure for Anglo-conformism (Gordon, 1978: 184; Australian Schools Commission Committee on Multicultural Education, 1979: 6). All individuals, no matter what their ethnic origin, were expected to adopt the norms of the dominant Anglo culture (which derived from the British Isles), and to give up their own cultural heritage. Schools were consciously seen as one of the most effective instruments of achieving the cultural assimilation of ethnic children, not only through 'immersion' in the ways of the majority, but also by elimination of their native cultures (Martin, 1978).

In several countries assimilation policies are now regarded as both outmoded and as failures. There is, however, a tendency among those who still favour assimilationist and monistic outcomes to adopt the multicultural phraseology but to attempt to achieve their ends by relegating ethnic cultures to residues (Kovacs and Cropley, 1975: 123). Through the breaking of such cultures into fragments, their impact upon the majority is reduced, while at the same time the transmission to the next generation is made less likely. This type of reductionism is characterized by a policy of discouraging ethnic or minority languages, since in many cultures the loss of the native tongue represents a prelude to their disintegration. Under the guise of multiculturalism, the goals of assimilation can then be brought nearer without incurring the odium of denying cultural rights to the minorities.

Hybrid monism

Theoretically, it is possible to conceive of the emergence of another form of cultural uniformity throughout society. Under the ideological orientation of cultural blending or synthesis (also labelled as *hybrid monism*), all the different cultures present in society would be welded together in some mix or hybrid, containing elements of each, in different proportions and combinations. Society would thus eventually become monistic, with a single culture. The new generation growing up, or perhaps its children, would come to the point where different cultural heritages would have little bearing on its current activities, since all would share instead the newly-evolved hybrid culture.

It is not clear, of course, which elements of each culture would be retained or in what form, nor who would decide these issues. What language, for example, would be used? In literate societies with standardized written forms, it is difficult to envisage the evolution of some new kind of jargon, creole or patois. It seems likely, therefore, that this approach would result in children being brought up to communicate in the language of the dominant group, and that alone. Hence, at least within the linguistic sphere, the situation would be that of dominant, rather than hybrid, monism (Smolicz and Lean, 1980a).

Cultural pluralism

(i) Separatism

Where ethnic cultural differences persist in society, at least two main types of pluralism may be distinguished. One form is the coexistence of distinct cultures within the same society, but almost in separate compartments, and with very little interaction between them. For example, if this kind of pluralism were to develop in the Australian, New Zealand or Canadian settings, it would imply the existence of two main categories. Individuals labelled 'Anglo-Australian' would speak nothing but English and follow exclusively British cultural traditions. Such people would collectively represent the majority or dominant group in this country. The other category would be made up of various 'minority ethnics' who adhered to their native traditions and ignored the majority culture as far as possible. Some of their children might reject their ethnic culture and might try to join the majority group. Alternatively, it would be possible for these minorities to maintain and develop their heritage into the second and future generations and thus perpetuate cultural separation of society.

Under this arrangement, separate government agencies and school systems would be established to ensure that children had maximum immersion in their home culture, with little consideration being given to interaction with children from other ethnic groups. Thus, even though society as a whole would be pluralistic, the members of the various dominant and minority backgrounds would remain largely within the confines of their own ethnic cultures. Those belonging to minority groups would become involved in the culture of other groups only in so far as it was necessary for economic and political coexistence.

The underlying assumption behind this theory is that of cultural separatism. Individuals are considered to be immersed either in the Anglo or in the ethnic cultural tradition. Society is pluralistic, but not at the individual level, since each person has to cope with only one language and only one cultural tradition. The concept of this type of separatism within the confines of one state is not a 'purely' theoretical one, but must be viewed as a possible outcome in a number of societies (such as Great Britain or West Germany) which until recently had mainly homogeneous populations and which received 'injections' of new arrivals from vastly different cultural or racial sources.

(ii) Multiculturalism

According to the second interpretation, cultural pluralism is seen to be a characteristic not only of society as a whole, but also of its individual members. In a society where one group predominates, members of minority groups would come to acquire the dominant culture, up to the level appropriate to their personal needs and aptitudes. What multiculturalism means, however, is that these same minority group members would be allowed and even encouraged to maintain and develop their native languages and cultures alongside the dominant one. The best example of such bicultural individuals is provided by a 'balanced' bilingual who can switch from one language to another with ease. Bilingualism is, however, only one facet of biculturalism, because other aspects of the heritage and family relationships may also be involved.

In such a society, multiculturalism would also entail at least some members of the majority group acquiring aspects of minority cultures and internalizing them for their own special purposes. As the example of several South-east Asian countries suggests, biculturalism can be accepted as a perfectly natural phenomenon in society (Llamzon, 1979). It is the monocultural individual who is regarded as unusual, rather than vice versa.

Multiculturalism, as defined here, implies that individuals from both majority and minority backgrounds would have the opportunity to make use of more than one culture in their everyday lives, be it in language, family life, social manners, ideology, or the higher spheres of cultures, such as literature and art. This approach does not assume that every individual is a bicultural, as in the case of the balanced bilingual, although the greater the number of such individuals the better. It *is* assumed, however, that everyone is positively disposed towards the idea of a multicultural society and participates in it to the extent that his ability and desires permit. Such a multicultural orientation may also be termed internalized cultural pluralism (or dualism), since the cultures concerned are internalized within one and the same person.

The discussion of this type of 'internal' multiculturalism shows that cultural diversity need not be divisive; it is assimilated at the most intimate, personal level, through being reconciled within each individual and transmuted by him in his daily life. Such biculturalism may create tensions but, as T S Eliot has pointed out, the greatest creativity often takes place at the 'friction-edge of cultures'.

A recent education report issued in Australia underlines the valuable aspects of such creative tension. It maintains that:

> the diversity which throws into daily juxtaposition varied beliefs, attitudes and approaches to living can be an enriching force in society. . . . Major intellectual, social and other developments have often occurred when there has been creative tension among competing ideas and approaches to life. (Australian Commonwealth Education Portfolio, 1979: paragraph 2.10)

Shared values in a multicultural society

In countries such as the United States, Canada or Australia, multiculturalism has been internalized within many individuals, although ethnic diversity is mainly concentrated in domestic and family life, and within neighbourhood and friendship networks, youth and folklore organizations, and social clubs.

However, in the sphere of political, economic, legal and educational affairs, mainstream national institutions exist which act as unifying forces in society. Underpinning such institutions and giving them meaning are shared values to which members of all ethnic groups generally subscribe (Smolicz, 1979: 15-17). These provide a kind of ideological umbrella which is especially important in a democratic society, since it is only such an agreement upon fundamentals of life that can guarantee stability and cohesion in a culturally plural setting. Authoritarian societies can manage their affairs by coercion, but even they usually search for some set of shared beliefs, be they religious or political, to reinforce their rule. One of the most important of such supra-ethnic or universal values is commitment to the political unity of the state.

It may be that the supra-ethnic values concerned were originally shared by members of only one of the ethnic groups, and that in the course of time the group concerned managed to have its values accepted by all the others. However, the origin of shared values is of lesser importance than their acceptance by all the ethnic groups. The nature of such shared values differs in various societies. For example, the Spanish and Byzantine empires transmitted the acceptance of Christian religious values (Roman Catholic and Greek Orthodox respectively) as fundamental for all peoples within their reach. The USSR has formally accepted the doctrines of Marxist Leninism as applying to all its constituent republics and nationalities. In Islamic countries it has become expected that all citizens will observe religious codes.

Likewise, Britain saw itself as guardian of Western style democracy and succeeded in maintaining and strengthening this value in territories peopled by European immigrants, many of them from its own shores. It may be argued that this ideal is now entrenched as a shared value in countries such as Australia, Canada, New Zealand and the United States of America. Other shared values which are held by the populations of these countries, irrespective of background, include a belief in opportunity for all individuals to better themselves economically and socially, according to their own ability and resourcefulness. The freedom of individuals to pursue their own private lives within legal and political constraints is also acknowledged. In addition, the English language is accepted as the common means of communication for all Australians, Americans and New Zealanders. All ethnic groups in those countries recognize the importance of English as the national language and lingua franca that is necessary for communication and for the political, economic and legal activities of society. In a society of this type, however, the acceptance of English by all ethnic groups must be taken as conditional on the understanding that, for those who wish to preserve their mother tongue, English represents an additional language, rather than the sole and unique means of communication.

Of the various supra-ethnic values mentioned above, the desirability of multiculturalism itself is still insufficiently understood and appreciated in many societies, and it is this value that needs special emphasis in the future. Indeed, without the acceptance of cultural diversity as a shared value by the majority group and by society as a whole, there can be no multicultural society. Otherwise, the way is left open for the pitfalls of assimilation or separatism.

Core values and ethnic cultural retention

Census data and empirical studies from a number of ethnically plural societies demonstrate variations in the degree to which ethnic minority groups adhere to their native tongue at the first and subsequent generation stages (Fishman, 1966; Clyne, 1972, 1976; Smolicz and Harris, 1977). For example, it was found that in Australia, Greek-Australians maintained their native language to a greater extent than other ethnic groups, while Dutch-Australians relinquished it most (Clyne, 1980).

In this connection the relationship between the ideological orientation of the dominant group and that of a given minority may help to explain why children of some ethnic groups are more likely to retain their ethnicity than members of others. The concept of 'ethnic tenacity' has been suggested to account for this phenomenon. This implies that some minority groups are more insistent than others on preserving their cultural integrity in any plural society. However, the concept of ethnic tenacity is not satisfactory on its own, because it does not take into account the relationship between the culture of the minority group and that of the majority.

When examining the relationship between cultures it is useful to postulate the existence in each culture of certain core values which are characteristic of a particular culture and which cannot be abandoned without endangering one's membership of the particular ethnic group (Smolicz, 1979: chapter 4; 1980). Such core values can thus be regarded as characteristic of the cultural group in question. In a plural society, the relationship between the core values of different groups helps to account for variations in the degree of ethnic cultural maintenance and assimilation.

The basic division in this respect is between language-centred cultures — cultures for which the native tongue constitutes a core value — and other cultures which are based upon family, religion or some other ideals — political, historical or structural. Most European cultures appear to be language-centred, for example, Polish, French and Greek cultures. In these cultures, language has become equated with affiliation to the group. Such close ties between ethnicity and language can have various origins; in the Polish case, these are historical and relate to the language persecution during most of the nineteenth century by the neighbouring occupying powers.

Frequently a culture is served by more than one core value, though one of them usually appears as of outstanding importance. In Greece and Greek Cyprus, the Greek language, the family network, and Orthodox religion can be seen as core values. The fact that religion has become elevated to the cultural symbol of national survival and autonomy in modern times found its most visible expression in the election of the Archbishop of Cyprus as the first President of the Cypriot Republic.

In Italy, regional distinctions are much greater than in many other European countries; in Southern Italy at least, the primacy of the Italian family as a core value remains unquestioned, with language as a second core (Vecoli, 1974). Jewish and Irish groups both stand out because of their non-linguistic cores. In the Jewish case, a distinct religion, the feeling of historic continuity, and the concept of peoplehood linked to a tradition of in-group marriage can be seen as providing the cores of Jewish ethnic continuity. The importance of the Catholic church for the Irish groups remains unquestioned, despite the existence of a small Protestant minority in the Republic.

One of the most interesting values is the group's orientation to other ethnic groups in the same society. Thus, for some groups, preservation of cultural purity has been elevated almost to the dimension of a core value, while in others the acceptance of cultural interaction, including the absorption of elements from other cultures, has been accepted positively.

The core values of the two main racial and cultural groups that make up the population of Malaysia form an interesting comparison in the way they pattern social relationships. Among the Malays, the Moslem religion and the native tongue constitute the key identifying values (Asmah, 1979). When a Malay marries a Chinese, the Chinese partner may become classified as Malay by accepting the religion of Islam and indicating a desire to learn the Malaysian language. The children of mixed Malay-Chinese parentage are then treated officially as Malays. Malays have for centuries lived mainly on the coast along international trade routes, and have evolved effective mechanisms like this for absorbing outsiders, while preserving their integrity as a cultural group (Nagata, 1977).

The Chinese in Malaysia appear to demonstrate a different core value system. It is perfectly acceptable within a Chinese family to have members belonging to different religions, including various brands of Christianity and Islam. In the past, the Chinese have also shown a greater openness to the English language, although Chinese schools have tried to conserve Mandarin as well. Unlike the Malays, the Chinese put greater emphasis on racial cohesion; although mixed marriages do occur, even those between Chinese Moslems and their Malay co-religionists are not particularly encouraged. It is the family in its widest sense, the clan, and the entire Chinese community, that represent the core values of the Chinese group.

Language-centred minority cultures

The concept of core values makes it easier to understand the varying degrees of 'ethnic tenacity' shown by various minority groups. In Anglo-dominated societies, for example, there has been, for at least half a century or more, a well developed tradition of religious pluralism. Minority groups with religion at their core have thus had a much greater chance of survival and development than groups centred on language, for example. It is significant that in Australia, both the Jewish and Irish groups have been able to establish their own day schools, which have been instrumental in helping to maintain Jewish and Irish ethnicity. In most instances this has been achieved ostensibly for religious reasons. In contrast, in the same societies there has been much less of a tradition of linguistic pluralism, with the result that language-centred cultural groups, such as the Greek, have not until very recently established a single secondary day school, despite the fact that Melbourne is claimed to be the third largest Greek city in the world.

Cultural maintenance in each group *must* be studied in relation to the core values of the culture concerned; the mechanism adopted for the preservation of one culture may not be suitable for another. As far as education is concerned, courses in ethnic languages are more necessary for the maintenance of language-centred cultures than they are for cultures with non-linguistic cores. For the latter groups, courses in heritage would assume greater importance than language.

For a language-centred culture, the loss of the native tongue usually heralds a cultural shift to the periphery. Ethnicity may still be maintained by appeal to the group's folk-lore, the preservation of family cohesion and in-group marriage. When such a shift occurs, however, the intellectual aspects of culture evaporate. In these circumstances, the cultural transmission chain tends to weaken in later generations. What is more, in its residual form, an ethnic culture is not very effective in interacting with the majority culture, at any other than domestic and folk levels. Significant cultural interaction can never occur on terms of equality, and the remaining pockets of ethnicity merely sustain structural division. It is when ethnic cultures have been reduced to such residues that they come to be associated with other variables like social class, religion or some other life-styles.

This is not to denigrate the importance of folk-lore or family bonds as a supporting value, nor is it to disregard the importance of such values in helping to retain ethnicity at a time when external pressure could extinguish it, before it has time to reassert itself in a cultural sphere. But cultures cannot be maintained in their integral form if their core values are lost. For language-centred cultures this means that ethnic languages must be preserved as the vehicles or carriers of those cultures. In this case there is no substitute for linguistic pluralism. In educational terms, this means the necessity of teaching minority ethnic languages, either in a bilingual situation (Andersson and Boyer, 1978) or in an ethnic language programme.

Ethnic diversity in a socially cohesive society: a balance between shared and core values

Although core values must be preserved if cultures are to retain their integrity, one cannot expect, say, European or Asian cultures to be incorporated *in toto* into societies such as those of Canada, Australia or the United States. National cultures are concerned not only with languages or life-styles, but also with institutional aspects that are of political, economic or legal significance. It is these institutional aspects that all cultures must shed in a plural society in favour of the shared or supra-ethnic values that are acceptable to ethnic majorities and minorities alike.

Within such a shared structure or framework, ethnic cultures may flourish, although the term 'ethnic' carries an implication that a certain part of the culture has been surrendered towards the common values for the whole society — and that this process of sharing concerns not only the minority, but the majority group as well. However, the ethnic entities remain as cultures rather than as cultural residues or sub-cultures so long as they retain their cores. If and when such cores are lost, ethnicity is gradually reduced to a sub-cultural or residual level.

The loss of certain ethnic institutional forms in a plural society is inevitable since, if each group retained its political, legal and economic structures, there would be no society, but a loose confederation of states. However, such an acceptance of shared institutions by all the groups, and consequent modifications of the culture of each group, is of an entirely different order from the excision of core values that are fundamental to its survival and development. These values constitute the boundary between accommodation to plurality and assimilation to the dominant majority.

The balance between maintenance of an ethnic culture and its growth and interaction with other cultures is, therefore, an extremely complex and sensitive process. On the one hand, as was indicated previously, some institutional aspects of each culture must be merged into a single shared value system that enjoys the consensus of all the groups. On the other, the adjustment process must not be so severe as to prune away the heart of a culture. Once the core value boundary is crossed the cultures disintegrate into residues and the essence of cultural pluralism is lost. This model of multiculturalism stresses therefore both the preservation of ethnic cultures and their adjustment to the shared values of society as a whole.

Equal opportunities for ethnic minorities

In plural societies, fears are often voiced that ethnic groups could become stratified on the basis of the level of education and occupational status achieved by their members (Gordon, 1978: 205-9; Zubrzycki, 1976). This would lead to differential access to power and resources on the basis of ethnic group membership. Those immigrants who came to America and Australia from Southern Europe, for example, were for the most part peasant farmers, many of whom had not completed primary schooling. They swelled the numbers of the urban unskilled workers at the bottom end of the socioeconomic hierarchy. It has been argued that if the children of such immigrants were to retain their minority languages and cultures, they would not be able to learn properly those aspects of the dominant culture that are necessary for high educational achievement and occupational status. It has been further claimed that ethnicity may become a social and occupational handicap because it provides a label which could be used by the dominant group to discriminate against the minorities. The assumption is that equality of opportunity in life is only possible in a society that is culturally monistic; that in a plural society ethnicity retention and socioeconomic advance are incompatible. This, it has been argued, is the 'ethnic dilemma' faced by members of minority groups (Gilmour and Lansbury, 1978; Glazer, 1979; Kringas, 1980).

To insist on the inevitability and universality of such a dilemma is to ignore the possibilities of equality of treatment for minorities in a multi-cultural society. A framework of shared values in economic and political life means that the cultural background of individuals is discounted in economic and civic relations. In the occupational realm, for example, individuals are judged on their capacity and performance as workers, be it at the manual, clerical or professional level. The candidate's ethnic culture, as distinct from the shared values of society such as the command of English, ought to be quite irrelevant when employing a labourer for a factory production line or when electing a Head of State. Unless ethnicity is in some way directly involved in work effectiveness, what matters is whether the people concerned have the appropriate skills for their respective jobs. Both the retention of ethnic culture (including ethnic identity) and the acceptance of this state of affairs by minority and majority, are quite compatible with equality of opportunity in political and economic life. The condition is that ethnic groups be accepted as equal partners in society, and that the bicultural individual be recognized as being, if anything, *better* equipped to handle many important jobs in society because of his ability to make use of the cultural resources of more than one group.

A schoolteacher of minority ethnic origin — whether Italian, Greek or Spanish — who has been through the country's school system and university or college, may still be a competent speaker of his native tongue and may also possess a dual identity that reveals attachment to his ethnic group, as well as a sense of belonging to the society in which he lives. His ethnicity may be revealed in his attendance at the ethnic church and his use of the mother tongue when talking to his wife and parents, but it does not interfere with his ability to teach mathematics. Nor should the ethnic aspect of his identity be taken into consideration by his prospective employers, one way or the other, when he applies for such a vacancy, since it is irrelevant. The only time that ethnicity should affect the labour market is when it confers a specific advantage upon the applicant, as would be the case if there were a need for a bilingual mathematics teacher. In such instances there is no tension between ethnicity and social status and achievement.

There is yet another reason why the so-called 'ethnic dilemma' is false. The loss of core elements in an ethnic culture does not in itself guarantee equality of treatment in occupational and social life. Even if the school system could be made successful in overlaying most aspects of ethnic minority behaviour, it is not likely to obliterate all traces of ethnic origin, such as surname, physical looks, a parent's accent and mannerisms, ethnic affiliations, or deeply engrained ways of thinking and feeling. These cultural residues are often sufficient to single out an individual as not belonging to the majority group, even though he may have tried valiantly to embrace the dominant culture in its entirety.

Members of minority ethnic groups have frequently sacrificed much of their culture without achieving equality of treatment. American Negroes have lost most traces of their African cultural past, but this has not made them any more acceptable to the dominant group (Gordon, 1978: 207; Baldwin, 1971). Other minorities may not be so physically distinctive, nor so strongly discriminated against, as Black Americans have been in the past, but cultural as well as physiological differences usually single them out. Indeed, if a dominant majority wishes to exclude a minority, and refuses to share certain kinds of jobs with it, it can continue to do so, no matter how culturally assimilated the group might become. In some instances the dominant majority may even alter its speech patterns to make sure that it is not confused with the minority as the latter tries to 'catch up' and acquire standard speech patterns (Giles, 1977; Tajfel, 1978). No group could have been better assimilated than were the Jews into German culture, but this did not prevent the Nazis from launching the holocaust. In short, assimilation does not in itself help social mobility. Instead, it may increase existing antagonisms and force the ethnic minority to rely even more on its own structures, outside the shared overall structure.

Minority ethnic identity

Over the last decade, the degree of ethnic consciousness among minority groups has been rising steadily throughout the world. The phenomenon has been observed (with some surprise) in the United States, where in the not too distant past ethnicity has been equated with backwardness and low class, and has provoked bigotry and old-fashioned insular prejudices that had no place in modern American society (Greeley, 1971; Novak, 1972). The ethnic revival movements have more recently rocked such apparently culturally monolithic and centralized societies as those of France and Spain. In Britain itself, the successes of Welsh and Scottish nationalists have taken the English by surprise. Ethnic identity, long assumed to be dormant, is reasserting itself, and this has not been limited to places where it has been accepted as a recurrent 'problem', like Belgium, Quebec, the Baltic States, or Northern Ireland.

The question of identity in an ethnically plural society has raised much controversy. Some commentators have assumed that dual or multiple identity inevitably creates conflict, in that the individual is forced to choose which ethnic group and culture to identify with. When this approach is adopted, attention is concentrated on the traumas of changing allegiance from one group to another, and on the high risk of the loss of identity, which involves temporary or even permanent alienation from both groups. Other writers maintain that an individual may identify with more than one group.

Much of the confusion can be traced to a failure to distinguish between political commitment to a state and its institutions, and cultural affiliation to an ethnic group. In a mono-cultural nation, allegiance to the state and identification with the cultural traditions shared by all its people usually merge into one overall national identity. Anglo-Saxon peoples, with a long established unitary culture and single identity (apart from regional and social class variations), have expected to be able to maintain this tradition in the plural societies of America and Australia. On the other hand, it has been generally assumed that it is impossible to be both Irish and American, Ukrainian and Canadian, Italian and Australian.

In the present pluralist framework, however, the terms American, Canadian and Australian are now frequently being used to refer to a person's current allegiance to a nation/state — to its political institutions and economic structures. In contrast, labels such as Irish, Ukrainian and Italian indicate ethnic ancestry and current cultural traditions in other areas of life, such as family, friendship, religion, language and manners. Viewed in this way, the two types of identity are not mutually exclusive. 'Pluralism of identity' is indeed a widespread phenomenon. People are now *choosing* to identify themselves as both Irish and American; Ukrainian and Canadian; Italian and Australian (Smolicz and Lean, 1979, 1980b). What is more, even for groups with language-centred cultures, such as the Poles, the ethnic identity of young Polish-Australians or Polish-Americans appears to be outlasting their knowledge of the Polish language and literature. Thus many young people, with only a 'domestic' knowledge of Polish, still show a very strong affiliation to the Polish group (Harris, 1977; Smolicz and Secombe, 1977, 1981).

There are various factors that operate to maintain and strengthen minority ethnic identity, if not in its highly evolved form, then at least as an enduring social phenomenon. Research findings in both Australia and America suggest that ethnic identity is usually anchored and sustained by the ethnic family with all its extended ramifications of grandparents, cousins, relatives, and very close friends. The ethnic family, and a galaxy of other ethnic primary social relations, represents the bedrock for the maintenance of ethnic identity. Such ethnic primary clusters are also subject to change through interaction, but research shows that, although many minority ethnic children have only a limited command of their ethnic language, their primary relationships centred on family and friends often remain exclusively ethnic. General observation supports the research findings that it is only when children become estranged from their parents and the rest of the family that their ethnicity comes into question (Myerhoff and Simić, 1978; Simić, 1979; Smolicz and Secombe, 1981).

In addition, various ethnic organizations, such as dancing and other folk-lore ensembles, scout groups, choirs, Saturday schools, neighbourhood clubs and cultural organizations possess a dual function: one is manifest, namely that of furthering the activity for which they were founded, and the second is latent, namely that of furthering ethnic friendships and primary relationships and hence, ultimately, intra-ethnic marriage. It is the continued existence and flourishing of this structural factor, in the form of close familial and primary relationships, that helps to ensure the survival of ethnic minority identity.

Support for ethnic identity

By themselves, however, ethnic families and organizations cannot alone ensure the cultural underpinning of minority ethnic identity. In separatist plural societies each ethnic group, whether majority or minority, has a wide range of cultural and structural supports. One of the most important of these is the school system, which allows individuals to achieve literacy in their mother tongue and to develop intellectually within their native culture. In a multicultural society with a set of shared values that includes a positive evaluation of ethnic diversity, the national government is expected to provide this sort of educational support for all ethnic groups within society. The public education system, not just the particular ethnic group, is thus responsible for making courses in ethnic languages and cultures available to all interested students. It should be noted that state schools do not limit themselves to the teaching of shared values but that they already provide this type of instruction for the majority group. What is essential in a multicultural society is the extension of this educational provision to minorities, in so far as numbers and concentration permit.

In practice, however, in those societies where the Anglo-ethnic group is dominant, minority ethnic identity has been maintained largely without the state's institutional and educational underpinning. As a result, young people from minority ethnic groups have been denied the opportunity of learning to read and write in their native tongue and to study the more intellectual aspects of their culture. Ethnic languages in particular have suffered: studies reveal that there has been a marked decline in levels of literacy and language usage among young people of minority ethnic background (Fishman, 1966; Baetens Beardsmore, 1977). In Australia, where migration is still quite recent and mostly of the post-World War II period, many ethnic children learn to speak their native tongue in pre-school years, but never master the art of reading and writing it. Once they go to school they begin to speak English more and more, and use the ethnic language only when speaking to parents, grandparents and others of the older generation. Among children of their own age, they almost invariably speak in English, and balanced bilingualism is a rarity (Smolicz and Harris, 1977; Smolicz and Lean, 1980a).

The retention and strengthening of ethnic identity, accompanied by the denial of the means for its cultural expression, represents a potential threat to social cohesion. Failure to provide support for individuals to maintain and develop their own cultural heritage does not result in their increased identification with the state. Instead, it leads to frustration, perhaps conflict, and structural separatism. However, Canadian surveys provide evidence for the opposite view, namely that increased identification with an ethnic group is reflected in increased identity with Canada as a permanent homeland (Richmond, 1974). This suggests that conflict and division arise not out of difference, but rather out of denial of the right and opportunity to be different.

Young people of ethnic minority backgrounds are now realizing that, although their ethnic identity is secure in the sense that it is not likely to disappear overnight, such identity is not culturally complete but only partial, incomplete and truncated, since it lacks the necessary cultural support for full development. If an identity derived from a language-centred culture is divorced from the core value of that culture, its integrity is undermined, and the individual is subjected to stress. A young person may 'feel ethnic', but cannot express the feeling in terms of the culture that he holds dear. This perception of inadequacy, of having failed to achieve what would be expected of him by his group members, and of being cut off from the mainsprings of his culture and its literary tradition, can cause very serious resentment and anger. Some indication of what this involves can be seen in the militancy and activism of the American Negro and his search for his long lost 'African soul'. The creation of 'Black Studies' as a university subject has been the belated and inadequate attempt by the majority group to defuse an explosive situation and to pacify members of a minority group who have retained their identity, but who were denied the opportunity to develop its cultural complement – to feel whole persons in a cultural sense.

In contrast to this dissension, minority groups can act as a cohesive force in society, provided that their ethnic identity and cultural diversity are supported structurally by national rather than separatist ethnic institutions. Each ethnic identity and culture is then accommodated within the one overall framework of shared values that are acceptable to, and upheld by, members of all ethnic groups.

Implications for education

The educational programmes adopted by schools reflect the ideological orientations that prevail in a plural society as a whole. Where dominant monism is upheld, this orientation is transmitted to ethnic children via the peer group, the school, the mass media, and even through their own ethnic family which itself may succumb to the cultural dominance of the majority group and accept the elimination of its native language and most aspects of its culture. In this situation, schools teach only the language and cultural heritage of the dominant group, in order to ensure that all children, whatever their ethnic origin, master its rudiments, and that minority languages are excluded from the curriculum and hence from the students' linguistic repertoire. In addition, there is often – consciously or unconsciously – an attempt to devalue ethnic minority cultures. In its milder form this devaluation is seen in the assumption, displayed by teachers and peers, that minority cultures are relics from the past which are irrelevant in the present society. This attitude may even apply to those aspects of culture, such as language or social manners, that the school itself has not bothered to transmit.

There may be a more insidious form of devaluation, that seeks to persuade minority ethnic children and their parents that the continual use of their ethnic language at home is harmful to children on both personal and intellectual grounds, since it is deemed to hinder their cognitive development, confuse them, and isolate them socially from their peers. Probably the most potent weapon that the majority group can use to subjugate a minority group is to persuade it of its cultural and social inferiority. Schools, for example, may lead many ethnic parents to believe that ethnic cultural diversity is harmful and that they have to make a choice between their children's economic and educational advance, on the one hand, and the retention of their ethnic culture on the other.

Cultural monism of this kind may also be effectively implemented through the adoption of transitional multicultural education programmes. These programmes are intended to act as 'crutches' to help students over the period when they are deficient in their knowledge of English and the majority life-style, and to ensure that learning does not stop while these are being acquired. But once mastery of the majority language and local 'know how' are achieved, ethnic courses are phased out. This state of transitional pluralism may in the long run prove to be the most efficient method of attaining the objective of dominant monism. Indeed, educational programmes of transitional bilingualism have come to be regarded by several minorities as a surreptitious way of furthering the ends of Anglo-assimilation.

Where cultural separatism is accepted by all groups in society, independent ethnic school systems exist, often at tertiary as well as at primary and secondary school levels. Such structures may prove most efficient in safeguarding the cultures of numerically weaker groups, but they carry with them a disadvantage, in that they greatly reduce the chances of cultural interaction and confine the culture concerned to its parent group.

Education for multiculturalism

Cultural pluralism that is internalized at a personal level is not likely to be achieved unless the state makes provision for the transmission of ethnic languages and cultures within the national education system. In this way schools could fulfil the functions of reinforcing and developing the culture of the home for children of both minority and majority groups. Indeed, all children, no matter what their ethnic origin, could have access to more than one cultural heritage. Schools could also help to ensure the stability of society through programmes based on shared traditions which are upheld by all groups in society.

In this connection there is a need for co-ordination between the teaching of the dominant language on the one hand, and the maintenance of ethnic languages on the other. The dangers have been observed, for example, in Germany, where

> because there is no coordination of instruction in both languages, the learners are overtaxed and, depending on individual circumstances, they either settle on rapid language assimilation or adhere to the ghetto of the native language. Yet almost all the [Yugoslav, Greek and Turkish] learners have deficits in their command of German *and* the native language so that one can speak of a two-sided demi-lingualism. (Stölting, 1977)

Pitfalls of this sort can only be avoided by curriculum planning that takes into account literacy in both the majority and minority languages (Müller, 1979).

Under a balanced education for multiculturalism, minority ethnic content would be incorporated into the whole spectrum of curriculum and research studies. In the past, in societies dominated by Anglo-Saxon groups, what has been lacking is the integration of minority cultures into the mainstream teaching and research tradition of schools, colleges and universities. 'Ethnic research', for example, has long been suspect. The past, present and future of the country have generally been seen through the cultural perspective of the majority group which at times has been so self-assured that it has not even been aware that it has been using its control of educational resources to enforce a cultural perspective that is neither 'God-given' nor 'natural', but the simple product of its own narrowly perceived self-interest and historical accident. This single-minded vision, with its equation of 'fair', 'just', 'reasonable' and 'scholarly' with the virtues developed within the Anglo-Saxon tradition, is still an obvious feature of many school and university traditions.

The transmission and development of ethnic cultural cores is a necessary task for educational systems, since the home is not in a position to fulful this function on its own. Schools and tertiary institutions represent the structural support that is necessary to prevent the deterioration of cultures into fragments or residues. They must take up this challenge, since in the present climate of the renaissance of ethnic identity, if they fail to do so, the response of ethnic schools will lead to ethnic separatism. School multiculturalism is required to avoid structural separatism and division in society. It is also the best way to avoid ethnic stratification, as well as the relegation of ethnic cultures to inferior positions in society outside the reach of the majority group.

In summary, to achieve multiculturalism in an ethnically plural society, the education system must provide at every level (primary, secondary, and tertiary) opportunities for all individuals:

1. to learn the shared values of society, including the national language (which in Anglo-Saxon societies means English);
2. to study their mother tongue in its cultural context (including the acquisition of literacy);

3. to gain access to an ethnic community language and culture other than their own;
4. to understand and value the multicultural nature of society and learn to appreciate the various cultures within it.

Such educational provisions and programmes reflect a balance between the values shared by all members of society, on the one hand, and the particular languages and cultures of various ethnic groups on the other. To focus exclusively on shared values denies members of minority ethnic groups the opportunity to maintain and develop their own cultures. Such cultural discrimination is likely to result in frustration, division and conflict. Alternatively, promoting the development of separate ethnic cultures, and failing to support the teaching of shared values, may lead to fragmentation, and would deny many members of society the opportunity to participate on an equal basis in the political, legal, civic, economic and other aspects of society.

In multicultural education, the aim is to offer all students the opportunity of becoming bilingual and bicultural, so that individuals not only have the chance to broaden their own knowledge of people and deepen their understanding of life, but also to provide the community as a whole with living bridges between the different ethnic groups. They can work towards a creative and constructive interchange of cultures in a plural society.

References

Andersson, T and Boyer, M (1978) *Bilingual Schooling in the United States* (2nd ed) National Educational Library Publishers: Austin, Tex

Asmah, Haji Omar (1979) Languages of Malaysia *in* Llamzon (1979) Australian Commonwealth Education Portfolio (1979) *Education in a Multicultural Australia* Australian Government Publishing Service: Canberra

Australian Schools Commission Committee on Multicultural Education (1979) *Education for a Multicultural Society* Australian Government Publishing Service: Canberra

Baetens Beardsmore, H (1977) Anomie in bicultural education *in* de Grève and Rosseel (1977)

Baldwin, J (1971) *Nobody Knows My Name* Harmondsworth: Penguin

Clammer, J R (1976) *Sociological Approaches to the Study of Language and Literacy in South East Asia* Sociology Working Paper 56, Department of Sociology, University of Singapore: Singapore

Clammer, J R (1980) *Culture and ethnicity: values and the problems of modernization in Singapore* Paper presented to Australian and New Zealand Association for the Advancement of Science (ANZAAS): Adelaide

Clyne, M (1972) *Perspectives on Language Contact* Hawthorn: Melbourne

Clyne, M ed (1976) *Australia Talks: Essays on the Sociology of European and Aboriginal Languages in Australia* Pacific Linguistics, Series D23, Department of Linguistics, Research School of Pacific Studies, Australian National University: Canberra

Clyne, M (1980) *Language ecology in Australia: some insights from the 1976 census* Paper presented to Australian and New Zealand Association for the Advancement of Science (ANZAAS) Conference: Adelaide

de Grève, M and Rosseel, E eds (1977) *Problèmes Linguistiques des Enfants de Travailleurs Migrants* Aimau-Didier: Brussels

Fishman, J A ed (1966) *Language Loyalty in the United States* Mouton: The Hague

Giles, H ed (1977) *Language, Ethnicity and Intergroup Relations* Academic Press: London

Gilmour, P and Lansbury, R (1978) *Ticket to Nowhere* Harmondsworth: Penguin

Glazer, N (1979) Affirmative discrimination: where is it going? *International Journal of Comparative Sociology* **20** 1-2: 14-30

Gollnick, D M (1980) Multicultural education *Viewpoints in Teaching and Learning* **56** 1

Gordon, M M (1978) *Human Nature, Class and Ethnicity* Oxford University Press: New York

Greeley, A M (1971) The rediscovery of diversity *The Antioch Review* **31**: 352-63

Harris, R McL (1977) *Poles apart? An intergenerational study of selected samples of post-war Polish immigrants in South Australia* PhD thesis: University of Adelaide: Adelaide

Kovacs, M L and Cropley, A J (1975) *Immigrants and Society: Alienation and Assimilation* McGraw-Hill: Sydney

Kringas, P (1980) *Migrants' definitions of ethnic schools: Part B. Wider implications* Paper presented at Conference on Ethnic and Immigration Studies, University of New South Wales: Sydney

Lim Kiat Boey ed (1980) *Bilingual Education* Anthropology Series 7, South East Asian Ministers Education Organization (SEAMEO), Singapore University Press: Singapore

Llamzon, L T A (1979) *Education in a Multicultural Australia* Australian Government Publishing Service: Canberra

Malony, C, Zobl, H and Stölting, W (1977) *Deutsch im Kontakt mit anderen Sprachen* Scripton Verlag: Kronberg

Martin, J I (1978) *The Migrant Presence* Allen and Unwin: Sydney

Müller, H (1979) Ausländische Arbeitkinder in der Bundesrepublik *Kindheit* **1**: 169-84

Myerhoff, B G and Simić, A eds (1978) *Life's Career-Aging: Cultural Variations on Growing Old* Sage Publications: Beverly Hills, Cal

Nagata, J A (1977) Ethnic differentiation within an urban mercantile community in Malaysia *Ethnicity* **4** 4

Novak, M (1972) *The Rise of the Unmeltable Ethnics* Macmillan: New York

Richmond, A (1974) Language, ethnicity and the problem of identity in a Canadian metropolis *Ethnicity* **1** 1: 175-206

Simić, A (1979) White ethnic and Chicano families: continuity and adaptation in the New World *in* Tufte and Myerhoff (1979)

Smolicz, J J (1979) *Culture and Education in a Plural Society* Curriculum Development Centre: Canberra

Smolicz, J J (1980) Language as core value of culture *RELC* (Regional English Language Centre) *Journal of Applied Linguistics* (Singapore) (in press)

Smolicz, J J and Harris, R McL (1977) Ethnic languages in Australia *International Journal of the Sociology of Language* **14**: 89-108

Smolicz, J J and Lean, R (1979) Parental attitudes to cultural and linguistic pluralism in Australia: a humanistic sociological approach *Australian Journal of Education* **23** 3: 227-49

Smolicz, J J and Lean, R (1980a) Parental and student attitudes to the teaching of ethnic languages in Australia *ITL (Instituut voor Toegepaste Linguistiek) — A Review of Applied Linguistics* **35** (in press)

Smolicz, J J and Lean, R (1980b) Australian languages other than English — a sociological study of attitudes *in* Lim Kiat Boey (1980)

Smolicz, J J and Secombe, M J (1977) A study of attitudes to the introduction of ethnic languages and cultures in Australian schools *The Australian Journal of Education* **21** 1: 1-24

Smolicz, J J and Secombe, M J (1980) *The Australian school through Polish eyes: a sociological study of student attitudes from their own memoirs* Paper presented at Conference on Ethnic and Immigration Studies, University of New South Wales: Sydney

Smolicz, J J and Secombe, M J (1981) *The Australian School through Polish Eyes* Melbourne University Press: Melbourne

Stölting, W (1977) Die Sprachpolitik an deutschen Schulen für ausländische Kinder *in* Malony, Zobl and Stölting (1977)

Tajfel, H ed (1978) *Differentiation Between Social Groups* Academic Press: London

Tufte, V and Myerhoff, B eds (1979) *Changing Images of the Family* Yale University Press: New Haven, Conn

Vecoli, R (1974) The Italian Americans *The Centre Magazine* 7.8.74: 36-40

Veenhoven, W A ed (1976) *Case Studies on Human Rights and Fundamental Freedoms: a World Survey 3* Martinus Nijhoff: The Hague

Zubrzycki, J (1976) Cultural pluralism and discrimination in Australia, with special reference to white minority groups *in* Veenhoven (1976)

2. Psychological and linguistic aspects of minority education

John R Edwards

Summary: A minority group can be so designated only within a society of which it is a part. Implicit, therefore, in most discussions of such groups is the idea of comparative status. In this sense, the term *minority* may or may not refer to numerical size; it virtually always, however, includes the issue of relative dominance/subordination. Minority concerns typically involve both ethnicity and social class variables. In many cases, ethnic group membership and low socioeconomic status coincide, thus justifying discussion of both under the general rubric of educational and social disadvantage. The linguistic and psychological aspects of this disadvantage are many and varied, but all derive from comparisons drawn between the minority group and others; often these comparisons proceed from the assumption of the correctness of the norms and standards of the larger or more dominant group, and thus tend to reflect poorly on those of the minority.

The aim of this chapter is to explore aspects of minority-majority contact, with special regard to the dynamics of the comparison process. Since we are concerned here most directly with education, this means giving attention to such things as people's desires and aspirations, the presence or absence of home/school discontinuity, etc. Linguistically, or sociolinguistically, one should consider views of standard and non-standard speech and language and how these may affect (especially) children's comprehension and production of language in the school. Only after attending to such matters can one begin to consider how best to reduce the friction so often apparent in minority education.

Introduction

Access to education, once a privilege, is now a right. Indeed, children in most places *must* go to school until a determined age. The school must therefore cater for large numbers of children who do not always come from similar backgrounds. This simple fact alone means that pressures of many kinds are endemic within the educational process. There are of course different ways in which schools, and educational bureaucracies in general, can respond to issues raised by the heterogeneity of populations, but perhaps it is not unfair to see these as falling into two major categories.

The first involves pupils adapting to the ideas and methods of the school; the second involves the school showing, to a greater or lesser degree, a willingness to adapt itself to the pupils. The further back in time one goes the more likely it is that one will encounter examples within the first of these categories. Conversely, present-day education, in many parts of the world, is likely to show at least some tendencies towards the second.

Each of these possible ways of responding to what is essentially a discontinuity between home and school has positive and negative aspects. There is, for example, value in demanding that all pupils learn certain things if one can be sure that these things are of broad significance. The disadvantages of taking this line are obvious: are we sure of the rightness of our own angle on knowledge, of our norms and standards? By demanding that all children learn a given subject in a given way, do we not run the risk of making the activity at best boring and at worst valueless and unrewarding for all concerned? On the other hand, given a school system which is more adaptable, the apparent advantage of greater flexibility can be offset by the danger that children may not be exposed to things which will fit them for participation in the wider social milieu. Since many 'non-mainstream' families see their children's future directly related to success in the mainstream, this is a real danger. We do not, presumably, wish to see education *limiting* children's chances.

I have oversimplified the matter here. Nevertheless, it is worthwhile to simplify occasionally, since real situations are often so complex that any hope of salvaging original points of departure becomes almost impossible to attain. This is especially apposite here since the school can be seen as a particular arena in which larger social issues are debated. For example, the very simple possibilities that have been outlined above relate to the much broader concerns of cultural pluralism and assimilation. When one is dealing with contact between minority and majority groups, one is interested ultimately in such broad issues. In this connection, the school can provide a useful focal point: it is, after all, a strong and conspicuous bastion of mainstream values, and it is one which exercises considerable power over its charges.

Minority groups

Minority populations are commonly understood to be numerically inferior components of a larger society who are, on the basis of size alone, inevitably outside the mainstream. There are different types of minorities, and the differences often reside in the varying ways in which groups come into contact. One classification which may be useful here is that given by the Royal Institute of International Affairs (1963), which delineates five general categories:

1. frontier populations, within which dominance may shift as a function of changing boundaries and/or allegiances;
2. populations forming concentrated units within a larger society — eg the 'migrant' workers in Europe;
3. indigenous populations conquered by other, more numerous groups

— eg the Welsh, Bretons and Catalans;
4. immigrant populations;
5. relatively isolated groups or individuals in states having a predominant national character — ie immigration on a small scale. (See also Edwards, 1977a.)

For present purposes it is apparent that indigenous minorities and sizeable immigrant groups form the major concern. We can add to the latter population the 'migrant' workers noted under (2) above, since these show many signs of permanence (see Widgren, 1975). Within this grouping, the specifics of minority-majority interaction may obviously vary widely, although ethnicity usually figures in the equation. An allegiance to non-mainstream culture, or a mixed allegiance, means that immigrant populations and indigenous groups are, to some extent at least, *separate* — both in their own eyes and in the perceptions of the majority. In some cases, the separateness decreases over time, sometimes to such an extent that it is lost. This is not inevitably so, however. Some groups, or some group members, resist assimilation; for some, visible distinctiveness may mean a more enduring separateness. I shall return to these issues again.

Minority status may not always be inherent in small numbers. Groups holding subordinate positions in society, even though they may be numerically large, may equally be said to constitute minorities (see Rose, 1972). Majority-minority relations, while often reflecting differences in population size, are of primary interest and importance in terms of relative *status* and *power*. Class differences, therefore, must also be considered in any discussion of such relations. While distinctions between 'rulers' and 'ruled' are now not always so clear-cut as once they were, differences in class remain important. That is, while the hereditary aristocracies and élites may have had their day in many parts of the world, their places have been taken by others.

The area of interest here lies in the points of contact between those who dominate and those who do not. The issue turns on *comparative* status and the conjunction of one set of norms and values with another. When comparisons are drawn, therefore, between almost any aspect of the life-style of a (large) lower class population and of a (small) upper class one, the outcome is usually predictable. The assumed correctness of the standards of the powerful results from the position from which comparisons are usually made, and there therefore need be no consideration given to anything so trivial as numbers when one is deciding which life-styles are best. This, of course, has marked implications for those who, in status if not in numbers, seem to come off second-best. This remains true even when the lines are not drawn, as above, between class extremes. Comparisons between working classes and middle classes yield similarly predictable results.

There is a final, and perhaps obvious, point to be made here. A lower class worker in Germany need not be a *Gastarbeiter*, but a *Gastarbeiter* is usually a lower class worker. In many parts of the world, in fact, there is a relationship between low socioeconomic status and national or ethnic group membership. In such cases one observes a double minority status, as it were, comprising both the numerical and the power elements. The West Indians and Asians in Britain, and the Blacks and Puerto Ricans in the United States are further instances here. Moreover, each of these groups has a physical distinctiveness which exacerbates their difficulties.

In summary, the concept of a minority, and of minority status in society, is one which has at its heart the idea of comparative power. I am not particularly concerned here with which groups hold power, nor with the rightness or wrongness of power-wielding in principle, although these are issues of great concern. Rather, it is the consequences, especially those of a psychological and linguistic nature, of comparison within a particular society, which are of direct relevance here. This I think is a useful point to clarify. After all, ethnic minorities can be majorities elsewhere, and lower class populations may dominate in given circumstances. It is when groups stand in a relation to one another such that one may be judged inferior, that minority issues cause concern. It is at this point that we can introduce the idea of disadvantage as a major theme of the discussion.

Disadvantage

Disadvantage, as referred to in psychological and educational literature, usually signifies a relatively enduring condition descriptive of the lifestyles of certain social groups — including ethnic minorities and members of the working classes — whose 'knowledge, skills and attitudes . . . impede learning' (Passow, 1970: 16). Why are such groups at a disadvantage compared with others? Three major forms of explanation have been offered (Edwards, 1979a).

The first view is that some groups are inherently less able than others and are, in fact, genetically inferior. This is a view which has been widely accepted throughout history, and has been proposed to account for the perceived deficiencies of the masses and of certain ethnic and racial groups. It is a view which holds, in effect, that observed inferiorities in all manner of things — from culture to language to achievement potential — are in fact *deficits*. The position has had its most recent support in the work of Jensen (1969, 1973). Taking his cue from the alleged failure of compensatory education in the United States, Jensen has argued that this failure occurred because of ignorance of genetic group differences operating along racial and social class lines.

Jensen has argued that there exists an inferiority in basic intelligence (as measured by intelligence tests) within certain groups and that differential forms of educational treatment are therefore called for. The chief difficulties here are, first, that tests of intelligence are notoriously culture-specific and even the most 'culture-free' among them have been constructed within a given context, which inevitably implies certain assumptions about intelligence. Secondly, tests of intelligence must be administered, and the different situations involved have been found to influence scores; and finally, even assuming that an accurate partition of the hereditary and environmental components of intelligence could be made *within* a population, this would say nothing about intelligence in other populations. Kagan (1969: 275) has noted that 'the essential error in Jensen's argument is the conclusion that if a trait is under genetic control, differences between two populations on that trait must be due to genetic factors'.

Finally, even if one were to grant Jensen's claims, these would not justify any large scale educational changes. Thus, a difference of 10-15 IQ points between Black and White children is not generally sufficient to warrant Jensen's proposal for different educational treatments (see Anderson, 1969; Kagan, 1969). Cronbach has stated that, educationally, 'it is pointless to stress heredity' (1969: 345; see also Bloom, 1969; Wiseman, 1973). The claim that genetic differences among ethnic and class groups may lead to their difficulties in school and elsewhere is therefore not only doubtful but also of no practical import.

The second major view of disadvantage is that it is a product of faulty environment. Children from certain groups are disadvantaged because of the unsatisfactory nature of their physical, social and psychological surroundings. Their deficiencies are therefore real, but may be ameliorated. This, one might think, offers to the disadvantaged more of a chance than is forthcoming from the genetic deficiency position; although observed differences are, once again, seen as real deficits, they are products of inferior contexts and not of inferior genes. Thus the 'environmentalist' position stresses the need to isolate and remedy those environmental factors which lead to poor cognitive and social functioning (see Deutsch, 1967). It is no surprise that this is the viewpoint which was primarily responsible for programmes of compensatory education.

As with the first view, however, there are difficulties with the environmentalist position. For example, whenever characteristics of the 'poor' environment are noted, it is assumed that these are related to such things as lack of school success. In fact, such links are almost always impossible to verify. Many children who live in lower class or ethnic minority areas do well at school and Wiseman (1968) has noted that there are many 'good' homes in the working class and many 'poor' ones in affluent surroundings. Characteristics considered to be deficits (or to lead to deficit) can only be so viewed from the standpoint of a middle class bias that assumes the rightness of its own standards. Consider the term 'cultural deprivation'. Since it clearly cannot signify that one is deprived of one's *own* culture, it must mean that one group is seen to be deficient because it is deprived of *another* culture. Do we say that a French child is culturally deprived because he does not understand things common to a Fijian child? Should we not, therefore, be wary of making any such judgements, even when the groups being compared are both participants (to some degree, at least) in a larger common culture?

This is the standpoint of the third major perception of disadvantage —

that disadvantage is *difference* and not deficit. It argues that just as it may be unfair to compare the French and Fijian child because their environments are so dissimilar, so it is unfair to compare the middle class child with the working class child, or the immigrant with the native. Those espousing the difference viewpoint are aware that, although sociocultural differences exist among sub-groups within a society, these sub-groups do not belong to entirely different cultures. The disadvantaged share much in common with mainstream society and are constantly in touch with it. In fact, it is this which gives definition to disadvantage — it arises when groups which share certain elements, by virtue of proximity if nothing else, and yet which differ in some respects, come into contact with each other. If such contact did not exist, then disadvantage as considered here would not exist; it is only when contact leads to comparison that disadvantage takes shape. And this, of course, is exactly what occurs: minority group members constantly come into contact with the larger society, are forced to do so and, indeed, often wish to do so. It is then that social evaluations make themselves evident. A useful summary of this can be found in Wax and Wax (1971: 138):

> If the Indian child appears as 'culturally deprived', it is not because he is lacking in experience or culture, but because the educational agencies are unwilling to recognize the alienness of his culture and the realities of his social world. It is not that the child is deprived of culture, it is that the culture which is associated with his parents is derogated because they are impoverished and powerless.

For 'Indian child' one could read 'Black child', 'immigrant child' or 'lower class child'.

Overall, I feel that the difference position is the most reasonable view to take of disadvantage. It is important, of course, to note that to recognize this is not to solve the problem. For, while adherence to this position denies the validity of biological or environmental inferiority, it admits that the disadvantaged *do* suffer deficits, of a social nature. This conception hardly makes the problems associated with disadvantage any the less real or important. Indeed, difficulties whose very existence depends upon social standards and social comparisons are among the most intractable (Edwards, 1979a). They prove, for example, singularly resistant to rational explanation and objective identification.

Non-standard speech

I should preface my remarks on speech and language by pointing out that I shall exclude from discussion children who do not speak the mainstream language at all, or who are of what is sometimes called 'limited English-speaking ability'. While such children are clearly at a disadvantage in the school system and elsewhere, their very real difficulties are less subtle than those encountered by speakers of dialect varieties. It is at the point when children are (at least minimally) able to benefit from instruction in the *regular* classroom that the social and psychological factors with which I am chiefly concerned here — and which are relevant for all minority children — come into play. Readers interested in the problems associated with the transition from one language to another (eg from a foreign mother tongue to English) will find useful recent discussions in Brown (1979), Edwards (1979a), Edwards, V (1979), and Khan (1980); see also the section on social change later in this chapter.

Undoubtedly, language is one of the most important contributors to disadvantage among minorities. Of all the characteristics of disadvantage, this is one of the most visible, and it has therefore attracted considerable attention. Perceptions of it parallel those of the larger issue of the life-styles and cultures of minority groups; thus, the classic controversy in the area has been the so-called 'difference-deficit' debate. Is it the case that certain language varieties are inferior in some ways to others, or are they merely different?

The realization that *languages* simply differ from one another, and cannot reasonably be seen as comparatively better or worse, has been current for some time. This is largely due to the work of anthropologists and linguists. No one, for example, would claim that French is better or more logical than English, and similar sentiments can be expressed for any pair of languages. Gleitman and Gleitman (1970: 45-6) have pointed out that:

> No one has succeeded in finding a primitive language . . . . No one has convinc-ingly demonstrated that there is some thought or idea, expressible in some language, that cannot be expressed in another.

On the same point, Lenneberg (1967: 364) asks:

> Could it be that some languages require 'less mature cognition' than others, perhaps because they are still more primitive? In recent years this notion has been thoroughly discredited by virtually all students of language.

It is only relatively recently, however, that a similar sort of acknowledge-ment has been generally made with regard to varieties of the same language. Here, linguists and psychologists have had to work against some strong opposing interpretations. Class and regional differences in accent and dialect have always attracted attention, and often derision. For minority groups, whose general backgrounds are often perceived as not merely different but also deficient, it is not surprising that speech styles have also been viewed in this way. Two important features of this perception are the alleged linguistic and aesthetic failings of low-status speech varieties.

The first argument has it that the language of the disadvantaged is linguistically inferior. In a general way, this follows from anecdotal judgements often made about the 'poor' or 'odd' speech patterns of class and ethnic minorities. These were considerably reinforced and brought to academic attention by the British sociologist Basil Bernstein. On the basis of his studies of middle class and working class speech he formulated the now well-known notion of 'elaborated' and 'restricted' codes. He appeared to be claiming that the working class were largely limited to a restricted code which was characterized by poor syntax and vocabulary, and non-symbolic, concrete modes of expression. Middle class speakers, on the other hand, also had at their disposal access to the more formal elaborated code — having a wide range of symbolic expressive techniques and a more fully-formed and explicit grammar (see Bernstein, 1959). Although in later writings Bernstein asserted that his codes were sociolinguistic rather than linguistic (1972), that therefore they reflected differences in performance rather than competence (1973), and that he supported essentially a difference rather than a deficit position, his work influenced much of the verbal deprivation literature, especially in the United States. For example, Hess and Shipman (1968) noted that lower class speech was characterized by a deprivation of meaning, and Bereiter and Engelmann (1966) stated that, for the Black child in America, language was in some instances dispensable and not of vital importance.

Such sentiments gave rise to compensatory programmes to repair children's speech — an approach which obviously has strong deficit-theory underpinnings. It was in order to dispel what they felt to be a myth of verbal deficiency that linguists and others began to look more closely at language varieties. Of great importance here is the work of Labov (eg 1973). He stressed that, for one group (American Blacks), verbal proficiency was not inferior or in need of repair and, indeed, was highly developed.

This work, on what is often referred to as Black English Vernacular (BEV),* makes a useful test case for the verbal deficiency/deprivation notion in general, since BEV has for a long time been seen as a substandard and illogical approximation to Standard English (the dialect most often spoken by the educated mainstream). The thrust of Labov's work was to show that, although we may fairly refer to BEV as non-standard English, it is clearly not substandard because it is a valid dialect with its own rule-governed structures. One example of these is BEV's different but regular treatment of the verb 'to be'. A Standard English sentence like 'He is nice' may be rendered in BEV as 'He nice' — the 'is' has been deleted. However, there is no BEV deletion in a sentence like 'I was unhappy'. The applicable rule here is that, in circumstances in which Standard English allows verb contraction ('He is nice' can become 'He's nice'), BEV permits deletion (to 'He nice'). In cases in which Standard English contraction is incorrect, there is no BEV deletion.

Through such examples, BEV can be seen to demonstrate consistency; although it differs from that of Standard English, its regularity is no less 'logical'. The overall import of such demonstrations has been to scotch the myth of verbal deprivation or deficiency, and to show that language varieties hitherto seen as substandard should be seen as non-standard — a non-pejorative term which simply acknowledges differing social status within society. There are, of course, many non-standard varieties, most of which have not been nearly so exhaustively studied as BEV. Nevertheless,

---

* Previously Non-standard Negro English (NNE).

findings thus far point strongly to the view that, just as there are no linguistic reasons for arguing the superiority of one *language* over another, so there are none for the superiority of *dialects* within languages (Trudgill, 1975).

It has also been argued, however, that some dialects are aesthetically less attractive than others. This, although a weaker issue than the linguistic one, would nevertheless provide at least some rationale for dialect superiority/ inferiority, if it could be demonstrated. To do so it is necessary somehow to remove social connotations from speech, so that unconfounded judgements of an aesthetic nature may be made. Giles and his colleagues did this by presenting speech samples to judges who were not speakers of, and were unfamiliar with, the varieties concerned. Thus, Giles *et al* (1974) had two Greek dialects — the Athenian and the Cretan — evaluated on aesthetic quality by British raters who knew no Greek. Although in Greece the Athenian is clearly the prestige standard and the Cretan is a low-status, non-standard variant, the judges' responses to the two dialects were not significantly different; if anything, there was a slight tendency to favour the Cretan variety. In a second study, Giles, Bourhis and Davies (1975) asked Welsh adults to evaluate the voices of European French, educated Canadian French and working class Canadian French speakers. Again, no variety was singled out as more attractive or pleasant, even though there were strong social connotations for each variety within the Quebec context where all were familiar.

As with the linguistic evidence, therefore, the aesthetic qualities of different varieties seem to be based upon social convention and connotation only. This lends support to the more general difference view of disadvantage *in toto*. Having rejected linguistic and aesthetic arguments for the superiority of standard over non-standard language and speech, one is left with social evaluations which evidently say nothing of the inherent qualities of speech itself. Rather, they reflect what are often stereotyped views of those who possess non-standard styles. One is not, of course, saying that it is unreasonable for individuals to find some dialects or accents more attractive than others; it should be realized, however, that these are matters simply of taste and convention (see also Edwards, 1979a; Giles and Powesland, 1975).

Minority education: psychological and sociolinguistic implications

With regard to the information presented in the preceding sections, we can see that disadvantage and non-standard speech are social issues which take shape when comparisons are drawn between majority and minority groups. One of the most frequent and enduring points of contact which allows such comparisons is the school. The disadvantaged child's life-style and language are not reflected or encouraged in the school; difficulties may start at once.

For many children, school is a rather natural continuation and extension of home life. Disadvantaged children, however, often experience a sharp discontinuity between home and school. It is important to realize that this is not something which can easily be overcome; the discontinuity will remain so long as there exists a difference between home life and school life, between the playground and the classroom. For some disadvantaged children, particularly those from immigrant or ethnic minority backgrounds, the discontinuity may constitute a type of 'culture shock' — that phenomenon one experiences on finding oneself in a foreign and unfamiliar context (Ashworth, 1975; Edwards, 1979a). In addition, such children may very well be the recipients of prejudice, especially if they are in some way physically distinguishable from others. Thus the first day of school for a child may be like going to a new country in which the inhabitants are not only strange but perhaps hostile as well.

Not only may this new country be alien and forbidding, it may also operate along lines quite different from those to which the child is accustomed. The home may not stress the value of academic education at all, for example, or it may place different emphases upon education for boys and girls. The responses children make to their elders, including parents and teachers, may not be similar to those expected at school. The competitive atmosphere which exists in many schools may be frowned upon in the child's maternal culture. Religious beliefs may lead to confusion and embarrassment. Even culinary habits and varieties of clothing and ornament may contribute to difficulties outside the home environment; and so on. There are, however, two general factors of importance which underlie all the specifics. The first is that all these aspects of life may create, or emphasize, home/school discontinuity. The second is that backgrounds are heterogeneous, and cannot be taken for granted by those (eg teachers) concerned with minority education.

The point here is that, in their efforts to understand children whose backgrounds are unfamiliar, teachers and others should not assume that labels like 'ethnic minority', 'immigrant' or 'lower class' indicate homogeneity; quite the contrary. Thus, Ashworth (1975) notes that Chinese parents in Canada are extremely keen to see their children do well at school; East Indians, on the other hand, may wish their children to go on to work as soon as is legally possible. Such differences in educational aspirations may also be found among indigenous working class populations. Some see little value in formal education and the things it represents (this is perhaps the stereotypic view), while others perceive the school (perhaps naively) as the most important avenue of upward mobility. Some groups may value what they see as healthy competition for high marks or teachers' attention; others, like the American Indian children discussed by Philips (1972), may not show up well in classrooms where this is stressed.

The heterogeneity of minority groups can thus complicate the educational process, even in cases in which teachers are sensitive to discontinuity in general. An awareness of this points to the great need for establishing and maintaining liaison between home and school. This is an issue which has most often been addressed by those concerned with community relations as a whole, but it is clearly of importance at a more individual level as well. In a way, however, the heterogeneity of the backgrounds of minority children serves to *reduce* their separateness from others; teachers are well-used to dealing with classes comprising assortments of abilities, motivations and achievement levels.

When language differences are also in evidence, the situation becomes more confused. The teacher, experienced in dealing with diverse patterns of interests and talents, often calls upon his or her knowledge of the children (and their backgrounds) to form expectations of likely progress and success. Where these backgrounds are roughly similar to the teacher's own, these expectations are often effective and accurate shorthand devices; where backgrounds are dissimilar the expectations may be ill-founded. The work of Rosenthal and Jacobson (1968) purported to show that teachers, given false information about children in their classroom, formed different expectations for what they believed to be groups of bright and not-so-bright children; these were seen to have an effect upon the children's subsequent progress. I say 'purported' because the work has since been subject to a good deal of criticism. However, there seems little doubt that teachers do form expectations, (whatever the verdict may be on manipulated expectations), and that these may have harmful consequences when inaccurate or stereotypic perceptions of language (or other 'visible' characteristics) are involved. Indeed, numerous studies have demonstrated that teachers do form expectations (whatever the verdict may be on basis of speech samples, downgrade disadvantaged children on dimensions ranging from intelligence to happiness (see Edwards, 1979b; Seligman, Tucker and Lambert, 1972; Williams, 1976). All of this may lead to what Rist (1970) has termed the self-fulfilling prophecy: teachers expect certain children to do less well than others, the children become sensitive to this, respond to the expectation and thus confirm the initial diagnosis. In this way, disadvantage is perpetuated.

Clearly, the concern here is that teachers, and the educational system in general, may unfairly categorize minority children. The language issue is particularly relevant because teachers, more than most, tend to have rather well-formed ideas about what is and what is not correct usage. They may complain to children that their speech is 'wrong', 'careless', 'vulgar' or even 'gibberish' (Trudgill, 1975), or they may feel that minority children are 'non-verbal', although the children's lack of speech production in class may have absolutely nothing to do with their competence or ability — indeed, it is easy to observe 'non-verbal' children being extremely verbal in other situations. In either case the danger is that the teacher may impute cognitive deficiency to the child whose speech is not 'normal'.

It is therefore an important task to make teachers aware of current sociolinguistic and psychological findings; to encourage in teachers a flexibility of outlook which will prevent too early and too rigid categorization of pupils; to show teachers that judgements of 'normal' speech patterns require a knowledge of the speech community to which the child belongs; and, in general, to ask teachers to consider each case on its own merits and not unnecessarily exacerbate the disadvantage suffered by their pupils.

One may reasonably ask, of course, if increased awareness and sensitivity are all that can be brought to bear on the problems of minority children at school. In reply one should say that, first of all, these qualities are not insignificant; the fact that they are somewhat intangible does not lessen their importance. We can, after all, recognize a good teacher, even though attempts to isolate elements of this 'goodness' have mostly proved trivial. Also, while we may wish to take active steps to combat disadvantage at school, two things at least should make us pause. The first is that disadvantage is a feature of social comparison which extends far beyond the school; the school can (and should) try to prevent it from becoming worse, but it has limited hope of decreasing it. Secondly, and with specific regard to language, active attempts to counter disadvantage make its presence more conspicuous, and more likely to be interpreted as deficiency. Many, for example, who reject the notion of compensatory education, with its emphasis upon a replacement or an enrichment policy, nevertheless endorse an *addition* approach, which assumes that, while there is nothing in the speech of the minority child which requires compensation or remediation, an expansion of his linguistic repertoire could well prove useful. This is a pragmatic view which recognizes that, whatever occurs in school, society at large is not likely to abandon its perceptions of disadvantage or disadvantaged language.

To want to expand, or add to, a child's linguistic store, is a commendable motive, but one runs the risk of stigmatizing the child's original speech pattern. How, the child might ask himself, can my language at once be merely different, and not deficient, and yet at the same time require expansion? Children *can* solve this riddle, but they are likely to be better able to do so when active attention is *not* paid to dialect differences. With regard to speaking in class, children should be permitted to use their own dialect without penalty, even when they are reading from a Standard English text. Reading is not a process of decoding to sound, but of decoding to meaning (Smith, 1973). If the child has grasped the meaning, then there is nothing wrong in his encoding of this meaning in sounds most familiar to him; indeed, it is most natural. Tolerance of difference and the desire to promote meaningful communication should be the concerns of the teacher here. Some have suggested that to ease reading development itself, texts should be produced which are written in non-standard dialect. There is no good evidence, however, to show that this aids the development of reading skills among non-standard speakers (eg Edwards, 1977b). Clearly the practical difficulties would be large; how many varieties should be catered for, how should a transition to Standard English texts be accomplished, and so on? Also, there are some indications that such a course of action would not be welcomed by minority group parents, on the grounds that the school *should* be an agent of the mainstream society in which they wish their children to move (Covington, 1976).

How, then, can a minority child's linguistic repertoire be expanded, if active approaches are to be ruled out? It must be remembered here that the child is not living entirely apart from mainstream society; he is, in fact, inundated with Standard English-speaking models. Further, much evidence has demonstrated that many disadvantaged children are able to understand Standard English, even if they do not customarily use it, from an early age (see Edwards, 1979a). The issue is not so much one of comprehension of the standard as it is of the *production* of it. The child, in a sense, has a choice as to whether or not he uses Standard English — even though home and peer pressure may not always be conducive to choosing. The teacher, in particular, acts as a model from which the child may gradually come to understand in which contexts Standard English is most appropriate and where, therefore, its use is likely to be most beneficial. As with other important and personal aspects of life, much must be left to the discretion of those most directly involved. This does not mean that the teacher cannot act as a guide to the child, but the process of becoming bidialectal — if this is what is desired by child and family — is not one which responds well to force or suggestion. Finally, lest it be thought that all this is much too *laissez-faire*, bear in mind that any more formal approach is not likely to work and/or may widen a gap which already too often exists between the disadvantaged child and the school.

Social change

What has been discussed in the last section involves attempted change — in attitude, if nothing else — on the part of the school in order to improve the treatment of the problems of disadvantaged children. I mentioned that the school's ability to combat disadvantage itself was quite limited, however, and this factor has led some to advocate much more thorough-going social change. Widespread social alteration is sometimes seen as the ultimate solution to material and social class inequities. Here, however, the gist of the discussion should raise a cautionary note. Although large scale upheavals dislocate social classes, one often observes in their aftermath that new inequalities have been created: although the characteristics may change, disadvantage itself may well remain. It is as well, then, to remember that relativism of one sort or another seems to be a long-enduring aspect of society.

An awareness of history, coupled with the realization that disadvantaged populations themselves are often keener to succeed within the system than to run the risks involved in overturning it, has directed more and more attention towards broader attacks on minority problems *within* society. These often retain, interestingly enough, a central focus on the school, but they see the school in a less isolated and more socially involved role. I refer here in particular to the renewed interest, especially in the United States, in cultural pluralism — in which the school's role is to provide bilingual and bicultural education. Related movements can be seen in Britain, continental Europe, Canada and elsewhere.

At its inception, American bilingual education was essentially an anti-poverty measure designed to help minority children of limited English-speaking ability adjust to, and succeed in, the mainstream. In this 'transitional' mode, bilingual education has achieved some success, although proponents of cultural pluralism note that this has actually hastened the assimilation of minorities. It has not, therefore, overturned the 'melting pot' (for some recent comments see Fishman, 1980). The cultural pluralists hope for bilingual education in a 'maintenance' mode — ie a continuing programme which will sustain and encourage a permanently pluralistic society. There are, however, some difficulties here.

The first is that many of those who participate in bilingual education do not appear to be particularly concerned with pluralism. It has been argued that, in coming to a new country, immigrants made an implicit choice regarding the relative priorities of language and culture on the one hand, and of more immediate economic considerations on the other. Thus many of them essentially agree — at least in principle — with assimilation (see Edwards, 1979a). The proponents of cultural pluralism are, indeed, often ethnic minority group members themselves, but are usually well-assimilated, secure and in a position to reflect at leisure on questions of culture and tradition (Edwards, 1977a, 1980a, 1980b; Higham, 1975; Weinreich, 1974).

Cultural pluralism itself is not always a well-thought-out phenomenon. Besides promoting 'roots' it may also act to keep people enclosed within ethnic boundaries (Drake, 1979) and may lead to the increasing fragmentation of society. Writings on the subject are often confused minglings of fact and value, since most authors have a particular axe to grind; indeed, many of them appear to advocate a return to some romantically-perceived past in which ethnic, spiritual and religious values are triumphant over the crass forces of materialism (Edwards, 1980a, 1980b).

Nevertheless, the sentiments from which a philosophy of cultural pluralism springs are not ignoble. The difficulty, according to Higham (1975: 232) is to resolve the 'opposition between a strategy of integration and one of pluralism'. He advocates 'pluralistic integration' in which diversity exists within a larger unity and in which general interests and specific claims may be attended to. In a way, this is a solution which many ethnic minorities seem to adopt themselves. I have pointed out elsewhere that the forces of assimilation do not entirely nullify ethnicity, and elements of original life-style remain (Edwards, 1977a). This, it may be argued, is a poor residue for groups who have traded away the visible and public aspects of their ethnicity — including the regular use of a mother tongue. Nevertheless, in the absence of legislated coercion (in the United States, at least) this trading seems to be a process willingly engaged in by many ethnic minorities. It would seem unwise to attempt, as do cultural pluralists, to push for more active affirmations of diversity until one is more certain that this is generally desired. A final, and useful, point to remember here is that the apparent tolerance towards ethnic groups which is found (or at least expressed) today cannot necessarily be equated with favourable dispositions towards pluralism (Drake, 1979).

Conclusions

My major purpose has been to consider some aspects of minority education in the light of evidence currently available. The point of this is to demonstrate that the linguistic and psychological difficulties of the disadvantaged are ones which arise mainly when comparisons are made. Given the nature of societies, and of status relationships, it is surely no surprise that, in comparisons of minority groups with mainstream members, the former often come off second-best. It is important to remember that these comparisons rest upon social convention, and not upon innate or logical deficiencies, while at the same time to realize that social problems are also pressing.

The next logical step is to consider what, if anything, should be done. Here the argument leads to the conclusion that active intervention is less apposite than tolerance and understanding — an unremarkable conclusion, since these are, in any event, widely-touted virtues. At least, however, in the present case it has been arrived at after other more active possibilities have been considered and it is not, therefore, merely a pious generality. If, after all, one accepts that the linguistic and cognitive capabilities of minorities are not deficient, then special attention of a compensatory or remedial nature is simply not called for. Within a tolerant society — and, especially, within a tolerant educational system which, on the evidence at hand, ought to be tolerant — minority individuals and groups should and will define themselves *vis-à-vis* the mainstream. Our task is to understand, and to promote further understanding on the part of others. This is a great, and a demanding, undertaking.

References

Abrahams, R and Troike, R eds (1972) *Language and Cultural Diversity in American Education* Prentice-Hall: Englewood Cliffs, NJ

Anderson, E (1969) The social factors have been ignored *Harvard Educational Review* **39**: 581-5

Ashworth, M (1975) *Immigrant Children and Canadian Schools* McClelland and Stewart: Toronto

Bereiter, C and Engelmann, S (1966) *Teaching Disadvantaged Children in the Pre-school* Prentice-Hall: Englewood Cliffs, NJ

Bernstein, B (1959) A public language: some sociological implications of a linguistic form *British Journal of Sociology* **10**: 311-26

Bernstein, B (1972) Social class, language and socialization *in* Giglioli (1972)

Bernstein, B (1973) A brief account of the theory of codes *in* Lee (1973)

Bloom, B (1969) The Jensen article *Harvard Educational Review* **39**: 419-21

Brown, D (1979) *Mother Tongue to English* Cambridge University Press: Cambridge

Butcher, H ed (1968) *Educational Research in Britain* University of London Press: London

Covington, A (1976) Black people and Black English: Attitudes and deeducation in a biased macroculture *in* Harrison and Trabasso (1976)

Cronbach, L (1969) Heredity, environment, and educational policy *Harvard Educational Review* 39: 338-47

Deutsch, M ed (1967) *The Disadvantaged Child* Basic Books: New York

Drake, G (1979) Ethnicity, values and language policy in the United States *in* Giles and Saint-Jacques (1979)

Edwards, J (1977a) Ethnic identity and bilingual education *in* Giles (1977)

Edwards, J (1977b) Reading, language and disadvantage *in* Greaney (1977)

Edwards, J (1979a) *Language and Disadvantage* Edward Arnold: London

Edwards, J (1979b) Judgements and confidence in reactions to disadvantaged speech *in* Giles and St Clair (1979)

Edwards, J (1980a) Bilingual education: facts and values *Canadian Modern Language Review* (in press)

Edwards, J (1980b) Critics and criticisms of bilingual education *Modern Language Journal* (in press)

Edwards, V (1979) *The West Indian Language Issue in British Schools* Routledge and Kegan Paul: London

Fishman, J (1980) Bilingualism and biculturism as individual and as societal phenomena *Journal of Multilingual and Multicultural Development* 1: 3-15

Giglioli, P ed (1972) *Language and Social Context* Penguin: Harmondsworth

Giles, H ed (1977) *Language, Ethnicity and Intergroup Relations* Academic Press: London

Giles, H, Bourhis, R and Davies, A (1975) Prestige speech styles: the imposed norm and inherent value hypotheses *in* McCormack and Wurm (1975)

Giles, H, Bourhis, R, Trudgill, P and Lewis, A (1974) The imposed norm hypothesis: a validation *Quarterly Journal of Speech* 60: 405-10

Giles, H and Powesland, P (1975) *Speech Style and Social Evaluation* Academic Press: London

Giles, H and St Clair, R eds (1979) *Language and Social Psychology* Blackwell: Oxford

Giles, H and Saint-Jacques, B eds (1979) *Language and Ethnic Relations* Pergamon: Oxford

Gleitman, L and Gleitman, H (1970) *Phrase and Paraphrase* Norton: New York

Greaney, V ed (1977) *Studies in Reading* Educational Company: Dublin

Harrison, D and Trabasso, T eds (1976) *Black English: A Seminar* Erlbaum: Hillsdale, NJ

Hess, R and Bear, R eds (1968) *Early Education* Aldine: Chicago, Ill

Hess, R and Shipman, V (1968) Maternal influences upon early learning: the cognitive environments of urban pre-school children *in* Hess and Bear (1968)

Higham, J (1975) *Send These to Me* Atheneum: New York

Jensen, A (1969) How much can we boost IQ and scholastic achievement? *Harvard Educational Review* 39: 1-123

Jensen, A (1973) *Educability and Group Differences* Harper and Row: New York

Kagan, J (1969) Inadequate evidence and illogical conclusions *Harvard Educational Review* 39: 274-7

Keddie, N ed (1973) *Tinker, Tailor . . . The Myth of Cultural Deprivation* Penguin: Harmondsworth

Khan, V S (1980) The 'mother-tongue' of linguistic minorities in multicultural England *Journal of Multilingual and Multicultural Development* 1: 71-88

Labov, W (1973) The logic of nonstandard English *in* Keddie (1973)

Leacock, E ed (1971) *The Culture of Poverty: A Critique* Simon and Schuster: New York

Lee, V ed (1973) *Social Relationships and Language* Open University Press: Bletchley

Lenneberg, E (1967) *Biological Foundations of Language* Wiley: New York

McCormack, W and Wurm, S eds (1975) *Language in Many Ways* Mouton: The Hague

Passow, A (1970) *Deprivation and Disadvantage* Unesco Institute for Education: Hamburg

Philips, S (1972) Acquisition of roles for appropriate speech usage *in* Abrahams and Troike (1972)

Rist, R (1970) Student social class and teacher expectations: the self-fulfilling prophecy in ghetto education *Harvard Educational Review* **40**: 411-51

Rose, A (1972) Minorities *in* Sills (1972)

Rosenthal, R and Jacobson, L (1968) *Pygmalion in the Classroom* Holt, Rinehart and Winston: New York

Royal Institute of International Affairs (1963) *Nationalism* Frank Cass: London

Seligman, C, Tucker, G and Lambert, W (1972) The effects of speech style and other attributes on teachers' attitudes toward pupils *Language in Society* **1**: 131-42

Sills, D ed (1972) *International Encyclopedia of the Social Sciences* (Vol 9/10) Collier Macmillan: New York

Smith, F (1973) *Psycholinguistics and Reading* Holt, Rinehart and Winston: New York

Trudgill, P (1975) *Accent, Dialect and the School* Edward Arnold: London

Wax, M and Wax, R (1971) Cultural deprivation as an educational ideology *in* Leacock (1971)

Weinreich, U (1974) *Languages in Contact* Mouton: The Hague

Widgren, J (1975) Recent trends in European migration policies *International Review of Education* **21**: 275-85

Williams, F (1976) *Explorations of the Linguistic Attitudes of Teachers* Newbury: Rowley, Mass

Wiseman, S (1968) Educational deprivation and disadvantage *in* Butcher (1968)

Wiseman, S (1973) The educational obstacle race: factors that hinder pupil progress *Educational Research* **15**: 87-93

3. Trends in educational response to multicultural challenge

Derrick Sharp

Summary: The present and the immediate future offer an exciting challenge and a great chance to make rapid progress in the education of minorities. Throughout the world the rights and needs of minority groups in all spheres of life are increasingly being recognized, while in many countries greater sums of money are being devoted to educational research and development in this field. Examples of work in progress in basic research, theoretical study, curriculum development and the implementation of language policies are given to indicate the scope of current work. Aspects identified as likely to be of particular importance during the next ten years are the need for information and its dissemination, evaluation of outcomes, the preservation of mother tongues, the language medium of teaching and learning, the involvement of parents and the wider community, the apparent conflict between the demands of basic and applied research, and the necessity of avoiding the harmful effects of backlash. Cultural considerations are borne in mind and mentioned, but not treated in detail. The final emphasis is on learning from a variety of language communities which differ from one's own but which have features in common.

Introduction

The present and the immediate future offer an exciting challenge and a great chance to make rapid progress in the education of minorities. Throughout the world the rights and needs of minority groups in all spheres of life are increasingly being recognized, while in many countries greater sums of money are being devoted to educational research and development in this field. Increased awareness may produce rapid results, for it indicates enormous potential and a scope which perhaps even now we do not fully appreciate. The scope may be suggested by the range of chapters in this *Yearbook*, which cover concepts and issues, matters of national policy, questions of relationship between minority and majority languages, a review of the research into educational opportunity for minority groups and an account of educational experiments.

The scope of worldwide concern is also indicated by the response to the launching of *The Journal of Multilingual and Multicultural Development* in 1980. During the 18 months of preparation for publication, this journal has received correspondence and articles from no fewer than

39 countries: Australia, Austria, Belgium, Canada, China, Denmark, England, Finland, France, Germany, Ghana, Greece, Holland, Hong Kong, India, Ireland, Israel, Italy, Japan, Malaysia, Mexico, New Zealand, Nigeria, Norway, Panama, Peru, the Philippines, Russia, Scotland, Senegal, Singapore, Solomon Islands, South Africa, Spain, Sweden, Switzerland, Tanzania, the United States of America and Wales. It is good to see India, a most complex pluralistic society for centuries, in the list, and to note a developing interest there following the first conference, in 1976, concerned with bilingualism (see Sharma and Kumar, 1977).

Increased awareness has been accompanied by recognition of the opportunities provided by, and the benefits to be gained from, added investment of all kinds in the education of minorities. A major contribution here has been made by Canadian French immersion programmes, not only through their fundamental work in curriculum development, language teaching research and evaluation, but also because of the scale and duration of the work.

Pike (1979) starts his article on 'Social linguistics and bilingual education' with a section of perspectives on the advantages of bilingual education. He juxtaposes the economic advantages with the psychological ('the developing or support of confidence in oneself as a valued individual') and sociological (the group identity of an ethnic community). The section is balanced by an awareness of the opposite point of view which sees ethnic identity in minority groups as a threat to national unity because it could be the road to separatism, and an appreciation of the practical problems which may result from a decision to maintain a mother tongue and to cater for mother tongue medium teaching at various levels in an educational system. Fishman (1980a) gives the effective counter-argument to those who would stress the dangers of separatism as a result of mother tongue maintenance.

There is a developing emphasis, therefore, on a progressive approach which seeks advantages in multicultural education; even so we still tend to think in terms of problems and disadvantages, an attitude traditional in many parts of the world. It is easy to sympathize with the feelings of the practising teacher who might have to cope with the problem of ten different native languages in one classroom but we must rapidly learn to think positively rather than negatively when we plan work, at whatever level, on the education of minority groups. This does not mean that we should ignore the difficulties, however.

The survey which follows as a preliminary to the identification of lines of development for the future is necessarily brief. The references are intended as examples, and although the reader may well prefer others, a clear pattern can be identified, which is that very little purely abstract work is being done. The examples chosen all demonstrate the close weave between theory and practice in this field, for all are firmly based on the relevant educational system and are concerned with practical outcomes, even when the basis of the study is essentially conceptual. The present writer's own work reflects the mixture of basic research, curriculum development and language planning which is a common formula (see Sharp, 1973; Sharp *et al*, 1973, 1977).

Theoretical study and basic research

Parts 3 and 4 of this *Yearbook* comprise contributions from eight different countries and give an appreciation of the many live issues and avenues being explored. In these chapters the emphasis is on theoretical consider-ations and fundamental investigation, but the issues appear elsewhere in the *Yearbook*.

The authors of the chapters in this volume speak for themselves. To their work must be added a mention, at least, of the immense and varied contribution of Professor Joshua A Fishman. It is impossible to attempt to summarize his contribution in a few words; in a recent article (Fishman, 1980c) he refers selectively to nine of his own articles or longer works which relate to his study of bilingualism and biculturalism, and the related concepts of diglossia and di-ethnia. Because his theoretical concerns are so firmly based in the social context and related to such practical matters as language planning, I shall refer to his work again later in this chapter.

Alongside Fishman we may place Professor W E Lambert, who has carried out invaluable study and investigation in Canada in recent years. Apart from his contribution to the St Lambert experiment, relevant also under the later heading of curriculum development, we may take as an example an article on the effects of bilingualism on the individual (Lambert, 1977). In this he uses the ideas of 'additive' and 'subtractive' bilingualism to suggest that the cognitive advantages of bilingualism accrue to the person whose strong first language is under no threat from his second language (additive bilingualism), whereas if the first language is eroded and perhaps replaced by a second language of higher status in the eyes of the world (subtractive bilingualism) cognitive disadvantages seem to follow. These concepts are of vital concern in the education of minorities.

French immersion programmes in Canada have stimulated and are stimulating a great deal of valuable work of various kinds, not least in the continuing evaluation of the results (see, for example, Swain, Lapkin and Andrew, forthcoming). The work of Merrill Swain, in this field, immediately brings to mind that of her colleague, James Cummins (eg Cummins, 1979a; Cummins and Das, 1977), whose range of interests is considerable but whose main concern has been the relationship between bilingualism and cognition, including such questions as whether bilingual-ism tends to make the individual more analytical in his approach to languages and perhaps more interested in language. Another from the same part of the world who is making an increasingly valuable contribution is Fred Genesee (eg 1979). In an important article on 'Bilingualism, cognitive functioning and education' (Swain and Cummins, 1979) the authors draw together threads from the work of many scholars. Extensive research and experimentation have been conducted in Europe over many years; some of this will figure in later parts of this chapter, but recent reports include Project Friesland (Wijnstra, 1978), Triglossia in Flemish Belgium (Baetens Beardsmore and Craen, 1979) and mother tongue teaching and learning in Finland (eg Skutnabb-Kangas and Toukomaa, 1976).

Interesting work is gaining momentum in many parts of the world including the USA. The Research Plan for Bilingual Education (1979-83) of the United States Department of Health, Education and Welfare was published as a possible model for other parts of the world of 'research and information gathering on education for persons of limited English proficiency'. Any reference to the United States of America embraces a great amount of work at both federal and state level which could probably never be assessed as a whole.

Curriculum development

In many countries, study proposals which have a practical outcome in classroom materials or teaching techniques more readily attract financial resources than do schemes of fundamental research. This means that curriculum development is likely to continue wherever operational programmes of any kind are pursued. In some ways even more important, though, is the evaluation and dissemination of the outcomes, for there are examples of the results of considerable investment being wasted for lack of follow-up resources. The problem is most difficult in those educational systems which do not have a high degree of central control, but there are signs, described in a later section, that this important aspect is at last receiving the attention it needs.

The work on immersion programmes in Canada has already been mentioned. The evaluation and dissemination of these programmes are extensively documented, in the references given earlier, and also in Lambert and Tucker (1972), Genesee (1978 and 1980) and Swain and Barik (1976). Nor should the Irish experience and its lessons be forgotten (Cummins, 1979b).

To list other examples (such as the substantial funding devoted by the Schools Council and the Welsh Office to curriculum development in both Welsh and English in Wales) would rapidly become tedious. Instead, let us examine briefly two very different straws in the wind.

The first is an article by Janice Yalden (1980) in which she identifies different developments in second language teaching, both theory and practice, in the United Kingdom and in North America. Halliday's suggestion that a language system w.ould be better seen as a system for making meanings than as a system for generating structures has led in Britain to the functional/notional or communicative approach. Yalden looks at this approach in her review of current research and teaching in the second language field in the United Kingdom and suggests that the present position represents a promising combination of theoretical developments and practical needs.

The other 'straw' is the production of a multicultural booklist (Ballin, Bleach and Levine, 1980) for the age range five to 16 years. Headings in the secondary section include general topics; the experience of the children; reggae, rasta and Black consciousness; Caribbean writing; African writing; South Africa; slavery; and other sources are also given. It is significant and encouraging that this is just one indicator of a growing literature.

Language policies

Language policies are a fascinating study because of their infinite variety. When they are policies for minority groups in varying types of community, the possibilities seem endless. Whether the policies are developed for predominantly educational reasons or not, the consequential needs in the educational system are vital to the implementation of the policy. Not least among these needs is an efficient and dedicated teaching force, essential when a minority group is in any sense oppressed or disadvantaged. Too often a fine language policy results in little or no development in practice because of a lack of properly trained and informed teachers.

The relevant points emerge clearly from Fishman's analytical approach to 'Bilingual education, language planning and English':

> In the USA Title VII Bilingual Education involves the admission of languages into the American public school that were never used there before, as well as the preparation of teaching-learning materials ... for languages, many of which lacked these before, rather than continuing with the exclusive use of English for populations not proficient in it. In the case of ethnic community schools bilingual education involves seeking more effective school-and-community outcomes − hopefully the reversal of language shift tendencies − by means of predesignated (ie planned) school-and-community experiences to counteract the English mainstream and its eroding effect on ethnic mother tongue. (Fishman, 1980b: 11)

After examples drawn from Ireland, Palestine, Quebec, Switzerland and Malaysia, Fishman continues:

> Thus, in many different ways, the authorities allocate resources to language in order to realise language status goals. Promotions, raises, appointments, awards, grants and publicity, on the one hand, and demotions, penalties, dismissals, fines and punishments, on the other hand, are utilized to implement status planning. (Fishman, 1980b)

Language planning is not new, as a process or even as a term (Haugen, 1966), but it takes on a new meaning in the light of such ideas.

Specific aspects

From time to time specific aspects of the education of minority groups receive attention in one country or several. Sometimes the issue is ephemeral, at other times it persists and develops.

One example — a highly controversial one — is semi-lingualism (see Skutnabb-Kangas and Toukomaa, 1976; Toukomaa and Skutnabb-Kangas, 1977). The concept of a bilingual child whose level of performance is so low that he may be said to have 'two second languages' is a useful one, but it raises serious questions. Any suggestion that bilingualism inevitably involves semi-lingualism for any substantial proportion of a population must be resisted, because it could become a self-fulfilling prophecy. Others maintain that any notion including 'semi' is bound to be prejudicial.

Another example of such work is the finding that in certain circumstances, as existed in the specially created bilingual schools in Wales, it seems that the minority language can be fostered at the apparent expense of the majority language but without in fact harming pupils' progress in that majority language (Sharp *et al*, 1973). A final example is the interesting explanation of the role of the speech therapist in the language assessment of bilingual children (Abudarham, 1980).

The way ahead

All the areas outlined so far cover work which will continue in the future. In some cases it will develop and increase in importance, whereas in others it will perform a supportive, servicing role. Some aspects are likely to be of particular importance during the next ten years, and the remainder of this chapter will be devoted to an attempt to identify them.

The need for information and dissemination

'Growth industry' is a popular term in educational circles. Though often used pejoratively, it aptly describes the worldwide appearance of projects and centres devoted to the gathering of information and its dissemination in our field. It is sadly true that in the past we have all tended to be too parochial, but over the last 20 years or so, and especially in recent years, the need has been appreciated and action taken.

The Linguistic Minorities Project is directed by Dr Verity Saifullah Khan of the University of London Institute of Education. It has the task of gathering information about minority groups in England, but in addition its vital contribution will be in devising instruments for collecting the information and developing techniques of analysis to detect significance. The London Institute also houses the recently established (1979) Centre for Multicultural Education, with Dr J S Gundara as full-time co-ordinator, and the team directed by Professor Harold Rosen which has worked on the Survey of Language Diversity in London Schools and is studying the educational implications and opportunities.

There is also the Schools Council Development Unit in Multi-ethnic

Education based in the School of Education at the University of Nottingham. Under the guidance of Professor Maurice Craft its task is to consolidate and disseminate information on classroom and library materials of a pluralistic kind. We have already mentioned Project Friesland (Wijnstra, 1978), which included a comparative study of Welsh results, and to this we can add the project sponsored by the European Economic Community at the University of Cambridge Institute of Education concerned with 'Mother tongue and culture in Bedfordshire'. All this is in addition to the very many centres of various kinds established by education authorities and institutions of higher education to help teachers. Some have the specific brief of dealing with multilingualism and multiculturalism.

Other examples include the Research Centre for Multilingualism, established in Brussels in 1969 and directed by Professor P H Nelde; and in the USA, the Summer Institute of Linguistics, Dallas, Texas; the National Center for Bilingual Research at Los Alamitos, California; and the work of TESOL (Teachers of English to Speakers of Other Languages). The literature of these centres, combined with that of individual scholars noted earlier in the chapter, forms a major contribution in this field.

The evaluation of outcomes

It is obvious that we should measure the success of major investment in basic research and curriculum development. Nevertheless, in the past this simple fact has often been overlooked, and we have continued to devote resources to less worthy developments. The point does not need elaboration, except to draw attention to the importance of long-term evaluation (as in the assessment of French immersion programmes referred to under theoretical study and basic research) and to the continuing necessity to develop and refine instruments of measurement. (See also Tucker and Cziko, 1978).

The preservation of mother tongues

For minority groups the preservation of mother tongues is probably the most crucial aspect of language planning. In a recent article, Fishman (1980a) begins by stating:

> With the 'new ethnicity' movement that has developed in the USA (and, in addition, also in much of the Western world as a whole) since the late 60s, hopes for minority language maintenance have risen dramatically within minority language communities themselves.

He then analyses realistically the role of the ethnic mother tongue school, asking specifically whether it can make an *independent* contribution to language maintenance, and concludes by stressing that language maintenance must be a serious moral issue of national life. It is interesting to compare this article with that reporting one of Verity Saifullah Khan's early surveys (1976). In her examination of long-established mother tongue schools in England she mentions no fewer than 17 languages as *examples*.

Mother tongue preservation is a controversial issue, sometimes within minority communities themselves. Too often the differences reflect varying attitudes among the generations, the elders wishing to preserve their original language and customs, the younger members seeking rapid integration with the host country's language and culture. Any attempt to improve proficiency in the major language, particularly if the aim is true bilingualism, may be seen by the elders as a threat to the minority language and way of life. The vexed question of the language medium of teaching and learning in schools is a part of this hotly debated theme.

Involvement of parents and the wider community

The content of the last paragraph leads naturally to consideration of how to involve parents and other adults in the minority group in the education of the young. This is a problem area, and although the difficulties are not restricted to ethnic minorities they are often more complex in these cases because of a conflict of cultures in, for instance, marriage customs. The central issue is that of relationships, one aspect of which is dealt with in Part 3 of this *Yearbook*.

We are here in the realm of attitudes, the exploration of which is one important feature of the Linguistic Minorities Project's work. We cannot change attitudes directly in most cases, but we can alter the circumstances which condition attitudes and thus hope for long-term improvement. A high level of parental backing and involvement, of interest and concern, is clearly one important factor in the success of the bilingual schools in Wales.

The value of a positive approach is supported in a paper by Cummins entitled 'Research findings from French immersion programs across Canada: a parents' guide' (The Ontario Institute for Studies in Education). This not only gives information and sources of further information but also identifies clearly the issues which arise and anticipates in this way many questions parents are likely to ask. It is a truism in education that the parents we most want to see are the very ones who never attend meetings of Parent Teacher Associations. All we can do is keep trying in what is certainly one of the most difficult of our tasks.

Conclusion

The competing priority between basic and applied research is likely to persist as a major issue in the next decade. Should we wait for 'essential', fundamental information which it may take several years to gather and sift before we start curriculum development in the relevant area? Or should we press on in the light of existing knowledge and experience or intuition, running the risk that the foundation of our endeavours may be suspect or false? There is no easy answer, but practical and economic pressures have meant that it has become less difficult to gain funding for applied research, as suggested earlier. The solution in many parts of the world therefore resembles the 'typically British' compromise.

Another recurrent dilemma is an ever-present danger only too familiar to some minorities. If they press too hard for their rights and/or equitable treatment, they may suffer a backlash from the more powerful majority which will leave them worse off than they were before. Matters of nice judgement are involved, based on persuasion and patience, because militant methods are often sadly counter-productive. However, this consideration takes us back to the linguistic and educational fields, into political and religious issues which are raised elsewhere in this *Yearbook*, especially in the preceding chapter.

References

Abudarham, S (1980) The role of the speech therapist in the assessment of language-learning potential and proficiency of children with dual language systems or backgrounds *Journal of Multilingual and Multicultural Development* 1 3: 187-206

Alatis, J E *ed* (1978) *Georgetown University Round Table on Languages and Linguistics* University of Georgetown Press: Washington DC

Baetens Beardsmore, H and Van de Craen, P (1979) The development of triglossia in Flemish Belgium *in* Van de Velde and Vandeweghe (1979)

Ballin, R, Bleach, J and Levine, J (1980) *A Wider Heritage: a selection of books for children and young people in multicultural Britain* National Book League: London

Cummins, J (1979a) Cognitive/academic language proficiency, linguistic interdependence, the optimal age question and some other matters *Working Papers in Bilingualism* 19: 197-205

Cummins, J (1979b) Immersion programmes: the Irish experience *International Review of Education* 49: 222-51

Cummins, J and Das, J P (1977) Cognitive processing and reading difficulties: a framework for research *The Alberta Journal of Educational Research* 23: 245-56

Fishman, J A (1980a) Minority language maintenance and the ethnic mother tongue school *The Modern Language Journal* 64 2: 167-72

Fishman, J A (1980b) Bilingual education, language planning and English *English World-wide: a Journal of Varieties of English* 1 1: 11-24

Fishman, J A (1980c) Bilingualism and biculturalism as individual and as societal phenomena *Journal of Multilingual and Multicultural Development* 1 1: 3-15

Genesee, F (1978) A longitudinal evaluation of an early immersion school program *Canadian Journal of Education* 3: 31-50

Genesee, F (1979) Scholastic effects of French immersion: an overview after ten years *Interchange* 9: 20-9

Genesee, F (1980) *A Comparison of Early and Late Immersion Programs* Department of Psychology, McGill University

Haugen, E (1966) *Language Conflict and Language Planning: The Case of Modern Norwegian* Harvard University Press: Cambridge, Mass

Hornby, P A *ed* (1977) *Bilingualism: psychological, social and educational implications* Academic Press: New York

Khan, V S (1976) Provision by minorities for language maintenance *in Bilingualism and British Education: the dimensions of diversity* CILT Reports and Papers **14**: 31-47, London

Lambert, W E (1977) The effects of bilingualism on the individual: cognitive and sociocultural consequences *in* Hornby (1977)

Lambert, W E and Tucker, G R (1972) *Bilingual Education of Children: The St Lambert Experiment* Newbury House: Rowley, Mass

Pike, K L (1979) Social linguistics and bilingual education *System* **7** 2: 99-109

Rawkins, P M (1979) *The Implementation of Language Policy in the Schools of Wales* Centre for the Study of Public Policy: University of Strathclyde

Sharma, P G and Kumar, S eds (1977) *Indian Bilingualism* Kendriya Hindi Sansthan: Agra

Sharp, D (1973) *Language in Bilingual Communities* Explorations in Language Study, Edward Arnold: London

Sharp, D, Bennett, G and Treharne, C (1977) *English in Wales: A Practical Guide for Teachers* Schools Council: London

Sharp, D, Thomas, B, Price, E, Francis, G and Davies, I (1973) *Attitudes to Welsh and English in the Schools of Wales* Schools Council Research Studies, Macmillan/ University of Wales Press: London

Skutnabb-Kangas, T and Toukomaa, P (1976) *Teaching Migrant Children's Mother Tongue and Learning the Language of the Host Country in the Context of the Socio-cultural Situation of the Migrant Family* Tutkimuksia Research Reports **15**, Department of Sociology and Social Psychology, University of Tampere: Finland

Spolsky, B and Cooper, R eds (1978) *Case Studies in Bilingual Education* Newbury House: Rowley, Mass

Swain, M and Barik, H C (1976) *Five years of primary French immersion: annual reports of the bilingual education project to the Carleton Board of Education and the Ottawa Board of Education, 1972-1975* Ministry of Education, Ontario: Toronto

Swain, M and Cummins, J (1979) Bilingualism, cognitive functioning and education *Language Teaching and Linguistics: Abstracts* **12** 1: 4-18

Swain, M, Lapkin, S and Andrew, C M (1981) Early French immersion later on *Journal of Multilingual and Multicultural Development* (forthcoming)

Toukomaa, P and Skutnabb-Kangas, T (1977) *The Intensive Teaching of the Mother Tongue to Migrant Children at Pre-School Age* Tutkimuksia Research Reports 26, Department of Sociology and Social Psychology, University of Tampere: Finland

Tucker, G R and Cziko, G A eds (1978) The role of evaluation in bilingual education *in* Alatis (1978)

Van de Velde, M and Vandeweghe, W eds (1979) *Sprachstrucker, Individium und Gesellschaft* Akten des 13 Linguistischen Kolloquiums, Gent, 1978. **1**: 191-200, Max Niemeyer Verlag: Tübingen

Wijnstra, J M (1978) *Education of children with Frisian home language* Paper presented at the XIXth International Congress of Applied Psychology, Munich, 30 July – 5 August

Yalden, J (1980) Current approaches to second language teaching in the UK *System* **8** 2: 151-6

Part 2:
National policies for minority group education

4. The education of linguistic minorities in the USSR

Nigel Grant

Summary: The peoples of the USSR vary greatly in numbers, language type and level of development. There are obvious problems concerning language development, and less obvious ones in the connections between language and other cultural factors, such as religion. Current trends include different responses to assimilation, and demographic changes, notably the relative increase of numbers among the Central Asian peoples.

Legally, all are guaranteed the right to education in the language of their choice, and are also taught Russian, but there are problems of numbers. Complete education is feasible in the languages of the Union Republics, but for smaller groups native-language education is available only in part, and groups still lacking a written language have to use Russian or another language throughout.

The educational levels of the various groups show many inequalities. Some of these can be related to the degree of urbanization, to the proportion of the population with fluent Russian, or to the strength of the indigenous culture, but we still lack a full explanation in many cases. Developments since 1970 show a diminution of differences generally, and support the view that there is an admissions quota in operation, and also suggest a sustained policy of improvement in Central Asia, both part of a general policy of equalization. The implications of current trends are still uncertain; attempts to encourage 'convergence' could be dangerous, but the development of pluralism, though difficult, holds out more hope for the future of a multinational state.

1. Background

It should not really need to be spelled out that the USSR is, by definition as well as in fact, a multinational state. But the use of the terms 'Russian' and 'Soviet' as if they were synonymous (like that other familiar erroneous equation of 'England' and 'Britain') is so common that it might be as well to take little for granted. There are, then, over a hundred nationalities in the Soviet Union, ranging in size from the Russians themselves, who make up about half the total population, down to groups numbered in thousands or even hundreds, like the Selkup, Tofalar and Yukagir (Isayev, 1977). Details are given in Table 1; it is worth noting that some of the nationalities are small and scattered, which is bound to raise practical problems in education.

It is also relevant that they are varied and distinctive, for we are not

		Thousands	% of total
	USSR	241,720	100
1.	Russians	129,015	53.4
2.	Ukrainians	40,753	16.9
3.	Uzbeks	9,195	3.8
4.	Byelorussians	9,052	3.7
5.	Tatars	5,931	2.5
6.	Kazakhs	5,299	2.2
7.	Azerbaidzhanis	4,380	1.8
8.	Armenians	3,559	1.5
9.	Georgians	3,245	1.3
10.	Moldavians	2,698	1.1
11.	Lithuanians	2,665	1.1
12.	Jews	2,151	0.9
13.	Tadzhiks	1,846	0.8
14.	Chuvash	1,694	0.7
15.	Turkmens	1,525	0.6
16.	Kirgiz	1,452	0.6
17.	Latvians	1,430	0.6
18.	Bashkirs	1,240	0.5
19.	Estonians	1,007	0.4

Over 130 nationalities are listed in the 1970 All-Union Population Census, Vol IV. The above figures are adapted from Kravetz (1980).

Table 1 *Population of the USSR, showing nationalities of over one million, 1970 census figures*

dealing with dialects but with members of different and often unrelated language families. It could be argued that, emotional problems apart, there are few fundamental *learning* difficulties when closely related languages are involved, like Russian, Ukrainian and Byelorussian. Whether the aim is to *transfer* from one usage to another (as from Catalan to Castilian in Franco Spain, or from Occitan to French even now), or to develop competence in another usage *as well* (as in Norway or post-Franco Catalonia), the linguistic similarities can be used to help the process. But this is not the situation with most of the Soviet nationalities. Many, to be sure, belong to the same Indo-European family as the Slavs — the Baltic Lithuanians and Latvians, the Romance Moldavians,* the Germanic Yiddish-speaking Jews,† the Iranian Tadzhiks and Ossetians, and the Armenians, whose language forms a separate branch of the family; but so do speakers of English, Italian, Hindi and Gaelic. Beyond a certain point, affinity is of little help in learning. In any case, the others belong to different language families altogether. There are the various Turkic people,

---

* Moldavian is closely similar to the Romanian used across the frontier, but is written in the Cyrillic script.

† The vast majority of Soviet Jews are Russian-speaking and know no Yiddish. This form of German, transcribed in the Hebrew alphabet, is officially used in the Jewish Autonomous Province of Birobidzhan.

notably the Transcaucasian Azerbaidzhanis and the Uzbeks, Kazakhs, Kirgiz and Turkmens of Central Asia; there are many Finno-Ugric peoples, such as the Estonians and Karelians; there is an extensive Buryat-Mongol group; there are the small groups of the Far East and Far North, and of course the Caucasian group, of which Georgian is the largest and best-known. Linguistically, this is probably as great a variety as any single state can offer.

But linguistic differences rarely exist by themselves. They may be the most conspicuous characteristics, but are frequently one of a whole set of cultural factors, many of which carry practical and political implications for education. One of these concerns the suitability of the languages themselves for formal educational use. Obviously, this question does not arise in the case of the long-established cultures of the Caucasus and the Baltic Republics, for example; but in the case of the more remote Northern peoples, and at one time in Central Asia too, the question of viability has been raised.

This is not in any way to subscribe to the notion that some languages are inherently too 'primitive' — lacking perhaps a written form, or complexity and subtlety of grammatical structure, or the vocabulary to handle the concepts of a technological society and a formal school system. At first glance, this again should not need saying. Macaulay's dismissal of the Indian vernaculars as unsuitable media for modern education, or the reluctance of British or French (or Russian) colonial administrators to see the languages of the peoples they ruled as anything but primitive jargons, might well be thought to have died out in the nineteenth century; and advances in the study of linguistics should, surely, have demolished finally the idea that the indigenous tongues of Africa, Asia or the Americas lacked complexity. (Colonial administrators, of course, tended not only to be ethnocentric in their attitudes, but also to come across vernaculars in a basic 'pidginized' version.) But since such judgements are *still* being made about the viability of, say, Gaelic in Scotland, Kiswahili or Hausa in Africa or Hindi in India, this question should perhaps be dealt with. For a fuller discussion of this issue in relation to the USSR and the Third World, see Grant (1977).

Historically, of course, such devaluing of languages new to the educational mainstream is commonplace. English, German and Russian have all in their day been held inferior to French or Latin; and the latter, in its turn, was thought by its speakers of the early Empire to compare ill with the virtues of Greek. It is the social perception of the status of the speakers of a language, not its inherent qualities, that raise doubts about its capacity as a means of communication and learning. Nor is the lack of a written form all that serious; where that is lacking, it can be supplied — as, indeed, it has been by the Academy of Sciences of the USSR in many cases (Musaev, 1965). (Again, this is precisely what happened in the case of Western and Eastern Europeans alike, who adapted the Latin or Cyrillic forms of the Greek alphabet to suit their own circumstances.)

Vocabulary is another matter. Any language, being a social activity, is likely to be adapted to the social and natural environment in which it is used. (Consider, for example, the variety of words for 'camel' in Arabic or 'snow' in Inniut; these reflect differences which matter.) Many of the languages of the Soviet Far North were, at the time of the Revolution, admirably adapted to the exigiencies of shaministic religion and a nomadic pastoral economy, but lacked the equipment to deal with the realities of a twentieth-century industrial state. This, of course, is not an inherent lack: languages can and do form new words as new needs arise, either by building on native root material (the favoured method in Chinese, Arabic, German and to some extent in the Slavonic languages), or by borrowing and adapting from some convenient source. Thus, Soviet Turkic and Northern languages have drawn heavily on Russian, much as Swahili and Persian drew on Arabic, English on French and Romanian on Slavonic and Hungarian. There are *some* problems, of course. If the cultural levels of the two language groups are far apart, the indigenous language can be swamped with foreign material to the extent that communication between its speakers can be disrupted (as has happened with tongues as diverse as Hindi and Gaelic). It need not be a permanent problem, but until the borrowed material is fully assimilated, entry to the formal educational system can expose the learner to alienation and culture shock.

But if this is a short-term problem, other cultural variables can prove more intractable. It is recognized in the USSR that there are still serious inequalities in aspiration and achievement between urban and rural pupils. Many of those affected are, of course, Russians; but where minority populations are disproportionately rural in their composition, consequent inequalities can take a particularly acute form. It has been widely noted that the problems of minority groups are in large measure those of peripheral areas, and this is frequently found in the Soviet Union also. Strictly speaking, of course, the 'rural problem' in the USSR is quite distinct from the problems of nationalities; but when these coincide — as they often do — difficulties can be compounded.

There is also a religious dimension. Halevy and Etsioni-Halevy (1974) have examined the different levels of educational attainment among the Soviet nationalities, classified by religious background rather than language, in an attempt to test the 'Hans hypothesis' that the formal educational attainment of a group is correlated with actual or traditional religious affiliation, in descending order from Jewish to Protestant to Catholic to Orthodox to Muslim. On the whole, their findings confirm the hypothesis up to fairly recent times, when the Central Asian peoples began to close the gap. It is possible to argue, of course, that the differentials reflected levels of social advance as much as attitude in the first place, and that these have become less important as religious belief dwindles among the various Soviet peoples. But the correlation up to recent times is intriguing, considering that the actual observances of the religions had fallen out of favour, and in many cases out of use. Religious affiliation, like language, may often serve as the main identity symbol in a whole cluster of values and attitudes, which may or may not be connected with the theology itself. Warring Protestants and Catholics in Northern Ireland, for instance, seem to have little interest in converting anyone, for their disputes have little to do with belief but a great deal to do with identity and power, religion being a convenient label. Similarly, many American Catholics, Jews and agnostics cheerfully subscribe in their social and professional behaviour to what is still known as the Protestant ethic, though its connections with religious values of any kind are now obscure. In Muslim societies, the 'traditional' attitudes towards women are particularly marked, though not all go as far as forbidding them to work with men or drive cars. It can be questioned whether such attitudes have any basis in the Qur'an at all — they are certainly a good deal older — but that is not really the point here: they exist, they have become part of the folkways associated with Islam, and thus can survive even the decay of belief. Even now, one still hears of plenty of cases from Soviet Central Asia of girls being kept away from school, forced into arranged marriages, and even of such quite illegal practices as the exaction of bride-price; and significantly, the price seems to go *down* the higher the girl's qualifications are (Grant, 1974). It can happen, then, that when the central authorities are dealing with a linguistic minority, they are tackling not only language but cultural differences of a kind that can run deep, and may pose more of a challenge — since they impinge on the aims and content of education — than the question of the language of instruction.

2. Current trends

Before going on to look at the position in education, we have to take account of current trends, linguistic, cultural and demographic, which affect the background factors. Quite apart from official policy and government action, the push-and-pull effect between cultural assimilation and self-assertion seems to have a dynamic of its own, and it works differently in different cases. For example, the legal policy towards Ukrainian and Armenian is identical, and in both Republics the indigenous language is in conspicuous official use; yet one rarely hears Ukrainian spoken in the streets of Kiev or Russian in the streets of Erevan. About 80 per cent of the schools in the Ukraine use Ukrainian as the medium of instruction, and teach Russian as a second language; but in Kiev itself the position is reversed, and most of the inhabitants speak Russian with a Ukrainian accent. In Armenia, by contrast, only some 3 per cent of the schools use Russian as the medium, though children are taught it. The normal language of communication is, overwhelmingly, Armenian (personal observation in Kiev and Erevan, 1976).

The reasons for such disparities are a matter for speculation. It has been suggested (and forcefully) that the Ukraine, being large and in a sensitive area, has long been subjected to Russifying pressures in order to contain potentially disruptive nationalist aspirations, while Armenia is too small and remote to pose any threat. This is quite possible, though hard to prove;

but there must in any case be other mechanisms at work. It is quite
credible that Ukrainian, being closer to Russian, is more open to cultural
penetration, rather as Scots was by English or Norwegian (for a long time)
by Danish. The contrast between the Ukrainian-speaking countryside and
Russian-speaking Kiev is suggestive, and is paralleled in miniature by a
similar contrast between English-speaking Edinburgh and the nearby
areas of Lothian and other parts of Lowland Scotland where Scots survives
(albeit in dialect form), though in this case without any official sanction
at all. Armenian, however, is quite distinct; it has its own script, its own
high culture dating from the fifth century, and it serves a small but
compact population. There is a growing body of international evidence
that the conventional picture of steady assimilation of smaller to larger
groups, though partly valid, is much too simple, and that pressures to
assimilate may produce, by reaction, the assertion of identity by minority
groups (Grant, 1978). It would be astonishing if the USSR were exempt
from either of these trends, official positions notwithstanding.

The balance of population is changing also. Fertility rates differ
considerably among the peoples of the USSR. Details are given in Tables 2
and 3, but broadly the non-Russian peoples, notably those of Central Asia,
are increasing at a much faster rate; it will not be long before the Soviet
Union is indisputably a country of minorities, the Russians included.
Ideally this is not supposed to matter, as all are 'brother-peoples' together.
But in practice no group likes to see its relative position weakened, and
there must be many looking at the birth-rate figures with some anxiety.
Doubtless — since the survival of past attitudes is not confined to
minorities — some will see this as a good reason for aiming at greater
Russification, while others may see it as an argument for developing

Republic	Birth rate	Death rate	Increase
RSFSR	14.2	8.5	5.7
Ukraine	14.6	8.6	6.0
Byelorussia	15.9	7.4	8.5
Uzbekistan	32.7	5.9	26.8
Kazakhstan	23.5	6.2	17.3
Georgia	18.7	7.5	11.2
Azerbaidzhan	29.3	7.0	22.3
Lithuania	17.4	8.7	8.7
Moldavia	18.9	7.4	11.5
Latvia	14.0	11.1	2.9
Kirgizia	30.1	7.5	22.6
Tadzhikistan	34.7	6.1	28.6
Armenia	22.8	5.2	17.6
Turkmenistan	34.3	7.0	27.3
Estonia	15.5	11.3	4.2

Note: All rates are expressed as a number per thousand, and are based on
1970 census figures.

Table 2 *Birth, death and increase rates by republics (1970)*

Nationality	1959 population	1970 population
Russians	114	129
Ukrainians	37.3	40.8
Uzbeks	6.0	9.2
Byelorussians	7.9	9.1
Tatars	5.0	5.9
Kazakhs	3.6	5.3
Azerbaidzhanis	2.9	4.4
Armenians	2.8	3.6

Note: All figures are in millions, and are based on 1970 census figures.

Table 3 *Increases in population in selected nationalities, 1959-1970*

further-reaching pluralism as a way of living with a situation that cannot readily be altered. Either way, developments in nationality policy are bound to reflect *Realpolitik*, and in turn are bound to affect educational policy and practice.

3. Constitutional and legal position

As far as the medium of instruction is concerned, there is no great problem about the legal position of minorities: all citizens have the right to use their mother tongue if they so wish, and this includes the education of their children. Actually, it is a little more complex than that (quite apart from practical difficulties, which will be considered presently); strictly speaking, every citizen of the USSR has the right to use any of the languages of the country he or she chooses, not necessarily the mother tongue. It may of course be Russian, and often is for a host of practical reasons, or it may be another vernacular. Most of the small ethnic groups of the Far North who lack a written language use Russian, but the Barabas show a preference for Tatar, the Dolgans for Yakut, and the Kereks for Chukchi. In the Caucasus, only the Aisor are listed as making exclusive use of Russian for this purpose; Avar is preferred by the Andi, Archi, Akhvakh, Bezhita, Botlikhe, Ginukhe, Gunzib, Godoberi, Dido, Karati, Kisti, Dagestani Tat, Tindi, Khvarshi and Chamali peoples; Azerbaidzhani by the Budukhes, Kryz, Rutul, Talysh, Tats, Khinalugs and Tsakhurs; similarly the Aguls use Lesgin, and the Bats, Svans and Udis use Georgian. In Central Asia, most of the small groups use Tadzhik, while the Baluchis use Turkmen and the Dungans Kazakh. In some of these cases, Russian is listed as the *second* literary language, but for many it does not appear at all. Language of choice, then, usually means the mother tongue, but there are cases where this is not so (see Table 4).

If Soviet policy is pluralist, it is pluralism on the British or Spanish model rather than the Swiss, Belgian or Yugoslav; that is, Russian, as the

Written languages	Peoples
1. Far North and Siberia	
Russian	Aleuts, Alyutor, Itelmen, Kets, Nganasans, Negidals, Oroks, Orochi, Saami, Tofs, Udege, Chulyms, Enets, Yukagir
Tatar and Russian	Barabas, Kamasin
Yakut and Russian	Dolgans
Chukchi and Russian	Kereks
Russian and Khakas	Shors
2. Caucasus	
Avar and Russian	Audi, Archi, Akhvakh, Bagvlals, Bezhitas, Botlikhes, Ginukhes, Gunzibs, Godoberi, Dido, Karati, Kisti, Tats (Dagestan), Tindi, Khvarshi, Chamali
Lezgin and Russian	Agul
Georgian	Bats, Svans
Georgian and Azerbaidzhani	Udi
Azerbaidzhani	Budukhes, Kryz, Khinalugs
Azerbaidzhani and Russian	Rutuls, Talysh, Tats (Azerbaidzhan)
Azerbaidzhani and Lezgin	Tsakhurs
Russian	Aisors
3. Central Asia	
Tadzhik	Oroshores, Yagnobes, Yazgulam
Tadzhik and Russian	Bartanges, Wakhi, Ishkashim, Rushan, Shugnes
Turkmen and Russian	Baluchi
Kazakh and Russian	Dungans
4. Others	
Russian	Vepsians, Izhorians
Russian and Lithuanian	Livonians
Ukrainian and Lithunian	Karaimes

Source: adapted from Isayev (1977)

Table 4 *Small ethnic groups by written languages used*

majority language and the language of the Soviet state, is taught in all non-Russian schools, and may be used as the main medium of instruction if parents so wish. (The frequency of this has already been noted in Kiev; it is also common in Kazakhstan and Latvia.) This can be urged on grounds of national cohesion and communication, and certainly reasonable competence in the language is widespread. There are, certainly, minorities among the old and the young who do not speak it at all; more surprising, perhaps, is the low incidence of fluent Russian among the other nationalities. According to the 1970 census, only among urban Tatars,

Byelorussians, Moldavians, Lithuanians, Latvians and Kazakhs did more than 50 per cent claim fluency in Russian, and even among these groups the figure for the rural population was much lower. If the aim is to foster Russian as the 'second native language' of the non-Russian peoples, there is clearly a long way to go. But its use as a secondary medium of communication is developed by the school system, and its practical currency is of course much wider than claims to fluency might suggest.

Pluralism does extend some little way beyond language to include literature and artistic and musical idioms, but emphatically not indigenous value systems if they conflict with the official ones. There is no question, for instance, of accepting the 'traditional' Muslim view of the role of women just because (for whatever reason) it is part of the culture. There may be concessions, like the not infrequent seating of boys and girls separately in class, or the retention of the odd women's pedagogical school; but they are tactical, not a sign of acceptance. Stalin's famous formulation about developing 'a culture national in form but socialist in content' is significant here; the structure of the school system, and the value system it seeks to promulgate, are uniform and centrally determined; and if sometimes it is decided to hasten slowly, to try gradualism and persuasion rather than coercion, this is a question of the best means to the end, not a rejection of the end itself. Pluralism in this case is of form, while the approach to content is essentially unitary.

4. Constraints and limitations in practice

But policy thus defined is still constrained by practical problems of level of development and of numbers. Neither of these is much of a problem in the Ukraine, Armenia, Georgia or the Baltic Republics. All of these have well-established literary forms, and populations (even in the case of smaller groups like the Armenians or Estonians) sufficiently numerous and compact to make the full range of schooling in the vernacular a practical possibility. The Central Asian languages have had a more chequered career. Before the Revolution, some were not written at all, since the few who were literate tended to use the related literary forms of Turkish or Persian or the unrelated Arabic; those with a written form used the Arabic script. When the written languages were being developed after the Revolution, the Latin alphabet was used at first, then the transition was made to modified forms of the Cyrillic alphabet. This was attacked in some quarters as an attempt to break links with the Islamic world and Russianize the Central Asian peoples; but even if there was an element of this, it can be argued that the Arabic alphabet, aesthetically beautiful though it is, is complex in its own right, and, being based on an essentially consonantal system, adapts ill to the phonemically quite different Iranian and Turkic languages. This at least was the view of Kemal Atatürk in Turkey, and the reason for switching to the Latin alphabet as a basis for mass literacy; and from this point of view there is little to choose between

Latin and Cyrillic, both (with Greek) alphabets of the same type.* They
have now, in any case, had long enough experience of literary use to be
viable, and they are also read by sufficient numbers to make it practicable.

The extent of usage varies somewhat. In Kazakhstan, where a high
proportion of the population is Russian, the preference for Russian-
medium schools is said to be on the increase, even among Kazakhs. (Urban
Kazakhs have, after the Tatars, the highest proportion of fluent Russian
speakers of all the major Turkic peoples.) In Uzbekistan, the vernacular
appears to be stronger. Other groups again, as already mentioned, have had
scripts designed for their languages and used in the schools. Even this,
though, has not always proved sufficient. The written Karelian language,
for instance, has never become viable, as the closely related Finnish is
available (as well as Russian). Yet others, like the small groups of the Far
North, the Caucasus and Central Asia, still lack a written language, and
therefore receive their schooling either in Russian or whatever vernacular
they generally use as their literary language.

But whether languages have a written form or not, there comes a point
where paucity of numbers limits the feasibility of full-scale vernacular
schooling. Instruction in Georgian or Latvian or Uzbek or Ukrainian, from
kindergarten to university, is quite a reasonable expectation on practical
as well as legal grounds, but is clearly not possible for tiny groups like the
Orochi, the Tofalar or the Selkup. In practice, there is therefore a great
deal of variety in the extent of vernacular schooling. The whole range is
available in the languages of the Union Republics, though not always
outside their own territories (there are some 5,000,000 Ukrainians living
in other parts of the USSR, some of whom complain that schooling in
their own language is available only in the Ukrainian SSR itself, while
Russians can be taught in their own language almost anywhere). The
extent to which it is *used* varies from one republic to another, depending
on other factors (we have already seen some of the differences between
the Ukraine and Armenia, for example) but at least it is a feasible
proposition. For the rest, it is largely a matter of numbers. In the larger
ASSRs,[†] with (say) over 100,000 speakers per language, it is usually
possible to offer vernacular schooling throughout the eight-year school,
ie classes I—VIII of the General Educational School up to the end of the
compulsory period. In the smaller ones, with over 10,000 speakers, the
primary stage (classes I—III or IV) may be taught in the vernacular, the
rest being given in Russian, or sometimes in another vernacular such as
Georgian or Tadzhik, depending on the area.

There is some evidence, not as yet conclusive, that the incompleteness

---

* This point is treated in both Musaev (1965) and Isayev (1977). The Greek, Cyrillic
and Latin alphabets all give equal weight to vowels and consonants. The Arabic
alphabet does not, reasonably enough in view of the structure of the Semitic
languages; but there are problems in its use for other language families, especially
the Turkic, where fine distinctions of vowels are grammatically significant.

† Autonomous Soviet Socialist Republics, subordinate entities within certain
Republics (mainly in the RSFSR).

of such vernacular schooling leads many parents to opt for Russian-medium schools on the grounds that the children will need it to complete their schooling anyway. (There are parallels to this in the West.) As for the very small groups, especially those with no written form, Russian (or whatever) has to be used throughout, the native tongue being employed only as an aid until the children have enough Russian to proceed. This requires special training. In the Herzen Pedagogic Institute in Leningrad, for example, the Northern Department admits small groups of students from certain northern nationalities and trains them specifically for the problems of teaching in their own areas, with special reference to the children's competence in Russian. What we seem to be faced with, then, is a general policy of *linguistic* pluralism, as defined, within the practical constraints of numbers and developmental levels. It is now necessary to consider how the various peoples have fared scholastically, and to examine the implications of present trends for the USSR and for other societies also faced with the problems of reconciling unity and diversity.

5. Developments and implications

If one examines the various nationalities' levels of scholastic attainment — fuller details are given in Table 5 — it is clear that there are substantial inequalities. Some of them are surprising, however. There are various cultural reasons why Jews in the RSFSR* should be so far ahead of the entire field, and it has been suggested — though there is little hard evidence — that the Georgians' position as clear second in the league is the result of Stalin's special favour to his fellow-countrymen. (It is possible, no doubt; but Stalin has been dead for a long time, and it is a moot point how far he thought of himself as a Georgian anyway. Also, there is ample evidence from the study of the Soviet educational system in general that governmental action can achieve relatively little if other factors are unfavourable.) If we take as a measure the proportions with higher education, we find these groups above the USSR average: Jews in the RSFSR, an astonishing 39.9 per cent; Georgians, 10.5; Armenians, 7.5; Tatars in the Uzbek SSR, 6.8; Estonians, 6.0; Russians, 5.9; and Latvians, 5.6. Just below the average come the Azerbaidzhanis (5.3), the Yakuts (4.6) and the Lithuanians and Ukrainians (both 4.5 per cent). On the whole, the Central Asian Turkic peoples tend to score low (eg Chuvash, 2.4; Bashkir, 2.2); but so do the Moldavians (2.2). For those with complete secondary education, the pattern is similar but not identical. Once again, the Jews are ahead (30.7), with the Georgians this time much closer (30.0), followed by the Armenians (23.5), Uzbek Tatars (21.1), Russians (19.7), Ukrainians (19.2), while the Latvians, Estonians and Azerbaidzhanis come in close under the national average. Among the major nationalities, the Moldavians

---

*Russian Soviet Federative Socialist Republic, the largest of the constituent republics of the USSR.

	P-	P	P+	CS	HE
USSR	22.4	29.3	48.3	18.7	5.5
Russians	20.3	28.9	50.8	19.7	5.9
Ukrainians	24.1	28.3	47.6	19.2	4.5
Byelorussians	22.9	33.3	43.8	16.9	4.0
Estonians	10.1	43.7	46.2	18.2	6.0
Latvians	19.1	32.1	48.8	18.3	5.6
Lithuanians	26.1	38.5	35.3	11.9	4.5
Moldavians	31.9	34.3	33.8	8.6	2.2
Armenians	21.1	27.1	51.8	23.5	7.5
Georgians	18.6	23.6	57.8	30.0	10.5
Azerbaidzhanis	28.7	28.9	42.4	17.3	5.3
Uzbeks	30.8	28.0	41.2	16.2	3.7
Kazakhs	31.1	29.9	39.0	14.9	4.2
Kirgiz	31.5	28.5	40.0	15.2	3.8
Tadzhiks	31.4	29.6	39.0	13.8	3.2
Turkmens	29.1	27.9	43.0	13.6	3.6
Bashkirs	27.4	35.7	36.9	10.2	2.2
Chuvash	25.3	32.3	42.4	11.9	2.4
Jews (RSFSR)	6.0	11.6	82.4	30.7	39.9
Tatars (RSFSR)	24.0	31.8	44.2	13.2	3.1
Tatars (Uzbek SSR)	18.8	27.4	53.5	21.1	6.8
Yakuts	30.6	32.0	37.4	14.3	4.6

The figures show the percentages of the population aged 10 or over with less than primary schooling (P-), primary only (P), more than primary schooling (P+), and of the latter, the percentage of population with complete secondary schooling (CS) and with higher education (HE).

Table 5 *Educational levels attained by selected nationalities, 1970*

once again bring up the rear.

Kravetz (1980), in his thorough examination of current trends, has examined these figures in relation to the level of urbanization (on the well-established assumption that rural populations have disproportionately acute problems in the USSR) and the extent of fluency in Russian. (He calls this the 'ratio of linguistic Russification'; this is rather an unfortunate term, since the figures cited are of those claiming fluency in Russian as a *second* language. But, with that reservation, the figures have their uses (see Tables 6 and 7).

Now, if we take the conspicuously most successful group, the Jews living in the RSFSR, we find them scoring very high on both counts: 97.9 per cent urban, and over 70 per cent with Russian as their *first* language. (There is no upper secondary or higher education in Yiddish anyway.) Of the other above-average groups, the Russians are highly urbanized (68 per cent) and obviously use the Russian language; but after that the correlation begins to break down. The Tatars have a high incidence of fluency in Russian (81.2 per cent of the urban and 38 per cent of the rural population), but only a moderate level of urbanization

Nationality	% Urban	% Rural
USSR average	56.0	44.0
1. Jews	97.9	2.1
2. Russians	68.0	32.0
3. Armenians	64.8	35.2
4. Estonians	55.1	44.9
5. Tatars	55.0	45.0
6. Latvians	52.7	47.3
7. Ukrainians	48.5	51.5
8. Lithuanians	46.7	53.3
9. Georgians	44.0	56.0
10. Byelorussians	43.7	56.3
11. Azerbaidzhanis	39.7	60.3
12. Turkmens	31.0	69.0
13. Kazakhs	26.7	73.3
14. Tadzhiks	26.0	74.0
15. Uzbeks	24.9	75.1
16. Moldavians	20.4	79.6
17. Kirgiz	14.6	85.4

Source: 1970 census.

Table 6 *Percentage of urban-rural distribution by nationality, 1970*

Nationality	% Urban	% Rural
Jews (Russian first, no Yiddish)	72.8	56.9
Jews (Yiddish first language)	14.2	17.6
Armenians	31.6	9.5
Estonians	36.5	16.7
Tatars	81.2	38.0
Latvians	52.4	37.8
Latvians (Russian as first language)	13.7	0.6
Ukrainians	48.5	25.1
Lithuanians	51.1	21.8
Georgians	35.6	8.2
Byelorussians	55.9	50.1
Azerbaidzhanis	29.6	4.3
Turkmens	30.7	7.4
Kazakhs	59.5	35.2
Tadzhiks	33.7	10.6
Uzbeks	32.0	6.9
Moldavians	62.2	27.8

Sources: Kravetz (1980) and Silver (1975).

Table 7 *Percentage of selected nationalities claiming fluency in Russian as second language, 1970*

(55 per cent, below the USSR average). Armenians score high on urbanization (64.8 per cent), but low on Russian fluency (31.6 per cent urban, 9.5 per cent rural), while Georgians score low on both criteria (44 per cent urban, of whom only 35.8 per cent claim to be fluent in Russian). At the other end of the scale, the Moldavians have a high level of Russian fluency (62.2 per cent of the urban and 27.8 per cent of the rural population), but are overwhelmingly rural (79.6 per cent, one of the highest proportions in the USSR). The level of urbanization does seem to be a useful guide in many cases, but the correlation is by no means close. As for the level of access to Russian, this seems to be a minor factor in many cases, but quite irrelevant in some. It is reasonable to assume that numerically less precise criteria, such as the strength of the indigenous cultures, carry more weight in determining educational advance.

The difficulty of attaching achievement to any particular criterion can be illustrated by comparing the major Central Asian nationalities. On the higher education measure, the Kazakhs lead with 4.2 per cent, and the Tadzhiks come at the end with 3.2; in between come the Kirgiz, Uzbeks and Turkmens (see Table 8). Taking proportions with complete secondary schooling, we find the Uzbeks in the lead this time (16.2 per cent); the

% with higher education		% with complete secondary education		% urban		% with fluent Russian	
1. Kazakhs	4.2	Uzbeks	16.2	Turkmens	31.0	Kazakhs	59.5
2. Kirgiz	3.8	Kirgiz	15.2	Kazakhs	26.7	Tadzhiks	33.7
3. Uzbeks	3.7	Kazakhs	14.9	Tadzhiks	26.0	Uzbeks	32.0
4. Turkmens	3.6	Tadzhiks	13.8	Uzbeks	24.9	Turkmens	30.7
5. Tadzhiks	3.2	Turkmens	13.6	Kirgiz	14.6	Kirgiz	?

Source: Figures adapted from Kravetz (1980) and modified from the 1970 census returns.

Table 8 *Central Asia, major nationalities: educational attainment, urbanization and currency of fluent Russian compared*

Kirgiz now come second, and the Kazakhs have fallen to third place, but the Tadzhiks have risen, leaving the Turkmens at the bottom with 13.6 per cent — not a vast discrepancy, but considerably greater than that applying in higher education. Generally, then, the Uzbeks, Kirgiz and Kazakhs do relatively well for the area, the Turkmens and Tadzhiks worse; but the connection with the two criteria mentioned by Kravetz is not close. The Kazakhs are *relatively* urbanized (26.7 per cent), but the Tadzhiks come near (26 per cent), while the Turkmens are actually ahead (31 per cent). As for fluency in Russian, this is very high among the Kazakhs (59.5 per cent urban, 35.2 per cent rural), as might be expected in view of the high proportion of Russians in Kazakhstan; but the others come much lower (a little over 30 per cent). Finally, it has been suggested that the Uzbek and Tadzhik cultures are stronger and better developed than the rest. Thus, tentatively, one might suggest partial explanations for the relative success of the Kazakhs (urbanization, use of Russian) and the Uzbeks (indigenous culture); but that is about as far as it goes. Explanations of any precision depend, it would appear, on combinations of factors, some of which are as yet not fully understood. For future work, much more information is needed, especially on the extent, use and *quality* of native-language instruction in the various republics.

The role of government policy, it has already been suggested, is necessarily limited, but it can account for developments that are difficult to link closely with such factors as urbanization, the currency of Russian, or for that matter the strength of the cultures or the religious factor examined by the Halevys. The next census should provide fuller information, but already there are indications that the relative positions of the groups are changing and that the gaps are narrowing. Kravetz has taken the census of 1970 figures for higher education enrolment and compared them with 1976-77 (still a time of increase); these are given in Table 9. Most show an increase, some a spectacular one. The most striking are among the Central Asian peoples. Chuvash, Bashkirs, Tatars, Tadzhiks, Kazakhs and Kirgiz all have ratios of over 120; increases above the USSR average of 108

| | 1970-1 | | 1976-7 | | 1976-7 figure as a percentage of the 1970-1 figure |
	Thousands	Percentage	Thousands	Percentage	
USSR	4,580.6	100.0	4,950.2	100.0	108
Russians	2,729.0	59.6	2,926.1	59.1	107
Ukrainians	621.2	13.6	655.1	13.4	105
Byelorussians	131.2	2.9	155.3	3.1	118
Uzbeks	150.7	3.3	176.5	3.6	117
Kazakhs	100.3	2.2	124.0	2.5	124
Georgians	87.8	1.9	82.6	1.7	94
Azerbaidzhanis	86.0	1.9	90.8	1.8	106
Lithuanians	49.8	1.1	58.6	1.2	118
Moldavians	30.8	0.7	33.0	0.7	107
Latvians	21.8	0.5	24.1	0.5	111
Kirgiz	26.4	0.6	32.1	0.6	122
Tadzhiks	28.1	0.6	34.7	0.7	123
Armenians	81.5	1.8	82.1	1.7	101
Turkmens	22.0	0.5	24.9	0.5	113
Estonians	17.9	0.4	19.3	0.4	108
Bashkirs	14.8	0.3	18.9	0.4	128
Dagestan peoples	20.3	0.4	23.8	0.5	117
Tatars	87.0	1.9	108.2	2.2	124
Chuvash	16.0	0.3	20.6	0.4	129
Jews	105.8	2.3	66.9	1.4	63
Other	152.2	3.3	182.6	3.7	120

Table 9 *Higher education students (undergraduate) by nationality*

	End 1970		End 1975		1975 figure as a percentage of the 1970 figure
	Number	Percentage	Number	Percentage	
Total USSR	99,427	100.0	95,675	100.0	96
Russians	59,517	59.9	59,120	61.8	99
Ukrainians	12,248	12.3	11,863	12.4	97
Byelorussians	2,540	2.6	2,634	2.8	104
Uzbeks	2,493	2.5	2,628	2.7	105
Kazakhs	1,780	1.8	2,011	2.1	113
Georgians	1,846	1.9	1,638	1.7	89
Azerbaidzhanis	2,036	2.0	1,820	1.9	89
Lithuanians	1,195	1.2	1,056	1.1	88
Moldavians	619	0.6	565	0.6	91
Latvians	700	0.7	615	0.6	88
Kirgiz	452	0.5	446	0.5	99
Tadzhiks	489	0.5	502	0.5	103
Armenians	2,292	2.3	2,036	2.1	89
Turkmens	480	0.5	450	0.5	94
Estonians	657	0.7	480	0.5	73
Bashkirs	236	0.2	259	0.3	110
Dagestan peoples	528	0.5	499	0.5	95
Tatars	1,380	1.4	1,419	1.5	103
Chuvash	267	0.3	247	0.3	93
Jews	4,945	5.0	2,841	3.0	57
Other	2,727	2.8	2,546	2.7	93

Source: Narodnoe khozyaistvo SSSR 1977 godu: Statisticheskii ezhe godnik
(Gosstatizdat, Moskva, 1979)

Table 10 Graduate students, by nationality

include the Byelorussians, Lithuanians, Latvians, Uzbeks, Turkmens and the peoples of Dagestan. The Estonians are on the average, the Moldavians, Ukrainians and Russians just under it, and the Armenians well below. The Georgians show an actual, though small, decrease, and the Jews a substantial one, a cut of nearly 40 per cent of the 1970 figure (Kravetz, 1980).

Admittedly, enrolment in higher education gives an incomplete picture of a group's educational advance (as witness the discrepancies between proportions with higher and complete secondary education given in Table 5). But it is a useful indicator nevertheless. The improvement of the position of the Central Asian peoples is consistent enough to argue the existence of a deliberate policy of positive discrimination; and, since the expansion of higher education does not happen overnight, it can hardly be a simple matter of adjusting the enrolment quotas, but a further-reaching policy of intervention, including presumably a major diversion of resources. At the other end of the scale, discrimination against Jews and, to a lesser extent, Georgians is clear enough. The mechanism is clear also; increases may not be effected by the imposition of quotas, but reductions can —

indeed, it is not easy to see how else they could be achieved. Most of the commentary so far has emphasized the declining position of Soviet Jews — unsurprisingly, in view of their prominent participation in the educational system up to the present, and the deterioration of their social and political situation. Anti-Zionism there certainly is, anti-Semitism there may be, but once again this is not the whole story. Viewed as a whole, the figures strongly suggest attempts (with varying success) to reduce inequalities both by favouring the disadvantaged and pulling back the more advanced groups, by a variety of measures including the use of a quota system.

As far as language policy in the narrower sense is concerned, even if one discounts accusations of deliberate Russianization, developments could take one of two roads. It is denied that there is any intention of moving towards assimilation of the linguistic minorities, but there is a school of thought that talks of 'convergence', the eventual mingling of the Soviet peoples in one new language community. Isayev (1977) mentions the fact that large numbers of people have moved from their original homelands to live elsewhere in the USSR (omitting to mention that in many cases the move was hardly voluntary); and, indeed, mobility does tend to encourage linguistic convergence. He also instances influences of Russian on the minority languages, and vice versa. Borrowing vocabulary is one thing, however; changing basic grammatical structures quite another, and it is hard to see how 'convergence' would really differ from assimilation into the Russian speech-community. This, even with some modifications, carries considerable danger. It is obvious that prejudices can survive for a long time, and resurface in ideologically 'respectable' forms. 'Convergence' could easily become a recipe for neo-chauvinism — and, by reaction, its nationalist mirror-image too.

Genuine pluralism, linguistically at least, would seem the more viable option in the long run. Clearly, there are limits: we have seen how numbers, rather more than developmental levels, can limit the use of vernaculars. But, equally, it does appear that there are minorities with long-standing viable cultures, and others which have emerged from illiteracy to full educational viability in the last half century or so. At the level of *Realpolitik*, it is understandable that central authorities can become anxious about possible future fissiparous tendencies, especially in sensitive border areas; but, in realistic terms, the temptation to solve this through covert Russianization could be counter-productive. In the long run, a large multinational state has to be run on a pluralist basis, or face the prospects of tensions of an increasingly serious kind.

The question of pluralism in content is more difficult, and is still unresolved. Strictly speaking, it falls outside the scope of this inquiry, but in practice language is but one aspect of a culture, not readily separable from the others. In theory, the content of schooling in the USSR is informed by an over-riding value system of Marxism-Leninism and Soviet Patriotism, which means that (for example) traditional attitudes towards women cannot be left to pass unchallenged, whether they are held by Tadzhiks or Russians. But in practice Soviet Patriotism contains a good deal of what looks to the naked eye like old-fashioned Russian patriotism, and the treatment of national figures in history, for example, invites contrast with the far more cautious handling of key figures among the minorities. Uzbek and Caucasian children are taught in their own languages, but not about such stalwarts of resistance to Tsarist expansion as Yakub Beg or Shamyl. (Yakum Beg and Shamyl, though much more recent, occupy places in Uzbek and Caucasian history and legend not unlike those of William Wallace in Scotland and Wilhelm Tell in Switzerland.) While appreciating anxieties about maintaining unity and cohesion, one must ask if genuine pluralism can stop at the language of instruction. This is always a difficult point for majorities to accept — minorities too, sometimes — but will have to be considered carefully if more dangerous forms of self-assertion are to be avoided.

The problems of reconciling cultural diversity and some kind of political unity are to be found far beyond the confines of the USSR. In Western Europe, for instance, we are all minorities now, and the passage of time makes it ever clearer that the either/or model does not work any more — French *or* European, Catalan *or* Spanish, Scots *or* British; increasingly, we are having to be aware of, and educate for, several levels of identity. The European Community has barely begun to work out the practicalities of co-operating pluralism yet, and that long-standing multinational state, the United Kingdom, has hardly grasped the point either. The multinational groupings to which more and more of us belong need not be threatened by diversity, but can best be unified *through* it, as both unity and diversity are fundamental attributes of any human group. The concepts are not easy to formulate as policy, let alone to work out in practice, which is one reason why the experience of the Soviet Union, with its faults and limitations as well as its successes, must be of continuing interest in an increasingly multicultural yet shrinking world.

References

Corner, T C ed (1978) *Education in Multi-Cultural Societies* Conference Proceedings of the Comparative Education Society in Europe (British Section): Edinburgh

Grant, N (1974) Sexual equality in the Communist world *Compare* 4 1: 24-30

Grant, N (1977) Language and education *in* Lowe *et al* (1977)

Grant, N (1978) Education for multi-cultural society *in* Corner (1978)

Halevy, Z and Etsioni-Halevy, E (1974) The 'religious factor' and achievement in education *Comparative Education* 10 3: 193-200

Isayev, M I (1977) *National Language in the USSR: Problems and Solutions* Progress Publishers: Moscow

Kravetz, N (1980) Education of ethnic and national minorities in the USSR: a report on current developments *Comparative Education* 16 1: 13-24

Lowe, J, Grant, N and Williams, T D eds (1977) *Education and Nation-Building in the Third World* Scottish Academic Press: Edinburgh

Musaev, K M (1965) *Alfavity Yazykov Narodov SSSR* Nauka: Moskva

5. The education of minorities in Canada: an examination of policies

Alison d'Anglejan

Summary: This chapter examines the present state of educational policy with respect to three categories of minority groups in Canada: the 'official' minorities, that is the English in Quebec and the French in the other provinces; the native peoples — the Inuit and Indians; and the 'non-official' minorities — the various non-British and non-French immigrant groups. Although education of Canadian children other than those of the native peoples is under the exclusive jurisdiction of the ten provincial governments, present policies have been influenced by federal government policies on bilingualism and biculturalism. Against a background of overlapping and occasionally conflicting provincial and federal policies, minority group education has evolved in a rather fragmented way, lacking a clearly articulated set of common goals.

Perhaps the most salient characteristic of the Canadian Federation is its linguistic, cultural and geographic diversity. The second largest country in the world, Canada's population of approximately 22,000,000 is irregularly dispersed with enclaves of high density in the industrial areas along the United States border and vast, sparsely inhabited areas in the central prairies and northern regions. This geographic and cultural diversity is reflected in a tendency towards the decentralization of political powers and in regional distinctiveness and autonomy.

Canada's constitution, the British North America Act of 1867, makes no specific reference to the language of education in schools and places education under the exclusive jurisdiction of the provincial governments. As a consequence, the federal government cannot determine a national policy for education, nor can it mobilize the educational system, as is done in some countries, to implement federal policy goals. However, it can and does act informally to influence education through recommendations to the Council of Ministers of Education of the ten provinces and other educational bodies. But the provinces are free to ignore, if they choose to do so, any recommendations or the offer of federal funds which are not compatible with provincial policies or which appear to undermine provincial authority. The granting of federal funds for such specific objectives as minority education or the teaching of the official languages to immigrant children involves delicate negotiations with the provincial governments. Supplemental funds for education are channelled through the provincial ministries of education which closely control their allocation. However, these constraints on the federal government's power to intervene in the formal educational system do not prevent the allocation of funds at the request of non-official educational groups such as ethnic or cultural organizations which operate outside the public school system.

It is against this complex backdrop of interacting and occasionally conflicting federal-provincial policies that this chapter will examine minority education in Canada. While the term 'minority group' is commonly used today to refer to any group on the margin of mainstream society (eg the handicapped, the poor, or women) this chapter will deal only with the ethno-linguistic minority groups. For the purpose of this analysis, a distinction must be drawn between three categories of minority groups: 1) the 'official' minorities, that is the English in Quebec and the French in the other provinces; 2) the native people, including the Inuit and Indians; and 3) the 'non-official' minorities — the various immigrant groups such as Ukrainians, Italians or Germans. It is necessary to examine these categories separately since their problems differ, as do official policies with respect to the education of their children.

The official minorities

Although Canada is a bilingual country with French and English as the official languages, this does not mean that most Canadians are bilingual, but rather that they are entitled to services provided by the federal government in the official language of their choice (Government of Canada, 1969). The vast majority of Canada's native speakers of French live in the province of Quebec and are descendants of the settlers who came from France mainly during the seventeenth century. Of Quebec's population of 6,000,000, approximately one-fifth claim English as their mother tongue. Thus, French is the majority language and English the language of the minority in Quebec, while the converse is true when Canada is considered as a whole. Table 1 shows the distribution of the official minority populations by province.

According to statistics provided by the Council of Ministers of Education (1978), Quebec's English-speaking (Anglophone) citizens constitute the country's largest minority group in absolute numbers. At 12.8 per cent of the total population of the province they represent the second largest group in terms of proportion in the provincial population. New Brunswick's 223,785 French speakers (Francophones) represent the largest percentage of the total population (33 per cent) and the third largest minority group in absolute numbers.

Ontario has the largest number of Francophones outside Quebec (462,075). Although they represent only 5.6 per cent of the total provincial population, Ontario's Francophones constitute the second largest minority group in Canada. Moving eastward from New Brunswick

Province	Minority language population*	Minority language population as a percentage of total population
British Columbia	38,430	1.6
Alberta	44,440	2.4
Saskatchewan	26,705	2.9
Manitoba	54,745	5.4
Quebec	800,680	12.8
New Brunswick	223,785	33.0
Nova Scotia	36,870	4.3
Prince Edward Island	6545	5.5
Newfoundland and Labrador	2755	0.4

Source: Council of Ministers of Education (1978)
* English in Quebec, French in all other provinces.

Table 1 *Official minority language population by province*

and westward from Ontario, the number of French-speaking citizens tends to be less and the proportion they represent of the total population decreases. Given these variations in the density of official minority populations, it is not surprising to find considerable variation from province to province with respect to provisions regarding minority language education. Thus, New Brunswick — an officially bilingual province — guarantees to its French and English citizens instruction in their own language. The law provides that the provincial language of instruction in every school shall be the mother tongue (English or French) of the majority of the students, and that the other children shall be given instruction in their own language, either in that school or in another school. In Prince Edward Island, Ontario, Manitoba and British Columbia, at the request of the parents, the school board now has a legal obligation to provide instruction in French, provided a specified minimum number of students can be assembled. In Alberta and Saskatchewan the law *permits* a school board to provide French-language education. The laws of Newfoundland and Nova Scotia make no specific reference to the language of instruction, but traditionally school boards have been free to grant permission for French instruction.

The case of Quebec, where the official minority language is English, is particularly interesting. The Quebec Education Act requires a school board to provide English education for every *eligible* member of the English-speaking minority. According to the terms of Quebec's Charter of the French Language (Gouvernement du Québec, 1977) eligibility is limited to three categories: (1) the children of parents who themselves received their elementary education in English in Quebec; (2) the children of parents domiciled in Quebec at the time the law came into force who were educated in English outside the province; and (3) children, or their brothers and sisters, who the previous year were enrolled in the province's English schools. This new legislation, and its predecessor Bill 22 (Gouvernement du Québec, 1974) placed restrictions which did not previously exist on access to minority language education. Whereas previously it was possible for all Quebec residents to have their children educated in English, migrants from other provinces and other English-speaking immigrants must now enrol their children in French schools. While at variance with the spirit of the federal government's Official Languages Act, this new policy is consistent with the broader linguistic and cultural goals of the present provincial government which has declared French the sole official language of the province and advocates a form of political sovereignty for Quebec. The growth of the Anglophone majority over the years through the assimilation of immigrants from other countries was perceived as a threat to the demographic make-up of the province. The present legislation was designed to stem the flow of immigrant children into the English school system and, as a consequence, to enhance the likeliness of their integration into the French-speaking community.

In Quebec, nearly all English students who are eligible under the provisions of Bill 101 attend English schools which offer elementary or secondary programmes within school-bus range of their homes. Quebec has traditionally been the most liberal of all the provinces in terms of educational opportunities for the official minority population. At the present time, most of Ontario's Francophone students are able to attend a French school or a mixed-language school within bus-range of their home. In the other provinces, the practical possibility of being educated in French while living at home depends largely on whether a sufficient number of French-speaking students can be assembled in one locality (Council of Ministers of Education, 1978).

The gradual evolution of *de jure* or *de facto* recognition of official minority education rights in the provinces of Canada is the result of a continuous struggle on the part of the Francophone minorities. The Royal Commission on Bilingualism and Biculturalism, set up in 1963 to study the state of bilingualism in Canada, drew attention to the lack of services in French for the French minorities outside Quebec. The report recommended that the federal government institute a policy of systematic language planning which would assure, among other things, the right of parents to educate their children in the official language of their choice. Such a policy, it was felt, was essential in order to prevent further assimilation of Francophones outside Quebec as well as to promote equality in education for Francophone children.

A report by the Association Canadienne d'Education de Langue Française (1978) cites the lack of federal authority in the area of education as the cause for regional disparities in educational provisions for Francophones. Since the provision for minority education is under the jurisdiction of the provincial governments, and is often left to the discretion of local boards, facilities are often inadequate. Parents, as well as such organizations as the Fédération des Francophones hors Québec, continue to do battle with local education authorities who are often reluctant to recognize minority rights and, when they do so, opt for minimal provisions. While the authorization of French-medium classes within the English schools was initially viewed as a victory, Francophone minorities now tend to perceive such classes as an inadequate bulwark against assimilation. The totally Francophone school, administered by Francophones for Francophones, is now the goal of pressure groups, many of whom feel that it will not be achieved until, and unless, minority education rights are legally protected and federal funds are directly available.

The native peoples

Canada's native peoples are a culturally and linguistically varied group. According to information provided by the Canadian Association in Support of the Native Peoples (1976) they include more than 280,000 status Indians, that is native people who are individually recognized by the government to have special rights under the provisions of the Indian Act and various treaties. In addition, there are some 18,500 Inuit People who have a similar relation to the government as status Indians. Finally, there are some 750,000 Métis and non-status Indian people for whom the federal government has no special legal responsibility but who often live on the periphery of the status Indian communities.

According to Burnaby (1976) these groups speak a wide variety of different languages and dialects deriving from 11 different language families. There were no indigenous writing systems at the time of contact with Europeans; however, writing systems have since been developed for many of the native vernaculars.

The native peoples have been described as 'the most economically deprived groups in Canada and far behind other Canadians in every respect' (Canadian Association in Support of the Native Peoples, 1976, quoted in Burnaby, 1976). The breakdown of the traditional hunting, fishing and agricultural economies has been paralleled by rising levels of family breakdown, illness, unemployment, crime and school drop-outs — all the correlates of extreme poverty and deprivation.

According to the provisions of the British North America Act and the Indian Act, the federal government is responsible for the education of status Indians. Since it is also responsible for administration and education in the Territories (the extreme northern regions of Canada) the education of many Inuit and non-status Indians also falls under its jurisdiction. Local governments have been set up in the territories which function much like provincial governments and have their own departments of education. Thus, the government of the North West Territories has the responsibility for Inuit education, except in Arctic Quebec where this is exercised by the Kativik School Board, an Inuit-controlled provincial board set up under the terms of a special agreement.

During the 1950s, the federal government began to exercise more direct control over native education, which previously had often been contracted out to religious organizations. The government moved to bring the education of native children more into line with that of other Canadian children. According to this policy (Burnaby, 1976) teachers in native schools were to be certificated to teach in that province in which the school was located and the curriculum was to follow that established by the province. Agreements were made between local school boards and the Department of Indian Affairs for Indian children to be enrolled in provincial schools wherever possible.

In 1969, the federal government made public its willingness to divest itself of all administrative responsibility for native peoples. According to the policy proposed by the Minister of Indian Affairs and Northern Development the administration of education for status Indians would be formally placed in the hands of the provincial education authorities. The policy met with considerable opposition on the part of the native groups who felt that it would undermine their chances for special educational provisions reflecting their specific needs. This led to the publication by the National Indian Brotherhood of a position paper entitled 'Indian Control of Indian Education' (1972). At the heart of the paper lie the concepts of parental responsibility and local control by the native people over the education of their children as well as the importance of the reinforcement of Indian identity. The principles outlined in the paper have been accepted by the federal government which now works closely with Indian associations and bands to meet the particular educational needs of native children. Discussions are now under way between the Department of Indian and Inuit Affairs and Indian people to revise the educational sections of the Indian Act (personal communication, Assistant Deputy Minister Indian and Northern Affairs, July 1980). Changes in legislation under consideration would permit Indian communities to become legal, autonomous educational authorities, and consequently they would be in a position to set their own education policies.

As can be seen from the above analysis, three levels of administration are involved in the shaping of education for Canada's native peoples. Although the federal government holds the legal responsibility for native education, the Indian Act as it now stands does not make adequate legislative provisions to assure the unique cultural and linguistic goals of the native people. Although there is reason to believe that changes in the Act are forthcoming, Burnaby (1976) points out that the government must act with caution in providing special legislative support for the languages and cultures of native peoples which goes beyond that which it is prepared to give to other citizens with particular ethnic interests. Indeed, the provincial governments which are involved contractually in native education face a similar problem. However, there is ample evidence, both anecdotal and statistical, to show that programmes designed for majority children are not providing native children with satisfactory basic skills, and that they are contributing to the erosion of ethnic identity and to assimilation. Sensitive to these problems and to the high drop-out rate, some provincial governments are beginning to develop curriculum guidelines and materials specifically oriented toward the needs of children of native ancestry. Quebec's new language legislation (Gouvernement du Québec, 1977) formally authorizes the use of Amerindian languages as teaching languages, and recognizes the right of Quebec's native peoples to education in their native tongue. Programmes involving the use of the native languages as the medium of instruction for the early grades are already being implemented in several places (eg Ontario, Alberta, Quebec, North West Territories). The importance of early literacy training in the native language is being recognized, as is the appropriateness of specialized training for teachers and the involvement of native teachers or assistants in the education process.

While the position paper prepared by the Indian Brotherhood does not necessarily reflect the unanimous opinion of the native peoples with respect to their educational aspirations, it does demonstrate the emerging desire and ability of some native groups to define and articulate their own policies. Future growth in educational opportunities for native peoples will call for constructive dialogue between articulate native representatives and government officials sensitive and responsive to their needs. In the absence of such dialogue, many of today's blatantly inappropriate programmes will perpetuate themselves.

The non-official minority groups

Over the past century, immigration from a variety of countries has played a vital role in Canada's development. The importance of the contribution made by Canada's immigrant groups, and their desire that their contribution should be recognized, was documented in Volume IV of the report of the Royal Commission on Bilingualism and Biculturalism (1970).

Palmer (1976) has identified three phases in the history of relationships between English Canada and the 'other ethnic' groups: Anglo-conformity, the melting pot, and cultural pluralism. During the first of these phases, assimilation of all immigrant groups to British culture was considered as the appropriate model and this view was transmitted through the public school system and school textbooks. Later, the melting pot ideology was imported into Canada where it never achieved the popularity it enjoyed in the United States (Palmer, 1976). A third ideology, that of cultural pluralism, developed during the 1960s. Identified by the catchword 'cultural mosaic', this ideology was based on the belief that recognition of the cultural contribution of the non-Anglo-Saxon groups would heighten the groups' feeling that they belonged to Canada and that it would thus strengthen Canadian unity. This view became official policy with the adoption in 1971 of an official federal government policy of multiculturalism within the framework of French-English bilingualism.

In accordance with this policy, the government committed itself to providing support in four ways: it would assist all Canadian cultural groups that had demonstrated a desire and effort to continue to develop, a capacity to grow and contribute to Canada; it would assist members of all cultural groups to overcome cultural barriers against full participation in Canadian society; it would promote creative encounters and interchange among all Canadian cultural groups in the interest of national unity; and it would continue to assist immigrants in acquiring at least one of Canada's two official languages to enable them to participate fully in Canadian society. The announcement of the policy triggered considerable response. There was general support for the policy among the ethnic groups (Palmer, 1976; O'Bryan, Reitz and Kuplowska, 1975). The potential negative impact of the policy on French Canada was strongly articulated by Rocher (1972, 1976). The cultural support now being offered to the other groups was seen as undermining that available for French Canadians, and the logical outcome of the policy was seen as multilingualism. The effect would be to dilute the cultural and linguistic impact of the French Canadian group in Canada. These attitudes among French Canadians were documented in an empirical study carried out by Berry, Kalin and Taylor (1976).

In several Canadian provinces, the non-official minority groups out-number the official minority. This is especially true in western Canada where Germans outnumber French Canadians in all four provinces, while the same is true of the Ukrainians in three of the four (see Table 2). Heavy concentrations of diverse ethnic populations are also found in the industrialized centres of Ontario and Quebec (see Table 3).

Province	British (Anglo-Celtic)	German	French	Ukrainian
British Columbia	57.9	9.6	4.4	2.8
Alberta	46.8	14.2	5.8	8.3
Saskatchewan	42.1	19.4	6.1	9.2
Manitoba	41.9	12.5	8.8	11.6

Source: Lupul (1976)

Table 2 Percentage of selected ethnic groups in western Canada

The growing awareness of ethnicity which swept North America in the 1960s and 70s (see Glazer and Moynihan, 1975; Novak, 1972) combined forces with the gains made by the official minority groups in the field of education; thus it is not surprising that non-official minority groups should also lay claim to support for educational programmes designed to enhance cultural identity through the use of ethnic languages as a medium of instruction in the schools. Increased pressure for the creation of such programmes also stems from the philosophical position which is gaining support in Canada and has already been legally recognized in the United States (Teitelbaum and Hiller, 1977) that the right to education in a language which the child understands is a basic human right and an

Province	Total population	Non-official language population as percentage of total population
British Columbia	2,184,620	37.7
Alberta	1,627,875	47.4
Saskatchewan	926,245	51.8
Manitoba	988,250	49.3
Ontario	7,703,105	31.0
Quebec	6,027,765	10.4
New Brunswick	634,555	5.3
Nova Scotia	788,960	12.4
Newfoundland	522,100	3.3

Source: O'Bryan, Reitz and Kuplowska (1976)

Table 3 *Non-official minority language population by province*

essential ingredient of equality in education.

As is the case for Canada's native peoples and French Canadians outside Quebec, children of immigrant families entering the Anglo-dominated public school system are often confronted by linguistic and cultural hurdles which may seriously undermine their chances of academic success. For many who arrive at school without a knowledge of English, the language barrier is not easily overcome in spite of special classes in English as a second language. Others, in order to be accepted by their schoolmates, reject the cultural values of their parents. The disparity and conflict between the home culture and that of the school undermines family relationships and exacerbates communication problems between the ethnic family and the school. Masemann (1975) and Wright (1970) have studied the problems which immigrant children in Ontario encounter in their early school years, as well as in their later school and work careers.

For generations, ethnic groups across the country have organized programmes outside the school system to teach ancestral languages and cultures. Many such programmes have been highly successful and have received support through the federal government's multiculturalism policy. More recently, various provincial governments have moved to make legislative provisions for the teaching of languages other than English and French in the public schools. For example, as a result of legislation enacted in 1971, successful bilingual education programmes in which English and Ukrainian are used as teaching languages for school subjects have been set up in schools in Alberta. In an analysis of the evolution of policies regarding the language of instruction in western Canada, Lupul (1976) draws attention to an interesting spin-off from the liberalized legislation in Alberta. He points out that the establishment of Ukrainian-English bilingual programmes, with the concurrent acceptance of the notion of Ukrainian-English bilingualism, was soon followed by the setting up of French-English bilingual programmes. In other words, the promotion of multicultural goals has had a positive impact on public acceptance of the federal policy of official bilingualism which has traditionally met with some hostility in the western provinces.

At the present time, several provinces have instituted programmes for the teaching of minority languages as subject matter within the public school curriculum. These programmes, available on a voluntary basis to minority group children of non-British, non-French ancestry (eg Quebec's Programme d'Enseignement des Langues d'Origine; Ontario's Heritage Language Programme) differ from those in Alberta and Saskatchewan described above in that they do not involve the use of the minority language as a teaching medium for other subjects. The focus is on the development of oral and literacy skills in the minority language.

The evolution of Quebec's policy with respect to non-official minority groups is particularly interesting. For historical reasons, and as a result of their preoccupation with their own cultural survival, French Canadians were not particularly receptive to other ethnic groups, which they viewed as a threat to their own demographic position. The impact of Quebec's recent language legislation (Gouvernement du Québec, 1977) which declared French the sole official language of the province and which restricted access to the English school system, was particularly felt by the ethnic communities which over the years had integrated with the English and sent their children to English schools. Many of these groups reacted with hostility to the legislation requiring that their children attend French schools unless they were legally eligible for English schooling; therefore the provincial government embarked on a policy of support for the cultural aspirations of the ethnic groups, together with a programme of consciousness-raising for French Canadians designed to promote greater acceptance of ethnic minority groups and to emphasize the contribution of these groups to the province's development. At the same time, a pilot programme for the teaching of selected ethnic languages within the French public school system was set up. While these provisions for ethnic language teaching are not enshrined in any legislation, there is reason to suspect that provincial government officials will continue to temper the impact of the language legislation by increasing their support for the cultural aspirations of the ethnic minorities within the French milieu.

It is clear from published reports of specific current programmes that efforts are being made by some local school boards and provincial authorities to recognize and respond creatively to the needs of Canada's 'other ethnic' populations. However, it is interesting to note that such special education programmes as have been described above are often created with the interests of national unity in mind or as cultural enrichment programmes. Rarely are they designed specifically to assure better educational opportunities for ethnic minority children. If the experiences of the French Canadian minorities can be taken as an indication of the degree of cultural and linguistic support necessary for cultural well-being, it may well be that programmes involving only the teaching of the ethnic language *per se* may prove to be primarily of symbolic value. While the importance of the acceptance of the ethnic communities by the schools, symbolized by the teaching of ethnic languages as subject matter, should not be underestimated, it seems unlikely that such programmes alone would significantly reduce the barriers to equality in education faced by large numbers of non-official minority group children.

Since Canada's immigration policy recognizes the importance of immigration for future national development and the country has traditionally opened its doors to political refugees, the problem of providing effective education for non-official majority children will continue to challenge policy-makers.

Conclusion

The existing provisions for minority group education in Canada have been influenced, albeit indirectly or unofficially, by at least three pieces of federal legislation: the British North America Act of 1867 which gave official recognition to the cultural duality of Canada, while placing education under the exclusive jurisdiction of the provincial governments; the Official Languages Act of 1969 which recognized English and French as the two official languages of the country; and the 1971 Multiculturalism policy which gave formal recognition to the cultural aspirations of the non-official minority groups.

Concurrent with the evolution of the federal policies has been growing recognition, both official and unofficial, by provincial governments of the specific rights and/or aspirations of the various categories of minority groups with respect to education. In some provinces this has resulted in the removal of legal barriers to the use of languages other than English in education. Like their federal counterparts, provincial policies have not evolved in a vacuum but within a context marked by increasing militancy and occasional outbreaks of violence on the part of minority groups dissatisfied with their place in society.

Fundamental to the direction in which educational policies have moved are two basic assumptions: first, that the enhancement of ethnic identity through the use of minority languages in the schools will have positive social repercussions; and secondly, that the use of minority languages in the early school years will improve educational outcomes for minority group children. Epstein (1977), in his study of educational policy in the United States, warns that the validity of such assumptions has yet to be demonstrated. Yet, in spite of this, they have already given birth to national policies and laws which are placing heavy burdens on the American schools.

The high degree of local autonomy which is characteristic of education in Canada has allowed for the gradual development in some areas of programmes finely attuned to minority group needs. Paradoxically, this local autonomy has also made it possible for authorities to turn a deaf ear to minority groups and to subordinate their interests to those of the majority. The result is an educational system which may offer the best or the worst of possible programmes, depending on the constellation of social, demographic and political variables which come together in a given area. As noted by the Organization for Economic Co-operation and Development (1975) and by Greenfield (1976), minority education in Canada has developed in an *ad hoc*, fragmented way devoid of a clearly articulated set of national goals or of a sustained research endeavour to evaluate the quality of existing programmes. Clearly, the political conflicts between Canada's two official language groups as well as the long history of power struggles between the federal and provincial governments have monopolized much of the country's energy. However, given the enormous cost of education today, the uniqueness and complexity of Canadian society, and the close link between educational opportunities and self-fulfillment, Canada badly needs a concerted national effort to define educational goals, to identify common problems and to seek creative solutions.

References

Association Canadienne d'Education de Langue Française (1978) Pour un plan de développement de l'éducation française au Canada *Revue de l'Association Canadienne d'Education de Langue Française* 7: 1-29

Berry, J W, Kalin, R and Taylor, D M (1976) *Multiculturalism and Ethnic Attitudes in Canada* Government of Canada: Ottawa

Burnaby, B (1976) Language in native education *in* Swain (1976)

Canadian Association in Support of the Native Peoples (1976) *And What About Canada's Native Peoples?* Canadian Association in Support of the Native Peoples: Ottawa

Council of Ministers of Education (1978) *The State of Minority Language Education in the Ten Provinces of Canada* Council of Ministers of Education: Toronto

Epstein, N (1977) *Language, Ethnicity and the Schools* Institute for Educational Leadership, George Washington University: Washington DC

Fédération des Francophones hors Québec (1977) *Les Héritiers de Lord Durham* Vols 1 and 2: Ottawa

Glazer, N and Moynihan, D P *eds* (1975) *Ethnicity: Theory and Experience* Harvard University Press: Cambridge, Mass

Gouvernement du Québec (1974) *La Langue Officielle* (Loi 22) Editeur Officiel du Québec: Québec

Gouvernement du Québec (1977) *Charte de la Langue Française* (Loi 101) Editeur Officiel du Québec: Québec

Government of Canada (1969) *Official Language Act* Queen's Printer: Ottawa

Government of Canada (1971) Statement by the Prime Minister (Response to the Report of the Royal Commission on Bilingualism and Biculturalism, vol 4) Press release, 8.10.71

Greenfield, T B (1976) Bilingualism, multiculturalism and the crisis of purpose in Canadian culture *in* Swain (1976)

Lupul, M R (1976) Bilingual education and the Ukrainians in western Canada: possibilities and problems *in* Swain (1976)

Masemann, V (1975) Immigrant students' perceptions of occupational programmes *in* Wolfgang (1975)

National Indian Brotherhood (1972) *Indian Control of Indian Education* National Indian Brotherhood: Ottawa

Novak, M (1972) *The Rise of the Unmeltable Ethnics: Politics and Culture in the Seventies* Macmillan: New York

O'Bryan, K G, Reitz, J G and Kuplowska, O (1975) *Non-official Languages: A Study in Canadian Multiculturalism* Government of Canada: Ottawa

Organization for Economic Co-operation and Development (1975) *Educational Policy in Canada: External Examiners Report* Canadian Association for Adult Education and the Students Administrative Council, University of Toronto: Toronto

Palmer, H (1976) *Reluctant hosts: Anglo-Canadian views of multiculturalism in the twentieth century* Paper presented to the Second Canadian Consultative Council on Multiculturalism: Ottawa

Rocher, G (1972) *Les ambiguités d'un Canada bilingue et multiculturel* Paper presented to the Canadian Society of Sociology and Anthropology, Université de Montréal, May 1972

Rocher, G (1976) *Multiculturalism: the doubts of a Francophone* Paper presented to the Second Canadian Conference on Multiculturalism, Ottawa, February, 1976

Royal Commission on Bilingualism and Biculturalism (1967) Vol 1 *General Introduction: The Official Languages* Queen's Printer: Ottawa

Royal Commission on Bilingualism and Biculturalism (1970) Vol 4 *The Cultural Contribution of the Other Ethnic Groups* Queen's Printer: Ottawa

Swain, M ed (1976) *Bilingualism in Education: Issues and Research* Canadian Society for the Study of Education 3

Teitlebaum, H and Hiller, R J (1977) The legal perspective *in Bilingual Perspectives: Law* Centre for Applied Linguistics: Arlington, Va

Wolfgang, A ed (1975) *Education of Immigrant Students: Issues and Answers* Institute for Studies in Education: Toronto

Wright, E N (1970) *Student's Background and its Relationship to Class and Programme in School* Research Report 91, Toronto Board of Education: Toronto

6. Changing policies toward the education of minority groups in China

Keith Watson

Summary: Traditionally the Han Chinese have only occupied the eastern parts of China. The remaining 60 per cent of the country has been occupied by 54 ethnic minorities — or minority nationalities — ranging in size from several million to only a few hundred. Because of the strategic importance of these border regions — not only do they sometimes border hostile nations but they also contain precious oil and other mineral deposits — successive Chinese governments have taken great pains to win over the allegiance of the ethnic minorities. Education has been used as a weapon in this process. The Nationalists, in pursuing a policy of assimilation, began to develop a network of schools for the 'border nationalities'. The Communists have built on this network, and while policies have vacillated according to the vagaries of China's political leadership, and while assimilation is not acknowledged as official policy, it would appear that this is still the ultimate goal of the Chinese Communist Party leadership. This chapter seeks to discuss the importance of the ethnic minorities in China's strategic thinking and shows how educational policies, in spite of differences of emphasis, have had a remarkable degree of similarity under both the Nationalists and the Communists.

Introduction

Originally the Chinese occupied only a small area north of the China plain. The rest of what is today known as the People's Republic of China (PRC) was occupied by other ethnic groups — the Mon, Yi, Jung and Ti, 'the Barbarians of the Four Directions'. The westward expansion of Chinese civilization from the fertile valley of the Yellow River brought the Han Chinese (the name the Chinese race give to themselves) into contact with these and many other tribal and nomadic groups. Some were overwhelmed by the Han; others were strong enough numerically or sufficiently regionally isolated in mountain areas to be left alone by weak Chinese governments.

Until recently, most outside observers have viewed China as an entity — a nation blessed with a homogeneous culture and a common racial stock. Even the Chinese themselves sought to give this impression. They referred to themselves as having common origins which could be traced back to 'the old hundred surnames' (Pye, 1975) and chose to ignore mention of the many ethnic groups that had fallen under their influence since they were regarded as inferior and as 'barbarians'. However, as knowledge of China has grown during the twentieth century, this view has changed considerably. Observers have become increasingly aware not only of considerable linguistic and ethnic differences amongst the Han Chinese themselves but also of the existence of many ethnic minority groups within China's borders.*

That there were marked differences even amongst Han Chinese gradually became apparent as the Chinese began to move overseas into South East Asia. Certain scholars made a study of the different dialect groups that were to be found in South East Asia — Hakka, Hokkien, Hailamese, Cantonese, Tiochiu (Coughlin, 1960; Freedman, 1958; Purcell, 1966; Skinner, 1958), and arguments arose as to whether they were subdivisions of the Han or whether they could be classified as separate ethnic groups since they had all the attributes of ethnicity (Glazer and Moynihan, 1975). They married amongst themselves, spoke mutually incomprehensible dialects, undertook certain distinctive skills and occupations and retained all the attributes of separate communities. Divisions within Chinese society by region and dialect have so threatened the unity of the country that until this century, and more especially until the Chinese Communist Party (CCP) takeover in 1949, successive Chinese governments have had little time to worry about the ethnic minorities within their borders.

As a result, official policy towards these groups has vacillated considerably. Traditionally, imperial dynasties chose to ignore minority ethnic groups provided that they could exact tribute and recognition of imperial overlordship. Certain non-Han groups were given special privileges and ethnic precedence when their dynasties (eg Mongol Yuan (1260-1368) and Manchu Ch'ing (1644-1911)) were on the throne (Yong Yap and Cotterell, 1977; Dreyer, 1976). However, Han dynasties from the time of Mencius (c 390-305 BC) regarded the minorities with disdain as rude, barbarous and uncivilized, but believed that they could be civilized and reformed by the powers of Chinese culture. During the period of Nationalist rule (1911-49) the government pursued policies designed to assimilate minority groups into the mainstream of Han society, arguing that they should recognize the superiority of Han civilization and adopt its customs, language and culture accordingly. The Communists began by recognizing the right of self-determination of minority groups but gradually moved towards a position that has oscillated between cultural pluralism, national autonomy and assimilation. At the same time there have been concerted and often creative efforts to woo, placate and promote minorities out of all proportion to their numbers, to such an extent that they have been given special educational privileges, their languages have been preserved, they are allowed to marry earlier than Han Chinese, they are exempt from

---

* The terms *ethnic minorities, minority groups, minority nationalities, border nationalities* and *national minorities* have all been used at different times, and frequently interchangeably, by the Nationalist and Communist governments. Different expressions therefore appear in this chapter.

birth control regulations and they have not been forced to 'adopt socialism'
as rapidly.

This chapter seeks to trace education policies in the light of the
evolution of a more general policy towards the minority groups under
both the Nationalists and the Communists, and to show that, whatever
title has been given to this policy by both regimes, ultimately it has
intended (and still does) to assimilate, or at least 'to amalgamate the
minorities into the pre-existing dominant Han nation' (Connor, 1979).
The chapter also hopes to show why it has become so important for the
Chinese Communist Party (CCP) to solve its 'minorities problem'. This can
only be understood in the light of the locations and strategic importance
of these groups.

Ethnic groups within China

An ethnic minority group is 'a collectivity of individuals who, because of
their cultural characteristics and their common ancestry, are singled out
from others in society for differential treatment and therefore they regard
themselves as objectives of collective discrimination' (Wirth, 1945). In this
sense, China has a wide variety of ethnic groups.

Officially there are between 53 and 56 different national minorities
ranging in size from the Chuang (12,000,000) in the region bordering
Vietnam to 700 Hol-Chih who live in Heieung Kiang in the north-east.*
At least ten groups have populations of over 1,000,000 but the exact
size of many of the groups is not known. They range from the largely
assimilated Manchus to the nomadic Mongols and Uighurs, from the
formerly head-hunting Kawa to the primitive tribes of Miao, Yi, Chingpo
and the Teng, 'an outcast minority discovered only after the PLA entered
Tibet with a still lower status than serfs or slaves' (Burchett and Alley,
1976: 277-8). The major groups are the Chuang (Zhuang) mostly in
Kwangsi AR, the Hui (Muslims) predominantly in Ninghsia AR and Kansu
(though other Muslims include Uighurs, Kirghiz, Tajiks, Uzbeks, Tatars
and Pao-An), the Mongols in Inner Mongolian AR, Tibetans in Tibet AR
and Uighurs and Kazakhs in Sinkiang Uighur AR. Figure 1 shows the
major distributions of the national ethnic minorities of China.

A glance at the map will show why national minority groups are so
important in current government thinking. Although they account for
only 6 per cent of the total population they occupy almost 60 per cent of
China's land surface along the border regions. These border regions are
not simply those areas along China's political boundaries, strategically

---

* Dreyer (1976) cites sources giving 53 and 54 nationalities; Kang (1979) also cites
54; *The Guardian* (1979) refers to 55 nationalities but also comments on a new
minority, the *Jinuo* that had been discovered in South West Yunnan in 1979. Price
(1980) on the other hand only mentions 33 nationalities but his data base is now
inaccurate. Pye (1975) reckons that upgrading of numbers and classification
is a continual process as more information becomes available.

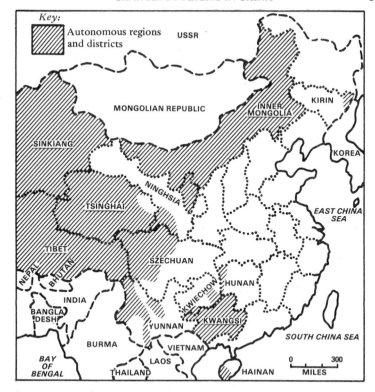

Autonomous regions

Singkiang Uighur AR:	Uighur, Kazakh, Hui, Uzbeks, Kirghiz*, Tajiks, Hsi-po, Tatars, Russians
Inner Mongolian AR:	Mongols, Daguors, Owenk'e, Olunchun
Kwangsi AR:	Chuang, Yao, Molao, Maonan
Ningsia Hui AR:	Hui
Tibet AR:	Tibetans, Menpa, Loyu, Teng

Autonomous districts

Tsinghai:	Tibetan, Mongol, Kazakh, T'u
Szechuan:	Tibetan, Yi, Ch'iang
Yunnan:	Chuang, Yi, Pai, Hani, Nahsi, Chingpo, Miao, Tai, Lisu, Lahu
Kweichow:	Miao, Tung, Puyi, Shui, Kolao
Kirin:	Korean, Manchu
Hunan:	Miao, T'uchia
Hainan:	Li, Miao, Yao, Ching

* CCP sources often refer to this group as 'Khalka'. This is an error since the Khalka are Mongol people of the Lamaist religion, whereas the Kirghiz are Turkic Muslims.

Figure 1 *Location of China's main ethnic minorities in autonomous regions (AR) and autonomous districts (Chou)*

important though these are, they are also 'a vast zone of China' embracing different ethnic groups, cultures and forms of livelihood. According to Deal, concern for and consciousness of border regions grew during the Nationalist period when all the ethnic minorities came to be labelled 'border nationalities' (*pien-chiang min-tsu*). In fact 'the view of the border lands deeply colours minority policy as frontier areas were seen as areas to exploit and develop for the benefit of the dominant nationality' (Deal, 1979: 33).

Some of the border areas are highly sensitive with weak demarcation lines, especially between the Shan states of Burma, Laos and China, the Mongol areas on both sides of the Soviet border and in the area where the Mongolian People's Republic meets the Inner Mongolian Autonomous Region and the Kazakh area of Sinkiang which adjoins the Kazakh Soviet Republic in the USSR. If peoples on these borders are hostile they could weaken China's security and increase the danger of foreign attack. Conversely, if the peoples in these regions are supportive of the central government they could make border defence that much easier.

Economically the border regions contain vast untapped mineral resources, oil and fossil reserves, the majority of China's timber forests, and 80 per cent of the meat, milk and wool supplying animals. Careful exploitation and husbandry of these resources could be of enormous benefit to China's attempts to project itself into the industrial and technological age. Geographically these regions are made up of mountainous and desert terrain, but are at the same time sparsely populated and could provide room for many millions of Han Chinese. The process of population transfer has been under way for 30 years now and has done little to ease the traditional hostility between minorities and Han Chinese in spite of the benefits of civilization and modernization that have been brought by the Chinese (Burchett and Alley, 1976). If anything it has increased the determination of minorities to retain their ethnic identity (Connor, 1979).

One final reason for interest in 'the minority problem' is that of propaganda. Because the 1949 Communist Revolution sought to transform Chinese society and to create an alternative socialist model of development, the eyes of the world have been focused on how successful these developments have been. A prosperous, contented and politically alert minority population can be shown as proof of the success of Chinese policies and socialist models. A discontented minority population can be exploited by opponents and critics of the regime. Thus Chinese governments have been concerned during much of this century, and especially since 1949, about how to integrate the minorities into the Chinese polity and how to win their loyalty and allegiance to the ideals of the Chinese Communist system.

Imperial policy

Traditional imperial policy towards ethnic minorities was a mixture of coercion and persuasion (Dreyer, 1976). Coercion included the suppression by force of uprisings (eg the Yi rebellion in Yunnan in the seventeenth century and two Muslim uprisings in the nineteenth century), by the billeting of troops in ethnic regions or by settlements of Han Chinese. Persuasion included exacting tribute and recognition of imperial overlordship. Amban officials, like colonial governors, were appointed to keep the peace in Mongolia, Tibet and Sinkiang with the assistance of local officials. In 1909 a Mongolian and Tibetan school was opened in Peking (Peijing) with the express purpose of training officials to serve in those areas. The curriculum included politics, finance, language training, and the literature, history and geography of Mongolia and Tibet (Brunnert and Hagelstrom, 1912). This was to be the forerunner of other Nationalities Institutes opened by both Nationalists and Communists for the training of cadres for ethnic regions.

In summing up the policy of the last imperial dynasty towards ethnic minorities, Dreyer says that it 'was a pluralistic form of integration that aimed at little more than control' (Dreyer, 1976: 12). In return for a vague commitment of loyalty to the Emperor and an absence of aggression towards the Han Chinese, traditional languages, customs and government systems were not interfered with. A few groups absorbed Han Chinese culture and became indistinguishable from other parts of Han China (eg the Manchus, Chuang and Pai). The Han, on the other hand, made little or no attempt to find out about the history, customs or language of tribal groups, believing that they would all move towards the Han Chinese because of the obvious superiority of Han culture.

Nationalist Chinese policy (1911-49)

A change in approach came during the period of the Nationalists. The new rulers of the Chinese Republic, largely Western-educated, offended by uprisings in Tibet (1910) and Mongolia (1911) in which hundreds of Han Chinese were massacred, were not so much concerned to preserve a multi-group empire based on loyalty to a dynastic ruler as to create a new, unified nation state based on the principles of nationalism and self-determination. The fact that these were inconsistent and opposing principles partly accounts for some of the confusion of Nationalist policies as well as that of subsequent Chinese Communist Party (CCP) policies.

The principle of self-determination for all peoples was enunciated by Sun Yat Sen in 1924 when he urged that the government should help 'the weak and small nationalities' within China to gain self-determination and self-government. This was reaffirmed in the First National Congress of the Kuomintang (KMT) (Tseng, 1930). Sun Yat Sen was strongly influenced by the ideas of national self-determination advocated by the US President Woodrow Wilson in his Fourteen Points (and as proclaimed in the Declaration of Rights of the People of Russia). However, to Wilson self-determination meant the political freedom of the smaller nations of

Europe, whereas to Sun Yat Sen it meant the right of minorities in China to be free from foreign domination (eg the Japanese in Manchuria, the Russians in Mongolia), though not necessarily from Chinese control. This policy was frequently resented by minority leaders who saw it as an excuse for Chinese imperialist aggression, which in fact it often was.

Sun Yat Sen exhibited typical Han chauvinism towards ethnic minorities. He regarded divisions as unhealthy and foresaw a time when there would be no divisions because all would have moved towards acceptance of the culture and language of Han China. He regarded China as 'really one nationality' and said:

> we must facilitate the dying out of all individual peoples inhabiting China ie Manchus, Tibetans, Mongols, Tatars . . . we must satisfy the demands of all races and unite them in a single cultural and political whole. (Sun Yat Sen, 1953)

It is interesting that he ignored the Hui, whom he regarded as a religious rather than an ethnic minority, and all the south-west tribal peoples whom he either did not know existed or regarded as insignificant (even though the Miao, T'ung and Yi had resisted assimilation for thousands of years). The five peoples that were recognized were given equal status in the five stripes of the Nationalist flag.

The ultimate aim was a situation where there was no distinction between Han Chinese and minorities. To help in the process of assimilation, ethnic place names were replaced by Chinese ones, minorities were encouraged to adopt Chinese surnames, and Chinese officials advocated the use of Mandarin, the wearing of Chinese dress and intermarriage. In 1928 the Ministry of the Interior sent a letter to provincial governors of the south western provinces asking them to comment on the most effective methods used to 'civilize' the tribes. Deal has observed that:

> There was stress on the unity of China's nationalities under the Nationalists and a desire to make the minorities aware that the best course for them to follow was to become part of a great Chinese nationality rather than to cultivate a sense of ethnic loyalty. (Deal, 1979: 34)

While administrative structures were only slightly modified — indirect rule was still permitted — and economic development was only minimal in the ethnic regions, education was seen as the chief means of bringing about assimilation and it has even been argued that in the process of providing schools and hospitals 'the Nationalists sought quite explicitly to emulate the policies and practices of Western missionaries' (Deal, 1972).

Nationalist handling of minority education varied according to locality and time. Schools for ethnic minorities were provided by local authorities and provincial authorities as well as by central government. For example in 1929 schools were established in Miao and Yao villages of Kwangsi province by a war lord. In Sinkiang in north-west China a number of schools were built in the 1920s and 1930s, though not until 1946 were these conducted in the native languages (Lattimore, 1950). In 1930 a Mongolian and Tibetan Department was established in the Ministry of

Education with responsibility for all 'border education'. It was responsible for establishing a network of primary schools in border regions to give instruction in 'modern education, citizenship, the Han language, vocational skills and hygiene'. Secondary schools were also established with an emphasis on technical skills and a 'clear understanding of the Chinese race and nation' (*China Handbook*, 1947). It was argued that since they had been psychologically prepared for assimilation through education, members of minority ethnic groups should be treated as Han.

The impetus for the development of 'border education' came as a result of the war with Japan, especially after Chiang Kai-Shek had moved his government to Chunking and realized he had to win the minorities' allegiance. Whereas only half a million yuan had been earmarked for border education until 1935, between 1936 and 1947 837,000,000 yuan were spent on ethnic minority education. While there was only one border school under Ministry of Education control before the war, 44 frontier schools of various grades were established or taken over by the Ministry after 1938 and in 1944 subsidies were promised for minority students. By 1947, food, book and clothing subsidies were available. A newspaper, the *Central Border Paper* was also established to stimulate literacy amongst Mongolians and Tibetans, and Chinese primary school books were translated into national languages while other materials on health, science and vocational education were developed for older pupils. Regardless of the type of border school — primary, middle, remedial, tertiary or vocational — the goals in all of these were the same: to promote Sun Yat Sen's Three Principles (Democracy, Nationalism and Livelihood) and to promote Chinese culture, history and morality.

Whatever shortcomings and weaknesses can be attributed to the Nationalists, for example their loss of Outer Mongolia and their inability to win the allegiance of the Tibetans, they did attempt to develop a policy for the education of minority groups. With the political and economic confusion of the 1920s and 1930s it is surprising that any policy evolved at all, but the Chinese government saw education as an effective weapon for bringing about assimilation and for reducing cultural differences. Unfortunately, there was too much emphasis on developing a uniform curriculum, and too little on developing local languages and materials. The arrogance of Han teachers alienated rather than encouraged minorities, to such an extent that Mongolians regarded modern education as bothersome, the Tibetans as an affront. Dreyer's assessment of Nationalist policy is that it was 'neither very good nor wholly bad' and that it 'might at its best be described as weak' (Dreyer, 1976: 41). Perhaps the fairest comment is that whatever the Nationalist shortcomings 'the Chinese Communists at least inherited from them a precedent for minority education, utilizing minority teachers and occasionally, minority languages' (Deal, 1979: 35), and were able to build on this rather than develop an entirely novel approach.

The Communist understanding of minorities

The CCP policy towards minority groups is based on Marxist-Leninist thinking, the experience of the Soviet Union and the modification of Mao's theories as a result of his own experiences in coming to power.

To Marx, ethnic national consciousness was merely a manifestation of bourgeois society. He believed that nations, nationalities and minorities would eventually disappear, though it is unclear whether this would occur by assimilation into a larger entity, by force, or through the inevitable workings of historical processes. He believed also that the economic advantages brought about through socialism would lead ethnic minorities to think less of their ethnic rights and more about the advantages of economic co-operation. However, because this was unlikely to happen overnight the need to recognize the rights of minorities was acknowledged, and the question of self-determination was discussed at the Second International in 1896 (Shaheen, 1956).

Unfortunately a degree of ambiguity crept into the discussions – and later into the writings of Lenin and Mao – which has caused confusion and vacillation in Communist societies. Self-determination could either mean the right to political independence or the right to only a degree of autonomy in the larger nation state. To Lenin the self-determination of minority groups initially meant the right to political independence (Lenin, 1916) though he genuinely did not believe many would exercise this right, because of the advantages of economic co-operation in a larger union. He also believed that if in Russia the rights and freedoms enjoyed by the Russians could be extended to minority nationalities, those nationalities would seek closer ties with Russia (Lenin, 1921; Pipes, 1953). However, as the full implications of the policy of self-determination began to dawn, and as Lenin opposed federalism on the grounds that it weakened the economic base of the nation (Lenin, 1922) he began to argue that self-determination was not the same as national separation but was a form of mutual co-operation in the interests of the proletariat of the larger state (Lenin, 1921; Pipes, 1957; Shaheen, 1956; Inkeles, 1960). According to Pipes,

> Lenin looked upon national problems as something to exploit and not as something to solve. But as a psychological weapon in the struggle for power . . . the slogan of self-determination . . . was to prove enormously successful. (Pipes, 1957: 49)

Before 1949 the CCP was more concerned with developing slogans that might gain the support of minorities in their struggle for power than with formulating a clearly defined policy. At the Second Party Congress in 1922, Mongolia, Tibet and Turkestan were proclaimed as 'autonomous states' and regional autonomy in a 'Chinese Federated Republic' was advocated. In 1930 the Ten Great Political Programmes gave the minorities the right to secede or federate and the 1931 Kiangsi Soviet Constitution (modelled on the 1924 Soviet Union Constitution) explicitly stated that minorities had the right of self-determination and of secession, as well as religious freedom and equality with all nationalities.

During the 1930s, as the Kiangsi Soviet came under increasing Kuomintang (KMT) pressure, the CCP sought more than ever to win the allegiance of national minorities. Between 1931 and 1938, however, there was a marked shift in policy from one recognizing the right of political independence to one recognizing autonomy within a unified China. As Mao was to argue, self-determination meant freedom to separate *or* freedom to unite. In the Chinese context only the second freedom was possible. Several reasons have been put forward for this change in policy. During the Long March, contrary to official reports, the Red Army was frequently harassed and on occasions was lucky to have survived (Dreyer, 1976; Wales, 1939; Wiens, 1962; Ekvall, 1965; Snow, 1937). The depth of hostility felt by the ethnic minorities towards the Han convinced the CCP leadership that if they were given the choice, the majority of minorities would opt *not* to join China. It was therefore better not to give them the choice. The CCP also began to recognize the strategic location of the minorities, especially along the Soviet border and in Sinkiang, and the need to develop a coherent policy towards them. More than any other factor, however, it has been argued that the Han inability to uphold their claims to Outer Mongolia led the Chinese leadership to link their 'minorities problem' with national security (Pye, 1975).

Since coming to power in 1949, CCP policy towards minorities has been described as assimilation through *Sinification*, ie the 'dilution' of existing cultures through Han colonization and settlement (Lal, 1970; Tien Hung-mao, 1974; Kang, 1979). The Chinese themselves have spoken about ultimate assimilation (Liu Chun, 1958) believing that because of increasing economic and political interdependence *all* minorities and the Han majority will ultimately 'coalesce into a hybrid nationality' (Hawkins, 1978). Educational policies have been designed to expedite this process, regardless of the dangers that they could lead to greater self-awareness and ethnic identity instead.

The evolution of a minorities education policy

During the early years after the CCP takeover, the party leaders were aware of the need to create a different policy from that of the KMT, to win the allegiance of the minorities to the new socialist state while at the same time strengthening their hold over minority regions; and to develop a knowledge base of minority areas, most Han being profoundly ignorant of the ethnic groupings in their midst. Initially, therefore, they set out to be moderate and accommodating in their approach. Minorities were urged to take a pride in their local culture, history and customs. Territorial rights, equality of all groups, representation in central government, the right to develop their own languages, culture and customs and the guarantee of religious beliefs were written into the 1949 Draft Constitution and reaffirmed in the Constitution of 1954. Cadres and commissions were sent to provincial areas to win the people's confidence, to discuss future policies and, in southern, south-west and south-east China, to learn more about the different tribal peoples.

Beginning in 1952 the CCP set about developing 'regional autonomy' for the 54 nationalities in China's borders. By the mid-1960s three types of autonomous area had been created:

1. five autonomous *regions* (*Ch'u*), areas largely inhabited by one minority or a combination of several minorities (eg Inner Mongolia AR (1947), Sinkiang Uighur AR (1955);
2. 29 autonomous *districts* (*Chou*), smaller concentrations of ethnic minorities within the larger regions;
3. 69 autonomous *counties* (*Hsien*), even smaller concentrations of ethnic minorities, some of which may be multinational (*China Reconstructs*, 1972). Over 90 per cent of national minorities are in some form of autonomous unit. The remainder, mainly Hui Muslims, are scattered throughout China (Winters, 1979).

Regional autonomy did not mean freedom to separate: it meant a certain freedom of control over internal affairs, the management of finances, the organization of local security forces, the use of the mother tongue, and a degree of autonomy over education and cultural affairs. 'The intent of this form of administration was not to liberate the minorities from central control but rather to integrate them more fully in the Chinese state' (Deal, 1979: 36). The move away from the Soviet concept of federation was justified on the grounds that it suited the Chinese situation better, especially considering that most of China's minorities reside on or near national borders and that the authorities have been preoccupied with maintaining border integrity in the face of mobile and often hostile minorities (Lattimore, 1962).* The policy of regional autonomy was thus a bold attempt at providing a degree of flexibility for minorities while at the same time seeking to win their co-operation in the common cause of creating a New China. The legal status of both minorities and regional autonomy in the People's Republic of China was confirmed in the 1976 Constitution which states that:

> The PRC is a multinational state. The areas where regional autonomy is exercised are all inalienable parts of the PRC. All the nationalities are equal.

---

* This was particularly true after 1962 when 50,000 Kazakhs and other non-Han groups fled across the Sinkiang border into the Kazakh Soviet Republic of the Soviet Union. Soviet propaganda warning that the Chinese were going to massacre and/or possibly remove them to other parts of China created panic amongst the tribal peoples and led to this mass exodus. As Pye has observed, 'The fact that such numbers would leave China demonstrated not only the failure of what Peking considered to be conciliatory policies toward minorities but also the vulnerability of China's borders. In the subsequent years the Chinese have increasingly seen the "nationalities problem" as one of guarding the sacred territory of the Chinese motherland' (Pye, 1975: 499).

Big nationality chauvinism and local nationality chauvinism must be opposed. (Min Yeh-wen, 1975)

During the first two decades after 1949, several conferences were held to establish educational priorities and policies for national minority areas. The All-China Minority Nationalities Education Conference of September 1951 stressed the need for training minority cadres to help develop a spirit of patriotism and to improve minority academic institutions, and a Central Institution of Nationalities was opened in Peking to train minority cadres. By 1958 there were eight Nationalities Institutes providing political training to minority cadres and language training to Chinese cadres. They were closed during the GPCR and were not reopened until 1972. They have been operating during the 1970s, though many of the cadres have been only semi-literate (Pye, 1975).

Other conferences stressed the need for literacy classes, universal primary education, middle schools where possible, and teacher training institutes. It was hoped that by 1968 the national minorities would have achieved parity at all educational levels with the national average (SMCP, 1956a). By the late 1960s, however, a changed approach began to emerge. Increasing emphasis was placed on the notion that 'nationality struggle is a question of class struggle' and minorities at the height of the Great Proletarian Cultural Revolution (GPCR) were urged to distinguish between class enemies and friends regardless of nationality, and to be prepared to attend struggle and criticism sessions (SMCP, 1969). There was also a growing divergence of opinion between those on the one side who argued that the same progress from amongst minorities could not be expected since, because of poverty and economic backwardness 'they would require much aid and assistance from outside' (NCNA, 1969) and the extreme exponents of the GPCR who argued on the other side that national minorities should practise 'self-reliance' and 'hard-work' and for whom no excuses could be made (NCNA, 1970).

Although the Communists inherited a minority education framework from the Nationalists, it was a frail and patchy one. For example, in 1951, 92 per cent of all Koreans of school age were at school whereas virtually no education at all was available in Szechuan and Yunnan, and only a few schools were available in Tibet and Sinkiang; by 1955, only one primary and one middle school had been established in Tibet. Thus one problem facing the CCP was the need to develop entire school systems in areas where the socioeconomic base was low, where peoples were nomadic (north-west), where peoples were semi-feudal (Tibet) and where peoples were exceedingly primitive (south-west). The First Five Year Plan (1953-57) recognized the weak educational and economic base of the minority areas and the need to expand and transform school provision, especially in the curriculum content. During the period 1950-58 there was an intensive programme of building primary schools in most minority areas in an attempt to establish compulsory UPE (universal primary education). It is difficult to assess the true picture. Undoubtedly much progress was made, especially in urban areas, but because figures were deliberately inflated during the 'Great Leap Forward' (GLF), the matter should be treated with caution (SCMP, 1958). Nevertheless in the south-west China border regions, between 1951 and 1958, numbers enrolled at primary schools rose from 1,200,000 to 4,200,000 and at middle school from 44,000 to 990,000 (Deal, 1972) while in the Inner Mongolian AR and Sinkiang Uighur AR considerable numbers of 'tent schools' were established to accompany the herdsmen. These were considerable achievements. By 1952, 700,000 textbooks had been produced in the Mongolian, Tibetan and Uighur languages, a process that has continued spasmodically ever since. Following the upheavals of the GPCR, the 1970s saw a return to an emphasis on primary and middle schools, experiments with both formal and non-formal instruction and an expansion of colleges and technical institutes.

In the early 1960s, as the commune system was extended to minority areas, the aim was to open one primary school in each commune and one middle school in each *hsien* (county). Attempts were also made to stop mobile tent schools for nomads and to introduce fixed primary schools so that UPE could be declared to have been achieved, even if it was not compulsory. In spite of the upheavals of the GPCR many claims have been made that primary education is at least almost universal in most minority areas (Hawkins, 1978). However, in the light of recent revelations of inaccuracies in Chinese statistics, it is difficult to ascertain how far claims of UPE can be relied on. What can be said with certainty is that considerable efforts have been made to expand primary and middle school education in minority areas and there is little reason to doubt that there has been considerable success.

To overcome the lack of basic knowledge about so many of these ethnic minorities, it was agreed in 1951 to establish research institutes with the express intention of discovering more about the language, customs and culture of minorities. Previous derogatory terms used for minorities (eg 'Lolo' for the Yi, and 'Fan' (barbarians) for all) were banned and peoples were to be called by the names they called themselves. The term for assimilation (*hung-hua*) was replaced by amalgamation (*jung-ho*). During the 1950s a major attempt was made to classify ethnic groups, to study their languages and customs and to number them. Numbers initially ranged from 40 to 100+ but by 1963 it was generally acknowledged that there were 53 different groups. One interesting point that emerged from these studies was that where there were written languages, a study of books and journals revealed not only the influence of 'foreign materials' but also a stress on the ethnic cultures in preference to Han culture — a situation that greatly distressed Han Chinese leaders. There were also numerous complaints at this time of Han cadre arrogance and oppression. During the GPCR the research institutes were closed on the grounds that they were adopting a 'bourgeois academic approach' to their study, but they too have been reopened during the 1970s.

A further area of difficulty in CCP handling of national minority education has been that of language. There are over 50 distinct ethno-linguistic groups and most minority languages are significantly different from Han Chinese. Bilingualism has therefore been a major aspect of educational policy. The 1954 Constitution recognized the right of minorities to use their languages in both spoken and written forms, in all public proceedings, in the press and in schools. At the same time it was recognized that minorities needed to learn written and spoken Chinese (Mandarin). Han personnel working in the ARs were also expected to learn the local languages, though in many cases there were problems because of the lack of written script. The CCP therefore encouraged the development of glossaries and dictionaries. Policy has been to encourage the regional language as the medium of instruction wherever possible and to develop regional languages provided that Chinese is also learned. Ultimately, as was Lenin's dream for Russians in the USSR, it is hoped that *all* will speak, read and write Chinese, thus helping the process of unification. In an effort to ease the learning of Chinese, attempts were made during the 1960s to romanize the scripts of both Chinese and minority languages. The hope was that by learning a romanized version of a minority language it would be easier for minorities to switch to learning pin-yin Chinese. During the GPCR, however, cadres and Red Guards placed great stress on teaching through Mandarin and forced the minorities to learn it. To speed up the process thousands of local language textbooks were destroyed, thousands of Han Chinese were sent to the minority regions and thousands of minority youths were sent to learn Chinese (SCMP, 1960b).

We do not know exactly how many thousands of young people were transferred in this way, but it was hoped that mixed settlements and forced intermarriage between Han and non-Han would ultimately lead to erosion of ethnic distinctiveness. Following the GPCR, moderate policies were once again pursued. Minority rights, characteristics and languages were recognized. Broadcasts and newspapers in minority languages were restored. Major efforts were made to raise educational standards in minority areas, to increase the numbers attending school (SCMP, 1972) and to restore teaching through the medium of the mother tongue. Indications are that minority languages are used at the lower grades of primary school, or until sufficient literacy is achieved in the mother tongue to be able to transfer to Mandarin. During the 1970s considerable efforts have been made to train minority teachers, revive minority languages and introduce the pin-yin script and it has been recognized that minorities cannot be expected to learn Chinese overnight.

Whatever the language medium of instruction and whichever ethnic minority we might be considering, the curriculum in the schools has been remarkably similar throughout China. Emphasis has been placed on history, the rise of the CCP, Mao's thought, civics, politics, patriotism as opposed to local nationalism, Chinese language, history and geography, and class struggles. There have been variations according to local culture and customs but the knowledge and attitudes imparted have been remarkably uniform. During the Great Leap Forward great emphasis was placed on 'more, better, faster, cheaper' in every area of life. In terms of minority education this meant intensification of the Sinification of the curriculum. Art forms and dancing had to change to conform to Han revolutionary patterns (Dreyer, 1976). New methods of animal husbandry and agricultural production were introduced, often with beneficial results. Many minorities protested violently because they saw this as a form of Han Chinese assimilation and in 1959 there was a major uprising in Tibet, suppression of which outraged the world (Patterson, 1960); there have also been several uprisings amongst Hui Muslims (Winters, 1979).

However, the success of any language, curriculum or minority policy depends upon the calibre and effectiveness of the teachers. This point was recognized early by the CCP, and during the 1950s many Han cadres and teachers were sent to minority regions to establish formal teacher training institutions for the local populace (eg Sinkiang University and Teacher Training College), as well as to develop non-formal and in-service training programmes. By 1960 it was recognized that the speed of progress was too slow and 'only by the active fostering and training of teachers of minority nationalities can there be a strong foundation for a continued Leap Forward in the education of national minorities' (SCMP, 1960a). However, since most training materials were available in Chinese there was conflict over whether to teach through Chinese *before* moving to the minority languages (SCMP, 1962) or whether to translate materials and increase the training of minority teachers. During the GPCR the former policy predominated, but by the early 1970s it was apparent that an increasing number of minority teachers were being trained in their own languages, and in some regions 90 per cent of the teaching force is made up of minorities (SCMP, 1973, 1974). An exception has been Tibet: Han Chinese teachers are still being sent in large numbers to different parts of Tibet, and in the mid-1970s thousands of Tibetan students were being sent to study in Chinese universities (Dreyer, 1976).

One group that deserves special mention is the Hui (Muslims). Although Muslims belong to various minority nationalities, especially the Hui-Hui of Arab-Persian descent, who predominate in Ninghsia AR but who are also spread throughout the cities of China; the Uighurs, who form 75 per cent of Sinkiang Uighur AR; and the Turkic Muslims (eg Uzbeks, Tatars, Tajiks, Kirghiz), and although they are spread across the Autonomous Regions of China, they have frequently been treated differently from other groups such as the Tibetans, Miao and Li. For example, Uighurs are allowed to slaughter their livestock and engage in private transactions not allowed elsewhere in China (Winters, 1979: 24). The reasons are partly because of CCP desire to win the confidence of Muslim Third World countries, partly because of the strength of Muslim opposition in China, partly because not being Christian, they are regarded as less subversive of CCP policy, and partly because of the strategic location of oil deposits in north and north-west China (Winters, 1976). Special Islamic Institutes have been established for the training of *ahungs* (imams) so that they can learn theology and Arabic in the context of 'patriotism, fervent love for the fatherland and for socialism'. However, state-funded primary schools have gradually replaced Koranic schools. Arabic has been forbidden in state schools, and pin-yin romanized script has been introduced as the medium of instruction. As one observer has commented,

> intensive efforts have been made under the new regime to bring all Muslim children into government schools where the Chinese language is taught and used as the medium of instruction and where science is emphasized. (Winters, 1976: 20)

Where mosque schools do still exist, their role is to teach Arabic and religious instruction for those serving in the diplomatic corps in Arabic-speaking countries.

Evaluation

The policies of the Han Chinese towards the minority people in China have aroused considerable interest, not least because observers, impressed by Mao's alternative approaches to a socialist society, have been eager to see how the government handled minority relations. Although there are a few who believe that nothing but benefits have accrued to minority peoples since the Communists came to power (for example, Burchett and Alley) there are many others who are far less sanguine (Deal, Dreyer, Kang, Pye, Winters).

Although officially the CCP has insisted on the ultimate goal as one of integration or amalgamation (*jung-ho*) rather than assimilation, which still has too many associations with the Kuomintang, there is little doubt that in spite of fluctuations in policy the long term aim *is* for the assimilation and political integration of minority peoples into a unified Han state. In this way, the Communists have developed, extended and intensified the policy begun by the Nationalists. Every means possible has been used to try to bring Han Chinese and minority peoples closer together — radio, press, speeches, leaflets, cadre training, education. Equality before the law, respect for different customs, the solidarity of all the peoples of China, patriotism — all these have been stressed frequently. Whereas the constitution of the Soviet Union technically allows for Union Republics to secede from the USSR, the PRC Constitution states that the Autonomous Republics are inalienable and integral parts of China. It is thus essential to reach a satisfactory *modus vivendi*. The geographical and strategic importance of the minority areas makes such co-operation even more vital. Ironically, however, the more propaganda, economic investment and education have been used to bring about closer amalgamation, and the more education has stressed minority languages, history and customs, the greater has been the resurgence of ethnic identity and resentment of Han Chinese interference on the part of the minorities. Even as late as 1971, Mao in his *Correct Handling of Contradictions* identified 'Han chauvinism' and 'local nationalism' as representing 'a specific contradiction among the people which should be overcome'

(Kang, 1979). On the present evidence, the Chinese majority has not resolved the problem of its minorities. Assimilation is still an impossible dream while real autonomy for the different groups is unrealistic. Provided that border security can be guaranteed the immediate future is likely to reveal growing co-operation between the Han and ethnic minorities and a grudging acceptance of mutual respect between the different groups.

References

Brunnert, H S and Hagelstrom, V V (1912) *Present Day Political Organizations of China* Kelly and Walsh: Shanghai

Burchett, W and Alley, R (1976) *China: The Quality of Life* Penguin: Harmondsworth

China Handbook 1939-1945 (1947) Macmillan: New York

China Reconstructs December (1972)

Connor, W (1979) An overview of the ethnic composition and problems of non-Arab Asia *in* Kang (1979)

Coughlin, R J (1960) *Double Identity: The Chinese in Modern Thailand* Hong Kong University Press: Hong Kong

Deal, D M (1972) *Peking's policies towards ethnic minorities in South West China, 1927 to 1965* Mimeographed paper given at the Northwest Regional Seminar on China, University of Washington, 28/29.4.72

Deal, D M (1979) Policy towards ethnic minorities in South West China, 1927-1965 *in* Kang (1979)

Dreyer, J T (1976) *China's Forty Millions* Harvard East Asian Series No 87 Harvard University Press: Cambridge, Mass

Ekvall, R (1965) Nomads of Tibet: a Chinese dilemma *in* Harper (1965)

Freedman, M (1958) Chinese communities in Southeast Asia: a review article *Pacific Affairs* 31: 300-4

Glazer, N and Moynihan, D P (1975) *Ethnicity: Theory and Experience* Harvard University Press: Cambridge, Mass

The Guardian (1979) *New minorities learn the hard way* 24.9.79

Harper, F ed (1965) *This is China* Dragonfly Press: Hong Kong

Hawkins, J (1978) National minority education in the People's Republic of China *Comparative Education Review* 22 1: 147-61

Inkeles, A (1960) Soviet nationality theory in perspective *Problems of Communism* 9 May/June: 25-34

Kang, T S ed (1979) *Nationalism and the Crises of Ethnic Minorities in Asia* Greenwood Press: New York

Lal, A (1970) Sinification of ethnic minorities in China *Current Scene* 8 4: 1-25

Lattimore, O (1950) *Pivot of Asia* Little, Brown: Boston, Mass

Lattimore, O (1962) *Inner Asian Frontiers of China* Beacon Press: Boston, Mass

Lenin, V I (1916) The significance of the right to self determination and its relation to federation *Collected Works* XXII Progress Publishers: Moscow (1964 edition)

Lenin, V I (1921) *Selected Works* International Publishers: New York

Lenin, V I (1922) The question of nationalities or of autonomization *in National Liberation Movement in the East* Foreign Languages Publishing House: Moscow (1957 edition)

Linton, R ed (1945) *The Science of Man in the World Crisis* Columbia University Press: New York

Lui Chun (1958) On the question of national assimilation *Jen-min-jih-pao (People's Daily)* 28.1.58

Min Yeh-wen (1975) Strengthen the unity of the peoples of all nationalities and consolidate the dictatorship of the proletariat *Jen-min-jih-pao (People's Daily)* 14.2.75

New China News Agency (1969) The educational revolution in the minority areas of China *Hsinhua News Agency* 9.11.69

New China News Agency (1970) Central China national minorities build new socialist mountain region through self-reliance *Hsinhua News Agency* 21.4.70

Patterson, G N (1960) *Tibet in Revolt* Methuen: London

Pipes, R (1953) Bolshevik National theory before 1917 *Problems of Communism* **2** May: 22-7

Pipes, R (1957) *Formation of the Soviet Union: Communism and Nationalism 1917-1923* Harvard University Press: Cambridge, Mass

Purcell, V (1966) *The Chinese in South East Asia* Royal Institute of International Affairs, Oxford University Press: London

Pye, L W (1975) China: ethnic minorities and national security *in* Glazer and Moynihan (1975)

Shaheen, S (1956) *The Communist (Bolshevik) Theory of National Self-Determination* 'S-Gravenhage: The Hague

Skinner, G W (1958) *Leadership and Power in the Chinese Community in Thailand* Cornell University Press: Ithaca, NY

Snow, E (1937) *Red Star over China* Random House: New York

Sun Yat Sen (1953) *Memoirs of a Chinese Revolutionary* China Cultural Service: Taipei

Survey of China Mainland Press (1956a) National Minority Education Conference *No 1304* June 4

Survey of China Mainland Press (1956b) Educational progress for national minorities *No 1313* June 17

Survey of China Mainland Press (1958) Rapid educational development in minority areas *No 1790* May 29

Survey of China Mainland Press (1960a) Actively foster teachers of minority nationalities *No 2263* May 9

Survey of China Mainland Press (1960b) Standard spoken language has blossomed in national minorities areas *No 2365* Oct 26

Survey of China Mainland Press (1962) Han language phonetic scheme promotes the cultural development of fraternal nationalities *No 2692* March 7

Survey of China Mainland Press (1969) Strengthen the unity of the masses of nationalities and consolidate the dictatorship of the proletariat *No 4498* Sept 18

Survey of China Mainland Press (1972) Constantly train teachers of minority nationalities *No 5110* Mar 27

Survey of China Mainland Press (1973) More schools for minority people in North-west China Region *No 5347* April 6

Survey of China Mainland Press (1974) More teachers of minority nationalities for Sinkiang *No 5598* April 9

Tien, Hung-mao (1974) Sinification of national minorities in China *Current Scene* **12** 11

Tseng, Yu-hao (1930) *Modern Chinese Political and Legal Philosophy* Commercial Press: Shanghai

Wales, N (1939) *Inside Red China* Doubleday, Doran: New York

Wiens, H J (1962) Some of China's thirty five million non-Chinese *Journal of Hong Kong Branch of the Royal Asiatic Society* **2** 54-74

Winters, C-A (1976) Islam in China *al-Ittahad* 13.7.76

Winters, C-A (1979) *Mao or Muhammed: Islam in the People's Republic of China* Asian Research Service: Hong Kong

Wirth, L (1945) Problems of minority groups *in* Linton (1945)

Yong Yap and Cotterell, A (1977) *Chinese Civilization: From the Ming Republic to Chairman Mao* Book Club Associates: London

7. Minority group interests within nation-building policies in Africa

Jeremy Greenland

Summary: Educational policy-makers in Africa claim to want a curriculum which is both flexible enough to draw previously under-represented minorities into school and yet sufficiently uniform to reinforce national institutions and development. Curricula developed so far strongly favour uniformity at the expense of flexibility. Practical reasons for this imbalance are cited: the high cost of producing and approving diversified instructional materials, the scarcity of appropriate personnel to design them, their complicating effects on teacher training, staff deployment, and the drafting of selective examinations. Political constraints on flexible curricula are then discussed: the study of regional languages and history threatens national unity, enhanced awareness of regional economic inequalities threatens the vested interests of national élites; there is resistance to the imported Western notion of minorities within a policy having 'rights' to schooling and to an adapted curriculum. Thirdly, it is argued that the dominant view of curriculum in Africa is so prescriptive and utilitarian in terms of intended pupil outcomes and assumptions about under-qualified teachers that it inevitably resists any move towards flexibility and innovation. Finally, it is suggested that renewed debate on the learning process and schooling could lead to a compromise between standardization and flexibility which is (a) realistic about the teachers involved, (b) free from the charge of being merely a Western import, and (c) congruent with the wider sociopolitical process of nation-building.

Ministers of education of the African member states of Unesco, meeting in Lagos in 1976, resolved as their first basic principle that 'since education is an inalienable right . . . systems of education and training should be designed on a properly planned basis, intended for *and equally well adapted for all individuals*, whatever their age, sex, social and occupational status, and wherever they live' (my italics). Their second basic principle is as follows: 'since education is a determining factor in economic, social and cultural development, the systems and structures whereby it is provided should express the national political will [and] . . . should be closely linked with the other systems upon which development depends . . .' (Unesco, 1977: 48).

The Lagos Declaration thus confidently assumes that member countries can establish a school system which on the one hand is flexible enough to equalize opportunity for access and achievement by its appeal to specific population groups, and which on the other hand is sufficiently uniform to foster national unity and supply the nation's requirements in terms of trained manpower. The purpose of this chapter is to discuss the part played by curriculum development in Africa (particularly the curriculum of the first basic cycle of schooling) in reconciling these apparently divergent aims.

It is important to note at the outset that in certain influential quarters attention to curriculum development is increasingly being seen as a blind alley. The effect of curriculum development on educational output, the World Bank argues, has failed to meet expectations; structural and administrative reforms are needed, not changes in curriculum content. Children not yet in school are to be reached by the application of school location planning techniques, by 'flexible modes of delivery' (for example, encouraging the Koranic schools of Kenya's semi-arid areas to 'feed into' Basic Education Centres), and, in the case of the final 5 to 10 per cent, by 'special measures' such as adapting the school calendar to the agricultural year and subsidizing instructional materials and school meals.

For children already in school, the argument continues, the priority is to improve the efficiency with which they learn. This can be achieved by 'qualitative measures' such as increasing the effectiveness of teachers, providing an adequate supply of instructional materials, exploiting distance teaching/learning resources, and 'remedying pre-school factors' in terms of improving standards of nutrition, health and housing; and by 'quantitative measures' such as reducing rates of repetition and drop-out, adjusting the teacher-pupil ratio and maximizing the use of classroom space.

This arsenal of structural and administrative reforms appears all the more impressive because of the 'hard' research findings on which it is based. The World Bank's own commissioned research claims to have shown that

> variation in the size of the class within a range of 20 to 40 makes little or no difference in average achievement

and that

> results from the Philippines indicate that after the first year learning in the first grade increased 12 per cent on tests in mathematics, science, and language after sufficient investments were made to alter the ratio of pupils to books from 10:1 to 2:1. (World Bank, 1980: 39, 35)

Research into the effects of changes in curriculum on enrolments and 'learning outcomes' simply cannot compete with this sort of thing. The 'Ife' project in Nigeria, which reached the modest conclusion that children learning through the medium of Yoruba achieved at least as good results as those learning through the more usual medium of English, is an isolated example. Research on differences in enrolments in apparently homogeneous areas of Cameroon showed that perceptions of the value of school differed sharply from one village to the next and were based on a number of factors. The most significant of these were (a) the degree of support from the traditional institutions, such as the chief and the secret societies, for the school, (b) the prospects for marketing the village's cash-crops, and

(c) whether the village school offered the full seven-year cycle or not (IPAR-Buea, 1977: 109).

There are good reasons, however, for persevering with a discussion of efforts to achieve a flexible yet standardized curriculum. One is that policy-makers in Africa tend only to adopt the World Bank's 'efficiency' model of 'educational output' when it is an unavoidable condition for securing an International Development Agency loan. The fact that every African capital boasts a Curriculum Development Centre, with a large staff producing syllabuses and materials and consuming a not insignificant part of the education budget, reflects a very different set of sociopolitical priorities from those of the World Bank and other aid donors. Another reason is that the tension between a flexible and a standardized curriculum involves, at bottom, discussion of the nature of curriculum itself. Some argue that this debate is a luxury best deferred until the education system has been made efficient; later in this chapter we hope to show that clarification of the curriculum issue now is an essential precondition for raising the efficiency of the system.

With the ambitious words 'systems of education . . . equally well adapted for all individuals' the Lagos Declaration implies a different curriculum for every child. And by qualifying 'all individuals' with 'whatever their age, sex, social and occupational status, and wherever they live' the Lagos Declaration accurately lists the main indicators of educational disadvantage in Africa — especially if ethnic identity is understood to be subsumed under social status. The outside observer, accustomed to approaching the notion of a disadvantaged minority with these indicators in mind, would conclude from Table 1 that in 17 of the 33 countries listed a majority, not a minority, of the 6-11 age group are as yet unschooled; and that the percentage of girls enrolled as opposed to boys is much lower in the Sahel countries, roughly equal in many countries and actually higher in Botswana, Lesotho and Swaziland. He would also be interested in the statistical validity of, for example, Heyneman's findings that the socio-economic status of a wide sample of Ugandan schoolchildren had remarkably little influence on their academic performance (Heyneman, 1979).

The Curriculum Development Centres, however, see things very differently, at least if their syllabuses and instructional materials are judged on the extent of their intention to redress the indicators of disadvantage outlined above. The only concession tends to be to regional variations, though some countries do not even allow that. The reasons for this highly unequal admixture of flexibility and standardization in the curriculum can now be discussed.

First, there are practical obstacles which hinder flexibility: a curriculum which allows local variants is highly expensive in terms of unit cost. Zambia has a vernacular language programme for each of its seven official languages, but the unit cost of producing instructional materials for the three 'minority' language groups is greater than for the four 'majority' ones. The alternative is to accept lower quality products, for instance

Region/country	All	Male	Female
Eastern Africa			
Botswana	86.9	80.7	93.0
Burundi	18.5	22.3	14.7
Ethiopia	17.4	22.8	12.1
Kenya	89.9	93.0	86.6
Lesotho	76.6	62.3	91.0
Madagascar	69.6	73.5	65.7
Malawi	43.1	48.8	37.4
Mauritius	90.0	91.9	88.1
Rwanda	49.9	52.6	47.1
Somalia	21.7	25.7	17.7
Sudan	30.6	35.5	25.5
Swaziland	79.8	78.2	81.5
Tanzania	53.8	57.5	50.0
Uganda	47.1	56.0	37.9
Zaire	65.7	74.6	56.9
Zambia	68.4	70.2	66.6
Western Africa			
Benin	41.8	57.0	26.8
Cameroon	85.5	93.2	77.9
Central African Republic	56.8	73.8	40.1
Chad	30.0	43.8	16.7
Congo, People's Republic of The	100.0	100.0	100.0
Gabon	100.0	100.0	100.0
The Gambia	28.7	38.4	19.0
Ghana	42.5	46.6	38.4
Guinea	26.0	34.8	17.3
Ivory Coast	70.7	85.9	55.7
Liberia	36.0	44.1	28.1
Mali	21.0	27.9	14.0
Mauritania	23.2	30.2	16.2
Nigeria	65.8	72.2	59.0
Senegal	35.4	42.6	28.3
Sierra Leone	34.8	40.9	28.7
Upper Volta	12.2	15.4	9.0

Source: World Bank (1980: 108)

Table 1 *Net enrolment percentages in developing countries of 6-11 year-olds by sex, 1977*

limiting the 'minority' groups to black and white illustrations only while the others have colour — something which is hardly likely to increase a child's love of the local. A British publisher expressed interest in publishing a teacher's handbook for school agriculture, but only if it could be 'de-Cameroonized' enough to appeal to the whole West African market. In Swaziland another publisher wanted one single textbook for school agriculture, not five regional variations, plus a guarantee that the course would stay unchanged for five years. There are other powerful but unequal pressures outside the control of the ministry of education: public broadcasting time for the seven Zambian languages is not divided equally between them — the inevitable consequence of uneven 'listener demand' and the availability of pop songs in Bemba; the cost of ensuring parity of output is simply prohibitive.

Local variations in curriculum are also costly in terms of the time required for their negotiation. It was not sufficient for the curriculum proposals submitted by IPAR-Buea to be approved by the Chief Education Officers of the two English-speaking provinces of Cameroon to which they applied; they had to be ratified — after laborious explanation, commentary and debate — by a national curriculum conference, a majority of whose delegates had virtually no knowledge of the provinces concerned.

Even when a degree of local input to the curriculum is sanctioned by the ministry, at best this is provided by a highly educated representative of Tribe x or Region y who has lived in the capital for years and may no longer be in touch with grass-roots feeling, and at worst — and more commonly — by expatriate technical advisers. The Buea curriculum development project in Cameroon which is frequently quoted with approval in the literature had a professional staff of 13 when the 'local' curriculum materials were being written: seven were Europeans, and the *technical* contribution of the six Cameroonian counterparts was restricted by the extent of their administrative and 'public relations' responsibilities. The illustrations for the curriculum materials were produced by an Australian visitor to Cameroon who made a rapid study of the local environment. Several of her drawings offended the Cameroonian staff members by the style in which Africans were portrayed and by the 'realistic' depiction of local housing, farms, etc, but, fortunately, or unfortunately, they went into print because the locals did not presume to challenge the foreigners' definition of artistic merit. A close look at curriculum texts dealing with local issues shows how much they rely on descriptions of these phenomena written years ago by foreign anthropologists or missionaries. In some countries an effort has been made to canvass local opinion as to what constitutes 'a well-educated child' — for example at the Nigeria National Curriculum Conference of 1969 — but once these qualities are enshrined in some well-meaning statement of educational aims, they tend to be ignored by the 'professionals' who are called in to write objectives for specific subjects and lessons.

A curriculum with significant local variations, even if backed up with teaching notes and instructional materials, makes additional demands on the already strained arrangements for training, posting and promoting teachers. In a number of countries college lecturers have not yet discarded their old methodology notes and adapted their lessons to the coursebooks produced by the Curriculum Development Centre. Posting teachers to the region of their origin and whose language they speak might seem essential for the success of a localized curriculum, but it arouses suspicions of 'tribalism' and also cuts across the preference of young teachers for jobs in the towns. Medical officers do a good trade in declaring teachers unfit to work in remote areas.

The content of the primary school-leaving examination is perhaps the most significant single constraint on the actual implementation of local variations in curriculum. Teachers of the final two years of primary school will only teach what they know will be examined. Booklets containing previous years' questions and 'model' answers sell more widely than the class textbooks themselves. Once multiple choice questions focus on common mistakes in English by eg Kenyan speakers, teachers will rehearse those particular speech patterns to the neglect of basic language skills. The timetable may declare that music, history etc are taught every week, but the unannounced visitor will never encounter such a lesson in examination classes, unless those subjects are part of the examination itself. And, as Hawes says,

> this is only half the story. The examination is set and marked in such a way that it excludes by its very nature from Science and Social Studies papers any questions based on the local environment. (Hawes, 1979: 103)

Lurking below these practical impediments to localized curriculum are a number of dilemmas involving wider political considerations.

In the immediate post-independence years it was a major concern of all curriculum development teams in Africa to replace the more obvious signs of a curriculum's Western origins with local examples and equivalents. However, substituting the flora and fauna of Burundi for their Belgian counterparts in a biology syllabus was essentially a cosmetic operation, since the authorities were even more anxious to maintain parity with 'metropolitan' standards and to dispel the feeling that 'African' syllabuses were an easy option. The motive, in any case, was to foster an awareness of *national* identity, to raise the flag and sing the national anthem every morning, to restrict the independence of the huge mission-controlled sector so that government, not mission inspectors, were the final arbiters — for example, pupils could be required to attend political rallies in school time and be inducted into the new national philosophy and view of the world. Zimbabwe, whose independence was delayed until 1980, is similarly keen that the curriculum for its emergency teacher training programme should be written by Zimbabweans so that the component of 'national political orientation' is not diluted by unsound technical assistance from abroad.

But all curriculum teams sooner or later face the problem that the constituent parts of the nation and the process by which nationhood was achieved have to be defined. This inevitably requires measures that militate against the quest for national unity. For example, although educational opinion now generally recognizes (reluctantly and belatedly in the case of the ex-French countries) that the skills of literacy and numeracy are best acquired and consolidated in the mother tongue, the decision whether or not to give a particular mother tongue the status of an official language for the purposes of education has enormous political implications. Can the history of ethnic or regional population groups be taught without making it clear that some collaborated more willingly than others with the colonizers? The authorities in Burundi are currently attempting to rewrite their own history by claiming that the ethnic antagonisms between Tutsi, Hutu and Twa — and even the consciousness of ethnic identity itself — are the direct result of the colonizer's predisposition to see Africa through ethnic spectacles. How the same authorities will explain away the abundant historical evidence for these antagonisms in Kirundi proverbs, poetry and legends is not yet clear.

If and when the curriculum succeeds in accommodating both local and national values, how does the product relate to the *pan-African* cultural values which the Lagos Declaration extols? In the World Bank's view, local culture is a useful adjunct to a consensus-type curriculum which enlists children's energies in the pursuit of socioeconomic development (presumably in a framework which leaves the present international power structure intact). By contrast, the insistence of African countries on cultural identity 'underlies the desire to install a new economic order in the world'. The Inter-governmental Conference on Cultural Policies in Africa, organized by Unesco at Accra in 1975, gave priority to 'African identity' as a means of rebuffing the cultural supremacy of the West. It is significant that the conference delegates saw 'the nationalist context within which the cultural activities of certain countries have been confined' as a threat. In their view, 'priority will be assigned to exchanges, to dialogue and to the bringing together, in free association, of cultural communities in the continent, or *within* a country. A new perspective will emerge, which can be qualified as pluralist' (my italics). The problem is the following: the delegates follow the logic of their plea for the promotion of local culture by arguing for 'decentralization of decision-taking' and the harmonization of educational policy with agrarian reform: 'what is needed is to devise an educational system where originality both of form and of content would derive largely from the sociocultural structures of the African countries, and to match their characteristic cultural pluralism with an educational pluralism'. On the other hand, in another passage in the same document, they encourage the authorities to 'single out those common elements which strengthen the national personality' (Unesco, 1975: 9-10). Nobody has yet defined how plural is pluralism.

In calling for equality of access to schooling and for a curriculum adapted to the needs of all children, the Lagos Declaration is using the language of individual human rights. The nature of this commitment, however, requires some qualification.

After the passing of two decades of independence in most of Africa there is not yet much evidence of a return to the much-vaunted democratic, egalitarian style of African life untouched by colonialism. Thus it is possible for the disinterested critic to see in the quest for *national* cultural identity on the one hand a legitimate reaction to the colonial past and continuing foreign domination but on the other hand a means whereby the nascent bourgeoisie in each country can consolidate its position. A Unesco publication surprisingly goes as far as to say:

> The degree of autonomy that can be afforded regional cultures and, above all, the degree of autonomy that they can themselves maintain, as well – and as important – as the extent to which they can contribute to the total national culture, is to some extent dependent on the balance of political and economic power as between the regions and the central authority. The cultural crisis, therefore, is also linked to problems of industrial development and the imbalance in economic development. (Unesco, 1976: 26)

Reference has already been made to the correlation between a Cameroon village's enthusiasm for schooling and its chance of marketing the farmers' cash-crops successfully. After piloting a programme of basic non-formal education for unschooled villagers in Mali, Belloncle and his team insisted that the project should only be implemented on a wide basis if the administration agreed to corresponding improvements in the supply of medical and agricultural services to the villages. Not to make this demand would have been a betrayal of the villagers' trust. They had been motivated to learn by the aspiration of being able to improve their negotiating stance *vis-à-vis* the outside world, for example having a say in how taxation scales and the prices of cash-crops were fixed (Belloncle, 1979). In a refreshing burst of (or lapse into?) frankness, the World Bank Report ends its review of the strategies for equalizing access to and provision of schooling by saying:

> Success will also depend on [the] willingness [of the political authorities, centrally and locally] to deal with various interest groups for whom the cost of an increase in educational opportunities would be a sacrifice of status, power or comparative advantage. (World Bank, 1980: 29)

That is to say, in the terms of reference of this chapter, the extent to which a curriculum accommodates local needs affects the overall balance of power between what is commonly called the centre and the periphery. The curriculum development team at Buea in Cameroon advocated raising the age of entry to school to seven years, on the grounds that if primary schoolteachers could achieve a smooth transition to adult work and community life at the age of 14 instead of 12, the risk of urban migration would be reduced. The disproportionately high potential for learning of the years between four and six is a powerful argument against this proposal, but in Cameroon the proposal was rejected by senior civil servants on other grounds, namely that their own children were exposed to the influence of the international kindergarten in Yaounde and could not be kept back from school for a further two years.

However, to see the Machiavellian forces of international capitalism as manipulating the national bourgeoisie via policies of centralized cultural domination does not give the complete picture. Another explanation competing with 'underdevelopment' theory for legitimacy is that the essentially liberal Western ideology of individual human rights is not easily reconciled with other 'traditional' considerations. The mutation of Westminster-style party politics into single-party government that has taken place in much of ex-British Africa is defended on the grounds that the authentic traditional democracy of the people concerned 'recognised no mechanical process of a majority outvoting a minority, but only a process of continued discussion until all had come to agreement' (Emerson, 1975: 210).

> Should one necessarily suspect an Ivory Coast textbook on civics of deliberate duplicity when its author claims that his country is fortunate enough to have a single political party since this proves that all Ivoriens are grouped around their leader and that they approve of him wholeheartedly? (Quoted in Emerson, 1975: 211)

Ironically, the contention that a preoccupation with *individual* human rights is both Western in origin and a luxury, is reinforced by the fact that governments wishing to give priority to economic, social and cultural rights see themselves justified in subordinating individual rights to those of the people as a whole.

This chapter has so far concentrated on the practical 'surface' obstacles to implementing localized curriculum and the underlying political ambiguities which the notion of localized curriculum accentuates. Of equal importance, however, in attributing responsibility for the present imbalance between flexibility and standardization is the prevailing view of curriculum itself, and it is to this issue that we now turn.

Ministry politicians and curriculum centre staff alike have inherited a view of curriculum whose main features are that it provides an exhaustive statement of lesson content and that this content has been prescribed by the authorities for the whole territory. This is particularly true of those educated in the French and Belgian tradition but applies also to the British-trained officials who were brought up on a voluntary-agency system where a high degree of conformity to centrally imposed standards was the criterion for the granting of government aid. *Ce n'est pas dans le programme* is the teacher's irrefutable defence against the suggestion that he should innovate. Such attempts as there have been to get teachers in training to make their lessons 'relevant' to the environment have not been underpinned by any real debate in the primary teachers' colleges about what constitutes a curriculum. Student teachers know better than to make provision in their lesson notes for the unforeseen consequences of their teaching.

Having found that 45 per cent of children in English-speaking Cameroon leave their home community within the first year of completing primary school, the Buea curriculum team piloted a series of English comprehension/social studies lessons on the problems of migration, the retention of 'country fashion', and the concept of the 'stranger' in urban areas. These materials have so far not achieved widespread currency in Cameroon. With reference to the earlier discussion, it would be true to attribute this to central government's reluctance to encourage what amounts to implicit criticism of its own social and economic policies. However, ministry officials have been able to impose their will by the simple bureaucratic act of refusing a set of curriculum proposals. They have not been compelled to send an army of inspectors to stamp out dissident teaching in the nation's classrooms. That task has been rendered superfluous by the conservatism of the teachers and training college lecturers alone. Similarly, African educators who return from study tours abroad impressed with, for example, the quality of English primary education, tend to see the problems of their own schools in terms of defective teaching techniques and equipment rather than in terms of differing underlying views of pupil-teacher relationships and of how children learn.

Although there undoubtedly are some educators in Africa who might patronizingly be said to hold an enlightened view of curriculum, they make a virtue out of the fact that the broad mass of teachers expects to teach a completely specific curriculum culminating in a highly predictable secondary entrance examination. It is generally accepted that the morale of primary schoolteachers in Africa, and its obverse which is professional discipline, has seriously declined over recent years. The rapid growth of the more prestigious and better paid secondary and tertiary sectors is one contributing factor, and the continuing influx of untrained colleagues is another. Although conceding that in-service training, improved pay and conditions of service, and a proper career structure based on merit, are the desirable remedies to this situation, hard-pressed education officials are, in the short term, using the curriculum and the school-leaving examination as expedient straightjackets with which to apply some discipline to the profession. Untrained and trained teachers alike can be held accountable if by Week 6 of Grade 5 the children have not memorized the constituent parts of the maize-cob. At secondary level in Burundi every pupil has a *journal de classe* in which he writes down, at the teacher's dictation, the 'aim' of every lesson. When the teacher returns from an absence of several days in the capital 'chasing his dossier', the 'aims' of several untaught lessons are solemnly invented and entered up for the inspector's benefit. The teacher of Grade 7 will lose face in the village if fewer children pass into secondary school than did so the previous year.

Where does all this leave the flexible, localized curriculum? In a psychologist's words, such a curriculum means 'structuring educational experience so that children can take full advantage of skills developed in their particular ecologies' (Triandis, 1974). The World Bank's view is far more conservative and in favour of standardization: although establishing as a 'general principle' that 'a curriculum should draw on the environment of the learner for the demonstration and application of its content', the Bank goes on to say that 'different curricula for different settings should be avoided' (on the expedient grounds that this would give populated groups 'unequal opportunities to advance to higher levels of education') (World Bank, 1980: 33). I would argue that the way forward should be one of compromise, but compromise first and foremost on the understanding of curriculum. On the one hand the totally closed, utilitarian view inherited from the colonial era — seeing education as a means to extrinsic economic, social or political ends — must yield to a more adequate educational view whose salient feature is a degree of openness — a learner exploring under the guidance of a teacher (Hodgkin, 1976; Greenland,

1980). On the other hand it means allowing the evolving political and cultural milieu to set a framework of boundaries within which this more open curriculum must work and with which it must interact.

The compromise is certainly untidy. Nyerere asserts that:

> the educational system of Tanzania would not be serving the interests of a democratic socialist society if it tried to stop people from thinking about the teachings, policies, or beliefs of leaders, either past or present

and yet the Party newspaper demands that

> pupils at all levels must be made to understand fully the principles of TANU and the Afro-Shirazi party. (von der Muhll, 1971: 51)

But in addition to arguing that this compromise view of curriculum is a necessary precondition for any meaningful introduction of local knowledge and skills, one can go on to advocate the compromise on three further grounds.

First, it attempts to be realistic about the speed at which a mass of under-educated and under-trained teachers can reform their teaching (Griffiths, 1975). Secondly, it is a defence against the charge that it represents an entirely Western, and therefore 'culturally imperialistic' approach to educational reform. Beeby's model of four 'stages' which he developed to describe the qualitative growth of primary school systems in developing countries has been accused of implying that the English 'progressive', 'Plowden' teacher represents the acme in this process (Guthrie, 1980). The four stages through which teachers can progress are labelled respectively 'dame-school', 'formalism', 'transition', and 'meaning', the final, most adequate stage being defined as follows:

> meaning and understanding play an increasing part in the pupil's day, and memorizing and drill, while still remaining, become subservient to them. Since passive understanding is thin and narrow, the child is encouraged to build up, by his own mental activity, the intricate web of relations that constitute real meaning: in other words he is taught to think. Unless his thinking is unnaturally circumscribed, it will inevitably lead to his making judgments of value. (Beeby, 1966: 67)

Beeby has recently argued, convincingly in my view, that stage IV can include educators who are 'traditional' as well as educators who are 'progressive' in their teaching methods. In both types of classroom one will find

> meaning and understanding stressed; variety of content and method to cater for individual differences; problem-solving plays an increasing part; pupils' own active thinking and judgment encouraged, and the control of language appropriate to this developed. (Beeby, 1980)

Thirdly, I would suggest, for example to the authors of the Lagos Declaration, that progress towards a 'Beeby stage IV' view of curriculum is far more congruent with their approach to sociocultural change than the view of curriculum which they hold at present. They continue to assume, just as it was assumed throughout the colonial era, that a curriculum for nation-building but adapted to minorities can be specified in advance.

Contemporary African history, however, shows that 'authentic' African society is being constructed in a very tentative manner — constructed not rediscovered. In the case of Burundi, the military regimes which have renewed themselves periodically since the 'revolution' of 1966 have had an approximate plan of the finished edifice of Burundi society in mind, but the use they have made of traditional materials is better described as *bricolage* than as building. Inventing a new three-word national motto to replace 'God, King, and Burundi' helped bridge the gulf from monarchy to republic, and a new habit of chanting political slogans three times and clapping speakers in three staccato bursts has somehow merged with the old tradition to become acceptable 'authentic' behaviour. If government spokesmen on the one hand refer to separate migrations of distinct peoples to Burundi, and on the other hand claim that 'we are all Barundi', they are accepting the reality of a process of transformation over time and should logically accept that this evolution is still continuing. Even their own less guarded statements confirm that they see 'we are all Barundi' as a reality which is still to be constructed out of the constituent parts of Tutsi, Hutu and Twa.

Whatever sociocultural goals a country may set itself, the attainment of those goals will be facilitated if, first, the political authorities admit the 'constructivist' nature of 'culture-making' and if, secondly, they accept a similarly open view of curriculum and encourage curriculum developers, teachers and pupils to participate in the experimental task of charting the way towards the nation's goals. Such a procedure would be infinitely preferable to the present practice of specifying and then transmitting a static but nominally flexible, localized curriculum in the hope that it will both foster national unity and encourage the unschooled disadvantaged minorities to enrol.

References

Beeby, C (1966) *The Quality of Education in Developing Countries* Harvard University Press: Cambridge, Mass

Beeby, C (1980) The thesis of stages fourteen years later *International Review of Education* **26** 4

Belloncle, G (1979) *Jeunes Ruraux du Sahel* Harmattan: Paris

Emerson, R (1975) The fate of human rights in the Third World *World Politics* **27** 2: 201-26

Greenland, J (1980) Western education in Burundi 1916-1973: the consequences of instrumentalism *Les Cahiers du CEDAF* (Brussels) **2-3**

Griffiths, V (1975) *Teacher-Centred: Quality in Sudan Primary Education, 1930-1970* Longman: London

Guthrie, G (1980) Stages of educational development? Beeby revisited *International Review of Education* **26** 4

Hawes, H (1979) *Curriculum and Reality in African Primary Schools* Longman: London

Heyneman, S (1979) Why impoverished children do well in Ugandan schools *Comparative Education* **15** 2: 175-85

Hodgkin, R (1976) *Born Curious* Wiley: London

IPAR-Buea (1977) *Report on the Reform of Primary Education* Institute for the Reform of Primary Education (IPAR): Buea, Cameroon

Prewitt, K ed (1971) *Education and Political Values* East African Publishing House: Nairobi

Triandis, H (1974) Psychologists on culture and thought *Reviews in Anthropology* **1**: 484-92

Unesco (1975) *Intergovernmental Conference on Cultural Policies in Africa. Problems and prospects. Accra 27 Oct—6 Nov 1975* United Nations Educational, Scientific, and Cultural Organization with the co-operation of the Organization of African Unity (OAU): Paris

Unesco (1977) *Education in Africa in the Light of the Lagos Conference* Educational Studies and Documents 25, United Nations Educational, Scientific, and Cultural Organization: Paris

Unesco Staff Association (1976) *Cultural Identity* United Nations Educational, Scientific, and Cultural Organization Staff Association Committee on Life-long Education: Paris

von der Muhll, G (1971) Education, citizenship and social revolution in Tanzania *in* Prewitt (1971)

World Bank (1980) *Education Sector Policy Paper* World Bank: Washington DC

8. Education and race relations in the UK

Alan Little

Summary: This survey of education and race relations in the United Kingdom starts with an examination of the political background of an all-party desire to combat racial discrimination and disadvantage. The task is both to meet the special needs of racial minorities and to prepare all pupils for life in a multi-racial society. Research evidence on the needs and achievement of Black children is presented under eight headings. In moving towards an effective educational policy to avoid racism, discrimination and hatred, government support and advice is needed, together with adequate funding earmarked for racially disadvantaged groups. Within this context, local authorities could develop comprehensive and co-ordinated strategies for helping schools to respond to the changing needs.

The political background: trying to avoid tension and hatred

All the major political parties in the UK recognize the distinction between racial discrimination and racial disadvantage, and the need for social policies to combat both. In parliament, for example, M. Alison, summing up the Second Reading of the Race Relations Act, 1976, referred to 'the other hazard, which is more intractable and in my submission, much more pervasive, . . . inescapable discrimination based upon disadvantage' (Hansard, 1976a). Alan Beith, speaking for the Liberals in the same debate, said: 'Anti-discrimination Laws in themselves are not enough. Actions must be taken to combat the disadvantage experienced by many people in minority communities — real disadvantages, not merely discrimination' (Hansard, 1976b). A Conservative Minister (Peter Walker), first in an open letter published in the *New Statesman*, and subsequently in an article in the *Guardian*, called for

> a programme to provide decent housing, job opportunities and a proper education for our coloured population. Let them [the Conservatives] set out a five-year programme for a Tory government in which the plight of those 80,000 West Indian families who are most deprived will be transformed.

The *Guardian* reprinted the article as a leader, 18 months after its original publication, under the title 'Under new management and getting worse'. Referring to immigration control, Walker argued, 'whether it is reduced or abolished, it will make little contribution to solving the racial tensions that exist in Britain today' (*Guardian*, 1979).

Despite the acceptance in principle of the need for positive policies designed to achieve racial justice and harmony in a multiracial society, little has been implemented. The Report of the Select Committee on Race Relations and Immigration in 1972-73 said:

> One conclusion that stands out above all others is that we have failed to grasp and are still failing to grasp the scale of what we have taken on. Far too many who are closely involved show reluctance to assess it realistically. They fear that such assessments may be used against the immigrant population. (Select Committee on Race Relations and Immigration, 1972-73: Paragraph 227)

This was said in relation to educational policies, and it is still relevant.

Education's contribution: to develop potentialities and understanding

The area of social policy of particular importance for achieving a racially just and harmonious society is education. This is again a point recognized by the government: for example, in its response to the Select Committee on Race Relations and Immigration, while admitting that 'it would be wrong to suppose that education alone could achieve all the objectives on which society may set its sights, or that it could function unaffected by conditions in society at large', government policy was:

> that the education service has important contributions to make both to the well-being of immigrant communities in this country and to the promotion of harmony between the different ethnic groups of which our society is now composed. This is because first the education service is made responsible to assist citizens of all ages to develop their opportunities to the full and within that responsibility has a special obligation to children who for one reason or another are most at risk of not achieving their true potential, and second, education would be a potent instrument for increasing understanding and well-being between races. (Department of Education and Science, 1974)

This points to the potential twin contributions of education, identifying and meeting the special needs of Black pupils and communities, and preparing all pupils for life in a multiracial society.

Educational research findings: 'Black achievement significantly lower'

What factors should educational policies for achieving relative justice between racial groups take into account? Among the wealth of facts and opinions about the educational situation of Black children, eight points seem to me to stand out in determining their educational needs.

1. Concentration

Ethnic minority communities make up a relatively small proportion of the total population (around 5 per cent) and a slightly larger proportion of the child population (around 7 per cent of births are to women who were born in the New Commonwealth). The concentration of Black people in relatively few areas means that proportions in particular schools and local authorities are much higher. Seven years ago, when the Department of Education and Science (DES) was counting the numbers of immigrant children in schools (immigrant children were defined as children born outside the UK, or born to parents who had been in this country for less than ten years), two local authorities defined more than 25 per cent of their pupils as immigrant, five between 20 per cent and 25 per cent, and a further six between 15 per cent and 20 per cent. In addition, some authorities with few children of immigrant origins overall had certain schools with large percentages; for example, in nearly one school out of 33 in 1972 more than a quarter of the pupils were of immigrant origin (Little, 1975). Current population figures take this point further (OPCS, 1980). In places like Bradford, Birmingham, Leicester, Wolverhampton and the entire Greater London Council (GLC) area, a fifth or more of school entrants are born to women from the New Commonwealth and Pakistan. For individual boroughs like Brent, Ealing and Newham, 40 per cent and over of children are born to women from the New Commonwealth and Pakistan.

In areas like these, Black children form not a small proportion of the school population but a sizeable element and the issue of their progress in school is a major one facing the school and the local authority. Uneven distribution of multi-ethnic communities means that the issues and problems of special need are unevenly shared; certain authorities therefore require support from outside.

2. Newness

Insofar as some of these children's difficulties, of culture and language for instance, stem from newness to this country, one should not be just looking at the coloured community but at all immigrant groups. For example, in the Inner London Education Authority (ILEA) two years ago, 7 per cent of all live births were to women from Ireland, 24 per cent to women from the New Commonwealth and Pakistan, and 12 per cent to women from other countries. Four out of ten (41 per cent) of all births were to immigrants. In the borough of Brent, the total in 1980 was 65 per cent (10 per cent, 45 per cent and 10 per cent respectively). Kensington and Chelsea had 50 per cent immigrant births and four other London boroughs had a figure of 50 per cent or more (OPCS, 1980). In areas like these, immigrant groups generally and coloured groups in particular make up a large element of the child and family populations. They are a significant part of the client group for pre-school and school services, and the public services must respond to their language, cultural, and religious differences.

3. Varied needs

Different areas (and, in particular, different schools) will have different educational needs as a consequence of the presence of children of different immigrant groups, and the nature of the responses of the educational system may therefore have to differ. Reviewing ILEA's experience, its leader, Sir Ashley Bramall, said:

> Inner London has 25 per cent of the West Indian population of the whole country: in Spitalfields 40 per cent of the population is Bengali and of 28 children taken into one primary school in the area this September, 23 knew no English at all; in one Church of England school in Soho, 50 per cent of the children are Chinese; in North Kensington and Paddington hotel owners are recruiting ever-increasing numbers of rural Moroccans whose children arrive in schools without even the most rudimentary knowledge of urban life. (Education, 1976)

A second but related point is that most of these schools are racially mixed and have pupils from the indigenous population as well as children of immigrants. Five years ago in the ILEA (one of the areas of highest concentration of immigrants and especially coloured immigrants) eight out of ten Black children attended schools where Black pupils made up less than one-fifth of the children in the school. Without doubt schools exist which are largely Chinese, Asian or West Indian, but these are rare. It is clear that a large number of schools have an ethnically mixed pupil body, and educational policies must reflect this: multiracial education must enable Black and White pupils to have equality of educational opportunity in an atmosphere of mutual tolerance.

4. Social disadvantage

The areas of concentrations of Black people tend to be areas of urban decay and social disadvantage. Black people have not created the problems of the inner cities, but for a variety of reasons (not least racial discrimination) they have been forced to live in them. The Department of the Environment's analysis of the 1971 census was that 70 per cent of the Black community are concentrated in 10 per cent of enumeration districts, in which they constituted roughly a fifth of the total population. When these 10 per cent of enumeration districts are compared with others on measures of housing deprivation, the Department found that they contain nearly three times the proportion of households which share or lack hot water, twice as many sharing or lacking a bath, nearly three times as many households living at a density above the statutory overcrowding level, and twice as many without exclusive use of basic amenities (Holtermann, 1975). Of the 12 urban areas with the greatest incidence of urban blight, nine are among the areas with the highest proportion of immigrants. These are the

multiracial inner-city areas of urban decay, and the educational consequences of this are profound. The leader of the ILEA, in summarizing the
'severe and deepening problems' that inner city schools have to cope with,
observed that:

> schools progressively deprived of their teachable and tractable children from
> stable home backgrounds have had to retain an increasing population of
> pupils from broken homes, one-parent families and other undesirable social
> conditions. To them have to be added succeeding waves of immigrants, each
> with their own complex of problems. (*Education*, 1976)

Examining Manchester, the Chairman of the Education Committee has
written:

> The city is left with fewer and poorer citizens to bear the burden of caring for
> those who remain, who include a disproportionate number of old or sick
> people, unemployed or low wage earners, large families and single parents. Yet
> it still attracts more disadvantaged; immigrants looking for − or forced into −
> cheap, inferior housing, drifters seeking the tolerance of the big city, those
> drawn by the illusory promise of work. The measure of this in Manchester is
> that over half our council tenants − and we have over one hundred thousand
> tenancies − are eligible for rent or rate rebates: 30 per cent of our school
> children claim free meals. Nearly half our schools are social priority schools:
> several have predominantly coloured pupils, others − or the same − find that
> more than half the pupils come from incomplete or broken homes. Many of
> these children inevitably bear the scars of social stress. Many are language
> deprived, under-achieving, display anti-social behaviour. (*Education*, 1976)

Similar points have been made by the Chairman of Wolverhampton Education Authority, when discussing the inner parts of his Authority:

> In Wolverhampton these areas are occupied by immigrants from far east and
> far west who have settled here in the past ten years or more. When we think of
> inner-city problems, these are the areas which we in Wolverhampton would
> automatically think of. To us they represent inadequacy in every sense,
> physical as well as socially, in terms which ten years ago we might have
> thought were behind us. Fifteen children in one primary school registered at
> the same address! Shocking. But one has to be prepared for shocks. (*Education*,
> 1976)

Professionals in these areas have had to respond not only to the long-
established problems of social disadvantage, but also to the issue of race
relations. They have responded with only limited aid from local authorities,
training institutions and central government.

5. The backlash

Schools face the problems of both social and racial disadvantage. Policies
must recognize this. The important question is why they have failed to do
so. In a review of policies for dealing with racial inequality in housing a
Community Relations Commission study concluded that there were 'two
major restraints on policy . . . central government restrictions and the need
to take into account the reactions of the majority population' (Community
Relations Commission, 1977). The majority attitude, according to the

report, 'did not always act as a restraint on policy, but it was certainly part of the context in which policy was formed'. The term used in the US for this is 'fear of the White backlash' (Glazer, 1975).

The fear of the backlash lay at the heart of demands for control of immigration. The MP for Bermondsey gave voice to fears of his own constituents in a parliamentary debate:

> We cannot go on like this. I do not care what those on this side of the House, or the Opposition side or anywhere else say. Problems at local level will become worse and worse for our own young people unless something is done. All Honourable Members know that people come to their surgeries describing the most distressing conditions − terrifying conditions − . . . . We must try to let the British people see that we are alerted to the problem . . . . Unless we do that, our own people will take action which all of us here will regret. (House of Commons Official Report)

A similar observation about people's fears and possible reaction was made by the Deputy Leader of the Opposition:

> In the long run, we have to take account of the very strong feelings in the country, so often based on that most damaging of emotions − fear − which notably flourishes on uncertainty. Fear breeds resentment and bitterness. It leads to cruel attitudes and even to violence. (op cit)

Recently the House of Commons debated a proposal for creating a special fund to help local authorities meet the need of ethnic groups and create conditions for equal and harmonious race relations. Although the majority of speakers were in favour of the Bill, opponents kept coming back to the issue of the backlash. One speaker warned that:

> It is no good thinking that ordinary, White, working-class people who exist in all the inner cities and who feel they are deprived, are not keenly aware that there is a form of discrimination that is likely to be codified . . . . The broad mass of White people in inner cities stand on one side and there are enclaves of coloured people to whom preferential allocation of funds will be made . . . .

Another member drew attention to the danger of 'appearing to discriminate in favour of certain groups . . . it offends the majority of the population and thereby sours rather than helps race relations'.

Similarly, one MP was anxious about the 'danger . . . that the reactions in areas in which people native to this country live will be extremely adverse'. This thought was echoed by another MP who suggested that:

> the indigenous population of this country will say, in relation to a particular ethnic group, whichever it may be, 'Extra money is being spent on these people. Why is it not being spent on us, the people who have lived here all our lives?'. . . There is no doubt that there is considerable resentment felt by many people in this country because of the underlying principles of the Bill.

This point was in fact made quite explicit by the Conservative spokesman for Home Affairs when he responded to the Queen's Speech in which the Bill was originally proposed: 'If there is the suggestion of limiting the money to any one group, there is always the danger of resentment building up . . .' (Parliamentary Debates).

Noting this resentment is not new. A circular from the DES to local education authorities in 1965 put this sentence in italics:

It would be helpful if the parents of non-immigrant children could see that practical measures have been taken to deal with the problems in the schools, and that the progress of their own children is not being restricted by the undue preoccupation of the teaching staff of the linguistic and other difficulties of migrant children. (DES, 1975)

Behind the official words clearly lie political and administrative anxieties about the reactions of the indigenous population in multiracial areas to both the presence of coloured pupils and policies to help them. The official feeling is that policies in the area of race relations must take note of these reactions and respond to people's fears and anxieties. However, not every response need be to reinforce or follow them. Politicians have a responsibility to lead and inform public opinion, not merely to follow or fuel it.

6. Minority demands

The White backlash is not the only reaction that has to be taken into account. It is increasingly clear that the reactions of minority communities themselves must be noted in policy development.

A significant pointer in that direction is the Community Relations Commission's study of the 1974 general election, indicating the potential and actual political influence of the minority vote (Community Relations Commission, 1975). This study concluded that without the support of ethnic minorities, Labour would not have won an overall majority in the October 1974 election. Despite this, when questioned on how Asians might vote in an election, the later Prime Minister, James Callaghan, is quoted as saying, 'It is not a matter which I wish to discuss. I do not think we should discuss these issues on a question of race at all' (Callaghan, 1978). But insofar as certain issues relate directly to racially distinct sections of the community, and insofar as the perceived anxiety of the majority population inhibits professional, administrative and political action on race relation matters, no one should be surprised (or dismayed) when minority communities themselves react in a vocal and organized manner on issues that affect them as ethnic minority groups. With the notable exception of various Select Committee inquiries and possibly the political discussions about the collection of ethnic statistics, official bodies have been slow to take up the idea of consulting minority communities about matters of policy that affect them.

Perhaps the most glaring illustration of this was the consultation on the first draft of the proposed EEC directive on mother tongue instruction. At the outset, no effort was made to canvass the views of minorities (and in particular non-English speaking minorities) on this sensitive, and to them, vital, topic. Views like that of the Association of Education Committees: 'We . . . reject the idea of a local education authority in this country accepting responsibility for teaching the children concerned their mother tongue and culture' (AEC, 1975), were repeated by organizations consulted by the DES, without any endeavour having first been made to discover what non-English-speaking clients for their services wanted or thought practicable. Minority community feeling is there, and if it is continually ignored will respond with the backlash that MPs and others are expecting from the indigenous population, if they feel that their views are not being heeded. Just how vocal and potentially influential minority communities can be is illustrated by the Southall demonstrations in the summer of 1976, and more recently, by their responses to Judge McKinnon. Increasingly, people in positions of authority are learning to respond to minority views and feelings on policy issues in race relations. For example, the DES is consulting minority communities about a proposed inquiry into the West Indian community, and the Department of the Environment has extensively canvassed minority opinion about ethnic records.

7. Underfunctioning

No comprehensive information is available about the performance of children in schools, and therefore the data on the comparative performance of White and Black children comes from a limited number of studies. The best known of these have been undertaken over the past ten years by the Inner London Education Authority. Several findings are of profound significance for developing an education policy for multiracial areas (Little, 1975).

First, there is a wide gap in performance between the children of minority backgrounds and the indigenous population. At the end of primary schooling, the children of New Commonwealth immigrants in the ILEA have been found to have a reading age of approximately one year below the national norms for their age group.

Secondly, the most important factor in determining educational functioning appears to be length of education in the UK, but even immigrant pupils fully educated in the UK are not functioning at the same level as the indigenous population. On transfer to secondary school, the ILEA bands pupils into three broad groups (top 25 per cent, middle 50 per cent and bottom 25 per cent), on verbal reasoning, English and mathematics. The percentage of immigrant children fully educated in the UK in the top 25 per cent are given in Table 1, for the three years 1966, 1968 and 1971.

	Verbal reasoning	English	Mathematics
1966	12	13	14
1968	10	12	12
1971	13	12	12

Table 1 Percentage of immigrant pupils fully educated in the UK placed in the upper quantile on transfer to secondary school

In all three years the percentage of immigrant children in the top 25 per cent is roughly half what should be expected, and half what indigenous children achieve. Further, there has been little improvement over the five year period under review. Admittedly, in one sense this is a relatively short time period to expect change, but in educational terms it is a long period, insofar as it is nearly the length of a child's primary schooling.

Thirdly, children from different ethnic backgrounds who are fully educated in this country appear to be functioning at different levels. Of the two main immigrant groups in the ILEA (West Indian and Asian), Asians who have completed all their primary education in this country appear to be doing as well as the indigenous population (see Table 2).

	English	Mathematics	Verbal reasoning
West Indian origin	9.2	7.4	7.2
Asian origin	19.3	20.2	21.1
Indigenous	25.0	22.9	19.8

Table 2 *Percentage of pupils fully educated in the UK placed in the upper quantile on transfer to secondary school, 1968*

Studies of smaller samples of secondary schools reinforce this conclusion. Comparing boys from South Asia with indigenous Whites at the end of secondary schooling in Newcastle, Taylor confidently states: 'Asians do better' (Taylor, 1976). As one commentator notes, 'Taylor shows that both educational achievement and commitment to educational success were a great deal higher amongst the South Asian respondents than they were amongst a matched sample of English boys' (Driver and Ballard, 1979). In a study of a 16+ cohort in Leicester, Singh found that the achievement of Asian pupils in 16+ exams was 'no worse than their White peers', despite the fact that 42 per cent had not received their primary schooling in Britain. Further, a very much higher proportion of Asians than Whites transferred to grammar school to take sixth form courses, and over half of those who left school enrolled at a college of further education (Brooks and Singh, 1978). Brooks studied Asian school-leavers in Walsall and concluded: 'It is the similarity between White and Asian educational performance which is impressive, rather than any difference.' In a study of three schools with large numbers of Asian pupils, Driver and Ballard reported that, with the exception of English language, the South Asian pupils consistently out-performed their English classmates. For example, in maths, 'their superiority could hardly have been more marked'. They also found in one school that 'while at 13+ the South Asian children came a full year behind the English children in mean reading age . . . by 16+ the situation had changed completely' (Driver and Ballard, 1979).

There are perhaps two reasons for the better performance of Asians, one of which is speculative, and one of which can be documented. The speculative reason concerns the children's background, the empirical one what they receive at school. Asian children come from stable cultural backgrounds with their own languages, religions, cultures and values, which include the prizing of learning for its own sake and the encouraging of self-improvement. Such a background gives the child a clear sense of his own ethnic identity and personal worth quite independent of the dominant culture's reaction to it. This is not true of West Indians, whose cultural background is essentially a variant of the dominant culture, which to no small extent disparages, and even rejects, their colour. Asian pupils bring to school a positive sense of their own worth. (How long that will be preserved if the system fails to support its survival is another question.) In a different way, Driver and Ballard make a similar point: they contend that South Asian pupils have been much less 'socialized to failure' than their White classmates, and ethnic affiliation, far from being a handicap or disadvantage 'must surely be regarded as a positive resource' (Driver and Ballard, 1979).

Further, it is not difficult for the educational system to identify and respond to the more obvious needs of Asian pupils. It is easy to see that non-English-speakers require additional help with the English language, and it is relatively simple to create the political climate within which this can be achieved. The same cannot be said for the needs of West Indians, which are more difficult to identify, subtle in nature, and possibly more threatening to the White culture because they will involve changes in it. That local authorities have made considerable strides to meet Asian needs, but not those of West Indians, is one of the major conclusions of Townsend and Brittain's study of school responses to the presence of Black and Brown children:

> It is apparent that the teaching of English to non-English-speaking pupils is seen by multiracial schools as their major task. Schools deal with this task in many different ways according to their own philosophy and to the resources made available by local education authorities. What is not so clear is the level of proficiency in English at which schools decide that no further special arrangements are necessary. The question of 'second stage' English, following the initial achievement of literacy, appears as yet to be imperfectly understood in either the need or the approach. Equally misunderstood perhaps are the need for, and approach to, teaching pupils of West Indian origin to use the English idiom, pronunciation and intonation. (Townsend and Brittain, 1972: 135)

There is no evidence to suggest that the situation of West Indians is improving with the children's progress through school. The ILEA Literacy Survey tested the same children aged 8+, 10+ and 15+ between 1968 and 1975. At the age of eight, the gap in the mean reading score between West Indian and indigenous children was 10.5 standard points; at the end of primary school it was 11.2, and at 15+ 12.3 points. If reading standards are an adequate indicator of intellectual development (and there is considerable evidence to suggest that they are), one must conclude that the gap in performance is widening with school career. Certainly there is no evidence of these pupils catching up, or narrowing the gap.

It has also been found that West Indian children are functioning at a level not only below the indigenous population, but also below socially disadvantaged sections of it. To take one example, a comparison was made on a standard reading test between West Indians fully educated in the UK tested at eight, ten and 15, and children from unskilled working-class backgrounds, on mean scores: the results are summarized in Table 3.

Age	West Indian fully educated	Children of unskilled background	Difference
8+	89.9	93.7	4.2
10+	88.7	93.5	4.8
15+	87.1	92.1	5.0

Table 3 *Mean scores on a standard reading test of children of West Indian and unskilled backgrounds*

At each age, the unskilled working-class child is on average reading at a significantly higher level than a child of West Indian origin. Given the wealth of evidence in the literature on the under-performance of White working-class children, this is a disturbing finding. This (and other points made earlier) has been confirmed by a study of 11+ year-olds in eight multiracial schools in one Outer London borough. The report notes that these schools are mainly situated in the poorer parts of the borough, and so,

> the indigenous pupils as a group scored below the national average. The Asian pupils as a group scored significantly below the Whites, and the West Indians scored significantly below the Asians. Bearing in mind the fact that the Asian group would include some very poor English speakers, the score of the West Indian pupils gives real cause for concern. (Community Relations Council, 1978)

This point was reinforced by an example of one secondary school in the borough: of first-year pupils, over one-quarter (27 per cent) received remedial help. Of children of West Indian origin, this figure was nearly half (46 per cent). By the time of O level/CSE — that is, 16+, the average number of passes for all grades was 4.2 for White pupils, and 1.0 for students of West Indian origin.

This gap in performance between Black pupils and socially-disadvantaged Whites can be demonstrated early in the pupil's school career. Levels 1 and 2 of the English Picture Vocabulary Test (ie the infant school and junior school stages) were used in the ILEA Educational Priority Study (Barnes, 1975), and the results are given in Table 4.

	Level 1		Level 2	
	Numbers	Mean score	Numbers	Mean score
All pupils	1341	94.5	1551	90.9
Non-immigrant	957	97.9	1162	92.9
West Indian	298	86.9	250	85.5

Table 4 *Relative performance in the English Picture Vocabulary Test*

Several interesting points emerge from this analysis: pupils in schools defined as educational priority areas (EPA) score over five points below the national norm on Level 1, and nine points below on Level 2. West Indians in infant schools (and therefore pupils who are likely to have a full United Kingdom education in the future) score 13 points below their national age peers, and 11 points below their indigenous classmates. In junior schools, the gap between them and their national age peers is nearly 15 points, and with class peers, over seven points. What stands out is that even at a very young age (ie in infant schools), the indigenous White pupil in the EPA school is performing at a significantly higher level than his Black classmate, but at a significantly lower level than his national age peer. It is worth noting that this finding is confirmed by a study completed in another EPA area using the pre-school version of the English Picture Vocabulary Test: 63 non-immigrants in the area (mean age of four years seven months) had a standardized score of 84.1. This indicates that the gap in passive vocabulary pre-dates school entry.

A similar point has been carefully documented by Pollak. In her Brixton survey she found that children of West Indian parentage were found to be developmentally disadvantaged at the age of three, compared to indigenous children living in the same inner-city working-class neighbourhood; on tests of adaptive behaviour, language and personal/social development given to three-year-olds in Brixton, West Indian children scored lower than other children (Pollak, 1972). Mabey in summarizing the ILEA longitudinal study (which involved testing pupils at 8+, 10+, 13+ and 15+) found that 'the broad level of attainment was settled at least by the age of eight years' and, if anything, the gap between pupils of West Indian origin and their White age peers widened between age 8+ and 15+ (Mabey, 1981).

The teaching profession is concerned not only with the educational performance of children of West Indian origin, but also with their behaviour in school. Research by Rutter and colleagues shows that teachers report a higher incidence of maladjusted behaviour in school (Rutter *et al*, 1974, 1975). In a study in South London, they found that: 'West Indian children showed rather more behavioural difficulties at school, but they did not differ from other children in terms of disorder at home. Nor did they differ from other children in terms of emotional disturbance in any setting.' A clue to the link between school performance and behaviour is given in a study by Varlaam, which examined the relationship between reading standards and maladjusted behaviour. The conclusion was that:

> when the two conditions (reading retardation and behaviour disorders) are found together, there is a better chance that reading retardation preceded behaviour difficulties than the other way round, and second, that such a chance is particularly strong when the children involved come from large families or have a West Indian background. (Varlaam, 1974)

Educational failure may create the maladjusted behaviour school report.

8. Discrimination

A final point to be taken into account is the fact of racial hostility and discrimination. This affects children at school in various ways. Initially, they experience the consequence of discrimination on their parents (who have had limited job opportunities, poor housing, etc). As a result, their own upbringing is less favourable than it might have been. We know, for example, that the incidence of multiple disadvantage is three times as high in the West Indian community as in the general population (Community Relations Commission, 1977).

Later, young people leaving school face discrimination in the labour market; the Office of Population and Census Survey is currently following up matched pairs of Black and White school-leavers, and it has shown that it takes four times as many interviews in careers offices to place a West Indian school-leaver as it takes his White counterpart, despite similar qualifications and education experience (Select Committee on Race Relations and Immigration, 1976-77: 462). Schools contain pupils of all ethnic groups, who have grown up in a prejudiced world, and are therefore prejudiced themselves: the development of racial prejudices and stereotypes, even in young children, has been extensively documented, and David Milner has recently shown how feelings of rejection threaten the identity of coloured children, and generate learning problems for them (Milner, 1975).

Finally, aspects of the school experience (the curriculum, teaching methods, etc) may unintentionally intimidate many coloured pupils. While, for example, the content of history or geography courses may be offensive, because of cultural bias, probably the most important influence is the attitude of the teacher: Elaine Brittain argued from her research that 'the needs of multiracial schools were not being fully understood and recognized by the teachers', and, more disturbing, she found, among teachers interviewed, evidence of 'large scale stereotypes of West Indian pupils'. It is clear (she argues) that teachers perceive West Indian pupils as 'of low ability and creating disciplinary problems' (Brittain, 1976). Therefore, apart from anything else, educational policy must respond to the fact of racial discrimination and negative stereotyping, which is often found within schools.

Towards an effective educational policy

The starting point for an effective educational policy in multiracial areas must be support and advice from central government and adequate funding for the special dimension of racial disadvantage. This would give a framework that would encourage local authorities to develop comprehensive and co-ordinated strategies for these areas, and in turn schools could begin to respond most effectively to changing needs. What should be the substance of such strategies? In my view, they must respond to the salient facts demonstrated by professional experience and research, which are:

1. the fact of under performance of children of West Indian origin and of special educational needs (language, culture) of children and adults from all minority backgrounds, ie the need for special educational programmes.
2. the fact of racial prejudice, hostility and discrimination within the majority population among both children and adults, ie the need for teaching programmes on race issues for all sections of the school population.
3. the fact of early detection both of under functioning amongst minorities and the emergence of racial stereotypes amongst majorities, ie the need for early intervention.
4. the fact of variation of need within and between different local authority areas, ie the need for local diagnosis and programmes.
5. the fact that we are ignorant about the scale of needs and, more important, ways in which they can be met, ie the need to improve our knowledge base for action.
6. the fact that given the nature of race relations, special provision cannot be imposed upon communities (either majority or minority) but must carry the communities with it, ie the need to involve communities in the diagnosis of need and provision of services.
7. the fact that racial disadvantage co-exists with general social disadvantage, ie the need for a co-ordinated and comprehensive approach to community development.

Perhaps the most significant fact is the uneven distribution of recent settlers in the system. As a result, efforts cannot be left to the initiative or resources of individual schools or local authorities but should be part of a national programme. This is why the government should reconsider its relationship with local authorities which have relatively heavy concentrations of peoples from minority backgrounds. To a large extent the initiative for action lies with the government (as do the necessary resources) and it has the responsibility to ensure that action is both taken and systematically evaluated. Further, any programme should combine development and research with action; we are not only ignorant about the nature of the disadvantages of the Black population (meaning that needs cannot adequately be diagnosed) but also equally ignorant about effective ways of improving our present efforts. Equally, we are ignorant about the social and psychological origins of prejudice and how it can best be combated in schools: action and development must therefore go in parallel.

References

Association of Education Committees (1975) *Letter to the DES on the EEC Directive on Migrant Education* 1.12.75
Barnes, J ed (1975) *Educational Priority, Volume 3: Curriculum Innovation in London's Education Priority Areas* HMSO: London

Brittain, E M (1976) Multi-racial education: teachers' opinions on aspects of school life, Part 2 *Educational Research* **18** 3

Brooks, D and Singh, K (1978) *Aspirations Versus Opportunities: Asian and White School Leavers in the Midlands* Walsall Council for Community Relations: Walsall

Callaghan, J (1978) Quoted in *The Times* 3.1.78

Community Relations Commission (1975) *Participation of Ethnic Minorities in the General Election, October 1974* HMSO: London

Community Relations Commission (1977) *Urban Deprivation, Racial Inequality and Social Policy: A Report by the Community Relations Commission* HMSO: London

Community Relations Council (1978) *Performance of West Indian Children: Cause for Concern: West Indian Pupils in Redbridge* Community Relations Council: London

Department of Education and Science (1974) *Educational Disadvantage and the Educational Needs of Immigrants* DES: London

Department of Education and Science (1975) *Circular 7/65: The Education of Immigrants* DES: London

Driver, G and Ballard, R (1979) Comparing performance in multi-racial schools *New Community* **11** 2

Education (1976) 3.12.1976

Glazer, N (1975) *Affirmative Discrimination: Ethnic Inequality and Social Policy* Basic Books: New York

Guardian (1979) Leading article, 20.8.79

Hansard (Commons) (1976a) **906** Column 1649

Hansard (Commons) (1976b) **906** Column 1606

Holtermann, S (1975) Areas of urban deprivation in Great Britain: an analysis of the 1971 census *Social Trends* **6**

House of Commons Official Report **912**: 112

Little, A N (1975) Performance of children from ethnic minority backgrounds in primary schools *Oxford Review of Education* **1** 2

Mabey, C (1981) British literacy *Educational Research* **23** 2

Milner, D (1975) *Education and Race* Penguin: Harmondsworth

Office of Population and Census Survey (1980) *Monitor* **80** 1 and 2

Parliamentary Debates **964** 69

Pollak, M (1972) *Today's Three-year Olds in London* Heinemann: London

Rutter, M L *et al* (1974) Children of West Indian immigrants I. Rates of behavioural deviance and of psychiatric disorder *Journal of Child Psychology and Psychiatry* **15**: 241-62

Rutter, M L *et al* (1975) Home circumstances and family patterns *Journal of Child Psychology and Psychiatry* **16**: 105-24

Select Committee on Race Relations and Immigration (1972-73) *Education Volume 1, Report*

Select Committee on Race Relations and Immigration (1976-77) *The West Indian Community, Evidence*

Taylor, J H (1976) *The Halfway Generation: A Study of Asian Youths in Newcastle upon Tyne* National Foundation for Educational Research: Slough

Townsend, H E R and Brittain, E M (1972) *Organisation in Multi-Racial Schools* National Foundation for Educational Research: Slough

Varlaam, A (1974) Educational attainment and behaviour at school *Greater London Intelligence Quarterly* **29** (December)

Part 3:
Issues in the relationship between majority and minority languages

9. Language and social structure in Welsh education

Glyn Williams and Catrin Roberts

Summary: There has been an unfortunate tendency for much of the work on the relationship between majority and minority languages in education to assume a liberal perspective. This defines the minority language as a 'problem' and tends to relate this 'problem' to the individual rather than to the power relationships associated with structured social inequality between majorities and minorities; it also tends to express the view of the majority language group. Recent work suggests an alternative perspective. If education is seen as the basis of both social control and ideological transmission, then the language of education must relate to the manner in which unequal relationships between groups are legitimized and institutionalized.

The evidence suggests that nineteenth-century state educational policies aimed at eliminating the Welsh language. This policy was justified by an appeal to liberal philosophy, English being hailed as the language of individual achievement and mobility. However, the potential revolutionary threat of a minority language employed to transmit a counter-ideology was not lost on those involved in planning the disappearance of the Welsh language. The exclusion of Welsh from certain spheres and the increasing differentiation of function between the two languages in Wales led to Welsh being relegated to informal community structures. The pressure for the extension of bilingual education derives chiefly from those who achieved upward social mobility and who had learned Welsh informally. The contentious issue of bilingual education should thus be seen in terms of the conflict deriving from class fragmentation.

Introduction

Conventional treatments of bilingual education and the role of minority language in the schooling process always treat minority language as a problem. Furthermore, the problem so defined is then traditionally couched in terms of the individual. Thus, individuals are seen to be hindered in the progress of their education by their 'problematic' functioning in a minority language. The failure of its individual members to achieve is explained in terms of their 'disadvantages' caused by knowledge of the minority language and/or culture — and their consequent limited competence in the majority language and/or culture. The insufficient nature of this explanation becomes evident under scrutiny, but because it is lodged within a philosophy of individual liberalism its validity — both at the level of public administration and at the level of academic analysis — is seldom questioned. Accordingly, attention is focused on education, and the social mobility of minority language speakers is duly studied.

Since education, viewed in liberal terms, is about the differential allocation of rewards to individuals according to their achievement, then inequality is also viewed in these terms. Thus an under-achieving minority language speaker is claimed to be losing out in the education system, and the reason proposed for this inequality is a cultural one involving language. If inequality is culturally derived in this manner, then it is hardly surprising that the egalitarian ideological thrust of liberalism should seek to rectify this inequality via programmes of cultural compensation such as minority compensatory education. It is held that through such programmes, minority group members may be 'educated' to a standard sufficient to allow them to interact adequately with majority group members and to capitalize on the subsequent benefits. The assumptions of inferiority and undesirability inherent in programmes to 'overcome' the disability of minority language speakers appear particularly in the revealing terminology: compensation, cultural deprivation, cognitive disadvantage and language deficiency for example.

It is surprising to find that assumptions concerning the deficiencies of minority languages — and hence their speakers — are still current, in view of the criticism of cultural deficit theories which followed Bernstein's work on the sociolinguistic codes of the social classes. It is also surprising that these assumptions persist not only in the context of academic debate but also clearly in language planning and educational programmes. It suggests that while social class prejudice is ideologically unacceptable, sufficient racial prejudice persists to legitimize evaluative distinctions based on language between majority and minority groups.

Yet it is again inadequate to say that minority language has been treated with 'prejudice'. If prejudice exists, then it indicates that a deeper level of analysis, of prior relationships etc, is required. It is here that we wish to locate our discussion: only through a consideration of the structural relationship of minority and majority groups can any explanation of the persistence or erosion of minority languages be achieved. Clearly, education is crucial to the process, but bilingual education must be studied in sociological terms.

Viewing a minority language, and all its attendant ramifications, as an inherent part of social structure, raises questions as to why it has always been defined as a problem. It also raises questions about who defines things as problematic in society, and how this definition gains general acceptance. Part of the answer may lie in the way concepts of majority and minority groups are formulated; in reality, the definition has nothing to do with numbers but reflects the distribution of power between the two groups. Similarly, the concept of 'bilingualism', while suggesting a situation of parity between two languages, may serve to mask a situation where, in reality, there is a manifestly unequal power distribution between two language groups. We are thus focusing on issues of power and control in society, and on how language may be used to articulate the interests of one group *vis-à-vis* another. While accepting the primacy of economic considerations in deciding issues of power and control, we are postulating a dimension of inequality in addition to the conventional dimension of class, in the form of an ethnic dimension which may or may not function in tandem with class. The articulation of class and ethnicity as dimensions of inequality is central to our analysis.

Thus it may be that a rationale presented in terms of individual identity, mobility and achievement serves to cloud the issues of actual relative power distribution between groups. Conversely, viewing issues of bilingualism in terms of the actions and interests of social groups rather than the individuals involved serves to highlight the actual and potential areas of conflict.

If we see social structure as involving the actions and interests of groups, then it becomes necessary to provide some explanation of how social and economic considerations constrain the choices or courses of action open to various groups in the pursuance of their interests. Marxism achieves this by distinguishing between the infrastructure and super-structure of a capitalist society. The infrastructure is regarded as the base, or the primary force in society, and consists of the productive activities in which that society is engaged. To simplify the theory, Marxism holds that the relationship between people engaged in the process of economic production can be seen, broadly, as the relationship between owners and non-owners of the means of production. That is, owners hold power and control the activities of non-owners, who produce in order to generate profits which consolidate the material distinctions between the two groups, and thus contribute to the power of one over the other.

Thus the relationship between owners and non-owners is one of exploitation: it is the non-owners who use their labour to produce for the benefit of the owners. Evidently, the polarized interests of the two groups means that their relationship is inherently one of conflict, and it is a central tenet of Marxism that whether this conflict is manifest or not, it is fundamental to the articulation of the two groups.

While the infrastructure is economically determined, the superstructure represents all the other social and cultural aspects of society — such as religion, law and education. But the superstructure is seen as a secondary force in society, that is, as a process which depends for its existence on the prior formulation of the base. Crudely summarized, it is argued that the infrastructure determines the form and content of the superstructure in order to ensure the successful continuance of the infrastructure. But this not only entails the reproduction of the process of production, but also the relations generated by that productive process. Thus Marxists argue that the fundamental distinction between owners and non-owners in economic production is reflected in all other spheres of social life, and thus serves to consolidate and reinforce the distinction.

The oversimplification of the above account is apparent in the mechanistic way in which the relationship between base and superstructure is presented: if base determines superstructure, and the process is continuous in the sense of being self-perpetuating, then it is obvious that some agency must exist which provides a dynamic for the process to ensure its reproduction and to make it acceptable to the groups involved. Furthermore, having claimed centrality for the inherent conflict between the interests of owners and non-owners, we must ask why non-owners are persuaded to accept their place in the productive process when this is manifestly serving the interests of another group. It is these procedures which constitute ideology, as the mediating agency between base and superstructure, and that which legitimizes the relations of production generated by capitalism.

Precisely how ideology is constituted and operates is a subject for debate. Essentially, however, it could be claimed — as in recent work on the sociology of education — that one of the areas where it is most evident is in the process of schooling. For it is currently suggested that education's primary function is to provide a legitimizing ideology, so that education becomes a focal point in the maintenance of the *status quo* and in the operation of social control. While the implications of this view are realized by certain sociological traditions, it is significant that educationalists still tend to regard schooling primarily as a process which aims to realize the self-potential of the individual, rather than as a means of guaranteeing the process of economic production by generating and transmitting an ideology of social control. Again, we see a philosophy of individual liberalism obscuring a process which ensures the oppression of certain groups.

Clearly, ideology is a dynamic quality which adapts to the changing requirements of the legitimizing process. Nonetheless, it is an inevitable force within certain social and institutional contexts, and therefore must be readily identifiable. It has long been established that there is a relationship between social structure and linguistic variation. While it is usually claimed that the former is the determining force, the use of language in ideological discourse to justify the existing social structure indicates that language and social structure interact. From this position we derive the relationship between class, language and ideology.

However, one of the weaknesses of conventional Marxism is its failure to accommodate a discussion of dimensions of inequality other than class. This is particularly evident if we acknowledge that ethnic differences cut across class distinctions. But acknowledging the existence of ethnic differences does not explain how individuals develop ethnic awareness and ethnic identity. If ethnicity is to be treated as a coherent dimension of inequality, then we must understand under which conditions individuals feel the need to redefine themselves in ethnic terms in order to counteract the power which controls those conditions. We would maintain that certain conditions are created within which ethnicity rather than class is highlighted as the significant dimension of inequality. Language becomes one of the more evident issues around which people can be mobilized and integrated into, or kept out of, the relevant ethnic group.

Our objective in this paper is to consider the issue of bilingual education in Wales within the preceding theoretical framework. We see bilingual education as the focus of a struggle not simply between ethnic groups but also between fractions of classes which constitute these ethnic groups. An understanding of the economic conditions which give rise to the salience of ethnicity as a dimension of inequality, and an analytical focus upon the *social* groups involved, should help to clarify the dynamics of bilingual education as a sociological entity. The link between education, language and ideology becomes evident in a consideration of the quest for legitimization between the groups involved in the struggles for control within existing conditions.

The historical condition

It was no coincidence that the sixteenth century in Wales witnessed the Act of Union, the Reformation and the translation of the Bible into Welsh. The Act of Union extended the administrative and territorial control of the English state over what had been designated a principality, while also laying the basis for the transition to agricultural capitalism. The Reformation facilitated the position of religion as the ideological fulcrum for the legitimization of the expansion of state interests, and the translation of the Bible into Welsh expanded this ideological function within a country whose population was virtually monoglot. Given that the limited amount of educational instruction was controlled and administered by the church, the potential sphere of its ideological influence was extensive. Despite the linguistic and cultural separation between the ruling class and the community within Wales, the power of the former ensured that it exerted almost absolute control over the economic and institutional life of the community. The ruling class was the patron of the church and also served as an essential intermediary through which the ideological control of the state over the community was implemented and guaranteed.

This situation was disrupted by the advent of industrial capitalism and nonconformism. The new economic order guaranteed a diversification of class positions. The intermediary positions were assumed by a certain number of independent farmers, tenants who farmed more than 50 acres and so employed a labour force, the factors and other officials of estate management, the clergy, schoolteachers, and some traders and merchants. What is interesting about this intermediary class was its tendency to fragment along lines which, through different religious affiliations, came to assume significant political dimensions. One fraction formed the leadership of the nonconformist movement, through which it expressed an opposition to the gentry, thereby leading to a struggle for the support of, or control over, the proletariat and peasantry. The vehicle for this opposition was Welsh ethnicity in general and nonconformism in particular. During the first half of the nineteenth century the nonconformist chapels were predominantly proletarian institutions with a part-time, often lay, ministry which was peripatetic. By the second half of the century, and especially after the religious revivals of 1840 and 1859, it was claimed that 90 per cent of the Welsh proletariat was nonconformist, being led by full-time resident ministers.

Despite the different world-views and organizational structures of the four main denominations (Calvinist and Wesleyan Methodist, Baptist and Independent) they united in expressing opposition to the control of the gentry over local government, and their hegemony in the world of ideas and social institutions. The opposition had a strong element of both cultural and political nationalism and tended to focus on the Welsh language, the Protestant chapels and, in time, the Liberal Party. It advocated action on behalf of a homogeneously defined Welsh *gwerin* (folk), a romantic concept which was compared to other nineteenth-century folk movements in Europe. It was not a movement which offered many radical alternatives to capitalism — although a degree of socialism was evident from time to time (Williams, 1979a) — but rather, it tended to involve a struggle over the control of capitalism within Wales.

In addition to their ideological activity, the nonconformist chapels as institutions formed the basis of a support system which focused upon a collective ethnic identity. They offered a number of support functions which did not carry the customary stigmatic connotations of the welfare system administered by the local authority, since they tended to be presented in terms of community membership and humanitarian assistance for worthy and needy chapel members. The poorer members of the congregation tended to be linked to the chapel through a series of patron-client relationships with those members of the deaconate who, as a result of their economic standing, were in a position to extend essential credit and other facilities in return for support of the chapels. Ability to take advantage of these facilities depended upon one's good name and regular participation in chapel activities. There is little need to underline the potential power of these institutions and their leadership.

The chapel leaders played a primary role in the formation and expression of aims, as spokesmen and brokers striving to achieve cultural mobilization through the development of a Welsh language press. The proletariat and peasantry were taught to read in the native language through Sunday schools, so that both political propaganda and religious ideology reached them in a unified form through a Welsh language press which was largely written and edited by members of the religious leadership.

Clearly a struggle was developing over control of the community and it appeared that the faction associated with nonconformism was achieving ascendancy. More important, perhaps, was the fact that this struggle tended to be expressed more and more in terms of opposition between community and state. This meant that the extension of the hegemony of the state through the mediation of the gentry and the ideological influence of the established church was under threat. The counter-ideology of Welsh nonconformism was in some respects a direct challenge to the territorial legitimacy of the state. In organizational terms, nonconformism lay outside the direct influence of the state, and for some sects power was vested in the individual community.

It is our contention that this development, and the crisis which it presented to the state, was partly responsible for the emergence of formal state-controlled education and the parallel decline of religion as the basis for ideological control within Wales. It should be no surprise, therefore, that the struggle which we have identified above developed into a struggle between the community and state over both religion and education.

As early as the second quarter of the nineteenth century, concern was expressed about the ideological role of education in Wales. While it was evident that a Welsh-medium religious institution was highly effective in its ideological influence upon a monoglot peasantry and proletariat, there was the additional problem of how to transmit an ideology which could serve as the basis for curbing industrial unrest. Indeed it was evident to some that these two issues were related. During the 1830s and 1840s various Welsh language nonconformist periodicals had supported Chartism and advocated its extension within Wales. The link between nonconformism and a movement which organized the proletariat, at a time when emerging industrial capitalism was generating a proletarian self-awareness, was particularly ominous for the ruling class and the state. Given the various examples of revolutionary unrest in Europe, an unrest which focused upon a heightening of ethnic awareness among dispossessed nations, the threat from Wales loomed large.

It is evident that as early as the second quarter of the nineteenth century education was seen as a basis for ideological control. In the 1839 education report Tremenheere noted that only a limited amount of English was taught in the schools where the Chartist 'riots' had occurred (Tremenheere, 1840). It was even more evident with reference to the Merthyr Rising (Williams, Gwyn, 1978). This was an obvious reference to the revolutionary potential of a minority language which could be employed to transmit a revolutionary ideology. With the majority of the Welsh population speaking only their native language, they clearly lay outside any ideological influence which was transmitted through the medium of the English language. When one Member of Parliament addressed the House of Commons in 1846 calling for a commission to investigate education in Wales, he referred to the role of education in Scotland in eliminating the cultural differences between Scottish and English people. The Tremenheere report went even further in quoting another government report to the effect that:

> It should be borne in mind that an ill-educated and undisciplined population, like that existing among the miners in South Wales, is one that may be found most dangerous to the neighbourhood in which it dwells and that a band of efficient schoolmasters is kept at much less expense than a body of police or soldiery. (Tremenheere, 1840)

Furthermore, the same Member of Parliament referred to the conclusion of the 1844 Commission of Inquiry for South Wales, that an ignorance of the English language was a major contributory force behind the Becca riots, a point reiterated by the London *Times*.

Given the revolutionary potential of a minority language, the state has only two solutions: to expropriate the minority language or to eliminate it. In this case, a series of policy decisions were made which could be construed as an attempt to eliminate the Welsh language. The strongest condemnation of both the Welsh language and nonconformism derived from the investigation which lay behind the publication, in 1847, of the government report which became known as the 'Treachery of the Blue Books'. This report of the Commissioners of Inquiry deplored the state of popular education in Wales. The criticism was couched in terms of the way of life of the Welsh people. Consequently, the main thrust of the report was to castigate the nonconformism of Wales, and reveal the Welsh language as the primary obstruction to the education of the masses. Historically, the Blue Books were tremendously significant, for they served to ostracize the language from education until well into the twentieth century. Thus the tradition of English-medium education in Wales was established, and it must be borne in mind that any incursions by Welsh into the curriculum since 1847 have thus taken the form of concessions, rather than being viewed as a right.

Not only was there a struggle *in* education, that is about which language should be the medium of education, but there was also a struggle *over* education. This was a struggle between the community and the state over who was to control and administer education. Prior to the law of 1870 which made education compulsory, the control of education was effectively in the hands of the local community. Given that the ruling class was losing the fight for the control of that community, there was every chance that the nonconformist faction would control education and thereby extend its ideological influence. Both the Independents and the Baptists, the most socialist and devoted of the nonconformist sects, criticized state intervention in education. They claimed that there was no justification for state involvement in either religion or education, both of which should be the responsibility of the community. Had they succeeded in controlling education, and had the movement to disestablish the Church of England succeeded, the state would have been deprived of its power over the two most influential bases of ideological control.

In furthering its interests, the state tied the issue of language in education to individual social mobility to the extent that it became the *raison d'être* of state control of education. In the eighteenth century there had been opposition to the extension of English language teaching in Wales on the grounds that it would stimulate migration, and thereby deprive the bourgeoisie of its labour force. By the second quarter of the nineteenth century, industrialization had progressed to the point where the demand for labour, together with the need for social control, could best be facilitated by relations of production which were conducted in the dominant language. Thus the most persuasive argument in support of English-medium education was to link the idea of 'progress' to the English language, while simultaneously presenting the Welsh language as a barrier to achieving such 'progress'. So strong was the argument in favour of the relationship between class position and language that it was claimed that a knowledge of English 'would liberate the now poor depressed monoglot Welshman from his mountain prison' (Williams, William n.d.). At the same time it was argued that a knowledge of Welsh hindered the effective learning of English. The medium of education in Welsh schools was English and a variety of punitive methods were employed to prohibit the use of Welsh as a medium of conversation in schools. The most notorious sanction, which − significantly − has its parallel in the Breton instance, was the Welsh Not, which was a piece of wood hung around the neck and passed on from pupil to pupil when they were heard to speak Welsh, with the wearer at the end of the day taking a beating. The explicit discouragement of the language in school was also extended, as far as possible, to the home.

A new domain had been opened up to the masses in Wales, the majority of whom were monoglot Welsh speakers. If we accept that a major function of the extension of education was to consolidate the process of centralized control and administration on the one hand, and to further the interests of a centrally controlled and financed capitalism on the other, then it is little wonder that English became the medium of education in Wales. It reflected the claim made in the middle of the nineteenth century, that 'under a common sceptre, a common code of laws with common interests it were desirable if but one common language prevailed' (Blackwell, 1851). It was not too dissimilar from the consolidation of centralized control associated with the growth of agricultural capitalism in the sixteenth century. The consolidation of industrial capitalism saw the legitimization or institutionalization of the Welsh language in certain domains of behaviour, and its elimination from other domains. The educational domain became exclusively English in language.

The contemporary period

It should be clear from the preceding discussion that bilingual education cannot be discussed in abstraction, but rather that it should be seen as a manifestation of a struggle between different social groups. This struggle is particularly evident in so-called democratic political systems where the control of the majority tends to be played against the interests and demands of minorities. Such minorities are obliged to press their claims continually, and it is only when this pressure reaches the point of crisis for the state that a response becomes evident within the context of the plural system. Sometimes this response represents a direct concession to the demands of the minority although, if the pressure is extreme, there may well be an attempt to extend the ideological control of the dominant group while appearing to accede to minority demands. These demands can be characterized as involving an attempt to reallocate the institutionalized relationship between the respective language within the education domain. However this is only part of the story, and there is an associated attempt at a wider domain extension of the minority language, this serving as the justification for the expansion of bilingual education. In order to pursue this sociological analysis further, it is essential to analyse the actions and interests of those involved in a language movement as a response to, and also as a part of, the relevant social and economic changes.

The most conspicuous feature of economic change in Wales since 1930 has been the increasing involvement of the state, especially with reference to its role in so-called 'regional development programmes'. It is within such features of economic 'planning' that we witness a collusion between the state and monopolistic capitalism. It has been demonstrated (Lovering, 1978) that consequent developments have created an enclave and a marginalized sector, leading to both geographic and social separation. As a result of growth policies, and the nature of the economic activities, the enclave tends to be concentrated in one place. In the main, its enterprises tend to employ a large labour force and to pay relatively high wages to mainly unskilled workers. These enterprises tend to be owned from outside Wales (Tomkins and Lovering, 1973), and tend to be managed by non-Welsh personnel whose structured careers involve a combination of social and geographic mobility. Such careerists consequently see little point in local integration. This is also true of the management of the monopolistic enterprises which have proliferated during the past 25 years, purchasing local enterprises which served as potential competition, or simply squeezing them out of existence by the sheer scale of their resources and transactions. As a result of the 'foreign' nature of the ownership of enclave enterprises, decisions concerning management tend to be made outside Wales and involve non-Welsh personnel. It is sometimes claimed that, because of the competition for public funds, there is an inherent conflict between this fraction of the bourgeoisie, and that employed in the expanding public sector which has been termed the 'new middle class'. In Wales, a substantial proportion of those employed in the public sector are Welsh-speaking, with some positions deeming a knowledge of the language a desirable qualification.

The proletariat in the marginalized sector is employed in small enter-prises and receives wages which average a third less than the wages of its counterpart in the enclave (Wenger, forthcoming). Several features of the labour force in the marginalized sector stand out. A high proportion are self-employed while simultaneously holding a number of jobs. This is not a manifestation of lucrative petit-bourgeois entrepreneurship, but rather of limited employment opportunities, especially secondary employment opportunities. The marginalized labour force tends to work extremely long hours for limited remuneration. It is this which is responsible for the high degree of mobility between the self-employed and skilled worker categories. This fluidity is also partly explained by the

tendency for the enclave, with its monopolistic and large scale characteristics, to squeeze out the small enterprise and to proletarianize the petit-
bourgeoisie in the process. However, the mobility may also serve as a
measure of opportunity access, in that it evidently operates in both
directions.

Within the marginalized sector the limited job opportunities oblige the
worker to accept lower-paid employment or to seek some form of
alternative employment, even if it be self-employment, outside the regular,
integrated market. Even self-employment can be seen as 'labour', and it is
often here that cheap labour is most evident (Bonacich, 1972). The self-
employed work long hours, as often do members of their families; they
sustain a low profit margin while limiting the profits that accrue from their
labour by putting a relatively large amount back into the enterprise. This
labour is cheap because of the use of family and even neighbour labour,
which is invariably loyal and unorganized. The advantage to the higher
income groups in the integrated sector which are serviced by such small
businesses is obvious.

The general condition in the marginalized sector is one in which the
majority of the local population does not participate in the new industrial
growth, together with a tendency to be made more remote from the scarce
infrastructural resources. This process is not a matter of the uninterested
being left behind, nor of certain geographical areas being neglected, but
rather a part of the process of uneven capitalist development: the growing
and the lagging sectors are inter-related, and thus disadvantages to some
derive from the benefits which accrue to others. Relevant factors include
the manner in which part of the petit-bourgeoisie is proletarianized; how
part of the local labour force may be used at one stage of the industrialization process before being discarded at a later, more lucrative stage; how
immigrants, transients and tourists make priority claims on the service
infrastructure; and how parts of the local economy are destroyed by new
developments. That the indigenous population, as represented by an
ability to speak the indigenous language, is over-represented in the process
of marginalization suggests the existence of a cultural division of labour in
which most of the benefits of the new developments appear to accrue to
the outsider.

Within the marginalized sector there is a tendency to draw upon the
resources of community as a basis for counteracting the effect of
marginality. Such resources frequently constitute the institutional
structure which serves as the basis for minority cultural and language
reproduction. As such, the advent of state intervention in the administration of welfare has tended to undermine these institutions, but it is no
coincidence that welfare distribution as a result of state intervention has
been divided along the enclave-marginal dichotomy, with the marginalized
areas being those which receive the poorest service (Grant, 1978). Thus the
salience of the relevant institutions remains relatively strong. Risk
minimization involves community institutions which operate through the
medium of the Welsh language, and community integration is not seen in

any way as a romantic element but rather as a necessary means of counteracting marginal status. It is this which transforms these institutions into political entities — and it is well to recognize that politics cannot be sustained by romanticism. Within the marginal areas and populations, regional and ethnic associations tend to be strong, mutual assistance is prevalent, and trust is retained among members of the ethnic group.

It should be evident that a consequence of this distinction between the enclave and the marginalized sectors is a fragmentation of classes. Relationships within classes tend to become disjointed and disorganized by the nature of the relationship between the two sectors. A disjunction develops, involving the separation of the economic aspects and the social aspects of the work situation, the relationships of production and those of reproduction.

The heterogeneity of the low-income groups in the marginalized sector, together with the false sense of economic opportunity associated with self-employment, serves to generate a cohesion which cuts across class and inhibits the development of a proletarian consciousness. The process also clouds the issue of what — or who — is responsible for their marginal status and relative impoverishment. The relationship between the dominant classes and the marginalized groups becomes increasingly precarious, unstable and fragmentary. For the marginals, the state, despite the limitations of its services, remains the major source of survival, but the majority remain outside, or marginal to, the state's compensatory mechanisms. It is also evident to many that it is the state, in its collusion with capitalism, that is responsible for their marginal position. The expressions of marginality are produced by the necessity of capitalist accumulations in the dominant sector, and this becomes increasingly obvious since marginality provides an effective means of reducing demands on scarce capital whilst contributing to its accumulation. The types of economic arrangements characteristic of marginalized economies tend to individualize the problem of making a living. This obscures the exploitation of the proletariat while emphasizing the limited opportunity for the enterprising individual.

The proletariat in the marginalized sector differs markedly from its counterpart in the enclave. Much of the marginalized population remains outside trade unions. The unemployed are not integrated, neither is much of the labour in the rural areas, hence the advantage to the 'new' industries in those areas. Among the workers who are unionized there are marked differences of advantage, awareness and integration. Thus the trade union movement is fragmented to the extent that the various fractions find themselves in competition with one another, and this competition works against the interests of those in lower-paid sectors, the unemployed and the non-unionized proletariat. Some of the demands pressed by the unions can be sufficient to liquidate the small enterprises employing many of the workers within the marginalized sector and thereby jeopardize their ability to earn a living. Thus workers are divided along lines which Touraine (1977) has referred to as 'defensive' and 'offensive'.

Under such conditions, the adversary can only be defined as the capitalist system imported and directed by 'foreigners', but the class which thus defines the adversary remains in the marginalized sector. Thus it is difficult to make a class struggle involve the idea of 'progress' since it argues against the means of achieving that 'progress'. It leads to a fragmentation of classes, which oppose one another because of their different relationships to the system of domination. This is strengthened by the disparities between workers in different industries and different regions — disparities which derive from the different relationships with the sectors that are linked to the flow of capital and (usually) the support of the state. It is in such situations that there will be a tendency to join forces along ethnic lines in opposition to both the master and the 'foreigner' — usually one and the same — the emphasis being upon community.

Here we are discussing the manner in which the status group is the community — a group drawn together across class positions. This community defines itself not only by exploitation but also by exclusion. The people involved are without recourse because they are enclosed within a dependent society which is not in control of its own means of production and mode of development, and whose resources flow either towards the 'foreigners' or towards the sectors which are dominated by them. This opposition is to a certain extent defined by a sense of exploitation on the part of the collectivity and by submission to a power which is in some way 'foreign'. Thus the conflict cannot simply be a class conflict within a 'national' economy, but it is equally the defence of the community against the external forces which serve to undermine it.

This process is particularly evident when the dominant indigenous stratum is threatened by the externally-based dominant élite of the enclave. Local identity will tend to be employed to create a local solidarity against the outsider. The dominant English bourgeois careerists define their aims and actions not in terms of Wales but rather in terms of the larger British entity which for most is conterminous with England. They are often supported by those members of the local entrenched bourgeoisie who are integrated into the enclave developments and who stand to benefit from them. Those of the local petit-bourgeoisie who find themselves not only excluded from the new developments but also increasingly marginalized as a result of such developments, rely on the idea of local community integration and solidarity as the basis for the retention of their own power. The issues which are the focus of the activities of varied pressure groups become the battleground for overt conflict between on the one hand the entrenched bourgeoisie and petit-bourgeoisie who emphasize the concept of community, and on the other hand the new bourgeoisie struggling to justify and legitimize their opposition to the concept of local community. It develops into a conflict of ideology between Welsh and British 'nationalism'; the latter is employed by the capitalist class, in collusion with the state, to mask and justify the maintenance of disparities in the geographic division of labour.

Community identity is based on language, religion and culture — all of which may serve as manifestations of a claim of devotion to a distinctive 'way of life' which is the basis of the status group. Identity does not necessarily focus upon any single marker. Language can serve as the basis for the closure of the status group with the result that the language becomes politicized. Within the marginalized sector, the Welsh language is the medium for a risk minimization service within institutions and networks which compensate for the ineffectiveness of the state's welfare system. These institutions can also serve as the basis for the mobilization of the community, and within them the local petit-bourgeoisie achieves its leadership potential, a function which also cuts across the various local communities to the wider ethnic community, thereby generating a local or regional leadership role.

It is in this context of the politicization of language as representative of certain interests within the community that we locate the struggle over the extension of Welsh in education. Particularly significant is the fact that it was not until a new phase of structural economic change, associated with state intervention, took place during the post-war era that bilingual education re-emerged as a central issue in Wales. This is not to imply, however, that the language's cause in education had not been championed by individuals and groups prior to this period, and corresponding concessions granted, but that formerly the language was never at the centre of the political stage to the extent that it is today. Certainly the 'Treachery of the Blue Books' generated a backlash in Wales and led to the founding of several Welsh societies and institutions during the latter half of the nineteenth century — among them being the first college of the University of Wales in 1872; directives on bilingual teaching are to be found in the Codes of Regulations even during this period. The weight of the Liberal camp behind claims for the extension of Welsh in education, and the impetus of Lloyd George and other Liberal MPs at the turn of the century prompted the establishing of a separate Welsh Department of the Board of Education and the provision of separate Codes of Regulations for Wales in 1907. Another feature of this period was the transfer of responsibility for education from central government to the local authorities in 1902, which we may again regard as a facet of the relationship between state and community.

In any event, the net gains from these moves, as far as the Welsh language was concerned, were minimal. Although the Codes for Wales continued to advocate bilingual education under certain circumstances, it was not put into practice. The Welsh language was excluded from education and relegated to domains within the community, and education became the primary agency for institutionalizing the separation of Welsh and English in Wales.

In 1927 language in education formed the specific area of investigation of a Report of the Departmental Committee of the Board of Education which incorporated the notion that Welsh-medium education should be encouraged. All the evidence, however, suggests that this policy was not implemented in schools, and the reason conventionally suggested is the lack of teachers trained to do this. A further reason would seem to be that as far as individual schools were concerned, decision-making about school policy lay in the hands of school governors who were invariably representatives of the English-speaking bourgeoisie. Thus despite the apparent devolution of control over education to local authorities, it is possible to identify a degree of retention of control over the community on the part of the state operating through this agency.

The first Welsh-medium primary school was opened in 1939, as a result of concern about the possible erosion of the Welsh language deriving from the presence of English war evacuees. Opened as a private venture, the school was established through the activities of a group of Welsh middle class parents in conjunction with Urdd Gobaith Cymru (Welsh League of Youth). The first state-controlled Welsh-medium primary school was opened in 1947, by which time the pressure for Welsh-medium education was rapidly gathering momentum. Clearly, there was a realization on the part of the state that the various pressure groups involved had to be appeased. Also, it was obvious that the attempts to eliminate the Welsh language embodied in the reports and Acts of the nineteenth century had failed. Thus a new strategy was emerging, which sought to expropriate the language from the control of the community through extending the domain of Welsh into state-financed education. Again we claim that the potential threat posed by a marginalized population which mobilizes on the basis of the Welsh language is not lost on those who are responsible for language planning and educational policy in Wales. This is evident in the way that prior provision is even now never made for Welsh in education: provision is made solely in response to the demands of various pressure groups and then only to a degree sufficient temporarily to appease these factions.

The demand for and provision of Welsh-medium education has increased prolifically since 1947. In the nine years from 1970-79 alone, the number of children receiving their education at Welsh-medium primary and secondary schools has more than doubled, from 8270 to 17,326. In addition, many secondary schools in naturally Welsh-speaking areas now offer instruction through the medium of Welsh in anything up to ten subjects. Although progress is slower at the level of higher and further education, many colleges are now able to offer a certain number of courses through the medium of Welsh, while specialized vocabularies are being developed under the auspices of the University of Wales to cope with the demands on a language hitherto excluded from the subject areas of education, science and technology.

As far as curriculum content is concerned, the syllabuses taught in Welsh-medium secondary schools are effectively standardized by the existence of the Welsh Joint Education Committee as the body responsible for school examinations in Wales. Founded in 1948 by the amalgamation of the old Central Welsh Board with other existing educational advisory agencies in Wales, the WJEC is held to be able to speak for education in

Wales as a whole. However, despite the inevitable centralization of the curriculum which derives from a system dependent upon examinations external to the school, the limited degree of autonomy of individual schools in deciding curricular matters guarantees a slightly different interpretation of curriculum in the Welsh-medium secondary schools from that of their English-medium counterparts. Given that their explicit aims incorporate first and foremost a commitment to the Welsh language and culture, it is hardly surprising to find the Welsh-medium secondary schools emphasizing different aspects in, for instance, the teaching of history, geography or music. Thus it seems that increasing the significance of specifically Welsh aspects of subjects such as these may contribute to the fact that children at these schools were found to have attitudes towards Welsh significantly more favourable than their peers in other types of schools in Wales, including schools located in naturally Welsh-speaking areas (Sharp, 1973). Once again this would seem to underline the salience of education in the production of ideology and the reproduction of culture.

However, while the demand for extending the use of Welsh in education continues to flourish, a counter-movement has developed which seeks to resist such developments. Pressure groups such as POW (Parents for Optional Welsh) have formed in areas where the demands for bilingual education are at their most fervent, aiming to act as watchdogs in safeguarding the interests of non-Welsh-speaking children. The significance of these polarized pressure groups lies in their composition. They cannot be regarded solely in terms of groups in opposition over the issue of bilingual education, but need to be viewed as representatives of the struggle over the community. While those campaigning for the extension of Welsh are drawn from the Welsh-speaking bourgeoisie, groups such as POW draw their support from English migrant careerists who see no value accruing to their children from learning Welsh, since they will anyway follow careers in England. Accordingly, the conflict between the two factions, while couched in terms of disagreement over the value of bilingualism, is a political manifestation of economic considerations. Within the marginalized sector, the community continues to serve its informal function which focuses on the agencies of Welsh cultural reproduction, and the process of proletarianization continues with the resultant displacement of the indigenous leadership. In the enclave, on the other hand, the bourgeoisie is fragmented into a new Welsh-speaking bourgeoisie involved in the public sector, and the English-speaking bourgeoisie associated with externally controlled capitalist development. The struggle over the Welsh language may be seen therefore as a manifest struggle for power between those factions of the bourgeoisie. It is in the light of the above that we contend that bilingual education lies at the heart of this struggle.

References

Blackwell, J (1951) *Ceinion Alun* (Works) In Welsh: London

Bonacich, E (1972) A theory of ethnic antagonisms: the split labour market *American Sociological Review* 37: 547-59

Grant, G (1978) The provision of social services in rural areas *in* Williams, Glyn (1978)

Lewis, E G (1978) Bilingualism in education in Wales *in* Spolsky (1978)

Lovering, J (1978) *Dependence and the Welsh economy* Paper presented to the SSRC Seminar Group on Wales: Gregynog

Ministry of Education, Welsh Department (1927) *Welsh in Education and Life — Report of the Departmental Committee* HMSO: London

Sharp, D *et al, eds* (1973) *Attitudes to Welsh and English in the Schools of Wales* Schools Council Research Studies, Macmillan/University of Wales Press: London

Spolsky, B and Cooper, R *eds* (1978) *Case Studies in Bilingual Education* Newbury House: Rowley, Mass

Tomkins, C and Lovering, J (1973) *Location, Size, Ownership and Control Tables for Welsh Industry* Cyngor Cymru: Cardiff

Touraine, A (1977) *The Self Production of Society* University of Chicago Press: Chicago, Ill

Tremenheere, S (1840) *Report of the Committee of the Council on Education on the State of Elementary Education in the Mining Districts of South Wales* Her Majesty's Stationery Store: London

Wenger, C (forthcoming) *Rural Industrialisation: Development and Deprivation* University of Wales Press: Cardiff

Williams, Glyn *ed* (1978) *Social and Cultural Change in Contemporary Wales* Routledge and Kegan Paul: London

Williams, Glyn (1979a) *The ideological position of nationalism in nineteenth century Wales* Paper presented to the SSRC Seminar Group on Wales: Cardiff

Williams, Glyn (1979b) *Economic development, social structure and contemporary nationalism in Wales* Paper presented at the First Conference of Europeanists: Washington DC

Williams, Gwyn A (1978) *The Merthyr Rising* Croom Helm: London

Williams, William (n.d.) Quoted *in* Evans, D *Life and World of William Williams, MP* Llandysul

10. The Chinese community in Malaysia: language policies and relationships

John T Platt

Summary: There are at least three types of relationship between majority and minority languages in regard to the Chinese community in Malaysia to be considered: the position of the dominant Chinese dialect of a region as against the other Chinese dialects spoken there; the relative position of all the Chinese dialects and Mandarin, and the relationships between the other speech varieties used by the Chinese in Malaysia.

The first relationship has developed in an unplanned way: throughout Malaysia, the dialect of the majority Chinese sub-group has become dominant and serves as a lingua franca. The second has developed through Chinese-medium education. Mandarin is the native speech variety of virtually no Malaysian Chinese, but most accept it as a prestige variety, and it is also the official language of Taiwan and the People's Republic of China.

The third relationship includes: (a) the relationship between all Chinese speech varieties and Bazaar Malay, the unplanned inter-ethnic pidgin lingua franca; (b) the relationship between all Chinese speech varieties and English, the former official and prestige language; and (c) the relationship between all Chinese speech varieties and Bahasa Malaysia, the planned and official national language of Malaysia.

The chapter attempts to explain how the earlier relationships developed and how these have been and are being modified both by the developing Chinese sense of identity and by the national language policies of Malaysia. The main agencies for the spread of Mandarin, English and Bahasa Malaysia have been educational, both private and governmental.

Any consideration of the relationship between majority and minority languages in regard to the Chinese community in Malaysia must take into account at least three main types of relationships:

1. the position of the dominant Chinese dialect of the particular region of Malaysia under consideration as against the other Chinese dialects spoken there;
2. the relative position of all the Chinese dialects spoken in Malaysia and Mandarin; and
3. the relationship between the other speech varieties used by the Chinese in Malaysia, namely the dominant Chinese dialect, Bazaar Malay, English and Bahasa Malaysia.

These relationships are, of course, all interconnected, with each having a bearing on the other, but for convenience it will be appropriate to consider them separately at first before attempting to present an overall picture and a prognosis. Furthermore, although the emphasis will be on Chinese in Malaysia it is not possible to ignore the language situation as it affects other communities in Malaysia or the language position in neighbouring Singapore.

Chinese immigration and the dominant dialects

It is difficult to establish how far back there has been Chinese contact with the Malay Peninsula, but it is known that Yin-Ching, an envoy of the Ming emperor, visited Malacca in 1403. The local ruler, Parameswara, established an orderly mercantile system which attracted Chinese as well as other merchants. Parameswara developed a relationship with China which continued under later rulers of Malacca and trade continued to increase. A Chinese settlement developed in Malacca (Tan, 1975).

After the capture of Malacca by the Portuguese in 1511, Chinese, Indian and other merchants continued to trade, and when it fell to the Dutch in 1641 there were reputedly 400 Chinese there. In 1750, 45 years before the British took it over for the first time, there were 2000 Chinese out of a population of 9600 (Tan, 1975). Most of these Chinese were of Hokkien-speaking background from the Amoy region of Fukien province. Britain handed Malacca back to the Dutch after the London Convention of 1814 but took it over again in 1824.

With the establishment of Penang as a British colony in 1786 and of Singapore in 1819, many Malacca Chinese moved to these new colonies. The early Chinese arrivals in Malacca had often married Malay women and although they and their descendants retained many aspects of Chinese culture, they had, of necessity, to communicate with Malays, Indians and others. The lingua franca was a pidgin variety of Malay and this, with the retention of Hokkien words for distinctively Chinese objects and concepts, became the native language of their descendants, the so-called Straits Chinese or Baba Chinese.

With the arrival of more Chinese immigrants from the Amoy region, the Hokkien dialect also became important in the three colonies which came to be known as the Straits Settlements and which became the Crown Colony of that name in 1867. The Chinese who had come to Malaya were mostly merchants, traders and artisans with little or no literacy or awareness of educated standards of speech. Therefore the variety which they spoke was usually not a prestige one. Furthermore, without any strong normative influence, the Chinese dialect was modified, especially by the Bazaar Malay pidgin and the Baba Malay creole of the Straits Chinese.

Although Chinese immigrants of other dialect backgrounds arrived, eg Cantonese, Teochew, Hakka and Hainanese, the local varieties of Hokkien remained dominant in the three colonies and those of other dialect backgrounds needed to acquire at least a basic competence in it.

The earliest Chinese schools in the region taught literacy through the medium of the dialects. These schools were established by private individuals, Chinese organizations and Christian missions. Besides literacy, most of them taught only Chinese history, literature, geography, politics and culture (Tan, 1975). However, until around 1920, when the Republic of China adopted Mandarin as the national language, the schools were not a linguistically unifying force, except in regard to literacy. Most Chinese in the nineteenth century, especially girls, had, in any case, little or no access to education. In addition, the various dialect groups were inclined to settle in different sections of the towns and therefore communication among dialect groups was probably minimal.

In the Malay States there was already immigration of Chinese to work in the tin mines in the early nineteenth century and by 1851 nearly 3000 were arriving each year (Tan, 1975). Because of the increasing production of tin to meet rapidly growing world demands and because of unstable conditions in China, there was a rapid increase in Chinese immigration, especially for the tin mines but also for work on plantations. In the tin mining areas of the state of Selangor and southern Perak, the majority of immigrants were Cantonese although there were other groups as well, particularly the Hakka (Kheh), many of whom, both male and female, were employed in tin production. Cantonese became the dominant Chinese dialect in Selangor and the Kinta valley tin mining region of Perak, and remains so today.

With the gradual spread of Chinese throughout the Malay peninsula, a pattern of dominant Chinese dialects developed. Basically this is Hokkien in the south — Johore, Malacca and part of Negri Sembilan; Cantonese in the centre — Selangor, Pahang and southern Perak; Hokkien again in the north — northern Perak, Penang, Kedah and Perlis, and on the East Coast in Trengganu and Kelantan. However, in Kedah and Perlis and especially in the north-eastern states of Trengganu and Kelantan, Chinese are very much in the minority except in certain towns.

In certain rural areas, other groups such as Hakka or Hainanese may be dominant but the overall pattern is of Hokkien or Cantonese as the dominant Chinese dialect.

Thus the unplanned relationship which developed *within* the overall Chinese community was one of a dominant dialect with a number of other dialects spoken by numerically smaller groups. Within the extended family and with others of the same dialect group, the 'native' dialect was spoken, but in communication with speakers of the dominant dialect or with members of other locally minor dialect groups, the dominant dialect (or a reduced form of it) was the lingua franca, eg a Hakka would typically communicate with a Hainanese in Hokkien in Penang. However, even in larger towns there would typically have been an area, possibly only one street, peopled by members of one minority dialect group. Thus, in the overwhelmingly Hokkien population of Penang Island, Chulia Street in the urban area of George Town is mainly Cantonese, while there is a considerable Hakka population on the west side of Penang Island, in a rural area. However, no Chinese can function adequately in Penang without some competence in Penang Hokkien. Even Hokkien speakers from other parts of Malaysia, eg Malacca, or from Singapore are instantly recognized as outsiders.

In regard to Chinese dialects, the concept of majority-minority languages is a simple one. Majority dialects are the ones which are the native varieties of a majority of Chinese of a region and are also used by other Chinese as a lingua franca. Although the term 'dialect' is commonly used of speech varieties such as Hokkien, Cantonese and Hakka, many of these 'dialects' are not, in their spoken form, mutually intelligible.

The growing importance of Mandarin

Even before the revolution of 1911 which ended the Manchu regime and led to the foundation of the Chinese Republic, there had been moves in China for modernization of education, and educational reforms also affected Chinese schools in Malaya (Loh, 1975). These reforms included the introduction of new subjects and the politicization of Chinese schools. After the 1911 revolution, the government of China encouraged an extension of Chinese education in areas of overseas Chinese population such as Malaya.

In 1920, because of concern by the authorities about the political nature of the Chinese schools, the Federated Malay States government brought in the Registration of Schools Enactment which gave the Education Department control over the Chinese schools. However, the amount of federal government funding to Chinese schools remained low, eg 1.6 per cent of total federal expenditure on education in 1924 and only 5.1 per cent even in 1938 (Loh, 1975).

Mandarin had become the national language in China after the 1911 revolution and the Chinese schools in Malaya adopted this more and more as the medium of instruction. However, Winstedt, the Director of Education, made it a condition that aid would be given only to Chinese schools which taught in the Chinese dialects and not in Mandarin (Loh, 1975). Most Chinese schools were unwilling to accept this condition, but some had to in order to survive. Although the government gave far greater assistance to English-medium schools, there was an official unwillingness for English to be taught in Chinese schools.

After 1929, Sir Cecil Clementi, the Governor, introduced measures further controlling Chinese education, including the restriction of employment to teachers born in Malaya and the appointment of extra inspectors; on the other hand, federal grants to Chinese schools were to be extended to schools teaching in Mandarin. However, after 1932 no further applications for assistance were to be accepted from Chinese (or Indian) schools.

Under the next Governor, Sir Shenton Thomas (who succeeded

Clementi in 1935), greater financial assistance was given to Chinese schools
and Mandarin was recognized as 'a language qualifying for federal grants,
and federal funding ... for teacher training "Normal Classes" ' (Loh, 1975).

After the period of Japanese occupation (1942-45), Mandarin-medium
education continued to expand and more students continued to secondary
education. In 1956, 34.4 per cent of students at government-aided
secondary schools were at Chinese-medium schools (23,282 out of a total
of 69,214); by 1960, although the percentage had dropped slightly (to
33.4 per cent) the number had increased to 38,828 (figures based on
Educational Statistics of Malaysia, 1938-1967, quoted in Platt and Weber,
1980). Government-aided Chinese-medium secondary education ceased to
be available but primary education enrolment continued to increase.
Official figures are no longer available but in a comment on the teaching of
the national language, Bahasa Malaysia, the English language newspaper,
New Straits Times (16.11.79) said:

> The position of mother tongue schools in Tamil and Chinese medium is
> guaranteed in the constitution and substantial numbers of parents still prefer
> to send their children to these schools. In fact the enrolments of Chinese
> schools are increasing rapidly.

In an investigation of language use by Chinese tertiary students in 1975,
I found that 68 per cent of those with Chinese-medium primary education
claimed to have used Mandarin with fellow students at secondary school in
out-of-class situations, 58 per cent to use it with friends in their home
town and 63 per cent with fellow students at the university. Although
only 5 per cent of this group claimed to use Mandarin at all with either
parent, 53 per cent claimed to do so with siblings (Platt, 1976a). Numbers
of Malaysian Chinese reported that they attended or had attended evening
classes in Mandarin and there appears to have been a growing attitude
towards Mandarin as a unifying symbol of Chinese ethnicity and culture.
Kuo (1979) quotes figures from a survey of 8454 Malaysians over the age
of 15, carried out in 1978 by a market research group (Survey Research
Malaysia): 66.3 per cent of Chinese mentioned Mandarin in answer to the
question: 'Are there any other languages or dialects you understand
besides ... (the language of the interview)?'

If these figures are an accurate reflection of language competence, then
Mandarin has already reached the status of a majority language among
the Malaysian Chinese in the sense that a majority have at least some
competence in it, even if mainly receptive. If present trends continue it
seems likely that the proportion of those understanding it and able to
speak it will increase. Singapore has been conducting a vigorous 'Speak
More Mandarin and Less Dialects' campaign and this could encourage
trends towards it in Malaysia. Kuo (1979) gives figures for Singapore
based on a similar survey by Survey Research Singapore; 69.5 per cent
(1972) and 82.1 per cent (1978) of Singaporeans claimed to understand
Mandarin. Furthermore, as English-medium education has been progressively replaced by Bahasa Malaysia-medium education as from 1970, some

Chinese parents have evidently felt that their children should receive a Chinese-medium primary education (with Bahasa Malaysia and English as compulsory second languages), followed by Bahasa Malaysia-medium secondary education.

There have been moves for the establishment of a Chinese university, but the government has not permitted this as it would be a private institution and would use Chinese as the medium of instruction. (*Asia Week* 4 4, 13.10.79). Even though the establishment of such an institution is highly unlikely, it is clear that Mandarin has become a symbol of Chinese identity.

In terms of diglossia (Ferguson, 1959) or more strictly polyglossia (Platt, 1977a, 1977b, 1978), Mandarin is in many respects a high-status speech variety within the Chinese community. The dialects are of considerably lower status, with regionally dominant ones being higher than the others, eg Cantonese would have a higher status than Hakka or Hainanese overall among the Chinese of Kuala Lumpur.

The inter-ethnic speech varieties of Malaysia

In this section, those speech varieties which have had or which have the function of inter-ethnic lingue franche between Chinese and others will be considered. Some of them have also been used or are used *among* the Chinese as well.

Chinese dialects as lingue franche

Although the Chinese were, and still are, numerically dominant in the urban areas of Malaysia, Chinese dialects have acted only to a limited extent as inter-ethnic lingue franche. Typically, the Chinese and Indians lived in different sections of the larger towns, and Malays, during the colonial era, formed a small minority in urban areas. Except for those employed in clerical and administrative positions, more particularly in the Unfederated Malay States, their usual occupations were those of driver, gardener or office attendant, a reflection of the fact that only a small élite were able to obtain more than a basic vernacular education. However, some Malays and Indians whose occupations involved frequent verbal interaction with Chinese did acquire the necessary amount of competence in the dominant Chinese dialect, and one can observe, for example, Indian sales people in Penang using Penang Hokkien with customers, or Malays working at hotels using the dominant Chinese dialect with Chinese guests and fellow staff. Kuo (1979) gives the following percentages for 1978:

Malays understanding	Hokkien	0.4 per cent
	Cantonese	1.5 per cent
Indians understanding	Hokkien	2.0 per cent
	Cantonese	1.5 per cent

However, in general, although the dominant Chinese dialect would be spoken by a majority of a town's inhabitants this would be because the majority were Chinese and it would serve mainly an intra-ethnic function.

Bazaar Malay, the old lingua franca

As mentioned before, the lingua franca which developed in Malaya when the need arose for communication between Malays and traders from India and China and then between Indians and Chinese was Bazaar Malay (Bahasa Pasar). This is a lexically and syntactically reduced form of Malay, different from the colloquial Malay used among Malays and far removed from the High Malay of earlier times or modern Bahasa Malaysia. The pronominal system was reduced, ie instead of the range of first and second person pronouns appropriate to the relative statuses of the inter-locutors and the widespread use of personal names and kinship terms as terms of address or self-reference, one Malay pronoun *saya* or Hokkien *goa* was used for first person singular and Hokkien *lu* for second person. Malay verbs were stripped to their stem forms, the Malay possessive system was modified to a Chinese one, eg *saya punya rumah* 'my house' instead of *rumah-ku* and the syntax was greatly simplified. Phonetically, Bazaar Malay varies considerably according to the language background of the speaker.

Although this was not a language used in education, and although it had no literature, no official status and only a very low prestige, it became the majority language of Malaya and remained so until after independence and the introduction of Bahasa Malaysia as the medium of education. It was the language used by a Tamil Indian buying in a Chinese shop, the language used by a Sikh watchman to a Chinese merchant and it was the language that every European had to acquire in order to function in this multilingual setting.

Although it was very definitely a majority language in terms of number of speakers it was, of course, not a majority language in terms of *native* speakers. A development from pidginized Malay was, however, Baba Malay creole, spoken as native language by the Babas or Peranakan Chinese (Straits Chinese). This group was always a minority one overall, but especially in Malacca it was extremely important and may have formed a numerical majority at some periods. Speakers of Baba Malay could, and can, modify their speech towards Bazaar Malay but most of them had little or no competence in a Chinese dialect. Thus, to this extent, Bazaar Malay performed an intra-ethnic function in communication between Peranakan Chinese and other Chinese. Interestingly, some Peranakan Chinese became literate in a romanized form of their language and a newspaper, *Bintang Timor* (Eastern Star) was published in Singapore, commencing in 1894 but lasting less than a year (Turnbull, 1977).

English as prestige lingua franca and world language

With the establishment of the British Straits Settlements colonies (Penang in 1786, Singapore in 1819 and the taking over of Malacca from the Dutch in 1824) English became the language of administration and the law. Although British officials were expected to acquire some competence in Malay (some achieved a very high degree of competence) the services of interpreters, often Indians, were necessary. English was also an important language in commerce and banking. In addition to British staff, English-speaking Indians were also employed in lower clerical positions (Platt and Weber, 1980).

The first English-medium school to be established was the Penang Free School in 1816. This was followed by the Singapore Free School in 1823 and the Malacca Free School in 1826. English-medium schools were later available in the Federated Malay States, eg in Kuala Lumpur in 1894 and Taiping in 1906. Schools were established by various Christian missions and these eventually received government grants. In addition, government schools were established and by 1931, in Singapore and the Federated Malay States, there were 82 English-medium schools, 20 being government schools with an enrolment of 6248 and 62 grant-in-aid schools with an enrolment of 21,823.

These schools were established in the larger urban centres and most of the pupils enrolled at them were Chinese, Indians or Eurasians as there were few urban Malays. However, a school for Malay boys was opened in 1905 in Kuala Kangsar, the royal town of the state of Perak, and by 1909 it had become Malay College and was a fully residential institution catering mainly for the sons of the Malay aristocracy (Loh, 1975).

English language newspapers had commenced in the early nineteenth century, eg *The Prince of Wales Island Gazette* in Penang in 1833, and eventually the readership of these newspapers included those locally educated at English-medium schools. With the expansion of government departments, especially after the federation of the four Malay States of Selangor, Negri Sembilan, Perak and Pahang in 1896, and with increasing commerce and communication systems, more and more English-medium educated local personnel were employed. Similarly, with the expansion of English-medium education, teaching positions were filled more and more by those locally educated. Gradually an English-medium educated élite developed, particularly among the Baba Chinese community, many of whom had little or no competence in a Chinese dialect but saw English-medium education as important. Some Chinese were able to undertake higher education at British universities and return to practise law or medicine (Turnbull, 1977).

In 1905, the Singapore Medical School (which became the King Edward VII College of Medicine in 1915) was opened, and in 1929 Raffles College, a tertiary arts and science institution, was opened officially. Both of these were English-medium institutions and although situated in Singapore they also attracted students from the other Straits Settlements and the Malay States.

After the period of Japanese occupation (1942-45), English-medium education expanded further. In 1951, there were 42,201 students at English-medium secondary schools in the Federation of Malaya (61 per cent of total secondary enrolment) and by 1962, 90 per cent of secondary enrolment was in English-medium schools. By 1967, with the establishment of more Malay-medium secondary schools, the percentage had decreased to 69.1 per cent but enrolment had increased to 286,254 in a total population of about 7,250,000. Kuo (1979) gives figures based on Survey Research Malaysia data showing 24.5 per cent (1972) and 37.9 per cent (1978) Chinese aged 15 and over claiming to understand English. These figures may be somewhat high as it is possible that the sample population interviewed by a market research organization may have included rather too low a proportion of rural Chinese and those at the lowest end of the socioeconomic scale. However, the proportion would probably have continued to increase if English-medium education had continued to be available.

Although English never became a majority language in the sense of most of the population having some competence in it, it became the language in which inter- and intra-ethnic communication could be performed on a wide range of topics, including those which could not be discussed in Bazaar Malay or the Chinese dialects. It was the language giving access to the wider world and in this sense it made those with adequate competence in it members of a wider speech community. Within Malaysia itself, it achieved the status of being the majority language of those with secondary education or above. Within the Chinese community it also had the function of being, in terms of diglossia or polyglossia, a High variety but whereas Mandarin became an intra-ethnic High variety, English was an intra- and inter-ethnic High variety. In inter-ethnic communication it formed a High and Low pair with Bazaar Malay.

The rise of Bahasa Malaysia

Before considering the rise of Bahasa Malaysia it is necessary to explain briefly the relationship between Bahasa Malaysia, Malay and Bahasa Indonesia. The Malay language (Bahasa Melayu) had many dialects and naturally there were considerable differences between the everyday speech of ordinary people and the literary style. Both Bahasa Malaysia (Malaysian language) and Bahasa Indonesia (Indonesian language) are based on educated Malay. Although Bahasa Malaysia and Bahasa Indonesia developed independently and there are grammatical and vocabulary differences between them, there has, for some years now, been consultation between the language planning agencies of both nations and a common spelling system in the Latin alphabet was agreed upon to replace the separate Latin alphabet systems previously used. Both languages have introduced large numbers of new terms for technical, scientific and commercial purposes; many of these are of European origin (eg *ekonomi* — economics) but others are formed from Malay, Arabic and Sanskrit roots eg *pusat bahasa* (language centre) from Malay *pusat* (navel) and *bahasa* (language), a word originally from Sanskrit but which was long ago incorporated into Malay.

Article 152 of the Federal Constitution of Malaya states: 'The National Language is Malay . . . . Until 1967 English will continue to be the alternative official language . . .'. In the development of Malaysia's language policy:

> the first stage was characterized by moderate Malay nationalism and covered the period from 1959 to 1969 . . . . Notwithstanding the provisions of the Constitution and the proposals made in the report on education reforms, during this period the government did not actively pursue a national language policy. (Tan, 1978)

However in 1969,

> the then Minister of Education, Tan Sri Yaakob, announced his intention to carry out the three great tasks of (1) carrying out a National Education Policy with Malay as the medium of instruction; (2) establishing a National University with Malay as the medium of instruction; and (3) raising the status of the Islamic College to that of Islamic University. Several days later he also announced that the purpose of the National Education Policy was to establish 'One Country, One Nation, and One Language'. (Tan, 1978)

The Ministry of Education announced plans for the progressive replacement of English-medium education by Malay-medium. The first year of elementary schools would use Malay as the medium of instruction in 1970 and a gradual conversion throughout the primary and secondary levels was to be completed in 1982. National type Chinese- and Tamil-medium primary schools were to continue but all government supported secondary education was, in any case, by 1970 available only in English or Malay. English was to continue as the compulsory second language. The conversion has been slower in the East Malaysian (Borneo) states of Sabah and Sarawak but overall the picture is the same. At the tertiary level, too, there has been a gradual introduction of Bahasa Malaysia as a replacement for English but the lack of Malay language textbooks in certain disciplines will almost certainly ensure the continuing importance of English, even if mainly in its written form.

Of course, Malay is the native language of the largest ethnic group in the population of Malaysia — 46.8 per cent in 1970 (Tan, 1978) and over 50 per cent in Peninsular Malaysia; as mentioned earlier, Bazaar Malay was the inter-ethnic lingua franca. The choice of Malay not only as a symbolic national language but as the main language of education and administration can be justified on several grounds:

1. speakers of Malay or related languages form the majority of the population;
2. a form of Malay, however pidginized, was the early lingua franca;
3. a form of Malay is the national language of the far more populous neighbouring nation, Indonesia;
4. the only other inter-ethnic lingua franca which could have qualified

as national language is English. This, however, was mainly a language for the upper levels of the urban population and, in any case, is hardly an appropriate symbol of a newly independent nation.

The alternative would have been to follow a 'pre-1969' policy, a policy of having Bahasa Malaysia as the national language, increasing the availability of education in it and requiring it to be taught *either* as first or second language, possibly with requirements for certain standards to be met for promotion through school and entrance to tertiary education or government employment. There are indications that such a policy may have been more popular among some non-Malay groups in Malaysia. Mention has already been made of attempts at having a Chinese university, and the increased enrolment in Chinese-medium primary schools in recent years. This move towards Chinese-medium education can be attributed at least in part to the non-availability of English-medium education, although it is no doubt also due to an increasing awareness among the Chinese of the status and importance of Mandarin as a pan-Chinese speech variety, as noted earlier. Whether this trend towards Mandarin will continue or whether greater incentives for competence in Malay — and disincentives for Mandarin-medium education — will lead to a reversal of the trend is difficult to predict.

Thus, as far as the Chinese community in Malaysia is concerned, both unplanned and planned systems of language use have developed. Within the wider Chinese speech community, the majority Chinese dialect of each region became dominant. For wider inter-ethnic communication, Bazaar Malay was a low prestige majority language. With the wider availability of Chinese-medium education, Mandarin became more and more widely known and accepted as a prestige variety among the Chinese. The use of English increased with greater educational opportunity and would probably have become one of the majority languages for Malaysian Chinese if changes in language policies had not occurred. Bahasa Malaysia, as a compulsory first or second language at the level of primary education and the only medium of education in government-supported schools, is gaining more and more users. However, it appears that in towns with high concentrations of Chinese population, the dialects are still the main medium of everyday communication, with Bahasa Malaysia reserved for more official types of communication.

Future relationships between majority and minority languages as they affect the Malaysian Chinese

To forecast the future of speech varieties in a multilingual society is difficult, particularly when speech variety use is affected by government policies. However, the following trends would seem likely.

Chinese dialects

The minority Chinese dialects are likely to diminish and eventually to disappear, despite quite strong feelings of group identity among some of the speakers. This trend is likely, partly because intermarriage between members of different groups is far more common nowadays, and because outside the family domain, the dominant dialect of the region is of greater practical value. Also, where Chinese children attend Malay-medium schools, their competence in the 'home' dialect is diminished unless reinforced in out-of-school interaction. The minority dialects will probably survive longest in rural areas where the members actually form a local majority. The dominant or majority dialects will probably survive longer but if Mandarin-medium education increases and the Chinese use Mandarin more and more in intra-ethnic communication then they too will diminish.

Mandarin

The use of Mandarin is likely to increase as long as Chinese-medium primary education is available. It is, after all, a pan-Chinese symbol, a language of practical value in communication with Taiwan and the People's Republic of China and also with neighbouring Singapore, if the language policy there is effective. In addition, it is a variety in which spoken and written communication can take place beyond the confines of the dialect group.

Bazaar Malay

There is evidence that the use of Bazaar Malay is diminishing. As younger Chinese have had Bahasa Malaysia at least as a second language this has taken the place of Bazaar Malay. In communication with an older person, eg an Indian with no formal education, a simplified type of Bahasa Malaysia is used rather than Bazaar Malay.

English

Despite recognition on the part of the government that English is an important international language and necessary in many areas of higher education, opportunities for natural spoken communication in it are diminishing (Platt and Weber, 1980). It seems likely that English will soon reach a similar status to that which it has in some smaller Western European nations, ie main second language in education and main vehicle for the publication of learned books and articles and access to such works published elsewhere.

Bahasa Malaysia

Whatever may be the attitude of individuals or groups, competence in

Bahasa Malaysia has become vital in many spheres of activity and any Chinese working in the government or private sector and needing to communicate beyond the Chinese community must use it. If Bahasa Malaysia gains wide acceptance among the Malaysian Chinese, as at least one speech variety within their repertoire, then it is likely that functional varieties will develop, forming a range from a prestige variety for use in formal situations to a colloquial variety for use with friends and workmates (Platt, 1976b). This range may well be similar in some respects to the range of Singaporean (and the earlier Malaysian) English, with the more colloquial variety showing phonetic and grammatical influences from Chinese. However, even the colloquial type would be closer to standard Bahasa Malaysia than was the case with Bazaar Malay. If it is accepted as the *Malaysian* rather than the *Malay* language then it could become an inter-ethnic unifying force but, unlike English, a language for all social classes, rural or urban.

References

Dressler, W U and Meid, W eds (1978) *Proceedings of the XIIth International Congress of Linguists* Innsbrucker Beiträge zur Sprachwissenschaft

Ferguson, C A (1959) Diglossia *Word* **15**: 325-40

Kuo, E C Y (1979) Measuring communicativity in multilingual societies: the cases of Singapore and West Malaysia *Anthropological Linguistics* **21** 7: 328-40

Loh, P F-S (1975) *Seeds of Separatism: Educational Policy in Malaya 1874-1940* Oxford University Press: Kuala Lumpur

Platt, J T (1976a) Speech repertoires and societal domains of Malaysian Chinese *Speech Education* **4** 1: 1-23

Platt, J T (1976b) Some aspects of language planning in Malaysia *Kivung* **9** 1: 3-17

Platt, J T (1977a) Code selection in a multilingual-polyglossic society *Talanya* **4**: 64-75

Platt, J T (1977b) A model for polyglossia and multilingualism with special reference to Singapore and Malaysia *Language in Society* **6** 3: 361-78

Platt, J T (1978) Aspects of polyglossia and multilingualism in Malaysia and Singapore *in* Dressler and Meid (1978)

Platt, J T and Weber, H (1980) *English in Singapore and Malaysia: Status, Features, Functions* Oxford University Press: Kuala Lumpur

Tan, D E (1975) *A Portrait of Malaysia and Singapore* Oxford University Press: Singapore

Tan, T-S (1978) *Language Policies in Insular Southeast Asia: A Comparative Study* Southeast Asia Studies Programme, Nanyang University: Singapore

Turnbull, C M (1977) *A History of Singapore 1819-1975* Oxford University Press: Kuala Lumpur

11. Puerto Rican children in American mainland schools

Francesco Cordasco and George Bernstein

Summary: The contemporary American school's response to the bilingual child cannot be understood unless it is placed in the historical context of that society's earlier responses to the immigrant communities and their children: alongside the school's concerns with cognitive development must be placed the greater society's commitment to enforced assimilation (ie American-ization), English language acquisition (with concomitant neglect and rejection of the child's native language), and Anglo-Saxon conformism. The Puerto Rican child is the heir to a complex set of societal responses developed over a long period of time, and the success or failure of the American school's response to his needs depends on the careful management of forces which may preclude the implementation of programmes which incorporate empirically valid learning principles.

The chapter addresses itself to the educational needs of Puerto Rican children in American mainland schools, with a primary attention to the delineation of a programme which gives promise of cognitive developmental success and assures a psychological maturation congruent with the realities of American societal structure.

The migration and mainland experience: an overview

In February 1971, the US Census Bureau published its November 1969 sample-survey estimate that the 50 states and the District of Columbia had 1,454,000 Puerto. Rican residents — 811,000 born on the island, 636,000 born in the states and district, 1000 in Cuba, and 6000 elsewhere. In March 1972, the Census Bureau released preliminary (and a few final) state population totals from the 1970 census for three categories — persons of Spanish language, persons of Spanish family name, and Puerto Ricans. Puerto Rican counts were for three states only — New York (872,471; 5 per cent of the state population); New Jersey (135,676; 2 per cent of the state population); and Pennsylvania (44,535).

Puerto Ricans have been on the mainland for many years; in the nineteenth century, a small colony of Puerto Ricans, gathered largely in New York City, worked for the independence of their island. After the annexation of the island in 1898 by the United States, a continuing migration to the mainland began. In 1910 some 1500 Puerto Ricans were living in the United States; by 1930, they numbered close to 53,000.

The migration was reversed during the depression of the 1930s, and again was substantially impeded by World War II in the early 1940s. After the end of World War II (and concurrent with the advent of cheap air transport) it increased steadily until it reached its peak in the early 1950s (in 1953, 304,910 persons left the island and 203,307 returned, leaving a net balance of 74,603). The state of the economy on the mainland has always been an indicator of migration. The decline in Puerto Rican migration to the mainland in 1970 which continued through the 1970s resulted from economic hardship in the States. The pattern has not significantly changed between 1970 and 1980. A recent demographic study observes:

> Migration tends to decrease during periods of crisis in the United States and sometimes the current has reversed itself; more than 280,000 people of Puerto Rican extraction have returned to Puerto Rico, and the current of returning migrants seems to have increased considerably since 1970. An economy which depends on its ability to get rid of its excess population by means of migration cannot be expected to have great stability and finds itself on a very unsound base. (Vasquez Calzada, 1979: 235)

In a prescient book on Puerto Rican Americans, the Jesuit sociologist, Reverend Joseph P Fitzpatrick, observes that Puerto Ricans have found it difficult to achieve 'community solidarity' and suggests that they may work out adjustment 'in very new ways' differing from those of past immigrants (technically, as American citizens, Puerto Ricans are migrants to the mainland United States). Father Fitzpatrick cogently observes:

> A book about the Puerto Ricans in mainland United States, with a special focus on those in New York City, is very risky but also is very necessary. It is risky because the Puerto Rican community is in a state of turbulent change in a city and a nation which are also in a state of turbulent change. So many different currents of change affect Puerto Ricans at the present time that it is foolhardy to attempt to describe this group adequately or put them into focus. Nor is it possible to point out clearly any one direction in which the Puerto Rican community is moving in its adjustment to life on the mainland. Its directions are often in conflict, and no single leader or movement has given sharp definition to one direction as dominant over others . . . . What is most needed at this moment of the Puerto Rican experience, both for Puerto Rican and other mainland Americans, is *perspective*: a sense of the meaning of the migration for everyone involved in that migration, for the new-comers as well as the residents of the cities and neighbourhoods to which the Puerto Ricans come. (Fitzpatrick, 1971: xi)

How varied the Puerto Rican experience on the mainland has been can be best indicated by the sharp contrasts provided in four juxtaposed excerpts from Puerto Rican reactions registered over a period of time.

In 1948, J J Osuna, the distinguished Puerto Rican educator, on a visit to New York City schools, observed:

> As far as possible something should be done in Puerto Rico to discourage migration of people who do not have occupations to go into upon their arrival in this country, or of children whose parents live in Puerto Rico and who have no home in New York. Too many people are coming, hoping that they may find work and thereby better themselves economically, and in the

case of the children, educationally. It is laudable that they take the chance, but the experience of the past teaches us that as far as possible, people should not come to the continent until they have secured employment here. (Osuna, 1948: 227)

In 1961, Joseph Monserrat, at the time Director of the Migration Division, Commonwealth of Puerto Rico, in speaking on 'Community planning for Puerto Rican integration in the United States', cautioned:

If all Puerto Ricans were to suddenly disappear from New York City, neither the housing problem nor other basic issues confronting the city would be solved. In fact, without the Puerto Ricans, New York would be faced with one of two alternatives: either 'import' people to do the work done by Puerto Ricans (and whoever was imported from wherever they might come would have to live in the very same buildings Puerto Ricans now live in for the simple reason that there is nothing else); or industries would have to move to other areas where there are workers, causing a severe economic upheaval in the city. Obviously, neither one is a viable solution. Nor will the stagnation of the past resolve our dilemma . . . . The Puerto Rican, although he comes from a close knit neighbourhood in the Commonwealth, has found the best possibility for social action and self-improvement on the city-wide level. The community of Puerto Ricans is not the East Side or the South Side. It is New York City, Lorain, Chicago, Los Angeles, Middletown. City living is learned living. The migrants must be helped to learn the facts of city life and how to function effectively as a pressure group in a pressure group society. (Monserrat, 1961: 221)

Both of these statements are in stark contrast to the ideology of revolution and separatism evident in the animadversions which follow. First, from a spokesman for 'La Generación Encojonada':

Violence is the essence of a colonial society. It is established as a system in the interests of the ruling classes. Colonial society 'is the meeting of two forces, opposed to each other by their very nature, which in fact owe their originality to that sort of substantification which results from and is nourished by the situation in the colonies. Their first encounter was marked by violence and their existence together . . . was carried on by dint of a great array of bayonets and cannon.' Puerto Rican history has been witness to this violent confrontation between people and oppressor. We see it in daily events: in schools, churches, factories, the countryside, in strikes, demonstrations, and insurrections. As soon as an individual confronts the system, he feels its violence in the way of life colonialism imposes on him: the feudal-type exploitation in the countryside, the capitalist exploitation in the cities.

The lifeblood of every colonial society is the profit it offers to its exploiters. Its basis is the authority of an exploiting system − not the authority that comes from a majority consensus, but the paternal authority with which a minority tries to justify a system beneficial to it. Around that system is built a morality, an ethic, rooted in the economic co-existence of colonizers and colonized. Thus the system envelops itself in forms that create the illusion of sharing, of a brotherhood and equality that don't exist. The Puerto Rican elections held every four years exemplify this. We must not confuse the ox with the fighting bull, the causes with the problem, the root with the branches. (Silén, 1971: 118-19)

And from a theoretician for the Young Lords' Party, spawned in the socio-pathology of the urban barrio:

> To support its economic exploitation of Puerto Rico, the United States instituted a new educational system whose purpose was to Americanize us. Specifically, that means that the school's principal job is to exalt the cultural values of the United States. As soon as we begin using books that are printed in English, that are printed in the United States, that means that the American way of life is being pushed . . . with all its bad points, with its commercialism, its dehumanization of human beings.
>
> At the same time that the cultural values of America are exalted, the cultural values of Puerto Rico are downgraded. People begin to feel ashamed of speaking Spanish. Language becomes a reward and punishment system. If you speak English and adapt to the cultural values of America, you're rewarded; if you speak Spanish and stick to the old traditional ways, you're punished. In the school system here, if you don't quickly begin to speak English and shed your Puerto Rican values, you're put back a grade — so you may be in the sixth grade in Puerto Rico but when you come here, you go back to the fourth or fifth. You're treated as if you're retarded, as if you're backward — and your own cultural values therefore are shown to be of less value than the cultural values of this country and the language of this country. (Perez, 1971: 65-6)

It is no accident that this strident voice registers anger particularly with the schools; for it is in the schools that Puerto Rican identity is subjected to the greatest pressures, and it is the educational experience on the mainland which, for Puerto Ricans, is generally bad and from which despair and alienation emerge. It is in mainland schools that the dynamics of conflict and acculturation for Puerto Ricans are best seen in clear perspective; and it is a grim irony that, generally, educational programmes for Puerto Ricans have failed despite the multitudinous educational experiments that were a part of the new attentions, born in Johnsonian America, paid to the culture of the poor, and the massive programmatic onslaughts on poverty. In the Puerto Rican mainland communities, there has been a subtle shift (following Black models) from the campaign for civil rights and integration to an emphasis on Puerto Rican power and community solidarity.

And the Puerto Rican poor in their urban barrios have encountered as their chief adversaries the Black poor in the grim struggle for anti-poverty monies and for the participative identities in Community Action Programmes (funded by the Office of Economic Opportunity) which are often the vehicles and leverages of political power in decaying American cities; additionally, a Puerto Rican professional presence in schools and a myriad of other institutional settings has been thwarted by exiled middle class Cuban professionals.

> Most of the Cubans are an exiled professional middle-class that came to the United States for political reasons. They are lauded and rewarded by the United States government for their rejection of Communism and Fidel Castro. The Cubans lean toward the political right, are fearful of the involvement of masses of poor people. Being middle-class they are familiar with 'the system' and operate successfully in this structure. They are competitive and upwardly mobile. They have little sympathy for the uneducated poor. (Hidalgo, 1971: 14)

It is hardly strange that the Puerto Rican community has looked to the schools, traditionally the road out of poverty, as affording its best hope for successfully negotiating the challenges of a hostile American mainland.

Non-English speaking children in American schools: the children of the past

American schools have always had as students children from a wide variety of cultural backgrounds; and the non-English-speaking child has been no stranger in American urban classrooms. If we are to understand the problems which Puerto Rican children encounter in mainland schools, it is instructive to look at the experience of other children (non-English-speaking and culturally different) in American schools. A huge literature (largely ignored until recently) exists on the children of immigrants in the schools. No document on this earlier experience is more impressive than the Report of the United States Immigration Commission (1911), of which the *Report on the Children of Immigrants in Schools* (vols 29-33) is a vast repository of data on the educational history of the children of the poor and the schools. By 1911, 57.5 per cent of children in the public schools of 37 of the largest American cities were of foreign-born parentage; in the parochial schools of 24 of these 37 cities, the children of foreign-born parents constituted 63.5 per cent of the total registration. 'To the immigrant child the public elementary school was the first step away from his past, a means by which he could learn to assume the characteristics necessary for the long climb upward' (Thomas, 1954: 253). And by 1911, almost 50 per cent of the students in secondary schools were of foreign-born parentage. In American cities, the major educational challenge and responsibility was the immigrant child. (US Immigration Commission [1911] *Abstracts* 2 1-15).

In the effort to respond to the needs of the immigrant child, it is important to note that no overall programmes were developed to aid any particular immigrant group. Although there was little agreement as to what Americanization was, the schools were committed to Americanize (and to Anglicize) their charges. Ellwood P Cubberley's *Changing Conceptions of Education* (1909), which Lawrence A Cremin characterizes as 'a typical progressive tract of the era', saw the immigrants as 'illiterate, docile, lacking in self-reliance and initiative, and not possessing the Anglo-teutonic conceptions of law, order, and government', and the school's role was (in Cubberley's view) 'to assimilate and amalgamate' (Cremin, 1961: 263).

Those efforts which were made to respond to the needs of immigrant children were improvised, most often directly in response to specific problems; almost never was any attempt made to give the school and its programme a community orientation. The children literally left at the door of the school their language, their cultural identities, and their immigrant sub-community origins. A child's parents had virtually no role in the schools. This New York City experience was not atypical in the way it left the immigrant child to the discretion of the individual superintendent, a principal, or a teacher.

Considering this lack of understanding and co-ordinated effort on behalf of the children of the poor, it is hardly strange that the general malaise of the schools was nowhere more evident than in the pervasive phenomenon of the over-age pupil who was classed under the rubric 'retardation' with all of its negative connotations. The Immigration Commission of 1911 found that the percentage of retardation for the New York City elementary school pupils was 36.4 per cent with the maximum retardation (48.8 per cent) in the fifth grade. The Commission observed:

> . . . thus in the third grade the pupils range in age from five to 18 years. In similar manner pupils of the age of 14 years are found in every grade from the first of the elementary schools to the last of the high schools. It will, however, be noted that in spite of this divergence the great body of the pupils of a given grade are of certain definite ages, the older and younger pupils being in each case much less numerically represented. It may, therefore, be assumed that there is an appropriate age for each grade. This assumption is the cardinal point in current educational discussion in regard to retardation. If it were assumed that there is a normal age for each grade, then the pupils can be divided into two classes — those who are of normal age or less and those who are above the normal age. The latter or overage pupils, are designated as 'retarded'. (United States Immigration Commission, 1911: 32 608-9)

At best, it is a dismal picture whose poignant and evocative pathos is etched in the faces of the children imprisoned in the cheerless classrooms of the era. It could have been otherwise: in the lower East Side of New York City the efforts of District School Superintendent, Julia Richman, at the turn of the century, pointed to the more rewarding directions of community awareness, of building on the cultural strengths which the child brought to the school; and the near quarter-century tenure (1934-57) of Leonard Covello at Benjamin Franklin High School in New York City's East Harlem, dramatically underlined the successes of the community-centred school. But Julia Richman and Leonard Covello were the exceptions, not the rule; and it is no coincidence that they came out of the emerging Jewish and Italian sub-communities, for these very identities help explain their responsiveness to the immigrant child.

Puerto Rican children in the schools: the early years

It is in the perspectives of these earlier experiences that the educational failures of the Puerto Rican child are to be viewed and understood. Committed to policies of Americanization, the schools neglected the cultural heritage of the Puerto Rican child, rejected his ancestral language, and generally ignored his parents and community. And these policies were in keeping with the traditional practices of the schools.

The Puerto Rican community in New York City is the largest on the mainland, and its experience would be essentially typical of other mainland urban communities. As early as 1938, the difficulties of the Puerto Rican child in the New York City schools are graphically (if passingly) noted:

> Many Puerto Rican children who enter the public schools in New York speak
> or understand little English. The children who are transferred from schools in
> Puerto Rico to those in New York are usually put back in their classes so that
> they are with children who are two or three years younger than they are.
> Americans who are teaching Puerto Rican children express the opinion that
> these children have had less training in discipline and in group cooperation
> than American children. Lacking the timidity of many of the children in this
> country, they sometimes act in an unrestrained and impulsive manner. One
> large agency in the settlement, which has dealt with Puerto Rican children for
> many years, reported that under proper conditions Puerto Rican children are
> responsive, easily managed, and affectionate. In contrast to this, another large
> institution said that for some reason which they could not explain the Puerto
> Rican children were more destructive than any group of children with whom
> they had had contact. All the evidence obtainable shows the relation of
> unsatisfactory home conditions to difficulties at school. During the past few
> years the desperate economic condition of these families has caused them to
> move so frequently that it has often been difficult to locate the children when
> they did not attend school. (Chenault, 1938: 146)

In December, 1946, Dr Paul Kennedy, then President of the New York
City Association of Assistant Superintendents, appointed a committee 'to
study and report on the educational adjustments made necessary by the
addition of the 400,000 Puerto Ricans who have lately become residents
of this city'. The surprisingly comprehensive report prepared by this
committee considered native backgrounds; migration to the mainland;
problems of assimilation; the education of the Puerto Rican pupil; and
made a number of recommendations. That the report was anchored in the
past is evident in its caution that 'Although the Puerto Rican is an
American citizen, the adjustment he must make in this city is like that of
immigrants to this country from a foreign land'. The report counted
'13,914 pupils enrolled in the public elementary and junior high schools
of the city who originally came from Puerto Rico'; and further grimly
observed:

> there is no doubt but that many pupils coming from Puerto Rico suffer from
> the double handicap of unfamiliarity with the English language and lack of
> previous educational experience, sometimes approaching complete illiteracy.
> Malnutrition and other health deficiencies contribute to the educational
> problem of the schools. The overcrowding at home and the restlessness on the
> street carry over into the school in the form of nervousness, extreme shyness,
> near tantrums, and other behavior characteristics which are the more difficult
> for the teacher to understand because of the language barrier. (New York City
> Board of Education, 1947: 38)

The Committee also undertook the first study of 'reading progress'
among Puerto Rican pupils who were new admissions to the elementary
and junior high schools. It made a series of recommendations, chief among
which was the establishment of special classes ('C' classes) for Puerto Rican
children 'for whom at least a year's time is needed for preliminary instruction and language work before they are ready for complete assimilation in
the regular program'. Although the report was generally neglected, it
represented the first systematic study undertaken on the mainland to call

attention to the needs of Puerto Rican children.

Attention has been called to J J Osuna's *Report on Visits to New York City Schools* in 1948. In 1951, a Mayor's Committee on Puerto Rican Affairs in New York City was convened and considered the needs of Puerto Rican pupils; and in 1953, Dr Leonard Covello, then Principal of Benjamin Franklin High School in East Harlem, consolidated and articulated into schematic form the various proposals which had been made up to that time to deal with the needs of Puerto Rican children in the schools.

Finally, in 1953, the New York City Board of Education presented in booklet form the results of a study initiated by its Division of Curriculum Development. This brief report indicated a new awareness of the importance of using Spanish in instructing Puerto Rican children, of the need for knowledge of Puerto Rican cultural backgrounds, and of the need for bilingual teachers. But it equally made clear the critical need for a fully developed educational programme for Puerto Rican children; and it served as a prologue to *The Puerto Rican Study* (New York City Board of Education, 1959) which was initiated in 1953.

The Puerto Rican Study

The Puerto Rican Study was, for its time, one of the most generously funded educational studies ever undertaken. The Fund for the Advancement of Education provided a grant-in-aid of $500,000 and 'contributions equivalent in amounts authorized by the Board of Education made the study a vital operation in the school system' (Foreword). It was not completed until 1957, and it was finally published in April 1959. It is, unquestionably, the fullest study ever made of the Puerto Rican educational experience on the mainland; and, in a broader sense, it remains one of the most comprehensive statements yet made, not only of the Puerto Rican school experience, but of the educational experience of the non-English-speaking minority child in the American school. As such it is an invaluable document in American educational historiography, touching on all the contemporary issues which the 1960s and 1970s have highlighted — ethnicity, the minority child, the contexts of poverty, and the educational needs of the 'disadvantaged' child. It is strange that, in the proliferating literature on the minority child and the schools, *The Puerto Rican Study* has been neglected. This may be due to its appearance before the advent of the Johnsonian anti-poverty programmes of the 1960s with their educational components, and to the inevitable fate of sponsored reports whose implementation and evaluation are seldom realized or are avoided for a variety of reasons.

The Puerto Rican Study's objectives are clearly stated:

> In a narrow sense, *The Puerto Rican Study* was a four-year inquiry into the education and adjustment of Puerto Rican pupils in the public schools of the City of New York. In a broader sense, it was a major effort of the school authorities to establish on a sound basis a city-wide program for the continuing

improvement of the educational opportunities of all non-English-speaking pupils in the public schools.

While the *Study* was focused on the public schools in New York City, it was planned and conducted in the belief that the findings might be useful to all schools, public and private, that are trying to serve children from a Spanish-language culture. As the *Study* developed, it seemed apparent that it might have values, direct or indirect, wherever children are being taught English as a second language. (New York Board of Education, 1959: 1)

It sought answers to the following specific problems: (1) What are the most effective methods for teaching English as a second language to newly-arrived Puerto Rican pupils? (2) What are the most effective techniques whereby the school can promote a more rapid and more effective adjustment of Puerto Rican parents and children to the community and of the community to them?

As the *Study* progressed, its staff developed two series of related curriculum bulletins — *Resource Units* organized around themes and designed for all pupils, and a *Language Guide Series* which provided the content and methods for adapting the instruction to the needs of the pupils learning English (the *Study* lists the *Units* and *Series*). The *Study* also furnished a detailed description of the Puerto Rican children; devised a scale to rate English-speaking ability; and constructed a detailed programme for the in-service education of teachers (Chapter 17).

The recommendations of The Puerto Rican Study

The *Study's* recommendations are both a blueprint and design for effectively meeting the needs of Puerto Rican children, and they cover all those inter-related facets of the experience of the minority child which, if neglected, impede social growth and cognitive achievement. Simply listed (without the capsuled rationales which accompany them), they represent a skeletal construct as meaningful today as when they were formulated.

1. Accept *The Puerto Rican Study*, not as something finished, but as the first stage of a larger, city-wide, ever improving programme for the education and assimilation of non-English-speaking children.
2. Take a new look at the philosophy governing the education of the non-English-speaking children in New York City schools.
3. Recognize that whatever is done for the non-English-speaking child, is, in the long run, done for all the children.
4. Use the annual school census as a basic technique in planning the continuing adaptation of the schools to the needs of the non-English-speaking pupils.
5. Recognize the heterogeneity of the non-English-speaking pupils.
6. Formulate a uniform policy for the reception, screening, placement, and periodic assessment of non-English-speaking pupils.
7. Keep policies governing the grouping of non-English-speaking pupils flexible. Place the emphasis upon serving the needs of the individual pupil.

8. Place special emphasis on reducing the backlog of retarded language learners.

9. Recognize 'English as a second language' or 'the teaching of non-English-speaking children' as an area of specialization that cuts across many subject areas.

10. Use the curricular materials developed by *The Puerto Rican Study* to achieve unity of purpose and practice in teaching non-English-speaking pupils.

11. Capitalize on the creative talent of teachers in finding ways and means of supplementing and of improving the programme for teaching non-English-speaking pupils.

12. Recognize and define the school's responsibility to assist, counsel, and co-operate with the parents of non-English-speaking pupils in all matters pertaining to the child's welfare.

13. Take a new look at the school's opportunity to accelerate the adjustment of Puerto Rican children and their parents through advice and counsel to parents on problems normally considered to be outside the conventional functions of the school.

14. Staff the schools to do the job: to help the new arrival to make good adjustment to school and community; to help the non-English-speaking child to learn English and to find his way successfully into the mainstream of the school's programme.

15. Staff the proper agencies of the Board of Education to maintain a continuing programme for the development and improvement of curricular materials and other aids to the teaching of non-English-speaking pupils.

16. Staff, also, the proper agencies of the Board of Education, and set in motion the processes to maintain a continuing assessment or evaluation of techniques, practices and proposals.

17. Take a new hard look at the psychological services provided for non-English-speaking children, especially for Puerto Rican children.

18. Through every means available, make it clear that the education of the non-English-speaking children and their integration in an ever-changing school population is the responsibility of every member of the school staff.

19. Maintain, improve, and possibly expand the programme of in-service preparation initiated through *The Puerto Rican Study* for training special staff to assist in accelerating the programme for non-English-speaking children.

20. In co-operation with the colleges and universities of metropolitan New York, create a dynamic programme to achieve unity of purpose and more adequate co-ordination of effort in the education of teachers and of other workers for accelerating the programme in the schools.

21. Use the varied opportunities available to develop an ever-improving co-operation between the Department of Education in Puerto Rico and the Board of Education in New York City.

22. In co-operation with the responsible representatives of the government of the State of New York, continue to explore the mutual interests and responsibility of the city and the state for the education and adjustment of non-English-speaking children and youth.
23. Think of the City of New York and the Commonwealth of Puerto Rico as partners in a great enterprise.

No full scale implementation of *The Puerto Rican Study* was attempted. Much of what the *Study* recommended appears again in the New York City Board of Education pamphlet *Educating Students for whom English is a Second Language: Programs, Activities, and Services* (1965), a review of subsequent programmes which emphasized teacher training, particularly the exchange of teachers between New York and Puerto Rico. All kinds of reasons can be advanced for the failure to implement *The Puerto Rican Study*, and these might include teacher and Board of Education resistance; the struggles which were to ensue over community participation and decentralization; the rapidly politicizing community/school relations with their attendant ideological quarrels; the absence of qualified personnel; and the accelerating growth of the Puerto Rican community which simply overwhelmed many of the schools. Whatever the reasons (and no one reason or a combination of reasons provides an acceptable explanation), the *Study* was more than a million dollar white elephant. Its achievements (however incompletely implemented) included the following.

1. It developed two series of related curriculum bulletins — *Resource Units* and *Language Guides* — for use in teaching English to non-English speaking pupils. These are keyed to New York City courses of study but may be easily adapted to courses of study in other school systems. They are adapted to the maturity level of children, grade by grade in the elementary school, and in terms of need for special instruction in English during the early secondary school years.
2. It developed a guide for teaching science — resource units and sample lessons — to Puerto Rican pupils who are still trying to learn English; and a guide for teaching occupations to teenage Puerto Rican pupils in high school who wish to qualify for occupational employment.
3. It developed a battery of tests, measures, and data-gathering techniques for use with Puerto Rican pupils in the mainland schools. Among these were a tape-recorded test for measuring the ability of non-English-speaking pupils to understand spoken English, a scale for rating ability to speak English, a bilingual test of arithmetic, and a process for screening new arrivals and for following their progress through periodic reviews.
4. Through an educational-ethnic-social survey of several thousand children in New York City elementary and junior high schools, it obtained a profile of the characteristics of pupils of Puerto Rican background in relation to other pupils in the same grades and schools.

5. Through testing thousands of pupils, it obtained estimates of the potential abilities as well as of the present performance of Puerto Rican pupils in relation to their peers, ie other pupils of the same age and grade in the same schools.

6. Through a variety of studies of individual children from kindergarten through the tenth grade or second year of high school, it gained revealing information concerning the problems of Puerto Rican children in achieving cultural-educational-social adjustment in New York City schools.

7. Through a survey of the relations of schools to Puerto Rican parents, it defined the problems confronting the schools, formulated criteria for determining the schools' role, and made some estimate of the cost in terms of personnel needed to help facilitate or accelerate the cultural adjustment of Puerto Rican parents.

8. Through analysis of previously established positions and of new positions established on an experimental basis it developed criteria for determining the necessity for special staff in schools to enable them to serve the needs of Puerto Rican and foreign-born or non-English-speaking children.

9. Through two years of experimentation with different procedures, it developed proposals for an in-service programme to reach all teachers required to teach non-English-speaking pupils.

10. Through participation in three summer workshops sponsored in part by the Board of Education of the City of New York at the University of Puerto Rico, it formulated proposals for the development of the annual workshop as a continuing means of promoting better mutual understanding and co-operation between the school system of New York City and the school system of Puerto Rico.

11. Through the surveys and testing of thousands of children, it devised a plan for obtaining a uniform census of all Puerto Rican and foreign-born children in the schools. Administration of census, through consecutive years, will give the Board of Education data for predicting with a high degree of accuracy pending changes in the ethnic composition of pupil population by school, school district, school level, borough and city.

12. Through its scale for rating ability to speak English, it provided a basis, used by the Commissioner of Education of the State of New York in defining non-English-speaking pupils, for the distribution of additional state aid authorized by law.

In themselves, these achievements (and the recommendations) were to become the measuring criteria against which continuing needs were to be delineated.

The failure to implement *The Puerto Rican Study* led to great agitation and continuing demands from the Puerto Rican community. The first Citywide Conference of the Puerto Rican Community (April 1967) in its published proceedings (New York City Office of the Mayor, 1968) presented recommendations for the education of Puerto Rican children, essentially a repetition of those made by *The Puerto Rican Study*. And in 1968, Aspira (an organization founded in 1961 by the Puerto Rican Forum to promote higher education for Puerto Ricans) convened a national conference of Puerto Ricans, Mexican Americans, and educators on 'The special educational needs of urban Puerto youth'. The conference's published report (Aspira, 1968), in its recommendations, reiterated most of those of *The Puerto Rican Study*. The Aspira conference also commissioned a report on Puerto Ricans and the public schools (Margolis, 1968), which chronicles visits to 16 schools in seven cities and 'makes no explicit recommendations. Its purpose is to put the problem in sharper focus and on wider display, not to promote any single set of solutions.' Margolis' report is a devastating indictment of those schools which neglected Puerto Rican children, and of programmes which were largely encrusted with all the bitter abuses of the past: it appears inconceivable that the practices he describes could have been occurring a decade after the publication of *The Puerto Rican Study*.

Beyond The Puerto Rican Study: the Bilingual Education Act

Much of the effort on behalf of the educational needs of Puerto Rican children in the 1960s must be viewed and understood in the light of the massive federal interventions in education largely initiated by the enactment of the Elementary and Secondary Education Act of 1965, and its subsequent amendments (United States Congress, 1965).

The passage by the Congress in 1968 of the Bilingual Education Act (United States Congress, 1968) reaffirmed and strengthened many of the recommendations of *The Puerto Rican Study* even though the *Study* had largely fallen into undeserved neglect. The struggle for a national bilingual education act represented a continuing fight against the rejection of the use of native languages in the instruction of non-English-speaking children. The successful enactment of the Bilingual Education Act represented a movement away from the 'ethnocentric illusion' in the United States that for a child born there English is not a foreign language, and hence that all instruction in schools must be through the medium of English. More significantly, the Act was a national manifesto for cultural pluralism and bicultural education, and in this sense may prove the most socially significant educational legislation yet enacted.

The Act recognizes 'the special education needs of the large numbers of children of limited English-speaking ability in the United States', and declared:

> it to be the policy of the United States to provide financial assistance to local educational agencies to develop and carry out new and imaginative elementary and secondary school programs designed to meet these special educational needs.

The main priorities of the Act are the provision of equal educational opportunities for non-English-speaking children; the strengthening of educational programmes for bilingual children; and the promotion of bilingualism among all students. A great number of programmes have come into being as a result of the Act, and although the programmes are of differing (and in some instances of dubious) quality, they affirm the practicability of meeting the needs of the non-English-speaking child.

Amendments to the Bilingual Education Act in 1974 strengthened bilingual-bicultural programmes, and clarified the federal role and commitment to bilingual education, despite continuing controversy:

> The 1974 Bilingual Education Act represented the Federal response to the educational needs of limited English-speaking children. The researcher found that the 1974 Act resolved many philosophical issues concerning the Federal role in bilingual-bicultural education. Those resolutions permit a determination whether the Act itself constituted a revolution, a reaction or a reform of past practices.
>
> A continuing Federal role in assisting states and localities in meeting the needs of limited English-speaking students was contained within the 1974 Act. Although the Federal government was not committed by the legislation to provide direct services to all eligible students, it did expand the number of local classroom projects and institute a major new Federal role in providing the resources — teachers, paraprofessionals, curricula, research — to enable localities and states to provide those services.
>
> The 1974 Act diluted the transitional limitations of the previous 1968 law, permitting bilingual-bicultural education programs to be funded through high schools, although the emphasis remained on elementary school instruction. The Act also made a full bilingual-bicultural approach the likely outcome in all instances, and specifically denied the sufficiency of an English-as-a-second-language program. All of these resolutions of issues concerning bilingual-bicultural education contributed to understanding the nature and character of the Act. (Schneider, 1976: 161-2)

Bilingual programmes in American schools exist within the mandated provisions of federal legislation: they are truly the progeny of the responses of Congress to perceived needs.

The realities of programme implementation

In the last analysis, it is the programme which addresses itself to the educational needs of the Puerto Rican child which must be evaluated with recommendations made for its continuing improvement. The evaluation of a particular programme for Puerto Rican children in a large urban school district and the recommendations which were made for its improvement and expansion are, in themselves, instructive: they delineate the contemporary educational experience for the Puerto Rican child, and they point the way to meet the needs.

The recommendations which are subjoined derive from a study and evaluation of the educational programmes for Puerto Rican students under way in the Jersey City (NJ) school district in 1971-72. Over 5000 Puerto

Rican pupils (out of a total school register of some 38,000) were in the city's schools. The recommendations provide a profile of contemporary Puerto Rican educational experience (practice that lends itself to improvement), generally encountered on the mainland. Most of the recommendations have been implemented across the 1970s.

Programme recommendations

Elementary level

1. The basic recommendation to be made for the elementary schools involves the establishment of functional bilingual programmes wherever there are Puerto Rican students in attendance. The basic premise of bilingual education involves the use of Spanish to provide instruction in most curriculum areas when English is not the mother tongue of the children and when there is insufficient fluency in English to profit from school instruction in that language. Thus, for example, instruction in basic curriculum areas such as mathematics, social studies, etc would be in Spanish. At the same time that instruction is given in the basic content areas in Spanish, an intensive programme in the teaching of English as a second language must be conducted. As children develop greater fluency in English, additional instruction in the basic curriculum areas should be given in English. This approach would assist children in becoming equally fluent in both Spanish and English, and at the same time it would also assist children to develop the appropriate knowledges and skills in curriculum areas other than Spanish and English. Bilingual education should also provide for the teaching of Spanish as a second language for those children who are dominant in English. Such programmes should begin in September 1972.

   At the present time in the bilingual classes in the Jersey City schools, this approach is not in widespread use. Teachers who speak Spanish are used for the most part to interpret what the English speaking teacher has said, and (as noted above) often at the same time, a practice resulting in considerable confusion. In addition, the practice of assigning two teachers to a room, one of whom functions as an interpreter, represents poor utilization of personnel, both educationally and financially.

2. The bilingual programme recommended by the evaluators would also necessitate the regrouping of participating children more carefully. In addition to using the traditional criteria for grouping in a bilingual education programme, it is necessary to develop parallel classes or sections of children who are dominant in either English or Spanish. In developing bilingual programmes, however, it is essential that priority be given in class assignment to children who are dominant in Spanish, rather than to those dominant in English, because the

greatest immediate need exists for children who are dominant in Spanish and who cannot derive as much educational value as possible from school programmes conducted solely in English.

3. It is recommended that two schools develop complete bilingual programmes beginning with the kindergarten and including each grade in the school. In other schools, bilingual classes should be established as needed.

4. A committee on bilingual education at the elementary school level should be established immediately in order to plan for the development of bilingual programmes in Public Schools Nos 2 and 16, and in other schools of Jersey City where there are large Puerto Rican enrolments. The bilingual education committee will also give attention to the development of a bilingual curriculum encompassing the usual curriculum areas as well as the teaching of English as a second language, the teaching of Spanish as a second language, and the history and culture of Puerto Rico as an integral part of the elementary school curriculum. The present Hispanic Culture Committee is a beginning; but it must deal with a Puerto Rican studies curriculum and only ancillarily with Hispanic cultures in general. Membership on the committee should include parents, teachers, principals, and should also make provision for student input.

5. A city-wide Puerto Rican advisory council composed of parents, high school and college students and community leaders should be established. The advisory council can advise school officials on the needs, aspirations, sentiments and responses of the Puerto Rican community insofar as educational matters are concerned. The existence of a community advisory council will assist in making public schools with large numbers of Puerto Rican students 'community schools', furnishing educational and other much needed services to the Puerto Rican community. Such an advisory council on a city-wide basis will provide much needed community participation in education in Jersey City for the Puerto Rican community.

6. Parochial schools with large numbers of Puerto Rican students should also participate in special programmes funded with federal monies.

7. All communications from school officials to parents should be available in both English and Spanish.

8. Additional Puerto Rican personnel should be recruited for positions at all levels in the public schools including teachers, principals, school secretaries, a curriculum specialist, teacher aides, etc. Special attention should be turned immediately to the employment of a curriculum specialist in bilingual education.

9. At the present time, no city-wide co-ordinating effort involving existing bilingual programmes is available in Jersey City. It is recommended, therefore, that a city-wide office at the level of co-ordinator for bilingual education be established. This office will

have jurisdiction over planning, developing, implementing, supervising and evaluating all bilingual education programmes, programmes in the teaching of English as a second language, and other special service programmes for Puerto Rican elementary school children and high school students. The office would also provide liaison with the Puerto Rican community.

10. Bilingual classes as envisaged in recommendation 1 should also be made available in the summer of 1972.

11. It is recommended that provision be made for the establishment of a continuing consultancy in the implementation of the recommendations contained in this report. Consultants would work with school officials and members of the Puerto Rican community in the implementation of the recommendations and would assist in the development of other programmes and special services that may be needed by the children of the Puerto Rican community.

12. Parent education programmes conducted in both Spanish and English should be developed for the Puerto Rican community.

13. An in-service programme for teachers and other school personnel should be developed as soon as possible. Current and past efforts in Jersey City in the areas of in-service courses include the offering of a course in 'Teaching English as a second language' that was to be given in the 1970-71 school year, beginning in November 1970, and a request to develop and finance an 'In-service course involving philosophy, approaches and methodology of bilingual education', to be given during the 1971-72 school year. In-service efforts should be expanded, and should include both professionals ' participating directly in bilingual programmes or English as a second language programmes as well as other professionals in the Jersey City public schools who may not be participating in special programmes for Puerto Rican children but who do work with Puerto Rican children in regular classes. Such an extensive in-service programme might be developed and offered during the regular school year, or might be given as a special summer institute for participating personnel.

14. Greater numbers of Puerto Rican student teachers should be recruited from Jersey City State College. An expanded student-teaching practicum drawn from the cadres of Puerto Rican students at Jersey City State College represents an important source for recruiting larger numbers of Puerto Rican personnel for employment in the Jersey City public schools.

15. A continuing and expanded liaison between the Jersey City public schools and Jersey City State College is recommended. Here, an important beginning and model (Title VII, at School No 16) has been provided by Professor Bloom and Jersey City State College personnel.

Secondary level

1. The city-wide Community Advisory Council described in recommendations for elementary schools should also turn its attention to secondary education and make recommendations relevant to the educational needs of Puerto Rican high school students in Jersey City.

2. A testing and identification programme should be developed at the secondary level. Such a programme would attempt to identify Puerto Rican students in need of intensive instruction in English as a second language or in other important school subjects such as reading.

3. A special committee to deal with secondary education for Puerto Rican students should be established, with the membership drawn from teachers, principals, guidance personnel and other school professionals; and including parents and students from the Puerto Rican community. The committee should give special attention to the current basic offerings: industrial arts, college preparatory, business and general studies. It should consider ways of increasing the holding power of the secondary schools so that greater numbers of Puerto Rican students remain in high school and graduate.

4. Special work-study programmes for Puerto Rican students might be developed in connection with the basic offerings now available. Such work-study programmes could become a very significant phase of the industrial arts and business education programmes, and should, consequently, carry high school credit.

5. An immediate attempt should be made to increase the number of Puerto Rican students in the college preparatory programme. This can be done by teachers, guidance personnel and administrators. More information about current high school programmes should be made available, and students should become familiar with the implications of selecting specific programmes and the out-of-school consequences of enrolment in any given programme. In addition, talent-search programmes might be initiated to increase the number of Puerto Rican students entering college.

6. Secondary school teachers should participate in in-service programmes dealing with the education of Puerto Rican students.

7. It is recommended that high school students having little fluency in English be given basic instruction in Spanish in the various classes required in the four curricula. Instruction in Spanish would be in addition to intensive instruction in reading, writing and speaking English as a second language. When high school students have achieved a sufficient degree of fluency in English, they may then receive all or most of their instruction in English. Bilingual education at the high school level at the present time is essential, and it is especially important when large numbers of students are dominant in Spanish rather than in English. It should be remembered that it

was not possible to secure from school officials data concerning the number of Puerto Rican high school students dominant primarily in Spanish.

8. At present, a secondary school curriculum committee is working on a course of study in Puerto Rican history. The work of this committee should be accelerated and a course of study in Puerto Rican history and culture should be developed as rapidly as possible. The committee might then turn its attention to the development of a course of study dealing with the Puerto Rican experience on the mainland. At present, there are no student members of this committee. Students should be a significant and contributing part of this committee. Indeed, greater participation by high school students in the decisions affecting their school careers is vital, and it becomes especially crucial when there are large numbers of students dropping out of high school programmes as is true for many Puerto Rican students.

9. The high schools should make available to all high school students without cost all special examinations such as the National Education Development Tests or the College Boards. Such examinations now require the payment of fees by candidates taking them. There may be many Puerto Rican and other students unable to take the examinations which require the payment of fees because of inability to afford the funds required.

10. The continuing consultancy referred to in recommendations for elementary schools should encompass secondary education as well as elementary education.

11. It is recommended that an experimental programme involving independent study be instituted for those students who are considering leaving high school before graduation. This programme would provide the opportunity for independent study under supervision, for which credit leading to a high school diploma would be given. Such a programme would also provide for attendance in organized classes in the high schools, especially where remedial or advanced programmes are required. Students would participate in developing their programmes. Such supervised independent study programmes could be related to jobs which students leaving high school before graduation may have secured.

12. It is recommended that additional Puerto Rican personnel be recruited for employment in Jersey City secondary schools. The two Puerto Rican guidance counsellors at Ferris High School are an important beginning.

These recommendations were, essentially, reaffirmations of the value of those made years earlier in *The Puerto Rican Study*. One cannot help but wonder how different educational opportunity for Puerto Rican children might have been had *The Puerto Rican Study* been implemented. In its cautions and admonitions, *The Puerto Rican Study* was prophetic:

A study, however good, never solves problems. At best, it finds solutions that will work. To translate proposed measures into practice is the greater task. At the very best it will take three to five years to translate the proposals of *The Puerto Rican Study* into an effective program . . . . The real question is, how rapidly can the school system move? . . . There are thousands of Puerto Rican children in New York City schools who have been here two, three, four or more years and are still rated as language learners. The task is twofold — to salvage as many as possible of those currently retarded, and to reduce the numbers that thus far have been added annually to the list. The time to begin is now — a year gone from a child's life is gone forever. (New York City Board of Education, 1959: 237)

References

Aspira (1968) *Hemos Trabajado Bien* Aspira: New York

Banks, J A (1973) *Teaching Ethnic Studies: Concepts and Strategies* Council for the Social Studies: Washington DC

Centro de Estudios Puertorriqueños (1979) *Labor Migration under Capitalism: The Puerto Rican Experience* Monthly Review Press: New York

Chenault, L R (1938) *The Puerto Rican Migrant in New York City* Columbia University Press: New York

Cordasco, F (1973) The children of immigrants in schools: historical analogues of educational deprivation *Journal of Negro Education* **42** 3: 44-53

Cordasco, F (1973) Teaching the Puerto Rican experience *in* Banks (1973)

Cordasco, F (1975) Spanish-speaking children in American schools *International Migration Review* **9** 3: 379-82

Cordasco, F (1976) *Bilingual Schooling in the United States* McGraw-Hill: New York

Cordasco, F (1978) Bilingual and bicultural education in American schools: a bibliography of selected references *Bulletin of Bibliography* **35** 2: 53-72

Cordasco, F and Bernstein, G (1979) *Bilingual Education in American Schools: A Guide to Information Sources* Gale Research Company: Detroit, Mich

Cordasco, F and Bucchioni, E eds (1972) *The Puerto Rican Community and its Children on the Mainland* Scarecrow Press: Metuchen, NJ

Cordasco, F and Covello, L (1968) *Studies of Puerto Rican Children in American Schools: A Preliminary Bibliography* Migration Division, Commonwealth of Puerto Rico: New York

Covello, F (1953) *Recommendations Concerning Puerto Rican Pupils in our Public Schools* Benjamin Franklin High School: New York

Covello, L (1967) *The Social Background of the Italo-American School Child* E J Brill: Leiden

Cremin, L A (1961) *The Transformation of the School* Alfred Knopf: New York

Cubberley, E P (1909) *Changing Conceptions of Education* Houghton Mifflin: Boston, Mass

Fitzpatrick, J (1971) *Puerto Rican Americans: The Meaning of Migration to the Mainland* Prentice-Hall: Englewood Cliffs, NJ

Gaarder, A B (1977) *Bilingual Schooling and the Survival of Spanish in the United States* Newbury House: Rowley, Mass

Hidalgo, H (1971) *The Puerto Ricans of Newark, New Jersey* Aspira: Newark, NJ

Kloss, H (1977) *The American Bilingual Tradition* Newbury House: Rowley, Mass

Margolis, R J (1968) *The Losers: A Report on Puerto Ricans and the Public Schools* Aspira: New York

Mayor's Committee on Puerto Rican Affairs in New York City (1951) *Puerto Rican Pupils in American Schools* Office of the Mayor: New York

Monserrat, J (1961) Community planning for Puerto Rican integration in the United States *in* Cordasco and Bucchioni (1972)

New York City Board of Education (1947) *A Program of Education for Puerto Ricans in New York City* Board of Education: New York

New York City Board of Education (1953) *Teaching Children of Puerto Rican Background in New York City Schools* Board of Education: New York

New York City Board of Education (1959) *The Puerto Rican Study: A Report on the Education and Adjustment of Puerto Rican Pupils in the Public Schools of the City of New York* Board of Education: New York

New York City Board of Education (1965) *Educating Students for whom English is a Second Language: Programs, Activities, and Services* Board of Education: New York

New York City Office of the Mayor (1968) *Puerto Ricans Confront Problems of the Complex Urban Society* Office of the Mayor: New York

Osuna, J J (1948) Report on visits to New York City schools *in* Cordasco and Bucchioni (1972)

Palante: *Young Lords' Party* (1971) McGraw-Hill: New York

Perez, D (1971) The chains that have been taken off slaves' bodies are put back on their minds *in* Palante (1971)

Richman, J (1910) The social needs of the public schools *Forum* 43 2: 161-9

Schneider, S G (1976) *Revolution, Reaction or Reform: The 1974 Bilingual Education Act* Las Americas: New York

Silén, J A (1971) *The Puerto Rican People: A Story of Oppression and Resistance* Monthly Review Press: New York

Thomas, A M (1954) American education and the immigrant *Teachers College Record* 55 2: 253-67

United States Congress (1965) 20 USC 241a; PL 89-10

United States Congress (1968) 20 USC 88b; PL 90-247

United States Immigration Commission (1911) *Report of the Immigration Commission* (41 vols) Government Printing Office: Washington DC

Vazquez Calzada, J (1979) Demographic aspects of migration *in* Centro de Estudios Puertorriqueños (1979)

Wagenheim, K (1975) *A Survey of Puerto Ricans on the US Mainland in the 1970s* Praeger: New York

12. Language policies in West and East Africa

Carew Treffgarne

Summary: Language policies in West Africa are contrasted with the East African region in which Swahili plays a unique role as the national language in Tanzania, Kenya and Uganda, and is used alongside English for some official purposes. In the light of the complex, multilingual and multi-ethnic situation in most developing African nations, the choice of local languages identified for language policy tends to be a compromise solution in reaction to the logistical and economic impossibility of providing education in every mother tongue. Yet even the compromise solution of choosing major ethnic languages, which serve as first or second languages of wider communication, is fraught with problems. In particular, current policies to introduce or consolidate the place of major African languages in education are hampered by the colonial language legacy, since English, French or Portuguese remains the target language of the educational system. This creates an imbalance in language policy with the status and function of the official language having a detrimental effect on current attempts to make local languages play a more dynamic role in curriculum development. It is argued that the successful integration of local languages into the educational system depends ultimately on greater government commitment to using these languages in areas of national life still monopolized by the official language.

The colonial language policy legacy

Language policy in the West African and East African regions differs in one major respect — namely, the absence in West Africa of a significant language of regional intercommunication like Swahili, whose wide currency in administration, the army, the police force and commerce *prior to* independence has enabled it to play a unique role in national life in Tanzania, Kenya, and more recently, in Uganda.* The precise role of Swahili in the government of these countries varies according to the particular combination of political, economic, social, cultural, linguistic and religious factors which determine language policy. However, a second difference can be discerned between those countries which formed part of

---

* This is documented in the following references: Wright (1965); Whiteley (1968, 1969); Brumfit (1971); Abdulaziz (1971); O'Barr (1976); Mhina (1979); Gorman (1974); Hopkins (1977); Mazrui (1979).

French West Africa (AOF), and Commonwealth countries in East and West Africa. Different emphases in colonial educational policies have had significant implications for the current state of the development of African languages, in both education and administration.

Indeed language planning in Francophone West Africa is in its infancy, compared to the well-established tradition in former British colonies of using local languages in primary education. The freedom accorded to missionaries in British territories to use local languages for educational as well as religious purposes tended to result in fairly arbitrary decisions on language choice and standardization (for examples see Epronti and Denteh, 1969; Itebete, 1974). However, their activities helped to establish official recognition for the pedagogical principle of mother tongue education. Thus, by the 1920s, influential bodies such as the Phelps-Stokes Commissions on Education in West Africa (1920-21) and East Africa (1924) were identifying the complexity of language policy in multi-ethnic and multilingual areas as necessitating education in the 'native language or dialect' at the lower stages of elementary school, with an African lingua franca where possible at middle level, and the 'Language of the European nation in control', at the upper level. In contrast, in French territories (apart from a brief experiment initiated by Jean Dard in 1818 at the Ecole Mutuelle, St Louis du Senegal), colonial education was conducted entirely through the medium of the French language, which was glorified as the embodiment of civilization and culture. The propagation of the sociopolitical concept of 'La Francophonie' during the colonial *mission civilisatrice* thus served to underline the prestige and status surrounding the unifying role of French as an international language. The widening of this concept during the 1970s to complement the teaching of French by teaching major local languages can be seen as a nationalistic reaction to linguistic imperialism.

Labels like Anglophone or Francophone, applied to countries where English or French serve as official languages, can give a misleading impression about the *actual* currency of these languages, which remains limited to a minority of the population in most developing African nations. The status of local languages, whether minor or major, is affected decisively in both West and East Africa by the presence and role of the former colonial language. Through its high prestige as official language of government and commerce and as target language of the educational system, this colonial language, which is in fact a minority language, continues to exert a significant influence on attitudes and commitment towards making local languages a dynamic part of the school curriculum.

Minority languages as official languages

The curious situation in which a minority non-African language still serves as the official language of government in most West and East African countries (or has been retained alongside Swahili, as in the cases of

Tanzania and Kenya), arose initially from its presumed neutral, unifying role, in contrast to the potentially divisive option of choosing one of several local contenders with strong ethnic connotations. National boundaries were fixed by the colonial powers, in many cases irrespective of traditional ethnic and cultural divisions. Consequently, on independence, the former colonial language became a means of ensuring continuity, and enhancing national unity.

Such paradoxes in the evolution of language policy abound, mainly because of the many functions that an international language like English and French can embody. In most African nations, the political expediency of using English or French has tended to outweigh any reactions against the European language seen as the symbol of the political, economic and cultural domination of the former European power. Thus, both the French and English languages have served as the medium for the growth of African nationalist movements, serving in the process to nurture wider language loyalties than those of the ethnic group or community. In Guinea-Bissau, Angola and Mozambique, Portuguese, which was considered as the language of oppression and exploitation during the liberation struggles of the 1960s and early 1970s, has subsequently come to be perceived by the ruling political parties (the PAIGC, MPLA and FRELIMO, respectively) as the only viable language of national unity in the complex multi-ethnic countries which they govern.

The continuing dominant role of the former colonial language in government is also enhanced by its utility in promoting international political, economic, social and educational contact. In consequence, the status and function of English, French and Portuguese, in relation to the more traditional languages of each West African or East African nation, emerge as fundamental variables in language policy formulation. So long as English, French or Portuguese continues to serve as the official language, and hence the target language of the educational system, concern to revitalize the traditional cultural heritage by improving, or introducing, the teaching of local languages may be given second priority.

Current strategies in language policy implementation

The imbalance in favour of English, French, or Portuguese had led to fluctuations in policy over this crucial relationship between a European language, with its modernizing, international connotations, and languages embodying traditional cultures and values. During the 1960s, policy in Senegal, Mali, Niger, the Upper Volta, the Ivory Coast, Togo and Benin was directed towards a total immersion primary cycle in French, which was matched in Sierra Leone, Liberia, the Gambia and parts of northern Nigeria by a 'straight for English', or 'maximum exposure to English' strategy. More dominant in Nigeria, Ghana, Uganda and Kenya have been policies advocating the 'bridging' role of local languages, on the one hand between home and school, and, on the other, to facilitate the learning of the official language. It is this second strategy which is currently emerging as the most popular alternative, following the shift in policy that occurred in many African states in the 1970s in a renewed attempt to establish greater cultural authenticity in the formal educational system.

The third type of response to the primary objective of teaching the official language questions the validity of the second, in which the local language generally serves as the medium of instruction for the first three years of primary school, prior to being replaced as a teaching medium by the official language. Renewed attempts to meet targets for universal primary education in many developing nations have drawn attention to the need to establish *permanent* literacy and numeracy skills in at least one language in primary schooling, which, for most students, will be all they receive. Illustrations of this third strategy, in which a local language serves as the medium throughout the primary cycle, are to be found in Guinea, Tanzania, and in some schools in the Oyo, Ogun and Ondo States of western Nigeria. Guinea started its ambitious policy of developing eight national languages (Pulaar, Malinke, Soussou, Kissi, Coniagui, Guerze, Toma and Basari) earlier than the other former French territories, as part of its ideological stand in opposition to the perpetuation of French political, cultural and economic influence in its external and internal affairs. In Tanzania, the promotion of Swahili, as one of the two official languages and as the sole national language, is reflected by its role as sole primary medium. However, although this policy disregards the 134 other languages spoken as home languages by an estimated 90 per cent of the population (Whiteley, 1971a: 147; Abdulaziz, 1971: 171; Polomé, 1975: 35), the wide diffusion of Swahili as a lingua franca and its polyethnic connotations (Whiteley, 1971a; Arens, 1975) have helped to make this acceptable. In Nigeria, the Ife project has led to children studying in desig-nated Yoruba-medium primary schools doing as well in the primary school leaving certificate and secondary school entrance examinations as their counterparts in three-year Yoruba-medium/three-year English-medium schools (Afolayan, 1976; Fafunwa, 1978). These comparatively successful examination results have helped to alleviate initial fears among parents that their children's performance in a predominantly English-medium system would suffer from the extension of teaching through the medium of their home language.

It has to be emphasized that, in each of these three examples, it is the dominant language of the area which serves as the medium (which may also enjoy wide currency as a second language), and that either English or French remains on the curriculum as a subject prior to becoming the medium of instruction at secondary and tertiary levels. In the first instance, some children will therefore be at a disadvantage if they speak a minority language or if their parents have moved into a language zone where their mother tongue is not spoken. The standardized form of the language chosen for teaching purposes may also present a handicap for children speaking more localized varieties of the language at home. For example, the Oyo variety of Yoruba may be difficult for children from some parts of Ogun and Ondo States in western Nigeria; just as the standardized literary form of Swahili may present difficulties for pupils speaking a more colloquial variety of the language. Hemphill (1974: 463) points out that such diglossia creates a learning problem in primary schools in some parts of Kenya. Brann (1975: 213) cites the anomalous situation in the Calabar area of south-east Nigeria, where Annang and Ibibio speakers have to study through the medium of Efik, which is the approved medium of instruction for the beginning of the primary cycle. The standardized form of the language, which has developed through missionary and educational practices, may thus present serious barriers to learning for some sectors of the community.

Passage through the educational system tends to depend unduly on competence in the official language. Although this is to a certain extent inevitable so long as French, English or Portuguese remains the target language, their predominant role in education does not warrant the virtual exclusion of tests in the local language. In most countries in West and East Africa, the examination for selection into secondary schools is conducted solely in the official language — even in countries with long-established policies of using local languages at primary level. In the case of Kenya, the English-medium primary examination consequently exerts a detrimental influence on the status of Swahili (and, by extension, other local languages) in the school curriculum (King, 1974: 125; Mulusa, 1978: 21). For teachers, parents and pupils, the teaching of local languages will continue to have low priority so long as the system of measuring ability reflects the overwhelming importance of competence in the official language.

Apart from the Republic of Guinea, most other African countries where French remains the official language are in the early stages of introducing their major ethnic or regional languages of wider communication into the initial years of primary school. Thus in West Africa, the Malian government is developing four major languages (Bambara, Pulaar, Songhay, Tamasheq); the government of the Upper Volta has identified three major languages (Moore, Dagari, Pulaar); the Senagalese government has chosen six major languages (Wolof, Pulaar, Serer, Diola, Mandinka, Soninke) and the Togolese government is working on two major languages (Kabre, Ewe) for formal and non-formal educational purposes. In contrast, some countries with a longer tradition of using African languages in education have been extending the number of languages taught during the colonial period, in order that their language policies might correspond more closely to national language distribution and patterns of usage. For example, Kenya has increased the number of languages in which primary school reading materials (TKK series) are available to 14 languages, while Ghana now has primary materials in 11 different languages.

While this increase in languages used as media of instruction is to be welcomed, primary school material in individual languages tends to be restricted to one or two readers per year. Few African languages can command the wide range of graded reading materials needed to stimulate, and hence consolidate, the acquisition of literacy skills. A notable exception is the Yoruba language, for which 150 titles have been produced for reading purposes in connection with the six-year Ife project. Despite attempts in Kenya and Ghana to pay greater attention to the needs of minority language groups, provision in either case is insufficient to allow for the ideal of enabling every child to study through the medium of his/her mother tongue or dominant home language. In parts of West and East Africa, such as the Ivory Coast and Uganda, which are characterized by extreme ethno-linguistic diversity, such a shift in policy would be an administrative nightmare.

For the time being, few African governments can command the necessary infrastructure for conducting research, training teachers, developing, publishing and distributing teaching materials (including supplementary readers) in *all* the languages spoken in their territories. The economy of scale that can be achieved on the basis of selecting a major ethnic first language, alongside those languages serving as second languages or lingue franche for speakers of minority languages, appears currently to be the most feasible solution. Although the commentary *Education in Africa in the Light of the Lagos Conference* of African Ministers of Education (Unesco, 1977) identifies 'the fundamental problem of promoting the use of mother tongue . . . as the language of tuition', the implementation of the conference declaration that education should be 'national and democratic, authentic and modern' appropriately calls for 'the full and complete restoration of the *national languages* as languages of instruction' (my italics). The alternative to using national languages only would be to develop language and dialect clusters numbering over 30 (in the case of Uganda), over 60 (in the case of the Ivory Coast), or over 390 (in the case of Nigeria).

It is open to speculation whether some governments have deliberately embarked on a long-term educational language policy designed to achieve a shift in language habits at the expense of ethnic languages; but the current revival of interest in promoting traditional cultures as constituent parts of a heterogeneous national culture, would seem to contradict this. The immediate concern to make the curriculum more relevant by intro-ducing the main local or national languages has resulted in a compromise solution by necessity rather than by choice. The economic cost of developing *all* home languages raises the question of how politically viable it would be to devote an increasing proportion of the national budget to language planning and development, when so many other sectors of the educational system require additional financial inputs.

Apart from the possibility that education may be conducted through a second, rather than the home language, the overwhelming prestige of the official language on the one hand, and the status of the particular variety of the language chosen as the standardized form on the other, accentuate the handicaps that pupils from remote rural areas may experience in the formal educational system. In contrast, children of ministers or top civil servants, who may be brought up in Abidjan, Accra, Nairobi or Yaounde, speaking French or English to the detriment of their mother tongue, will also be at an advantage in terms of scholastic achievement.

Nevertheless, although familiarity with the official language may be a reflection of class differentiation and urban/rural difference, the status and function of official languages in relation to local languages cannot be over-simplified as 'diglossia of a modern sort', as Fishman's (1968: 45) description of speech communities in Africa south of the Sahara would imply. His neat distinction between the role of the official language in formal contexts, with local languages reserved for more informal, familiar situations, may have characterized the colonial period and perhaps the early post-independence era; but nowadays such a categorization of language usage is contradicted by increasing evidence of more flexible, functional language behaviour, particularly in sociopolitical contexts – whether formal or informal (Treffgarne, 1978). Furthermore, such diglossia cannot be upheld in those situations in which governments have been taking conscious steps to alter the imbalance in function and prestige between official, national and local languages. Even after a particular language has been designated as the national language, problems arise when a comprehensive series of measures are taken in which the national language shares, or takes over, functions formerly reserved for the official language.

Kenya provides a vivid example of such an evolving relationship between the constituent parts of language policy, in its introduction of Swahili as an additional school subject in schools where other local languages serve as the initial medium of instruction. Elsewhere, in urban centres and in areas on the coast, Swahili is used as the teaching medium at the beginning of primary school, with English subsequently becoming the main medium in grades three or four. Problems over the lack of properly trained Swahili teachers have led to considerable variation in policy implementation and in consequent command of the language. In the public sphere, the absence of a comprehensive series of measures to consolidate Kenyatta's declaration in 1969 that Swahili should become the national language (Gorman, 1973; Hopkins, 1977) have led to fluctuations in usage. Swahili did not become the official language for the conduct of parliamentary proceedings until 1974, English remaining the language for written records of proceedings. However, in 1979, English was reinstated alongside Swahili for parliamentary debates. While this shift in policy may have been influenced by the fact that a generation of members of parliament may have had difficulties in expressing themselves in Swahili through its virtual absence from colonial education during the 1950s (Gorman, 1974: 431-5; Mulusa, 1978: 19), the proviso in the 1979 general elections that prospective candidates should be fluent in both English and Swahili may help to encourage its wider diffusion.

A similar situation exists in the Federal Republic of Nigeria. The return to civilian rule has witnessed the reconstitution of the National and State Houses of Assembly, some of which (for example, Anambra and Ogun State Assemblies) have made decisions to allow a dominant local language to serve as an official means of expression alongside English. Likewise, at federal level it is intended that Yoruba, Ibo and Hausa should eventually become languges of debate; but, as in Kenya, the infrastructure for implementing this decision has been slow to emerge. A fundamental aspect of the new role required of the language depends on how quickly language planning committees or agencies can be set up to adapt and extend the language to encompass political, economic and legal terminology; and how quickly provision for shorthand and translation facilities can be developed. However, despite the gap between nationalistic declarations of language policy and actual implementation, such declarations of intent are significant preliminary stages in bringing about a decisive move away from the over-riding prestige and status of English, French and Portuguese in contemporary African nations. Such a shift in language attitudes is essential to overcome the élitist tendency for active participation in public life to be dependent on command of what remains for most people a foreign language.

The balance in terms of language and learning outcomes is not easy to achieve. The strategy of dividing the primary cycle into two or three years in the medium of a local language, with the official language evolving from curriculum subject to medium of instruction, has been criticized for its failure to achieve permanent literacy in either language among primary school-leavers (eg Afolayan, 1976: 115). On the other hand, despite the 'terminal' nature of formal primary education for the majority of the enrolment, no government in West or East Africa denies the primary school pupil the opportunity of learning the official language, albeit to a limited extent. Tanzania has made enormous progress in initiating extensions in the role of Swahili in political and legal spheres (O'Barr, 1976; Dubow, 1976), but appears to have temporarily slowed down the extension of Swahili as sole medium of education from primary to secondary level. Faced with determining standards in English among primary school leavers (see Hill, 1981), current strategies focus on improving the specialist training of teachers of English in order to facilitate the eventual transition to Swahili-medium secondary education in which English will remain as a subject of study. The need for language policies in West and East Africa to reconcile the acquisition of learning skills in different languages with other priorities on the curriculum remains a crucial dilemma in curriculum planning.

Conclusion

It thus emerges that language policy implementation in education can be consolidated or undermined by language policy and usage in society at large. A major dilemma in language planning in West and East Africa arose over how to establish a more equitable balance so that the prestige of one language does not appear to undermine attempts to restore local languages and cultures to their rightful place in the curriculum. The renewed call for greater cultural relevance and national authenticity (as made at the Conference of Ministers of Education in Lagos, 1976) reflects policies oriented towards integrating major local languages into the educational system. The Lagos declaration comments on the complementary nature of African national languages and foreign languages, and specifies that the promotion of the former 'does not preclude, but on the contrary lends itself to a pragmatic functional use of foreign languages for the purpose of fruitful exchanges on the basis of equality' (Unesco, 1977: 50). Nevertheless, the tendency for language policies to perpetuate the determining role of England and France in educational achievement and in subsequent socioeconomic mobility, appears to undermine the concern of the Lagos Conference to combat élitism and to provide greater equality of opportunity for minority groups. Measures taken to enhance the significance of African languages, not only in the educational system but also in parliament, the civil service and the job market in general, could help to achieve greater democratization and what the Lagos Conference identified as the 'intellectual emancipation' of the societies in question (Unesco, 1977: 49).

The plea for linguistic self-determination, or individual language rights (Zachariev, 1978), cannot be met so long as the British colonial failure properly to train teachers of African languages or adequately to provide teaching materials, is in danger of being perpetuated. Even a language having such a well-established literary tradition as Swahili is plagued by the inter-related problem of provision of textbooks and opportunities for supplementary reading (Gachukia, 1970: 3; Wanjala Welime, 1970: 14; Polomé, 1975: 42). Although Hill (1981) reports an improvement in Tanzania in this respect, the problem of publishing and distributing materials so that they can be used in every school has not yet been overcome. The 'Survey of language use and language teaching in Eastern Africa', which led to publication of Studies of Language in Uganda (1972), Kenya (1974), Ethiopia (1976), Zambia (1978) and Tanzania (forthcoming), sought to initiate greater regional co-ordination in linguistic and sociolinguistic research; but co-operation in the crucial field of materials production and dissemination does not appear to be taking place. The way in which the East African Publishing House and the East African Literature Bureau have virtually ceased to fulfil their original regional functions illustrates how vulnerable such economic co-publishing ventures can be in the prevailing political climate.

So, for the time being, the struggle to establish a few regional or major ethnic languages takes precedence at national levels over any consideration of inter-state co-operation in language planning, not only for the languages identified for national and educational purposes, but also for the development of *all* languages, however minor. Moves to rectify the imbalance in West and East African language policies depend ultimately on how far passage through the educational system, employment opportunities, and participation in public life, can be achieved through African national languages. So long as English, French and Portuguese enjoy their current monopoly position in most developing African nations, the revival of a dynamic, national culture through the teaching of local languages will continue to be thwarted.

Acknowledgement

The author is grateful to John Cameron for comments on this paper.

References

Abdulaziz, M M (1971) Tanzania's national language policy and the rise of Swahili political culture *in* Whiteley (1971b)

Afolayan, A (1976) The six-year primary project in Nigeria *in* Bamgbose (1976)

Arens, W (1975) The Waswahili: the social history of an ethnic group *Africa* 45 4: 426-37

Bamgbose, A ed (1976) *Mother Tongue Education: The West African Experience* Unesco/Hodder and Stoughton: Paris and London

Birnie and Ansre eds (1969) *Proceedings of the Conference on the Study of Ghanaian Languages at the University of Ghana, 1968* Ghana Publishing Corporation: Accra

Brann, C M B (1975) Standardisation des langues et éducation au Nigeria *African Languages/Langues Africaines* 1: 204-24

Brumfit, A (1971) The development of a language policy in German East Africa *Journal of the Language Association of Eastern Africa* 2: 1-9

Court, D and Ghai, D P eds (1974) *Education, Society and Development* Oxford University Press: Nairobi

Criper, C and Ladefoged, P (1971) Linguistic complexity in Uganda *in* Whiteley (1971b)

Dubow, F (1976) Language, law and change: problems in the development of a national legal system in Tanzania *in* O'Barr and O'Barr (1976)

Epronti, E O and Denteh, A C (1969) Minority languages *in* Birnie and Ansre (1969)

Fafunwa, A B (1978) Mimeographed paper submitted to the Unesco *Symposium on the Coordination of Linguistic Research and its Application to the Teaching of African Languages* Ouagadougou, Upper Volta

Fishman, J A (1968) Nationality − nationalism and nation − nationism *in* Fishman, Ferguson and Das Gupta (1968)

Fishman, J A, Ferguson and Das Gupta eds (1968) *Language Problems of Developing Nations* Wiley: New York

Gachukia, E (1970) The teaching of vernacular languages in Kenyan primary schools *in* Gorman (1970)

Gaucher, J (1968) *Les Débuts de l'Enseignement en Afrique Francophone* Le Livre Africain: Paris

Guilavogui, G (1975) The basis of the educational reform in the Republic of Guinea *Prospects* 5 4: 435-44

Gorman, T P ed (1970) *Language in Education in Eastern Africa* Oxford University Press: Nairobi

Gorman, T P (1973) Language allocation and language planning *in* Rubin and Shuy (1973)

Gorman, T P (1974) The development of language policy in Kenya with particular reference to the educational system *in* Whiteley (1974)

Hemphill, R J (1974) Language use and language teaching in the primary schools of Kenya *in* Whiteley (1974)

Hill, C P (1981) Some developments in language and education in Tanzania since 1969 *in* Polomé (forthcoming)

Hopkins, T (1977) The development and implementation of the national language policy in Kenya *in* Kotey and Der-Houssikian (1977)

Itabete, P (1974) Language standardisation in Western Kenya: the Luluyia experiment *in* Whiteley (1974)

King, K (1974) Primary schools in Kenya — some critical constraints *in* Court and Ghai (1974)

Kotey, P F A and Der-Houssikian, H *eds* (1977) *Language and Linguistic Problems in Africa* Hornbeam Press: Columbia, SC

Ladefoged, P, Glick, R and Criper, C (1972) *Language in Uganda* Oxford University Press: Oxford

Mazrui, A (1979) Language policy after Amin *Africa Report* **24** 5: 20-2

Mhina, G (1979) The Tanzanian experience in the use of an African language in education: a case for Swahili *African Affairs/Langues Africaines* **5** 2: 63-71

Mulusa, T (1978) Adult education and Kiswahili *Kenya Journal of Adult Education* **6** 2: 18-22

O'Barr, J F (1976) Language and politics in Tanzanian government institutions *in* O'Barr and O'Barr (1976)

O'Barr, W M and O'Barr, J F *eds* (1976) *Language and Politics* Mouton: The Hague

Ohannessian, S, Ferguson and Polomé, E *eds* (1975) *Language Surveys in Developing Nations* Center for Applied Linguistics: Arlington, Va

Phelps-Stokes Commission on 'Education in Africa' (1922) Report by T J Jones, Phelps-Stokes Fund: New York and abridged version by L J Lewis (1962) Oxford University Press: London

Polomé, E (1975) Problems and techniques of a sociolinguistically-oriented survey: the case of the Tanzanian survey *in* Ohannessian, Ferguson and Polomé (1975)

Polomé, E *ed* (1981) *Language in Tanzania* International African Institute: London (forthcoming)

Prator, C M (1975) The survey of language use and language teaching in Eastern Africa in retrospect *in* Ohannessian, Ferguson and Polomé (1975)

Rubin and Jernudd *eds* (1971) *Can Language be Planned?* University Press of Hawaii: Hawaii

Rubin and Shuy *eds* (1973) *Language Planning: Current Issues and Research* Georgetown University Press: Washington DC

Treffgarne, C B W (1978) *Language usage and language policies in Senegambia: Local responses to the Anglophone/Francophone Division of a Multi-lingual region* Unpublished PhD thesis, University of London Institute of Education: London

Unesco (1977) *Education in Africa in the Light of the Lagos Conference (1976)* Educational Studies and Documents 25, Unesco: Paris

Wanjala Welime, J D (1970) Some problems of teaching Swahili at advanced level in Kenya *in* Gorman (1970)

Whiteley, W H (1968) Ideal and reality in national language policy: Tanzania *in* Fishman, Ferguson and Das Gupta (1968)

Whiteley, W H (1969) *Swahili: The Rise of a National Language* Methuen: London

Whiteley, W H (1971a) Some factors influencing language policies in Eastern Africa *in* Rubin and Jernudd (1971)

Whiteley, W H *ed* (1971b) *Language Use and Social Change: Problems of Multilingualism with special reference to Eastern Africa* International African Institute/ Oxford University Press: London

Whiteley, W H *ed* (1974) *Language in Kenya* Oxford University Press: Nairobi

Wright, M (1965) Swahili language policy 1890-1940 *Swahili* **25** 50: 40-8

Zachariev, Z (1978) Droits a l'éducation *International Review of Education* **24** 3: 263-72

Part 4:
Educational opportunity for minority groups:
the research reviewed

13. Equality of educational opportunity in Zimbabwe: past and future

Betty Jo Dorsey

Summary: The first section of this chapter examines those factors which have affected Black pupils' access to the opportunity structures in the formerly White-dominated society of Rhodesia. Differential access to schooling based on race is examined with the implications it has had for the 'life chances' of Black pupils. Factors other than race such as sex, regional and ethnic differences, quality and type of school attended and socioeconomic status are also found to have influenced differentially the opportunity of various groups within Black society. The effect of the War of Liberation in the closure of most of the Black schools in the rural areas is considered as well as the new Education Act of 1979. This Act, while it provided for a gradual integration of former White schools, is found to have created additional problems particularly in the area of social stratification of Blacks.

In the second section the possibilities for the future opportunity for Blacks in an independent Zimbabwe under a Black majority ruled government are considered. The ruling party Zanu (PF) have planned for a non-racial, wide ranging and all-encompassing educational system with vast expansion to compensate for the inequalities of the past. However, it is doubted whether it is possible to eradicate all inequalities in a developing country with limited resources; indeed, even developed countries have not been able to do so. However, Zimbabwe does possess economic and human resources to a greater extent than many Third World countries and, therefore, may be able to demonstrate that it is able to overcome many of the constraints which have frustrated the achievement of educational inequality elsewhere.

Inequalities in the social, economic and political context of the educational system

When Zimbabwe achieved independence in April 1980 under a Black majority government, it inherited an educational system based on inequality of opportunity for the four main racial groups which comprise the society. In this case the most disadvantaged 'minority' group has been, in fact, the numerical majority, the Blacks, who constitute 96 per cent of a population of approximately 7,500,000. Whites make up 3.5 per cent of the population while Asians and Coloureds constitute the remaining 0.5 per cent.

In former Rhodesian society, race was the main criterion for social stratification and it was the basis for ordering nearly all social relations.

Of particular importance was the fact that the four racial groups had different degrees of control over production and different degrees of access to the rewards which flowed from it. The Whites exercised most control and enjoyed the highest rewards and the Blacks at the other end of the scale had the least control and the lowest rewards.

From the beginning of White rule in 1890, Blacks were prevented from competing with Whites on equal terms. A very early act of the British South Africa Company which governed the colony until 1923 established a separate department to handle African affairs. This was later incorporated in the constitution of the self-governing colony of Southern Rhodesia which provided for a Native Affairs Department headed by a Chief Native Commissioner.

However, some Blacks were drawn into the modern economy and through mission schools acquired skills and education; they thus began to be potential economic competitors to Whites. As the threat of Black competition increased, the pattern of segregation became more explicit and separate agencies were established to handle the affairs of each race encompassing all aspects of life, including agriculture, education, housing, taxes, and medical and social facilities.

In 1931 this segregation culminated in the passage of the Land Apportionment Act which formally divided the country into discrete racial areas. The segregation of all land into White and Black areas dispossessed the Blacks of most of the more fertile land and undermined their economic self-sufficiency. Their areas were poorer in terms of welfare service as well as productive capacity and yet they had to support higher densities of population; 62.8 per cent of the total Black population lived in Black areas which constituted only half the country (Kay, 1972: 23). The rapid growth of the Black population (3.6 per cent a year) and the increasing deterioration of Black lands forced Blacks to seek work in White areas: in mining, industry, commerce, agriculture, and in the domestic service sectors. These factors have contributed to what Arrighi (1970) calls the 'pauperization' and 'proletarianization' of the peasant Black.

Thus national resources allocated by an all-White legislature channelled funds into the development of White areas at the expense of the development of Black areas. In addition, labour legislation secured a high wage for White workers by eliminating Black competition for skilled jobs. Under the Industrial Conciliation Act (1934), Blacks were excluded from effective bargaining and Whites were given a *de facto* monopoly over skilled jobs. This Act preserved an artificial scarcity of skilled labour which was then recruited from outside rather than trained from among the indigenous population. The control over unskilled Black wages was in the hands of the government, and these were kept artificially low, largely through a policy of importing migrant labour from neighbouring countries.

The incomes of White farmers were also protected from Black competition, first through the Land Apportionment Act and secondly through marketing arrangements which discriminated against Black farmers. Whenever necessary, legislation was enacted which ensured that

Black development did not pose a serious threat to White development and interests. In 1934 Godfrey Huggins, the Prime Minister, maintained,

> If I am allowed to protect my own race and find a niche in this country for every grade of white civilization, then I will dip into the pockets of the Hon. Minister of Finance and see that the native gets more money; but until I know that, I am not moving. That is why you find a standstill in the Native Development Vote . . . (Gray, 1960: 144)

White-dominated governments thus made decisions that limited and restricted Black acquisition of power while at the same time strengthening the position of the Whites. Continued manipulation of the economic, political and educational structures was particularly important in maintaining White dominance.

According to Murphree, (1975b: 259) 'white policies left the blacks largely undertrained, unskilled, underpaid, underemployed and the consequences for them has been a cumulative economic underprivilege'. As a result, in the past Blacks have essentially occupied a dependent and subordinate position in society.

The pattern of educational development for Blacks within a racially segregated system

The dual education system which developed thus mirrored the structure of Rhodesian society, in that separate systems of education evolved to serve the racially defined communities. Even though the 'European' and 'African' Education Departments were administered by a single Ministry of Education, each department developed as a separate and distinct system. Asian and Coloured pupils were administered by the 'European' department; however, they attended different schools from those of White pupils. There was very little racial mixing.

Perhaps more significant for the Blacks were the differences apparent in the quantity and quality of education which resulted from the different regulations and budgetary provisions for the two systems. The Rhodesian Front Government which took office in 1962 inherited an expanding Black educational system which it attempted to control by instituting a new fiscal policy relating expenditure for Black education (but not White education) to the economy of the country. The budget for Black education was pegged at 2 per cent of the gross national product and various economy measures were implemented in order to keep government expenditure within the allotted budget (Dorsey, 1975: 47).

The differential expenditure is indicated in Table 1, which shows that the government spent over 12 times more per primary school pupil in the 'European' system than in the 'African' system and nearly three times more per pupil at the secondary school level.

The racial disparity in educational expenditure reflected in Table 1 is by no means the complete picture; *per capita* expenditure in the Table relates only to enrolled students, and when expenditure is contrasted with

	European, Asian and Coloured Division	African Division	Ratio of Col 1 to Col 2
Primary school enrolment	39,613	810,908	
Expenditure	11,366,457	18,893,251	
Expenditure per pupil	287	23.3	12.32
Secondary school enrolment	29,448	37,462	
Expenditure	14,519,362	7,055,740	
Expenditure per pupil	493	188	2.62
Total enrolment	69,061	848,370	
Average expenditure per pupil	375	40	12.26

Source: Rhodesian Government (1975).

Table 1 *Government expenditure on education by racial group, 1975 ($)*

the total population figures the disparity is even greater. Black primary school enrolments for 1975 represented 133 pupils per 1000 of the Black population, whereas White primary school enrolments represented 142 pupils per 1000 of that population. At the secondary school level, Black enrolments represented six pupils per 1000 of the population while White enrolments represented 106 per 1000.

There was also an extremely high drop-out rate in the Black system, producing a broadly based educational pyramid in which pupils in secondary schools represented only 4 per cent of the system, while in the White system the corresponding figure is 43 per cent. Education for Whites was compulsory to the age of 15 and the White pupil proceeded automatically to a comprehensive secondary school and, if sufficiently bright, was assured of going on to the sixth form (advanced high school). On the other hand, the Black child entered a system that was voluntary and highly selective. Whether he continued at certain levels depended upon his ability to pass examinations with a high mark and his parents' ability to pay his fees (Dorsey, 1975: 53). Table 2 shows that in 1975 only 54.5 per cent of the Grade 1 cohort completed the seven-year primary school course. 9.9 per cent of the Grade 1 cohort went on to secondary school, 4 per cent completed Form Four, and the number in the sixth form qualifying for university entrance was 0.3 per cent.

In addition, at the end of primary school those Black pupils selected for secondary school were further selected on their primary school final examination performance for either academic secondary schools or vocational secondary schools, whereas White pupils proceeded automatically to comprehensive secondary schools. In the academic secondary schools, a four-year course of study led to a final qualifying examination set by an external examining board, the University of Cambridge Local Examinations Syndicate. The content of academic secondary education was narrowly determined by the demands of the school certificate examination and mirrored the curriculum offered in the European system.

Year	Grade 1 enrolment	Corresponding Grade 7 enrolment (6 years later)		Corresponding numbers entering secondary* school (7 years later)		Corresponding numbers completing 4-year secondary course (10 years later)		Corresponding numbers completing 2-year higher secondary course (12 years later)	
		Numbers	Percentage	Numbers	Percentage	Numbers	Percentage	Numbers	Percentage
1959	112,608							183	0.2
1960	113,941							221	0.2
1961	118,453					2525	2.1	285	0.2
1962	126,919					3069	2.4	318	0.3
1963	123,719					3945	3.2	350	0.3
1964	117,736	47,206	39.4	10,360	8.8	4038	3.4		
1965	119,934	53,018	43.2	11,356	9.5	4814	4.0		
1966	122,590	56,586	45.5	11,939	9.7				
1967	124,465	61,848	48.8	12,591	10.1				
1968	126,854	68,614	54.5	12,545	9.9				
1969	125,863								

* Includes enrolments in academic and vocational secondary schools.

Source: Rhodesian Government (1964, 1974, 1975).

Table 2 Drop-out rate in the Black educational system in Rhodesia, 1971-75

The limited nature of secondary educational facilities for Blacks was deliberate government policy for both fiscal and structural reasons. A broadly-based primary system for Blacks providing basic competence in literacy and numeracy served the purpose of providing an effective unskilled workforce for commerce and industry at fairly low wages. A restricted secondary school system provided for the limited demands for skilled Black labour while at the same time limiting potential competition with White skilled labour.

The dual system of education briefly described here had the important effect of minimizing contact between the young citizens of the country of different races. The only exception to this was found in the country's private schools, most of which were multiracial. Even in these schools (which were, under the terms of the Land Tenure Act, in White areas) enrolment of Black pupils was limited by legislation to 6 per cent of the student body. In any case, fees were so high that only a very few Black parents could afford to send their children to these élite schools.

Another important effect of the dual system was that the highly selective Black system produced an educational and social élite even more clearly than did its White analogue. The status of the élite in Black society tended to structure its members' aspirations and expectations in life. Their educational attainment also gave them the potential for competing for the same jobs as their White counterparts.

I conducted an extensive research study into the aspirations, academic achievement and career attainment of Black secondary school pupils in 1971-72 (Dorsey, 1975) with a follow-up in 1977 of the same group. The study covered the entire school-leaving population at the Form Four and Form Six levels which numbered 2557 pupils.

Aspirations

Not surprisingly these Black school-leavers were found to have high educational and career aspirations. Only 3 per cent considered a secondary school certificate as the terminal point of full-time education, while 65 per cent of the boys and 27 per cent of the girls aspired to go to university.

Pupils and parents of all socioeconomic groups were found to value education highly, as an avenue to occupational and status achievement in the relative absence of other means of mobility. The increase in school outputs had led to a rise in the amount of education required by employers for most jobs and particularly for the relatively well-paid and scarce prestigious jobs. The pupils' perception of educational attainment as a means to mobility was thus realistic, while the probability of fulfilling their aspirations was less so.

Academic achievement

Black secondary school pupils in this study did extremely well in the Cambridge School examinations with 96 per cent achieving a full certificate and over one-third achieving a first division pass. Black pupils at the Form Four and Form Six levels compared favourably with their White counterparts in examination results. In fact, at Form Four the overall failure rate was higher for White pupils, although at the other end of the scale a higher percentage of White pupils achieved distinctions in their subjects, particularly in mathematics and science subjects. At the Form Six level, however, Black pupils had an overall higher examination achievement than their White counterparts both in total percentage passes and in the quality of their passes in all subjects. Considering the greater selectivity of the Black pupils, these results are not surprising.

The comparison of the academic achievement of White and Black pupils was significant for two reasons. First, it indicated that the Form Four and Form Six outputs of the two systems were of comparable scholastic development and potential. Secondly, pupils from both systems had the potential for competing for the same jobs and for coveted places at institutions of higher education. These results therefore corroborated the belief, held by many Black school-leavers, that they were capable of competing successfully with White school-leavers for employment. Their belief that they were prevented from doing so purely on the basis of race and culture had important implications for society at large.

Employment opportunities

When employment opportunities for Black secondary school-leavers were compared with their high aspirations and academic achievements, it was obvious that a serious discrepancy existed in Rhodesian society which contributed to the frustrations of Black youth.

Six months after completing school, only 12 per cent of the Black school-leavers in this study, which covered the entire output of the system, had found jobs; 25 per cent were continuing in their studies, while 50 per cent were unemployed. A higher percentage of girls were unemployed after completing Form Four than boys. Unemployment was higher among Form Four school-leavers while a much higher percentage of Form Six school-leavers were able to continue their education.

Out of the 12 per cent of school-leavers who were employed at the time of the follow-up study, 55 per cent were employed in middle-level occupations (essentially white collar) while 45 per cent had taken up menial jobs and could be classified as 'underemployed' considering their level of education. A secondary school education tended to be an adverse factor in obtaining employment in lower status jobs and a number of respondents indicated that they did not admit to having a Cambridge School Certificate when applying for them.

In general, school-leavers reported that the single most important factor which enabled them to obtain a job was 'knowing influential people' and the single most important factor preventing them from obtaining a job was 'racial discrimination'. One young man, after describing in great detail his efforts to find a job, ended with this paragraph:

> These procedures are repeated and I have been repeating them since I left
> school. In spite of the fact that I have eight O-levels and a first division pass it
> seems Rhodesia has no jobs for African school leavers but for Europeans.
> (Dorsey, 1975: 165)

A secondary school education tended to increase Black pupils' self-consciousness, their social awareness and their aspirations. They perceived racial segregation as the significant factor frustrating the attainment of their aspirations. Initially they saw this operating at the educational level, with Blacks being provided with inferior schools and limited access to further education; but ultimately they saw this discrimination extended to their preclusion from many of the best jobs for Whites. Under such circumstances it is not surprising that tensions and antagonisms between these youths and the established social order arose. In the years 1972-79, thousands of Black youths, both male and female, left the country to join the armed struggle. Many left in the middle of their secondary school careers, relinquishing hard-won and coveted places in these schools. As Shibutani and Kwan (1971: 135) have noted,

> Systems of ethnic stratification begin to break down when minority peoples
> develop new self-conceptions and refuse to accept subordinate roles. As they
> become more aware of their worth in comparison to members of the dominant
> group, what they had once accepted as natural becomes unbearable. What had
> once appeared to be special privileges for superior persons, is redefined as the
> rights of all human beings . . . .

Other determinants of access to equal opportunity in education

Thus far this chapter has concentrated on the inequality of educational opportunity due to the racial structuring of the society. However, there were other factors operating which contributed to differential access to education — and by implication to broader social and economic inequalities — among various groups within the Black population. These factors include: sex differences, place of residence, school attended, religion and socioeconomic status (Dorsey, 1975).

Sex differences

In the study of Black secondary school-leavers, I found that sex differences in enrolment were considerable. At Form Four the ratio of boys to girls was 3:1 while at Form Six it had increased to 8:1. On the whole, girls came from slightly higher socioeconomic backgrounds than boys; presumably poorer parents are less likely to consider the education of girls as essential. Although girls performed as well academically, they had lower educational aspirations than boys: only 27 per cent aspired to go to university (compared with 65 per cent of boys). Girls tended to opt for training courses in nursing and teaching after Form Four. A number of factors — both cultural and economic — might account for the imbalance of the sexes in secondary schools, but the most important seems to be the parents' attitudes towards the education of girls and the self-image which girls have as a result of cultural conditioning.

Regional and ethnic differences

There has been considerable differentiation in educational provision between urban and rural areas and between the seven provinces into which the country is divided (Dorsey, 1975: 78-80). Within all urban areas, an average of 62 per cent of children of school age attended school while in the rural areas the average was 44 per cent. As might be expected, those provinces with the larger urban areas had the highest percentage of children in school. The more remote and less accessible provinces such as Mashonaland North and Victoria had the lowest school enrolments, 31 and 41 per cent respectively. It is interesting to note that these were also the provinces where the liberation war was launched and then spread throughout the country.

Inequality of access to schools among various ethnic groups was related to differentiation in educational development in the various provinces of origin and not to ethnicity *per se*. Provincial development, in turn, was seen to be related to various factors including the physical environment, remoteness from urban centres, demographic distribution, and the historical development of mission centres.

Differences due to quality and type of secondary school attended

The competition for selection to higher institutions and training colleges in the past was so intense that it was necessary to secure a very high pass in the Cambridge School Certificate in order for pupils to be able to further their education. The variation between schools with regard to academic success was considerable. In 1971 the top school achieved 83 per cent first division passes while the bottom school had only 7 per cent. The results of my survey showed that schools which were single-sex, boarding, denominationally affiliated and/or rural mission produced the best Cambridge examination results. Of the top ten academic schools, nine were rural mission boarding schools and seven of the nine were single-sex schools. Four were boys' schools and three were girls' schools. One of the ten was a government single-sex boarding school. Since to a large extent examination results conditioned career attainment, the type of school attended was an important factor in the ultimate occupational achievement of Black pupils (Dorsey, 1975: 170).

Socioeconomic status

Given the high drop-out rate, it can be inferred that pupils who completed the full primary course were not representative of local populations in general. In rural areas, particularly, it can be assumed that successful children were drawn from families who had access to a cash income and whose level of education was above average for the local adult population.

This assumption is confirmed at the secondary school level where pupils in my study had parents whose educational and occupational backgrounds were on the whole, above average for the general Black population (see Table 3).

Amount of education in years	Adult males* %	Fathers of pupils %	Mothers of pupils %	Adult females* %
Nil	35.1	8.1	12.5	45.9
1−5	30.2	42.3	58.5	33.2
6+	32.0	48.0	27.8	17.9
Not recorded	2.8	1.7	1.2	3.0
Total	100.1	100.1	100.0	100.0
Number	1,157,720	2557	2557	1,117,370

* Education figures for adults in the general population derived from Central Statistical Office (1969).

Table 3 *Comparison of education of parents of Black secondary school pupils with the general Black adult population*

Although it is apparent that the 'life chances' of pupils from higher socioeconomic backgrounds may be greater than those from more disadvantaged homes, it should be noted that a considerable proportion of secondary school pupils do come from humbler circumstances, as Table 3 shows; over 50 per cent of fathers and over 70 per cent of mothers had less than six years of schooling. The study also indicated that 60 per cent of fathers were in 'low' status occupations, and of these 16 per cent were rural peasant farmers.

Thus selection for secondary schools was not solely by academic merit. The ability of parents to pay school fees was obviously an element in selection. Particularly under-represented were children from peasant farm families. However, within the category of those who could 'afford' secondary schooling, selection was then based on academic merit and was not *intentionally* class-selective. Pupils from more disadvantaged homes actually did slightly better academically than others (Dorsey, 1975: 141). This was in contrast to Britain and America, where studies have consistently shown a positive correlation between pupils' achievement and the occupation and education of their parents. However, it was consistent with other studies in Africa which had not shown a strong correlation in this respect (Heyneman, 1976; Clignet and Foster, 1966).

Effects of the liberation war on the internal educational system 1977-79

As the armed struggle intensified in rural areas, more primary and secondary schools were forced to close. Table 4 indicates the extent to which the system was affected during the last three years of the war.

	1977	1978	1979	Total
Primary				
Schools closed	477	1094	1520	3091
Pupils displaced	92,654	265,675	403,250	761,579
Teachers displaced	2652	6058	9330	18,040
Secondary				
Schools closed	8	38	57	103
Pupils displaced	1553	10,157	16,834	28,544
Teachers displaced	61	512	838	1411

Table 4 *Effects of the liberation war on the schools*

In addition to the effects shown in Table 4, teachers' colleges and homecraft schools, involving 1966 students and 106 staff, remained closed (Rhodesian Government, 1979b: 2). It has been estimated that it will cost US $30,000,000 to repair war damage to the school system.

Two further important effects of the war were the influx into the urban areas of thousands of families which resulted in the rapid growth of many urban schools necessitating 'hot seat' classes in the afternoons and the loss of many teachers from the system, some of whom found alternative employment in commerce and industry.

The Coalition Government and the 1979 Education Act

In 1978 a Coalition Government was formed which incorporated in the Cabinet the leaders of the various internal Black political parties. The main impact on the educational system of this Coalition Government was through the Education Act of 1979. At an administrative level, the Act provided for the integration of the 'European' and 'African' divisions of education and for the 'gradual' integration of schools. Government schools were reclassified into Group A schools (essentially the former schools of the European division), Group B and C schools (former African division). These schools had differential fee-paying structures: Group A were high fee-paying, Group B were low fee-paying and Group C were non fee-paying. There were also strict zoning restrictions for Group A schools which limited enrolment to those pupils whose parents owned or leased accommodation in the area. The new structure reflected a gradualist and essentially élitist approach to racial integration in the schools, with consideration of White sensitivities continuing to dominate policy. As Chikombah (1980: 62) points out,

> One can only conclude that the classification of schools into these groups and the zoning of Group A schools were determined more by political considerations which are discriminatory and ethnocentric in nature than by educational considerations.

Blacks living and working in the Group A zones were not permitted to send their children to these schools if they did not own or lease accommodation — which effectively eliminated domestic workers' children. At the same time, Group A schools were increasingly under-utilized due to White emigration while Group B schools continued to be overcrowded.

The Act also created a fourth category of school called 'community' schools which essentially provided for the purchase of government schools by 'a community of persons'. The schools would then be administered by an elected board of governors. The boards were not permitted to discriminate in the enrolment of pupils on the 'grounds of race or colour alone: provided that, in determining the persons who may be enrolled as pupils, the board shall have regard to the religious or cultural identity of the school' (Rhodesian Government, 1979: 182). During 1979 the community schools issue was hotly and often acrimoniously debated in many communities. Approximately one-third of the primary and secondary schools of the former European Division of Education elected to become community schools. The schools were sold by the government to the communities for a nominal sum, thus providing at minimal cost a further mechanism for the effective cultural control of these essentially élitist schools by their largely White constituencies.

With regard to equality of educational opportunity, the 1979 Education Act created more problems than it solved. Although Group A schools were now open to Blacks, they were only open to those Blacks who could afford to purchase or lease property in the former White areas. The under-utilization of the Group A schools, which were only half-filled, was an uneconomic use of the country's limited resources. A legacy to the independent government which came to power in 1980, this structure contains the seeds of discontent, not only because it deprives a large sector of the population of a scarce commodity, but also because it encourages class stratification and divisions within Black society to an extent hitherto unknown.

This section of the chapter has examined those factors which have affected Black pupils' access to the opportunity structures of society. Initially we examined differential access to schooling by race and subsequently by other factors such as sex, regional and ethnic differences, quality and type of school and socioeconomic status; these also affect the life chances of Black pupils. In addition the effects on the educational system of the liberation war and the Education Act of 1979 were briefly considered. In the following section we will attempt to ascertain how far the factors affecting opportunity for Blacks can be changed and to what extent we can expect equality of educational opportunity in the new nation of Zimbabwe.

Possibilities for the future

The present government led by the Zanu (PF) party was elected by an overwhelming majority in April 1980. It faced, on the assumption of power, a number of formidable tasks with regard to education in Zimbabwe. First priority was given to the reconstruction and reopening of schools which had been closed during the war. During 1980, 3000 schools reopened and school enrolments increased to 63 per cent with 1,300,000 pupils in school.

The Party Manifesto (Zanu, 1980: 12-13) promoted a wide-ranging and all-encompassing educational system which included the establishment of free compulsory primary and secondary education, expansion of (largely free) university education and the establishment of the Zimbabwe Institute of Technology. Emphasis was also placed on the necessity for pre-school and adult education.

The Manifesto maintained that the government would support an educational system of high quality organization and content, and that it would abolish racial education and sex discrimination in the education system. The system would also be oriented to national goals and seek to develop in the younger generation non-racist attitudes, a common national identity and common loyalty. With the proposed expansion of the system a massive teacher training programme was envisaged.

Bureaucratic structures react slowly to change and for several months after taking office there were no visible changes. However, during the last four months of 1980 a number of measures were taken: first, primary schooling was made free (though not compulsory due to lack of facilities). Secondly, a vast expansion in secondary education is planned for 1981 with Form One enrolments increasing from 20,000 to 90,000, and thirdly, a massive exercise was commenced to train teachers on an in-service basis as well as to recruit staff from overseas to cope with anticipated increased enrolments.

In order to accommodate the increased number of pupils, the Minister of Education announced that all schools would be fully utilized, zoning laws would be changed, and Group B schools would have double-sessioning. He also said that fees for secondary school pupils were 'under consideration'.

It is too soon yet to assess the educational programme being proposed by the government. They are still at the embryo stage and no overall development plan has been produced which would indicate whether educational developments are being considered together with long-range economic development plans. It does, however, appear that popular demand for education is pressing the government to expand the system in much the same way as has happened elsewhere in Africa (Abernethy,

1969: 133). The difficult lesson to be learned is that if educational growth overtakes the expansion of job opportunities the result will be the frustration of aspirations.

It has been suggested that if popular demand for education, on the one hand, and economic circumstances on the other, are considered as constants, only one variable remains which can be manipulated to break out of this vicious circle: the make-up of the educational system. Since quantitative factors cannot be modified, a strategy for reform must be oriented towards the qualitative and structural aspects of education. The educational system must undergo curricular and organizational trans-formations which will enable it to respond to popular aspirations and at the same time to contribute effectively to an increase in economic productivity (Hanf *et al*, 1975: 87).

No concrete proposals have yet been put forward by the new government with regard to curricular changes; the present expansion seems to be along the lines of 'more of the same'. There is an overemphasis in Zimbabwe schools on the accumulation of knowledge useful for passing examinations at the expense of development of pupils' problem-solving capacities or practical abilities. Furthermore, practical subjects should not be limited to less academic pupils. If only part of the educational system is oriented to practical subjects and another part remains academic, the former will be considered second-rate and doomed to failure.

In its efforts to redress the inequalities inherited from the past, the major constraints on the government's efforts will undoubtedly be those of money and manpower. The realities of the situation were acknowledged by the Minister of Education when addressing a group of teachers: 'It will take us at least 20 years, if not more, before we can say that every Zimbabwean will be enjoying the quality of life that we would all of us wish to enjoy'. The Minister may be too optimistic. An assessment by the International Council for Educational Development (1979: 3) on the progress made towards wiping out inequalities in this last 30 years indicates that the amount of progress has been very disappointing:

> the whole world is still shot through with serious and widespread educational disparities and disadvantages, particularly for rural children, those from lower socioeconomic levels and within both these categories, girls and young women in particular. (1979: 3)

The conditions leading to this pessimistic overview obtain in Zimbabwe. At the same time, the country possesses economic and human resources to a higher degree than many Third World countries; its highly educated and dynamic new leadership may be able to produce a policy which will demonstrate that it is able to overcome many of the constraints which have frustrated the achievement of educational equality elsewhere.

References

Abernethy, D (1969) *The Political Dilemma of Popular Education* Stanford University Press: Stanford, Cal

Arrighi, G (1970) Labour supplies in historical perspective: a study of the proletarianization of the African peasantry in Rhodesia *Journal of Development Studies* 6

Baker, D G ed (1975) *Politics of Race* Saxon House/D C Heath: London

Central Statistical Office (1976) *Census of Population 1969* (Vol II) Government Printer: Salisbury

Chikombah, C (1981) Education in transition: the educator's problem in Zimbabwe *The Bulletin of the Institute of Education* 16 2: 62-6

Clignet, R and Foster, P (1966) *The Fortunate Few* Northwestern University Press: Evanston, Ill

Dorsey, B J (1975) The African secondary school leaver *in* Murphree (1975)

Gray, R (1960) *The Two Nations* Oxford University Press: London

Hanf, T *et al* (1975) Education: an obstacle to development? *Comparative Education Review* 19 1: 68-87

Heyneman, S (1976) Influences on academic achievement: a comparison of results from Uganda and more industrialized societies *Sociology of Education* 49 3

International Council for Educational Development (1979) The world educational crisis revisited: interim report on educational inequalities *Newsletter:* December

Kay, G (1972) *Distribution and Density of the African Population in Rhodesia* Miscellaneous Series 12, University of Hull: Hull, Yorks

Marx, G ed (1971) *Racial Conflict: Tension and Change in American Society* Little, Brown: Boston, Mass

Murphree, M W ed (1975a) *Education, Race and Employment in Rhodesia* ARTCA: Salisbury

Murphree, M W (1975b) Race and power in Rhodesia *in* Baker (1975)

Rhodesian Government (1964, 1974, 1975) *Annual Reports of the Secretary for African Education* Government Printer: Salisbury

Rhodesian Government (1976) *Report on Education* Government Printer: Salisbury

Rhodesian Government (1979a) *Act No 8* Government Printer: Salisbury

Rhodesian Government (1979b) *Annual Report of the Secretary for Education* Government Printer: Salisbury

Shibutani, T and Kwan, K (1971) Changes in life conditions conducive to inter-racial conflict *in* Marx (1971)

Zanu (PF) (1980) *Election Manifesto*

14. Educational opportunity for minority group children in Canada

Joti Bhatnagar and Arpi Hamalian

Summary: This chapter reviews research on the educational opportunities for immigrants to Canada who are members of cultural minorities. It examines the social situation of immigrants, attitudes of the majority group towards them and their status and power relationships in Canada. An analysis is then made of the condition of immigrant children in Canadian schools: points considered are their reception by school boards, teachers, and peers; whether there are problems of language, culture conflicts and social rejection, and how these interfere with the provision of equality of educational opportunity. Alternative answers to the problem — assimilation and multiculturalism — are discussed.

This is followed by a brief survey of special projects and programmes related to the development and democratization of educational opportunity structures for minority group children, such as the efforts to preserve the minority language and culture and to share cultural values in the formal educational structures of public schooling.

There are three types of cultural minorities in Canada: (1) the native people (the Indians, Inuits, Métis and others); (2) English Canadians in the Province of Quebec and French Canadians in provinces other than Quebec, acknowledged as the 'founders'; and (3) the immigrants. The life-style, culture, and social and educational problems of these groups are quite different from one another. In a chapter of this size it would be difficult to do justice to all these groups. Laxer (1979) has published an introductory text on English/French relations in Canada, while an extensive bibliography of work on natives has been published elsewhere (Brooks, 1976). This chapter will focus upon the third category of cultural minorities — the immigrants.

For a long time Canada has been one of the major immigrant-receiving countries of the world. In 1979, a relatively quiet year, Canada received 82,125 immigrants from 82 nations spread across six continents (Statistics Canada, 1980). In boom years more than 400,000 immigrants per year have arrived. Historically, immigrants from northern Europe and the USA have generally been regarded as the most desirable and have not faced the same problems of social and cultural adjustment as have the others. They are, therefore, excluded from this account of cultural minorities.

Recent political events in Canada had a direct bearing upon the definitions and rights of minority group children in general, including the educational rights and opportunities available to them. The Official Language Act of 1969 sought to define Canada as officially bilingual and bicultural, ie English and French. The declaration of a multicultural policy in 1971 implied some degree of official support for the maintenance of languages and cultures other than English and French. Legislative developments in the Province of Quebec since the election of the Parti Quebecois in 1976 have fortified the link between language, culture, and ideology, thus highlighting the salience of minority issues for the continued survival of Canadian society in its present form.

To a certain extent, schools reflect the opportunity structure in society at large, and what happens in schools can only be understood in the context of their social milieu. For this reason, before turning our attention to schools, we will examine status and power relationships in Canadian society.

Opportunity structure in Canadian society

The vertical mosaic

In his classic study Porter (1965) demonstrated the preservation over time of what he called a 'vertical mosaic' in Canada, a mosaic that at least until the early 1960s was structured very much in terms of ethnic group membership. On this model, the British were at the top, followed by northern Europeans with central and southern Europeans at the bottom. Indians and Inuits were so far removed from the centres of power that they were not even considered. Recent research seems to indicate that this vertical mosaic has become even steeper and harder to climb. Bancroft (1979) supports the view (Clement, 1975) that power in Canada is highly concentrated in few hands. The top 10 per cent of the population holds 42 per cent of the wealth and the mobility of the middle class – even of the Anglo-Saxon middle class – up into this power centre is decreasing. Unless there is a fundamental restructuring of Canadian society there is little hope for minority groups to enter the corridors of power. A study (McKinney et al, 1978) of the 1971 census data revealed that Canadian Black males were better educated than all other Canadian males, yet this educational advantage was not reflected in their socioeconomic positioning. Head (1978) found that Blacks who were born in Canada fared no better than immigrant Blacks. After reviewing numerous studies, Hughes and Kallen (1974) came to the conclusion that there is a great deal of both personal and institutional racism in Canadian society, and that ethnicity still constitutes an important criterion for social stratification. Although the relationship between ethnic group membership and social mobility is not restricted to immigrants, this factor plays an important role in the integration process of immigrants in Canadian society and affects the rate and direction of their social mobility.

Immigrants and the vertical mosaic

Berry *et al* (1977) interviewed a national sample of 1849 respondents. Most interviewees perceived the consequences of immigration as being more positive than negative, though concern was expressed about the possibilities of increasing unemployment and upsetting the balance between English and French Canadians. Most immigrants, including non-Whites, were rated acceptable, and those with skilled trades or high levels of education were considered most desirable. When asked about their behavioural intentions, respondents showed patterns of discrimination against immigrants. Discrimination was greatest against high-status immigrants in a business relationship, and was least against low-status immigrants in a business relationship. The combination of these results with those reported earlier suggests the paradox that while highly educated and skilled immigrants are considered highly desirable for admission to Canada, there is some reluctance to use their services. The study found a pecking order of preferences for different groups: northern Europeans, south and central Europeans, and non-Whites, in that order, and that although on the whole Canadians reject explicit racism, physical differences among groups are nevertheless important: 'Race appears to be one of the basic dimensions in the structure of perception of ethnic groups.' The authors conclude that, generally, the Canadian core is more tolerant of racial differences than the core in most other multiracial societies.

Berry and his colleagues employed a national sample; a different picture emerges from studies conducted in high-immigration areas. Richmond (1976) reported that Blacks and Asians were four times more likely than Whites to report employment discrimination and eight times more likely to report discrimination in housing. Buchignani (1977) traces the history of bigotry against East Indians in Canada, and many similar studies have established that the incidence of prejudice and discrimination of both the violent and subtle variety has increased substantially in recent years (Chandra, 1973; Ramcharan, 1974; Head, 1975; Ontario Human Rights Commission, 1977; Ubale, 1977; Henry, 1978; Jean-Baptiste, 1979). Lasry (1980) studied the occupational mobility of 469 North African Jewish immigrants to Montreal. On entering the job market, these immigrants experienced a significant drop from the occupational level they had occupied in their country of origin: the higher the level, the greater the drop. This stands in marked contrast with the experience of British immigrants.

> Because they entered Canada at a higher social status the British immigrants were theoretically more liable to suffer a decline in status and immigrants from other countries were more likely to experience upward mobility if other factors had not impeded them. In practice the opposite occurred. British immigrants were able to improve their position and those from other countries, particularly the ones who had been in professional or clerical occupations in their former countries, suffered considerable decline in social status in Canada in the large majority of cases. (Richmond, 1967)

Although well-documented studies (Parai, 1974; Green, 1976;

Ashworth, 1976) have clearly established how immigrants have helped Canada both to develop a viable population base and to prosper economically through availability of unskilled, skilled and highly-skilled manpower, public imagination has been caught by writings such as those of Collins (1979) who argued that the ills of Canada could be directly attributed to the dilution of British cultures through contact with non-Whites. Ramcharan has put the position forcefully:

> While Canada overtly prides itself on being a society tolerant of racial and cultural differences, in practice it is a society permeated with bigoted and prejudicial attitudes, overt racial discrimination, and negative stereotyping. Particularly in the last four years, the prevalent attitude has been that all social and economic ills have been caused by foreigners and strangers who have dared to enter Canada. (Ramcharan, 1979)

It does appear that race and ethnic relations have taken a turn for the worse in Canada, particularly in high immigration areas. To what extent are these patterns reflected in schools?

Opportunity structure in Canadian schools

What is the evidence on discrimination? Elliston (1978) recently conducted a study by giving a questionnaire to 1800 school personnel and interviewing 231 students. He was looking for evidence of racism in schools in Metro Toronto with the idea of suggesting remedies, and found that racism is less evident in schools than in the community but that, nevertheless, it does exist. 'The idea of genetic differences persists among teachers who continue to regard Black students as "intellectually inferior" and proceed to act accordingly.' The lack of equality of opportunity was clearly perceived by the minority group students and this led to conflict. However, where a school's policies clearly and explicitly rejected racism, the situation was considerably better:

> The overwhelming impression from the responses of the students interviewed was that where the school was engaged in multiracial or ethnic group activities and where minority group students had a chance to assume leadership roles, racism became a non-issue.

These difficulties are not confined to non-White children. Lack of social acceptability has been reported for immigrant children from the Soviet Union (Markus, 1980) and Czechoslovakia (Maijala, 1977).

Anderson (1975) reported that educational problems of West Indian children are the result of overt and covert acts of discrimination which produce alienation and indifference among these students. Similarly, Hughes and Kallen (1974) found that West Indian students' problems in school were only marginally related to their previous cultural or educational background:

> Recent West Indian immigrants are more likely to come from middle class families, and to have had an 'English' type of classical education. The West Indian child does come from a different culture and most make some

adjustments in their efforts to cope with the huge bureaucratic educational structures. However, the most difficult problems faced by many West Indian children in the schools are related to race and colour.

These findings were confirmed by Head (1978) who conducted interviews with 210 randomly selected Black adults and 54 Black youths in Toronto. The respondents were aware of widespread discrimination in education, and felt strongly about being denied equality of educational opportunity in Toronto schools.

The Toronto Board of Education (1975) acknowledged the problems of lack of equality of educational opportunity for immigrant children in its *Draft Report*. In a later publication (Toronto Board of Education, 1979) the Board's committee stated unequivocally: 'We condemn any expression of racial bias and . . . will use all authority . . . to eliminate it.' The committee went on to make 120 recommendations to expel racism from its schools. Similar problems were felt in Saskatchewan where a committee containing members from Saskatchewan Human Rights Commission, School Trustees Association, Teachers Federation and Department of Education was formed to find ways of combating ethnic stereotyping in schools. The committee came to a conclusion that the focus of action should be on in-service training for teachers, and on the provision of resource materials that teachers could use (Van Dyck and Arkell, 1979).

Streaming

Minority groups have long complained that the process of streaming works to their serious disadvantage. Immigrant students are channelled to vocational rather than academic streams. Harvey and Masemann (1975) in their survey of Toronto schools found that most immigrant students wanted to enter academic streams but ended up in technically-oriented vocational programmes which often did not result in the High School Leaving Diploma: 'They bear the scars of having been taunted by their Anglo classmates for not being proficient in English and finish with the stigma of having attended a school that "slow learners" also attend.' The minority group students are very much aware of the inadequate placement and streaming procedures and resent them. Head (1978) found that his Black respondents were upset by 'streaming' procedures:

> they felt that many Black students who are capable academically are directed into vocational courses. In a similar manner, there has been a tendency to associate Black students, again especially West Indians, with slow learners.

In his recent survey Samuda (1980) found serious problems in placing immigrant students.

> Administrators and teachers were suddenly required to alter long-held ethnocentric attitudes without any special preparation and had in a short time to begin accommodating a very different kind of new Canadian from Trinidad, Bangladesh, The Azores, Jamaica. There were no OSR cards to shape the direction of placement; there were no records whatsoever in a great many

instances; there was not even an adequate interview to provide a basis for placement into the system because, very often, the students knew little or no English, or the dialect was so different as to be almost incomprehensible to the average Canadian educator. There were no educational policies; there were no guidelines to help devise programs, no instruments for the assessment and placement of the atypical students. Furthermore, the teachers themselves were never prepared or trained to cater for such differences.

Textbooks

The inferior status of minority group students is further reinforced by social studies and history textbooks used in the classroom. Two such studies have been reported in Canada. Lupul (1976) analysed the textbooks used in Alberta high schools and found them to portray Canada's 'other people' in a most inadequate fashion. McDiarmid and Pratt (1971) analysed the content of all social studies textbooks authorized for use in Ontario schools. They found that the textbooks make scant reference to religious groups other than Christians; immigrants on the whole received positive treatment, but Negroes and other non-Whites were treated in negative terms. An analysis of the pictures in textbooks revealed that Asians and Africans were given negative treatment.

> A very high proportion of both Africans and Asians were shown engaged in manual work. Skilled or professional work seemed largely the preserve of whites, who accounted for almost three-quarters of those shown in this classification. There are scholars, engineers, and modern farmers in India, Malaysia, and Thailand, to choose just three countries. Portraying most representatives of other groups as primitive agriculturalists restricts important information which should be available for the students in our schools.

There is evidence (Shirley, 1968) to suggest that school texts are influential in the development of ethnic attitudes: much more needs to be done, therefore, to remove racial bias from texts currently in use in Canadian schools.

From the discussion so far it is evident that if there is to be genuine equality of educational opportunity in Canada, much more will have to be done by agencies of the government, school boards, community groups and teachers (Coelho, 1978). In the absence of such equality of educational opportunity many children learn helplessness. Minority group status often results in feelings of powerlessness, alienation, and frustration. Such feelings can affect an individual's motivation, and cognitive and emotional processes, and can lead to a state of passivity and apathy — feelings contrary to those required for constructive and productive citizenship (Sue, 1977).

Official policies of integration and the role of schools

Assimilation policy

Prior to the 1950s the dominant policy was one of assimilation of immigrant children into mainstream culture as quickly as possible. Palmer and Troper (1973) have described this ideology as 'Anglo-conformity', based on 'the desirability of sustaining British institutions and norms as the established bases for building Canadian society'. Such 'desirability' to all intents and purposes became the underlying principle of education for immigrants. As Lind (1974) points out:

> without ill will, almost coincidentally, immigrants became defined as problems. Their potential bilingualism became a stigma rather than an asset . . . the New Canadian approach bulldozed all the alien languages into one unrecognized heap.

Many believe that 'Anglo-conformity' is still the dominant approach. Cummins (1978) feels that school systems have promoted, and continue to promote, the assimilation process. 'Bilingualism' was widely thought to engender mental confusion, and was considered to be the major cause of the immigrant child's academic difficulties, and an impediment to the learning of the English language. The school system, therefore, actively discouraged the minority group children from maintaining their language and culture. In his recent survey of school personnel, Samuda (1980) notices that:

> In Metro Toronto, a strong assimilationist element was clearly evident. The solutions most frequently offered by Metro respondents included such statements as 'have a holding centre'; 'culturize them'; 'have a crash course in Canadian customs'; 'give them one year to adjust to Ontario culture'. Such statements would seem to imply that teachers, school principals, and − to a lesser extent − administrators, will continue to resist the changes in the educational system which are needed if the policy of cultural pluralism is to become a reality.

By and large the assimilation model failed to work. The vertical divisions in Canadian society continue to be along ethnic lines with British on top, followed by north Europeans, French, southern and central Europeans, and non-Europeans, in that order (Porter, 1972). He pointed out that the non-democratic, non-egalitarian nature of schools has contributed to the persistence of this pecking order. After reviewing studies dealing with the relationship between school and social structure in Canada, Murphy and Denis (1979) came to a similar conclusion. They found that:

> The striking feature of school in Canada is the way it has functioned to reproduce ascribed inequalities − and in so doing to conserve the distinct position of ethnic groups in the stratification system.

By and large, non-Anglo groups remain unassimilated in cultural, status and economic opportunity terms.

Multicultural policy

In the early 1970s the Government of Canada rejected the assimilationist policy and in its place adopted 'Multiculturalism within a bilingual framework' as the new state policy. Prime Minister Trudeau (1971) put it in no uncertain terms:

> The policy of multiculturalism within a bilingual framework commends itself to the Government of Canada as the most suitable means of assuring the cultural freedom of Canadians. National unity, if it is to mean anything in the deeply personal sense, must be founded on confidence in one's own individual identity; out of this can grow respect for that of others and a willingness to share ideas, attitudes and assumptions. A vigorous policy of multiculturalism will help to create this initial confidence. It can form the base of a society which is based on fair play for all.

The statement received enthusiastic support in many quarters including minority groups. It soon became the declared policy of most school boards. A Toronto Board of Education (1976) document declared that:

> In accepting the reality of multiculturalism in Canada, the workgroup on multicultural programs for the Toronto Board of Education believes in the right of each person to cultural integrity, to a positive self-image, and to an understanding and respect for differences. If we are to appreciate differences and commonalities, multicultural education must be a basis for our school system and must be directed to all students and teachers.

At the official level, it was clearly recognized that not only is a high level of self-esteem towards membership in one's cultural group necessary for healthy and wholesome development of the individual, it is also a prerequisite for harmonious and co-operative relations between groups.

As a consequence of multicultural policy the federal government began a programme to support after-school ethnic language classes, cultural festivals, music and dance classes and the like, all organized entirely within the various ethnic communities. But children generally perceived these as being outside their usual education; participation in these activities was often viewed as an esoteric exercise rather than as a manifestation of 'multicultural Canada'. Since the educational system in general and teachers in particular represent the authority of mainstream Canadian culture, it soon became evident that multiculturalism could not be implemented without the enthusiastic participation of schools. Such involvement from the child's vantage point would represent an endorsement of the concept of multiculturalism by society at large. The schools responded in three ways: by providing opportunities for cross-cultural contact, by introducing language classes in the schools, and by implementing bilingual and bicultural programmes.

In 1977 Harbourfront, an 86-acre tract of land in the central waterfront area of Toronto, was used to develop a series of activities to support the theme 'Growing up with dignity'. The activities allowed

> students to discover, appreciate, and enjoy the similarities and differences among the many cultures which make up the Canadian mosaic. Participation and involvement were stressed in the hope that children would not only see demonstrations but also participate in the activities which were many and varied. (McQuillan, 1977)

Students from Arab, East Indian, Chinese, Greek, Italian, Jewish,

Portuguese and several other ethnic groups presented folk heroes, history, dance, paintings, games, food and cultural traditions to other children. The programme is now running all year round.

A second decision aimed at raising the self-esteem of immigrant children through preservation of their language and culture was the provision of a number of languages as electives in the secondary school curriculum. Toronto, for example, offers German, Italian, Chinese, Hebrew, Polish, Portuguese, Russian, Ukranian, Greek, Hungarian, Latvian, and Croatian in its schools. Though such programmes are now well-established in high schools, they have been difficult to establish at the elementary school level. Ontario, the most populous of the Canadian provinces, adopted a Language Heritage Programme in 1977. Through this scheme financial assistance is available to any school board that decides to respond to parent groups' demand for ethnic language classes in the elementary school as part of the regular curriculum. Many school boards have been quick to take advantage of the offer while others have been hesitant.

Supplementary language classes by themselves have been found to be insufficient. Children view these as extra work and are, on the whole, unenthusiastic about them. If immigrant children are to develop pride in their cultural heritage more than language classes are needed. Several school boards across Canada recognize this and have begun to experiment with bilingual, bicultural programmes. (The two languages are that of the immigrant child in addition to *either* French or English.)

The Toronto Board of Education started an experimental programme in autumn 1965 in the Main Street school. At first, 75 students over 12 years of age were enrolled. Many of the teachers involved in the programme were themselves bilingual or multilingual, but more important all of them were very sympathetic to the concept of multiculturalism. The programme recognized that problems of immigrant children go beyond linguistic difficulties, and emphasized the need for communication, commitment and dialogue to allow students to be resocialized at their own pace. The school's philosophy is best summarized by Mr La Fountaine in an internal memo to the Board:

> The real fact of life in this question of the new immigrant population in our school system is that the problem it presents is not, never has been, and never will be, a language problem. It is a cultural problem. Furthermore, it insists that the new immigrant's culture and ours be integrated, made compatible, in the personality of the immigrant himself. This means that there is only one valid principle to which the Board can look for its solution. The new immigrant must be provided with the opportunity and the possibility to effect the integration of his own culture with the new culture — which the school represents — for himself, on his own terms and in his own time. (La Fountaine, 1976)

The methodology employed by the school is described by the Principal:

> At Main Street there is a great deal of sharing of experiences. Teachers and students do things together — they work out projects together, they visit the community library, stores, and shops together, they eat their lunch together, they go on field trips together. The students are encouraged to talk about the

way of life in their native land and of the changes Canada had meant for them and their families. There is no attempt to influence the students into adopting the clothes, food, and responses of other young Canadians. The fact that a boy's lunch consists of a thick chunk of meat and a slab of bread instead of a ham or cheese sandwich and an apple should not be a source of confusion and embarrassment, but an opportunity for an exchange of information and ideas – and perhaps an exchange of food. The round lunch tables provide a setting for developing dialogue as a pupil eats with teachers and classmates. Here, as elsewhere in the school, the aim is not assimilate these young people into our culture, but to integrate them. (Sterioff, 1976)

The school obviously had very commendable aims. But did it succeed in helping its pupils? Evaluation studies did not show any large differences in the academic achievement between the graduates of this school and those from other regular schools. However, the school proved to be very popular with the immigrant population and its enrolment increased. It also served as the inspirational model to other schools interested in experimenting in this way.

In two mid-town Toronto schools, 90 per cent of the children were of Chinese origin. In the early 1970s parents of these children began speaking out on the widening communication gap between themselves and their children – more and more, the children were talking in English, becoming part of a new culture and seeming to reject that of their parents. There were after-school Chinese classes in the community, but they required a great deal of extra work and were too expensive for most families. The parents appealed to the school board, and after much discussion the programme began in 1974. The board's document outlining the rationale of the bilingual bicultural programme states:

The existence of such a program in the school would place a recognition of integrity and worth of the Chinese culture within the child's frame of reference. Secondly it would represent compatibility between the home and school rather than a cultural competition for the children's allegiance. (Toronto Board of Education, 1976)

The programme consists of withdrawing the students from regular classes for half an hour per day for instruction in Chinese language and culture. The programme was evaluated a year after its inauguration, and the researchers found that most students, parents and teachers agreed that the Chinese programme was successful in making students more aware of Chinese culture. Receiving half an hour a day less instruction did not result in any lowering of academic achievement, while a very noticeable change in the self-esteem was observed. The students were both better informed and placed greater value upon their cultural heritage. The programme became a prototype of several other bilingual and bicultural programmes (Deosaran and Gershman, 1976). A similar Greek bilingual programme is now being run in two schools in East Toronto.

In 1973, an experimental Italian transition programme was started in a junior and senior kindergarten. In this programme, the children are initially taught in their mother tongue (Italian in this case). They are then gradually introduced to English and are expected to catch up with regular classes in oral and written English by grade three. Evaluation studies indicated that the lack of early instruction in the English language did not cause the children to suffer in English language comprehension, while their self-esteem improved considerably (Shapson and Purbhoo, 1977).

The Government of Quebec initiated a project ('Project d'enseignement de langues d'origine') to offer children of linguistic minorities the chance to maintain and develop knowledge of their family's language and culture. Three programmes in Greek, Italian, and Portuguese were developed. They were open to children who had knowledge of the language concerned, and whose parents recognized themselves as belonging to the particular ethnic group. The programme was offered on a trial basis in the 1978-79 school year in the first grade in seven schools of the Montreal Catholic School Commission and consisted of teaching ethnic language and culture for half of the school time. Preliminary results indicate a general satisfaction on the part of children, parents, teachers and organizers, and the programme was extended to the second grade in the 1979-80 school year.

Objections have been raised to multicultural education both at the conceptual and practical levels. Some disagree with the concept of multiculturalism. They argue that retention of ethnic identity impairs social mobility, thereby entrenching inequalities. In his brilliant analysis of the Canadian mosaic concept, Porter (1965) had argued that pluralism and equality of opportunity are incompatible. Holmes (1978) not only argues against schools as agents for producing multicultural society, he also argues against the provision of any special services for immigrants.

> In the long run, most special services to immigrants will, in my opinion, turn out to be patronizing, condescending and dysfunctional. They may provide separate and different education but surely we have learned by now that it is very difficult to produce separate but equal facilities if one of the separate parties suffers from some disadvantage whether it be social, psychological or financial.

In a later paper, Porter (1969) argues that cultural differences are exaggerated by English Canadians as an excuse for preventing minority groups from climbing the social ladder. He maintains that the myth of cultural differences is the major obstacle in the way of equality of opportunity in Canada, and that since multiculturalism implies maintenance of cultural differences, it will greatly help the cause of the continuing English-Canadian monopoly over their élite position in Canadian society.

A different view is taken by others who argue that it is not that multiculturalism has failed in Canada — it has never been tried. Lofty principles have been stated but never practised.

> Multiculturalism policies, established by the federal government, have been underscored by the provincial government of Ontario. Statements by Ministers of Education, Chairpersons of school boards, the various Work Groups on Multiculturalism within Metro Toronto, all illustrate the fact that the thrust for reform has developed outside and apart from the schools. And,

significantly, there exists a lag between the words of the politicians and the attitudes and practices of the teachers who are the principal instruments in the assessment, placement, and educational treatment of the new Canadian. (Samuda, 1980)

Deosaran (1977) had earlier observed a similar 'disheartening gap between the policies of equal educational opportunities and the realities' in Ontario in general and in Toronto in particular. Ghosh (1978) is of the view that:

Education has failed to appreciate differences between peoples and cultures. The pressures for integration into the dominant culture and evaluation of performance in terms of standards set by the values, beliefs and practices of that culture have resulted in education that focuses on the elimination of differences.

There seems to be little doubt that the concept of multiculturalism has neither affected educational policy-making at the school level nor the educational practice of a very large body of teachers.

Conclusion

Porter's criticisms are justified to a certain extent. A distinction could be made between a multi-ethnic pluralist society and an institutionally pluralist society. While there has been a great deal of discussion in Canada about the former, little thought has been given to the latter. In practice, English-Canadians, and to a lesser extent French-Canadians, still control the major institutions in Canadian society, and 'until every child in school has an equal opportunity to put his hands on the levers of power, multiculturalism is likely to remain but an empty slogan' (Hamalian, 1979).

References

Anderson, W W and Grant, R W (1975) *The Newcomers* York University: Toronto

Ashworth, M (1976) *The Settlement of Immigrants: The Need for a Policy* University of British Columbia: Vancouver

Bancroft, G (1979) A place to stand *Multiculturalism* 2: 17-21

Berry, J, Kalin, R and Taylor, D (1977) *Multiculturalism and Ethnic Attitudes in Canada* Department of Supplies and Services: Ottawa

Bosquet, M (1977) Personal correspondence

Brooks, I R (1976) *Native Education in Canada and the United States: A Bibliography* Office of Educational Development, University of Calgary: Calgary, Alberta

Buchignani, N (1977) Bibliography: a review of historical and sociological literature on East Indians in Canada *Canadian Ethnic Studies* 9: 17-31

Chandra, U K (1973) *Racial Discrimination in Canada* B and B Research Associates: San Francisco, Cal

Clement, W (1975) *The Canadian Corporate Elite* Macmillan Carleton Series: Toronto

Coelho, E (1978) Curriculum change for a multicultural society *Teacher Education* 12: 82-91

Collins, D (1979) *Immigration: The Destruction of English Canada* B M G Publishing: Richmond Hill, Ontario

Cummins, J (1978) Educational implications of mother-tongue maintenance *Canadian Modern Language Review* 34: 395-416

Deosaran, R A (1977) Educational aspirations: individual freedom or social injustice *Interchange* **8**: 72-87

Deosaran, R and Gersham, J (1976) *An Evaluation of the 1975-76 Chinese-Canadian Bi-cultural Program* Research Department, Toronto Board of Education: Toronto

D'Oyley, W ed (1978) *Black Presence in Multi-Ethnic Canada* Ontario Institute for Studies in Education: Toronto

Elliston, I (1978) Is racism increasing in schools? *Multiculturalism* **2**: 27-8

Ghosh, R (1978) Ethnic minorities in the school curriculum *Multiculturalism* **2**: 24-6

Green, A (1976) *Immigration and Post-War Canadian Economy* Macmillan: Toronto

Hamalian, A (1979) National integration in multi-ethnic societies: the differential role of schooling and non-formal educational agencies *Compare* **9**: 33-44

Harvey, E B and Masemann, V L (1975) *Occupational Graduates and Labour Force* Ontario Ministry of Education: Toronto

Head, W A (1975) *The Black Presence in Canadian Mosaic* Ontario Human Rights Commission: Toronto

Head, W A and Lee, J (1978) The Black presence in the Canadian mosaic: discrimination in education *Interchange* **9**: 85-92

Henry, F (1978) *The Dynamics of Racism in Toronto* York University: Toronto

Holmes, M (1978) Multiculturalism and the school *in* D'Oyley (1978)

Hughes, D R and Kallen, E (1974) *The Anatomy of Racism: Canadian Dimensions* Harvest House: Montreal

Jean-Baptiste, J (1979) *Les Haitiens au Canada* Ministry of Supplies and Services: Ottawa

La Fountaine, M (1976) quoted *in* Toronto Board of Education (1976b)

Lasry, J (1980) Mobilité professionelle chez les immigrants juifs Nord-Africans à Montréal *International Review of Applied Psychology* **29**: 17-30

Laxer, R M ed (1979) *Bilingual Tensions in Canada* Ontario Institute for Studies in Education: Toronto

Lee, D J ed (1979) *Emerging Ethnic Boundaries* University of Ottawa Press: Ottawa

Lind, L (1974) New Canadianism: melting the ethnics in Toronto schools *in* Martell (1974)

Lupul, M R (1976) The portrayal of Canada's 'other' peoples in senior high school history and social studies text-books in Alberta, 1905 to present *Alberta Journal of Educational Research* **22**: 1-33

Maijala, H M (1977) Experiences of an immigrant child in Toronto *TESL Talk* **8**: 48-52

Markus, R L (1980) Difficulties encountered by Soviet immigrant children in adapting to secondary schools in their new homeland *TESL Talk* **11**: 14-25

Martell, G (1974) *The Politics of the Canadian Public Schools* James Lewis and Samuel: Toronto

McDiarmid, G and Pratt, D (1971) *Teaching Prejudice* Ontario Institute for Studies in Education: Toronto

McKinney, D W, Connor, L and Hull, E (1978) A note on socio-economic position of 1971 census enumerated Black employed males in Canada *in* D'Oyley (1978)

McQuillan, B (1977) A cross-section of cultures: education week at Harbourfront *Multiculturalism* **1**: 13-15

Murphy, R and Denis, A B (1979) Schools and the conservation of the vertical mosaic *in* Lee (1979)

Ontario Human Rights Commission (1977) *Life Together: A Report on Human Rights in Ontario* Queen's Printer: Toronto

Palmer, H and Tropper, H (1973) Canadian ethnic studies: historical perspectives and contemporary implications *Interchange* **4**: 15-23

Parai, L (1974) *The Economic Impact of Immigration* Manpower and Immigration Canada: Ottawa

Porter, J (1965) *The Vertical Mosaic* University of Toronto Press: Toronto

Porter, J (1969) Bilingualism and the myths of culture *Canadian Review of Sociology and Anthropology* **6**: 111-19

Porter, J (1972) Dilemmas and contradictions of multi-ethnic society *Royal Society of Canada: Transactions* **10**: 193-205

Ramcharan, S (1974) *Adaptations of West Indians in Canada* Unpublished PhD dissertation, York University: Toronto

Ramcharan, S (1979) East Indian immigration to Canada *Multiculturalism* **2**: 14-16

Richmond, A H (1967) *Post-War Immigrants in Canada* University of Toronto Press: Toronto

Richmond, A H (1976) Black and Asian immigrants in Britain and Canada: some comparisons *Journal of Community Relations Commission* **4**: 501-23

Samuda, R J (1980) How are the schools of Ontario coping with a new Canadian population: a report of recent research findings *TESL Talk* **11**: 44-51

Shapson, S and Purbhoo, M (1977) A transition program for Italian children *The Canadian Modern Language Review* **33**: 486-97

Shirley, F O (1968) *The influence of reading on concepts, attitudes and behaviour of 10th, 11th and 12th grade students* Unpublished PhD dissertation, University of Arizona: Tuscon, Ari

Statistics Canada (1980) *International and Interprovincial Migration In Canada* Statistics Canada: Ottawa

Sterioff, J L (1976) Experiments on the main street *Toronto Education Quarterly* 1965-66: 2-3, quoted *in* Toronto Board of Education (1976b)

Sue, S (1977) Psychological theory and implications for Asian Americans *The Personnel and Guidance Journal* **55**: 381-9

Toronto Board of Education (1975) *Draft Report of Workgroup on Multicultural Programs* Toronto Board of Education: Toronto

Toronto Board of Education (1976a) *The First Report of the Workgroup on Multicultural Programs* Toronto Board of Education: Toronto

Toronto Board of Education (1976b) *We Are All Immigrants to This Place* Toronto Board of Education: Toronto

Toronto Board of Education (1979) *Report of the Sub-Committee on Race Relations* Toronto Board of Education: Toronto

Trudeau, P E (1971) Canadian culture: announcement of implementation policy of multiculturalism within bilingual framework *Debates 8 Canadian Parliament* 28th Parliament, 3rd Session, 8.10.71

Ubale, B (1977) *Equal Opportunities and Public Policy* Ontario Human Rights Commission: Toronto

Van Dyck, W C and Arkell, R N (1979) Stereotyping in the classroom *Multiculturalism* **3**: 22-5

15. Education and occupational aspirations of young South Asians in Britain

Gajendra Verma and Brandon Ashworth

Summary: This chapter reports on a larger study by the authors, which is concerned with the determinants of the vocational choices of adolescents of South Asian background in Britain, focusing on the roles of 'cultural conflict' and the British educational system.

The first part of the chapter covers the antecedent considerations of migration, indigenous reaction and patterns of immigrant settlement, particularly of the South Asians; these are related to the specific educational requirements of the group. Such background information is vital to an understanding of the educational problems both encountered and posed by South Asian children in the British educational system.

The second part consists of a report on several specific aspects of the education of South Asians which are at present under study, and concentrates upon the vocational aspirations of South Asian adolescents prior to leaving school. An examination of aspirations in relation to cultural, social and personal factors revealed that aspirational level represents a complex interaction between the adaptation of migrants and their children to the British educational and occupational system and the general patterns of socialization and moderating personality variables. The chapter concludes with a reflection on the current plight of South Asian youngsters in British social and educational hierarchies, and makes suggestions for both curriculum change and further research.

Introduction

Polarization between the native White and the non-White young members of British society is becoming increasingly evident. The growing alienation of the rising generation of Black and Asian youth can only be ignored at the risk of allowing the unhappy example of the United States ('too little and too late' policies) to be imitated in this country. The recent disturbances in Bristol and London are not merely a consequence of anti-authoritarianism but reflect some of the deeper social, economic and — though it has been denied — racial problems, all of which must be the concern of both the immigrant and the host communities.

Although the total community in Britain has been composed over the centuries of many diverse groups with varying social and cultural backgrounds, post-war migration from the New Commonwealth — the Caribbean, Africa, India, Pakistan, Bangladesh and South East Asia — has generated discussion about the nature of British society. Whenever a reference is made to immigrant groups in Britain, the assumption is made that the reference is to those people — Blacks and Browns — who have come from what are known as the New Commonwealth countries. The total number of immigrant people living in Britain is estimated to be about 3,000,000. Of these, about half are White immigrants from Europe, the Old Commonwealth (Canada, Australia and New Zealand), and Ireland. The other half have migrated from New Commonwealth countries and have attracted a great deal of attention from the indigenous population. The majority of these immigrants have settled in the major conurbations of London, the Midlands and Yorkshire, where both work and housing were available.

Many factors contributed to the post-war migration from the West Indies and the Indian sub-continent. In the 1950s, many industries in Britain were desperately short of semi-skilled and unskilled labour for their post-war economic revival. The lack of good employment and disparities of life-chances in their home countries, contrasted with the many opportunities and abundant wealth which seemed to exist in Britain were the main factors which brought a small proportion of people from alien ethnic and cultural backgrounds to Britain. But although the New Commonwealth immigrants had hoped for economic and social betterment in Britain, their entry was limited to the lower social strata.

The different ethnic groups in Britain can be categorized in the following way: Blacks — West Indians and Africans; Asians — Pakistanis, Indians, Bangladeshis, Sikhs, Malaysians and Chinese; Europeans — Italians, Cypriots, Greeks, Poles and Hungarians. Each sub-group relates in different ways to educational, social, occupational and cultural life in British society.

Because immigrant groups from the New Commonwealth countries were young, there was a higher proportion of families with younger children among them than within the indigenous population. This has meant a rapid increase in the number of Black and Asian children in both primary and secondary schools in Britain. The character of the school population, particularly in urban areas, has undergone considerable change; Britain has become a multi-ethnic, multicultural society. Moreover, given the age structure and cultural patterns of many immigrant groups, the proportion of ethnic minority pupils in schools is likely to rise. In London, the statistics for 1975 showed that 23 per cent of all births were to New Commonwealth mothers (Multi-Ethnic Education, 1977).

British thinking and policy-making must therefore be oriented towards multicultural education. Teachers and educational planners can no longer ignore the fact that a programme of educational reform emphasizing pluralism in schools is of utmost concern to *all* schools, whether or not the school contains large numbers of ethnic minority pupils. The number of advisers to education authorities concerned with 'multi-ethnic' or 'multi-cultural' education has grown steadily over the past decade in areas of high immigrant population. There is less clarity, however, over the exact implication of these labels for policy. The Department of Education and Science suggested in a discussion paper that 'our society is a multi-cultural, multi-racial one and the curriculum should reflect a sympathetic understanding of the different cultures and races that make up our society' (DES, 1977). Yet these curriculum aims have not been realized (Mallick and Verma, 1981), nor do the self-concepts of many Black children reflect a curriculum which meets their cognitive and affective needs (Jeffcoate, 1979).

Responses of the indigenous population

Government policy on immigration to Britain since the arrival in the 1950s of New Commonwealth immigrants in large numbers has been strict and has often shown a partisan control of certain groups. There has always been a hard core of racism in British society which has advocated the suppression, control and eventual repatriation of all non-Whites (Bagley, Verma, Mallick and Young, 1979; Bagley and Verma, 1979). But the largest section of the indigenous population holds an assimilationist policy, indicating explicitly that immigrants will be accepted if they give up their 'alien' social, cultural and religious characteristics and conform to the British way of life. Much British thinking and policy-making on race and education has been based on this broad conception, using interchangeably such terms as 'integration', 'assimilation' and 'adjustment'. The confusion which prevails in the field of multicultural education has been created by a complex set of factors, among which lack of policy at the national level is one of the most significant. A liberal minority of the indigenous population hold a pluralist position, suggesting that Britain should tolerate ethnic groups to the extent of allowing autonomy with regard to dress, religion and customs which are fundamental individual rights. They further argue that the immigrant groups have brought with them new perspectives which are of positive value to British society, which is in any case based on a mixture of many different cultures.

Ironically, the assimilationist view has been carried through in a discriminatory way. For example, West Indians come from a British dominated culture, are Christian and familiar with many British institutions including an educational system similar to Britain's own. Yet they have suffered considerable discrimination in education, employment and housing, and the assimilationist aspirations of the West Indian group have largely been rejected (Bagley and Young, 1979). Similarly, young Asians who have had all their education in Britain and who speak perfect English have been discriminated against in employment (Ballard and Holden, 1975).

The duality of the prevalent British attitude is documented by a study of those immigrants from Pakistan who are Christian (Jeffrey, 1976). These immigrants were refugees from a Muslim country which had not, by and large, respected their Christian identity. They had hoped that in

Britain, which is nominally a Christian country, they would receive more equitable treatment. But the British have failed to distinguish them from other immigrants from Pakistan, and the assimilationist hopes of Pakistani Christians have been rejected. Perhaps this may be the reason that they have tended to stress aspects of a Pakistani, rather than a Christian, identity.

This has been the general pattern of response by the indigenous population to many immigrant groups, irrespective of the latter's initial attitude to British culture. The research evidence is sufficient to reveal the critical, stiff and non-accepting attitude of the British. The reaction on the part of the immigrant communities has been to draw as far as possible upon their own resources, and re-establish religious, social and cultural traditions which were lapsing.

This chapter attempts to test some of the ideas outlined above. Our research has been with one particular immigrant group, the adolescents from a South Asian background whose parents settled in two major industrial cities in the north of England. Although broad generalizations about other immigrant groups cannot be made, examination of the experience of one particular ethnic minority group raises certain fundamental questions, not only concerning the education of ethnic minority pupils in Britain but also about British educational policy in general.

The South Asians in Britain

In order to understand the nature and determinants of the vocational aspirations, choices and achievements of adolescents from a South Asian background it would be useful to sketch the society and the educational background of their parents.

South Asian immigration (mainly from the Indian sub-continent) to Britain was at its peak in the 1960s. The poor prospects of employment in their own countries, and a definite hope of economic and social betterment in Britain, were among the factors that led to their coming in the first place. The vast majority of the early migrants were young men who had left their families and dependants behind, though when they settled down in the new environment some of them brought their families over to England. Their initial intention was often merely to work for a few years and then return to their own country; however, their children were less likely to return to their parents' country of origin.

Recent statistics (*The Sunday Times*, January 1977) show that there are approximately 618,000 Asians living in Britain, forming the largest single immigrant group. They have come mainly from four regions of the Indian sub-continent: Punjab (north of Delhi) and Gujerat (north of Bombay) in India, Pakistan and Bangladesh. Most migrants from the Punjab and Gujerat areas are in skilled and commercial jobs (some have their own businesses) whereas people from Pakistan and Bangladesh are often employed in factories, especially in the textile industry. People from Gujerat are usually educated (some have had university education) but very few have been able to obtain white-collar jobs.

In 1972, some 30,000 Asians in Uganda were forced to migrate to Britain (Swinerton, Kuepper and Lackey, 1975). This group, who settled largely in London and in Leicester, had well-developed entrepreneurial skills and have been particularly successful in setting up small and medium-sized businesses in manufacturing and retailing. They are an economically upward mobile group.

In East London Bengali immigrants have settled in the same houses and in the same clothing and textile industries where Jewish immigrants lived and worked in the early part of this century. These Bengali immigrants are often misunderstood and indeed persecuted by disadvantaged members of the indigenous community. A possible explanation of such behaviour may be that Bengali immigrants work hard and have the ability to rise economically and socially.

The South Asian community can be divided into three major religious groups — Hindus, Muslims and Sikhs. In addition, Christians are an important religious group among South Asian migrants, especially Pakistanis. Although there are distinct cultural, social and linguistic differences among these South Asian immigrant communities, their experience in British society is somewhat similar. They and their children, many of whom were born in this country, have been the target of discrimination in many spheres of life.

Having outlined briefly the general background of post-war migration, we must now examine some of the issues in the education of South Asian pupils.

Some issues in schooling

The debate concerning formal schooling of 'immigrant' children (despite the common label the majority are not immigrants) has centred for a number of years around the issues of language, race relations, achievement, religion, culture and disadvantage. Among the policies required to deal with these issues are those concerned with compensatory measures, designed to counteract disadvantage. However, this limited approach is inadequate for two reasons. First, all too often the sincere motive of attempting to offset disadvantage by compensatory education has misguided those interested in equality of opportunity into concentrating upon the weaknesses of ethnic minority groups. Secondly, despite its desirability, equality of opportunity may not be easily attained, given the prevailing role of education as a system of differentiation and classification of the workforce in an advanced industrial society. The recent studies of Halsey and Goldthorpe (1980) have served to emphasize the relative rigidity of the British social structure.

Some sociologists point out that the entire debate about the process of schooling is irrelevant, given the context of hierarchical roles and the extremely limited 'opportunity structure' in the world of work. Even a teacher in our Project school who had close links with industry aimed at helping the potentially 'unemployable', expressed misgivings about the views of industrialists:

> . . . industry has told us, and we'll put a question mark on it, that [these kids] are unemployable, because we don't do it right. Well, the same type of pupil ten years ago was employable, because the labour market was different, but now, it's very easy to put the blame on the school. I'm not saying the school is innocent but I think more blame is being put on the school purely because they can't find jobs for them.

The literature on ethnic minorities in the British educational system often describes the features of particular cultures, but very rarely attempts to explain the way in which education operates in the consciousness of different groups in society. This is a grave deficiency, and to compensate for this, the present study was designed to explore the nature and determinants of the vocational aspirations, choices and achievements of adolescents from a South Asian background, with special reference to the role of the school.

The present study

Background

The present study aimed to understand the 'differential aspiration' between adolescents of South Asian origin and their peers from the indigenous population. The implications of this are profound: it has been consistently shown that 'Asians' suffer from multiple disadvantage (Smith, 1976) and restricted employment opportunities. When aspirations are high but likely to be disappointed, there may be serious consequences for the adaptation of the individual to working life (Verma, 1981). It can also be argued that the adaptation processes of 'first-generation immigrants' are mediated through a diffuse network of interpersonal and institutional mechanisms (eg networks of friends and family, community-based self-help systems and, less significantly, government agencies) while children of immigrants are exposed to the institutionalized and culturally complex socialization system of schools and career preparation.

The concept of differential aspiration was first introduced by Beetham (1967) in discussion of aspiration on the part of 'immigrants', particularly 'Asians'. According to him, 'Asians' aspire to occupations which require qualifications 'beyond their reach'. He attributes this to various causes: a lack of acquaintance with the full range of occupations available in British society; a fascination with mechanical jobs (natural in those who come from a country where mechanization is not highly advanced); a reluctance to enter the lower occupations endured by an earlier generation; the influence of parents (whose conceptions are based on the occupational structure of the country of origin); and a tendency to aim for jobs which would provide money or status in the event of the family returning home. Beetham also pointed to the 'surprising diffidence' of native White children who saw substantial obstacles in the way of even modest ambitions and aspirations in life. Following Veness (1962) and foreshadowing Willis (1977) he pointed to the particular nature of the socialization fostered by the 11+ examinations, streaming, and in particular, the secondary modern school. His model has achieved a degree of respectability for its balance between 'cultural factors' derived from the 'country of origin', and factors derived from interaction with the education system.

Despite the criticism which has been levelled at this interpretation (eg Hiro, 1968) it has been treated as an empirical fact both at a policy-making level (House of Commons Select Committee on Race Relations and Immigration, 1968, 1969, Minutes 6.2.69, p 84) and at 'grass-roots' level. However, there is a degree of bias in Beetham's writing. He views 'depressed aspiration' in White working class children as the norm, and regards the aspirations of 'Asians' as 'unrealistic'. It is this aspect of his work which has been most severely criticized (Hiro, 1968); paradoxically it has also been most enthusiastically followed up by teachers, careers officers and researchers. Partly because of Beetham's work and partly because of the explanations by other researchers in this field, 'culturally determined' over-aspiration has become a prevailing conceptual orthodoxy.

This conceptual orthodoxy is evident in many subsequent investigations. Gupta (1977), Fowler et al (1977), Baker (1978), and the Commission for Racial Equality (1978) have all discussed the relevance of 'cultural' influences on vocational/occupational expectations. The results obtained by these studies are remarkably consistent in that they all conclude that Asian adolescents had 'higher' aims than their White counterparts. Fowler and her colleagues (1977) also reported a stereotyped viewpoint on the part of youth employment officers in Glasgow, where over-aspiration was seen as a barrier to appropriate job choice for 'Asian' youths. These researchers, however, found that this theoretical framework was inadequate to explain disappointment and failure in the labour market. They also produced evidence showing unfamiliarity, on the part of the sample studied, with application procedures, educational requirements and job availability. Gupta (1977) concluded that 'Asians', both male and female, expressed significantly higher educational as well as vocational aspirations. Compared with the native White sample, Gupta's Asian sample also showed higher occupational mobility between generations, which he attributed to parental attitudes and 'ethnic coloured minority status'.

What is lacking from most analyses is an adequate treatment of the way in which aspirations are constructed — socially and psychologically. For example, two individuals who express a desire to become doctors may have different motives — one may wish to gain social status and the other may have a genuine wish to help others. Similarly, the precise social and psychological consequences of failure to meet aspirations have not been carefully studied. However, serious concern has been expressed concerning the alienation and dissatisfaction of young Blacks and Browns of West

Indian and South Asian origins (Verma and Bagley, 1979; Bagley, Verma, Mallick and Young, 1979) with regard to their career prospects.

Scope of the present study

In our research we have been concerned with the following aspects of vocational adaptation of South Asian youngsters in British schools:

1. whether young South Asians underachieve compared with their White indigenous counterparts;
2. how far their aspirations are in keeping with their achievement level compared with their White peers;
3. the factors influencing the level of vocational aspiration;
4. the degree to which teachers and careers officers perceive South Asian youngsters in negative or positive terms;
5. the extent to which employers in the north of England view ethnic minority groups in negative or positive terms, and the degree to which some employers practise racial discrimination;
6. the impact which discrimination in different spheres has on individuals' and groups' perceptions of the host community as a whole, and the world of work in particular;
7. the extent to which young South Asians come into conflict with an education system which does not provide them with 'qualifications' to compete with their White peers;
8. the values inherent in the normative conception of a 'correct' level of aspiration, and the extent to which the British educational system 'downgrades' the expectations of working class British adolescents and acts as a filtering process by which stratification is reproduced.

The qualities which differentiate the aspirations of South Asian from those of indigenous teenagers are multi-dimensional, and reflect the complexity of the social situation which migrants and their children from the Third World have to negotiate in metropolitan society.

Research method

The methods of study consisted of case studies of schools and communities in two areas of the north of England which have dense South Asian settlements. In order to make studies in suitable depth we selected seven mixed-sex schools in the two areas. The techniques involved have included demographic analysis, analysis of the changing labour market, large-scale use of questionnaire techniques, observation of educational processes, and in-depth interviews with selected adolescents (both South Asian and indigenous), parents, employers, teachers, members of the community, careers officers and policy-makers.

The research was conducted at two levels. The first was concerned with large-scale data collection (a questionnaire was given to over 1000 pupils from the 1978 fifth forms of the seven schools). The sample comprised individuals from all ethnic and ability groups. At the second level we used a smaller cohort of 200 pupils, both males and females, from the 1979 fifth forms. The principal part of the research at this stage involved lengthy tape-recorded interviews (using a semi-structured interview schedule), and administration of standardized psychometric tests of academic motivation, attitudes toward school, self-esteem and achievement motivation. We also had a number of group discussions with the pupils which helped to high-light differences of opinion and social perception among the participants. The following section presents briefly the broad patterns emerging from our quantitative and qualitative data.

Findings and discussion

What emerged from the initial questionnaire (given to over 1000 youngsters in seven schools) and from the interviews is that South Asian adolescents in the two areas of the north of England tended to have realistic aspirations with regard to their vocation. Some did admit to having had fantasy aspirations, but these were not significantly different from the fantasies admitted to by indigenous pupils. However, in the earlier stages of immigration in the West Yorkshire area (the area of our study) when migrants from the Indian sub-continent took up jobs in the textile industry — often working nights and on piece work — there was an obvious reason for exhorting their children to set their sights higher. Indeed, this is a common enough attitude among working class parents.

Thus the 'over-aspiration' of South Asian youngsters which has frequently been explained in the literature in terms of cultural factors may simply be a reaction to the group experience of their parents who have been involved primarily in unpleasant and difficult work — the kind which indigenous workers were reluctant to tackle. Many of the South Asian youngsters in our study made this point explicitly. A Pakistani boy said:

> He [father] doesn't want me to go into textile because he says he doesn't think much about it, and I don't want to go to work in a mill either. He says it's not good there — you have to work all night and you don't get any sleep . . . .

The explicit rejection of the type of factory work done by their parents was highly marked among young South Asians particularly Pakistanis, but this does not necessarily mean that they were unrealistic about their future careers.

A majority of our South Asian sample anticipated difficulties in the way of achieving their goal, although they seemed highly motivated and were anxious to succeed in academic work. This high motivation set in the context of the socialization system may partly account for the currency of the concept of 'over-aspiration'.

Motivation in the context of academic achievement seems to have two main dimensions — hope of success and fear of failure (Atkinson, 1957; Heckhausen, 1977). A number of studies have attempted to link over-aspiration with high motivation to avoid failure (eg Moulton, 1965). Furthermore, it seems reasonable to assume that motivation in school depends partly on the belief that scholastic success is related to subsequent occupational level. The results of the *Motivation Attitude Intensity Scale* (Sumner, 1972) showed that South Asians scored significantly higher than the English, and that girls had a higher score than boys (a high score indicates high 'school morale'). The findings can be explained in a number of ways: differential educational traditions in the country of origin may associate schooling with success in life (Verma, Bagley and Mallick, 1980); depressed scores of the British adolescents may stem from a more pessimistic assessment of employment opportunities in the north of England; high motivation level on the part of South Asian adolescents may imply a favourable attitude towards the educational institution perceived as a vehicle for social mobility. The South Asians also expressed a desire to stay on at school longer which lends support to the results obtained on the MAIS.

Another aspect of our research was concerned with the social and economic status of South Asian immigrants in West Yorkshire. According to the orthodox criteria of housing, income level and family size, the South Asian population would seem to experience considerable deprivation, which one would expect to have an adverse effect on self-esteem, motivation and academic achievement. Self-esteem was assessed by the Coopersmith Self-esteem Inventory (Coopersmith, 1967). It is interesting to note that first generation young South Asians had significantly higher self-esteem than either the second generation or their White counterparts. The higher self-esteem may be explained by differences in 'cultural' norms between the South Asian population and the indigenous population — for instance, the mutual support networks in the South Asian communities. High self-esteem may also be indicative of a defence reaction. The lower self-esteem among the second generation (born in Britain) may be seen in terms of 'anticipated difficulties' in getting employment, as reported by many of our respondents. In answer to the question 'How difficult do you think it will be to get a job you like?', the majority of South Asian youths anticipated more difficulty than did their English counterparts.

When examining differences between culturally distinct groups it is important that the groups are not treated as homogeneous, as in all groups there are wide variations in the psycho-social attributes of individuals. Self-concept or self-esteem seems related not only to how people see themselves, but also how they would like others to treat them.

The problem is made more acute by the continuing underprivileged position of ethnic minorities in British schools, and a progressive decline in achievement in some Black and Asian pupils as they advance, increasingly alienated, through the school. Their location in the educational hierarchy is clearly demonstrated by the overview of a fifth form in one of our project schools: this distribution was mirrored throughout the schools we studied, and other research shows that a similar picture emerges nationally.

The most obvious factor seemed to be the existence of discrimination

Type of course	School class	Ethnic group				
		West Indian	African	Indian/Pakistani	Chinese	East European
GCE courses	5G1	–	–	–	–	–
	5G2	3%	–	–	–	–
	5G3	–	–	3%	–	–
	5G4	–	–	–	–	6%
GCE and some CSE	5G5	3%	–	6%	3%	6%
	5G6	12%	–	5%	–	5%
	5G7	3%	–	6%	–	–
CSE (GCE crafts) non-academic subjects	5S1	15%	5%	5%	18%	–
	5S2	14%	–	14%	–	5%
	5S3	17%	5%	–	–	–
	5S4	35%	–	20%	–	–
	5S5	30%	–	15%	–	–
	5S6	50%	–	42%	5%	–

Table 1 *Ethnic minorities in a streamed fifth form
(as percentages of each class)*

and prejudice on the part of certain employers and teachers who interpret the ambition of South Asian and Black people as 'unrealistic'. Racist tendencies were evident in interviews with many teachers and careers officers.

Teacher prejudice takes various forms. In the classroom, teachers often operate on the basis of stereotypes and unproven assumptions. American research on labelling (Rosenthal, 1973) suggests that such stereotypes are particularly prevalent in the teaching of minority pupils, and our research showed that many teachers hold negative stereotypes of Black and Asian pupils. Some teachers have a conventional view of immigrant children – they attribute all their problems to language difficulties, socioeconomic background and inherent lack of intelligence. One of the teachers in a Project school was emphatic:

> I still believe that there are such things as working class mentality, middle class mentality and an aristocratic mentality, and I don't think, whatever the sociologists and the people of this world try to hide or cover, you'll ever stop that kind of basic tripartite system of people. Now the people you are talking about, their sons and daughters, finish up in this school in classes which are non-examination or bottom CSE. They rarely have sons and daughters who are going to be bright GCE candidates and it isn't the fault of the education system and it isn't the fault of western civilisation, it's inherent in life.

It is also obvious from our research data that careers teaching receives scant attention on the curriculum in some schools and appears to have little impact on some children, particularly ethnic minority pupils, because of the incidental nature of such teaching. Many careers interviews are devoted largely to disabusing people of unreasonable aspirations. The problem has been particularly acute among South Asian teenagers. In one of our sample schools careers education was not included on the timetable at all.

On the basis of our study it is possible to question the role of careers education. Should careers teachers and officers devote their time to persuading children from an early age to lower their expectations? In many cases, such adjustment of expectations is performed by only partially trained personnel and could have serious consequences.

The accelerating industrial decline is also one of the factors which has to be taken into account in discussing vocational adaptation, because of the implications it has for the school-leaver and for the curriculum developer who may be attempting to modify the curriculum to cater more specifically for the needs of Asian and Black youth.

Thus the issue of the vocational adaptation of South Asians is not clear-cut. It is closely bound up with many social, educational and psychological factors.

Reflections

In this chapter we have set out the problems presented by the education of adolescents from a South Asian background in Britain.

The first point to be made is that the attitudes of the indigenous population to immigrants and their children in general, and to the education of ethnic minority pupils in particular, are often confused, and are of various types. Three broad kinds of attitude can be identified — a rejectionist view, an assimilationist view and a view which advocates cultural pluralism and its counterpart, multicultural education. The assimilationist view still dominates much thinking in British education and social policy.

In recent years, considerable attention has been focused on the problems of adaptation of ethnic minority pupils to British life. The findings of many studies and research reports show that the British educational system has failed to meet the needs of ethnic minority pupils, has ignored their linguistic backgrounds and their strengths, and has discriminated against them in other ways. This has resulted in increasing alienation of such children from the British educational system and an increasingly aggressive outlook towards a social system which is rightly seen as profoundly racist (Bagley, Verma, Mallick and Young, 1979).

Studies of teachers in British schools have found that they are likely to share the prejudices held by the majority of the population. A number of special courses have been designed by colleges and departments of education in Britain which give training in multicultural education, (*see Chapter 20*) but unfortunately such courses are still rare. The need for such training is well illustrated by an evaluation of curriculum innovation in the field of multicultural education (Verma, 1977). Our experience shows that only a minority of teachers hold liberal views in this field. Many indigenous teachers do not fully understand the needs and difficulties of Black and Asian children, and those who do understand are not adequately equipped with resources to educate pupils for a plural society.

Hence there is an urgent need to educate the educators. The broad aim of multicultural education is to create a situation in which people of all races, religions, castes and creeds have an equal place in a harmonious, multiracial society. Such a goal requires success in achieving a complex set of inter-related objectives (social, educational and political). If a policy of multicultural education is to be successful it must be supported by properly trained and adequately motivated teachers.

If the educational system is to meet the needs of the new generation of Black and Asian children it will have to change in quite fundamental ways. It will have to adopt an increasingly plural approach, providing both integrated and parallel instruction in the traditional values, culture and language of the various ethnic groups — Asian, African, West Indian, Irish, Cypriot and others. It should be acknowledged too that the failure of any child to acquire cognitive skills is a failure, by and large, of the school. School should be a place where children acquire positive self-esteem, not a negative view of themselves as failures. Immigrants and their children are not responsible for failure: failure is more likely to be caused by the oppressive and demoralizing influences of a racist society.

In the face of such an educational system, with teachers who may be passive or active supporters of racist ideologies and practices, and which not only fails ethnic minority pupils both academically and culturally, but also condemns many of them to exclusion, how are parents to meet the challenge? One solution, practised by Asian families who can afford it, is to have their children educated privately in English preparatory and public schools. While such schools make no pretence at offering anything other than a traditional Anglo-Saxon education, their small classes and concern for individual pupils do offer ethnic minority children a greater chance of academic, and hence perhaps vocational, success.

Note

The research reported in this chapter was conducted over a two year period (1977-79) and was funded by the Leverhulme Trust Fund, London. The Project was based in the Postgraduate School of Studies in Research in Education, University of Bradford, and was directed by Gajendra Verma.

References

Atkinson, J W (1957) Motivational determinants of risk-taking behaviour *Psychological Review* 64 359-72

Bagley, C and Verma, G K (1979) *Racial Prejudice, the Individual and Society* Saxon House: Farnborough, Hants

Bagley, C, Verma, G K, Mallick, K and Young, L (1979) *Personality, Self-Esteem and Prejudice* Saxon House: Farnborough, Hants

Bagley, C and Young, L (1979) The identity, adjustment and achievement of trans-racially adopted children: a review and empirical report *in* Verma and Bagley (1979)

Baker, A (1978) Asians are not all alike *New Society* 2.11.78

Ballard, R and Holden, B (1975) The employment of coloured graduates in Britain *New Community* 4: 325-36

Beetham, D (1967) *Immigrant School-Leavers and the Youth Employment Service in Birmingham* Institute of Race Relations/Oxford University Press: London

Brody, E (1969) Migration and adaptation *in* Brody (1969)

Brody, E ed (1969) *Behaviour in New Environments* Sage Publications: Beverly Hills, Cal

Commission for Racial Equality (1978) *Looking for Work: Black and White School Leavers in Lewisham* HMSO: London

Coopersmith, S (1967) *The Antecedents of Self-esteem* Freeman: San Francisco, Cal

Fowler, B, Madigan, R and Littlewood, B (1977) Immigrant school-leavers and the search for work *Sociology* 1 Jan 1977

Gupta, Y P (1977) The educational and vocational aspirations of Asian immigrants and English school-leavers *British Journal of Sociology* 28: 185-98

Halsey, A H and Goldthorpe, D (1980) *Origins and Destinations: Family, Class and Education in Modern Britain* Oxford University Press: Oxford

Heckhausen, H (1977) Achievement motivation and its constructs: a cognitive model *Motivation and Emotion* 1: 283-329

Hiro, D (1968) Unrealistic aspirations *New Society* 2.7.68

Jeffcoate, R (1979) *Positive Image Towards a Multiracial Curriculum* Chameleon Books: London

Jeffrey, P (1976) *Migrants and Refugees: Muslim and Christian Pakistani Families in Bristol* Cambridge University Press: London

Mallick, K and Verma, G K (1981) Teaching in the multi-ethnic, multicultural school *in* Verma and Bagley (1981)

Moulton, R W (1965) Effects of success and failure on level of aspiration as related to achievement motives *Journal of Personality and Social Psychology* 1: 399-406

Multi-Ethnic Education (1977) *Joint Report of the Schools Sub-committee and Further Education Sub-committee of Inner London Education Committee:* London

Rosenthal, R (1973) The Pygmalion effect lives *Psychology Today* 7: 56-63

Smith, D (1976) *The Facts of Racial Disadvantage* Penguin: Harmondsworth

Swinerton, E, Kuepper, W and Lackey, G (1965) *Ugandan Asians in Britain* Croom Helm: London

Sumner, R (1972) *Motivation Attitude Intensity Scale* National Foundation for Educational Research: Windsor, Berks

Taylor, J (1976) *The Halfway Generation: A Study of Asian Youths in Newcastle upon Tyne* National Foundation for Educational Research: Windsor, Berks

Veness, T (1962) *School Leavers* Methuen: London

Verma, G K (1977) Some effects of curriculum innovation on the racial attitudes of adolescents *International Journal of Intercultural Relations* 1: 67-78

Verma, G K (1981) The problems of vocational adaptation of 'Asian' adolescents in Britain: some theoretical and methodological issues *in* Verma and Bagley (1981)

Verma, G K and Bagley, C eds (1979) *Race, Education and Identity* Macmillan: London

Verma, G K, Bagley, C and Mallick, K (1980) *Illusion and Reality in Indian Secondary Education* Gower Publishing: Farnborough, Hants

Verma, G K and Bagley, C eds (1981) *Self-concept, Achievement and Multicultural Education* Macmillan: London

Willis, P (1977) *Learning to Labour* Saxon House: Farnborough, Hants

16. Educational opportunity for minority groups: Australian research reviewed

Millicent E Poole

Summary: Educational opportunity for minority groups in Australia has been embedded within a context of social and political policies designed to reflect the changing pattern of Australian society. Currently, in terms of access and outcome measures, minority groups are not, on average, disadvantaged, except in relation to achievement outcomes in language-related areas. Aspiration levels of immigrants tend to be high, with parents supportive of their children's schooling. However, there are other factors to be taken into account, such as social class and family resources (intellectual and economic), differences in commitment to schooling between and among different immigrant groups, and some evidence of differing cultural expectations for immigrant boys and girls. Overall, the evidence suggests that social class factors rather than minority group membership tend to inhibit equality of educational opportunity.

Introduction

The changing pattern of immigration in Australia since World War II has 'completely transformed Australia from being a homogeneous English-Scottish-Irish community into a heterogeneous nation composed of many of the cultural and linguistic streams of the world' (Taft and Cahill, 1978: 3). This influx of minority* groups, of course, made its imprint on the schools which, for the first time in their history, had to confront the problem of how to teach children with minimal knowledge of English and diverse linguistic backgrounds. There were, in addition, other connected problems, eg low levels of literacy, lack of parental secondary or tertiary education, different regional languages, and family mobility leading to frequent changes of school for children.

Martin (1978) hypothesized three shifts of focus in the way Australians perceived immigrants. The initial phase was assimilationist: immigrants and their children were expected to meld into an Anglo-conformist Australian society. The second phase was problem-oriented, focusing on the social, economic and educational difficulties that migrants experienced. The

---

* Minority = immigrant newcomers. A conscious decision was made to exclude aboriginal groups because of (a) the different historical circumstances involved, and (b) the added sets of disadvantage to those included here, which could not be encompassed within this chapter.

present focus is 'participatory': minority groups are demanding greater access to the economic, educational, social and political structures of Australian society.

Educational institutions have tended to reflect these emphases. For example, during the assimilationist phase it was assumed that immigrant children would soon fit into existing patterns of schooling and quickly 'pick up English'. Subsequently, when the 'problem phase' was identified, the federal government introduced the Child Migrant Education Program (CMEP), in 1970. The conception of this programme was, however, very narrow, focusing on the teaching of English as a second language (TESL or ESL). As a result, CMEP was perceived by many as a 'band-aid' approach to the multiplicity of educational problems facing immigrant children. Today, as ethnic membership and participation have been espoused as official goals, schools are responding by rethinking and restructuring their curricula.

Immigrancy *per se*, and official attitudes to immigrants, have not been the sole barriers to the distribution of educational opportunities for ethnic groups. A number of studies have suggested that immigrants to Australia, by and large, enter at lower levels of the socioeconomic structure. For example, Connell *et al* (1975), identified southern Italians, northern Italians, Yugoslavs and Greeks as being ethnic groups of predominantly lower socioeconomic status (SES). De Lemos (1975), in her study of immigrant achievement conducted through the Australian Council for Educational Research, found that a majority of children in the non-English speaking sample came from low socioeconomic status families. Likewise, the OECD draft report *Educational Policy and Planning: Transition from School to Work or Further Study in Australia* (1976), pointed to the high proportion of low SES families among recent arrivals. In assessing the educational opportunity structure in Australian society, then, in terms of equality of opportunity for minority groups, it is necessary to consider both social class and ethnicity.

Martin (1971) argued that although 'socio-economic position apparently improves with length of residence, the economic vulnerability of immigrants during their first years in the country provides the conditions in which a residual, non-mobile and seriously disadvantaged immigrant population is forming at the bottom of the economic scale' (cited in Connell *et al*, 1975: 242). Such circumstances, according to reproduction of social class theory, tend to perpetuate educational and economic inequalities (Ashenden *et al*, 1980).

With the exception of Marjoribanks (1979), who uses the term 'ethclass' to encapsulate class and ethnicity, very little research has addressed itself to this 'double disadvantage'. The impact of multiple factors producing and reproducing disadvantage is now, however, widely acknowledged, and reflects views summarized by Blakers (1978):

> Much of the disadvantage in schooling suffered by children of migrant origin arises from having poor and lowly educated parents, and often living in crowded, deprived inner city areas where school facilities and amenities have

been minimal. (Blakers, 1978: 66)

During the 'problem phase', there was little or no public recognition that assimilation was not occurring, and that immigrant children had special needs. Few attempts were made to understand the family's relations with the education system or vice versa. Burns and Goodnow (1979) attribute the slowness of official recognition partly to assumptions held about immigrants and about the nature of learning:

> In the area of schooling, for example, a concerted attack on the teaching of English did not begin until 1970. Until that time, both education authorities and migrant parents apparently shared the assumption that young immigrants and children born in Australia would have no difficulty learning English . . . . They would acquire it from television, from the neighbours, or if they came to school without English, from 'sitting next to Nelly'. (Burns and Goodnow, 1979: 132)

In analysing the climate of change that occurred in an Australia moving towards the 'participatory' phase, Burns and Goodnow (1979) attribute the process to changes within both the immigrant and native group, ie a readiness to be visible and assertive on the part of immigrants, and a greater knowledge and recognition by Australians of the needs and aspirations of immigrants. They embed these processes within a wider Western context of concern with 'identity', 'roots', 'equal rights for all', and with what Novak (1972) describes as a reaction against the highly industrialized and homogenizing aspects of mass culture.

In relation to opportunity and schooling, the distinction has been made between equality of *access* to educational opportunity and the equality of *outcome* (eg Coleman, 1966). Equality of access within the highly bureaucratized and centralized systems of education in Australia has not been a major issue, especially since the advent of the Karmel (1973) report advocating funding on a 'needs' basis. This resulted in special resources being channelled to disadvantaged groups (eg through the Disadvantaged Schools Project). It is equality of outcome measured, in Coleman's terms, as *school achievement*, and subsequent *job placement* on leaving school, which has come under closer scrutiny as an index of possible disadvantage.

Concern has been expressed about the perceived difficulties experienced by immigrant children, usually within a framework of equality of educational opportunity, especially for disadvantaged groups. Several studies have suggested that immigrant children perform at lower levels than their Australian counterparts (Wiseman, 1971; Hewitt, 1977; Williams *et al*, 1980). On the other hand, there is equally convincing evidence that, far from being 'at risk', immigrant children are performing at a higher level than their Australian counterparts (Martin and Meade, 1979; Taft, 1975). Some of this discrepancy may result from the pooling of results for immigrant groups, a potentially misleading practice since, as Martin and Meade (1979) and Poole (1981) argue, intra-ethnic differences are often extensive. In addition, it has been shown that large numbers of students from non-English-speaking ethnic groups reject the institutional ideology of school-related success by 'clinging to high aspirations and staying at school despite a low level of performance as the school assesses it' (Martin and Meade, 1979: 16).

Increasingly, emphasis is being focused on the structural parameters of equality of educational opportunity. The key question is whether tolerance of cultural diversity will extend to pluralism based on structural equality. To date, there are major inconsistencies inherent in state and federal policy documents on multicultural education which espouse both cohesiveness and plurality as goals to bring about equality of opportunity.

Using Paulston's (1976) paradigms of social and educational change, I have argued that such documents are anchored to conflicting paradigms which are educationally irreconcilable (Poole, 1979, 1980). Applying the functional paradigm to multicultural education, the focus for equality of educational opportunity becomes 'technocratic', in Paulston's terms, ie concerned with methods, techniques, curriculum and teacher training as a means of equalizing educational opportunity. The conflict model, on the other hand, is concerned with the relationship between education and economic, political and social justice (Paulston, 1976) and with equality of income (Jencks, 1972); ie on this model educational equality extends beyond the provisions and processes of schooling into the very class structure of society (see also Ashenden et al, 1980).

Theorists in the conflict tradition perceive education as part of an ideological structure which a ruling class controls to maintain its dominance over minorities. Translated into base-line concerns, the functionalist paradigm is concerned with ESL teaching and the multi-cultural curriculum; the conflict paradigm, with employment figures of immigrant youth leaving school and with early drop-out rates. The irreconcilable differences between these two visions of equality of educational opportunity is neatly caught in a metaphor by Lenski (1966): 'where functionalists see human societies as social systems, conflict theorists see them as stages on which struggles for power and privilege take place' (cited in Paulston, 1979: 210). To the conflict theorist, schools are microcosms of societal processes, and educational opportunity must be evaluated not only within the school system but also in relation to the employment options of school-leavers (work, further study, unemployment).

There is evidence of increasing reflection on the meaning of equality in education for minority groups in Australia, amid what Bullivant (1980) calls a 'mix of rhetoric and muddled thinking', and Hill (1979) sees as dangers of 'ghetto mentalities and ethnic protectionism'. What, then, is the current status of minority groups in Australia, in terms of educational opportunity along the following dimensions — cognitive style, identity and self-concept, lack of aspiration and parental attitudes?

Cognitive style

It has been argued that to achieve educational equality, it is necessary to understand and identify the cognitive style of specific socioeconomic and ethnic groups (Poole, 1975). Whether this should be a major starting-point for designing and implementing curricula for ethnic children, however, is debatable. I have argued elsewhere that teachers need to be aware of the combinations of learning strengths which a child possesses so that he or she will not be disadvantaged in the schooling process (Poole, 1975).

Unfortunately, however, very little research has been undertaken in Australia on the cognitive style of ethnic groups, especially if cognitive style is conceptualized as a stable preferred pattern or mode of processing information adopted by an individual. Most published studies focus on individual aspects of cognitive processing rather than on self-consistent and enduring differences in cognitive organization and functioning.

A few studies have examined cognitive strategies used in problem-solving and information processing tasks, comparing ethnic and Australian children. Philp and Kelly (1974), for example, contrasted the different strategies used by 'old' Australians and newcomers (parents born in non-English-speaking countries) on Olson's (1970) Buttonboard task (a task requiring players to press a series of buttons to determine which pattern is wired into a board). Although the instructions said nothing explicitly about avoiding redundant moves, the 'old' Australians (unlike the newcomers) showed from grades one to six an increasing reduction in the number of redundant moves.

Georgeff, Poole and Evans (1979) also examined redundancy as an aspect of information selection in a set of concrete tasks aimed at identifying strategies used in referential tasks. Using a sample contrasted on SES and ethnicity, the study found that children of low SES tended to select features that carried little or no information relative to the task, whereas children of middle SES more often selected features of high information content. No significant differences were observed between the lower SES Australian and immigrant groups on verbal or non-verbal encoding strategies. Cognitive processing strategies thus were found to be more aligned to SES differences than to migrancy *per se*. In a subsequent study, the researchers found that it was possible to train low SES and ethnic groups in more efficient information-processing styles (Evans, Georgeff and Poole, 1980).

The problem-solving strategies used by Australian and Greek children were analysed by Davis and Goodnow (1977). Using three tasks (memory for a set of 24 pictures, Olson's Buttonboard task, and 20 Questions) the authors found, among children drawn from the same classrooms, differential use of specific problem-solving strategies rather than gross differences in conceptual level or stage. Differences on the Buttonboard task disappeared under explicit instructions to minimize number of moves, but not so for 20 Questions. The differences appeared to reflect not the extent to which a strategy was known and could be used, but the extent to which it could be initiated or spontaneously used in a given task setting. The importance of shared understandings about the value and appropriateness of specific cognitive strategies was stressed.

The influence of ethnic mix on cognitive functioning (performance profiles) and attitudes in working class children was explored by Rosenthal and Morrison (1979). Three categories of schools were selected — high, medium and low immigrant density. The entire grade six population was tested. An interesting pattern of results emerged: reading achievement, but not non-verbal cognitive tasks, was high for non-immigrant children in the low group; in the high immigrant group, non-immigrant children displayed better attitudes to school and motivation to achieve. Performance of immigrant children on the cognitive tasks was highest in the medium group. In the high and low groups, non-immigrants performed better on the cognitive tasks. The results were interpreted in terms of a 'peer-language model, ie the availability to children of appropriate language models at school'. Perhaps similar influences could exist in relation to the use of cognitive strategies, a question needing investigation.

Several studies have explored the cognitive profiles of ethnic and Australian groups. In a study of fifth-year children from six schools in low SES areas, Evans and Poole (1975) differentiated three schools as high in immigrant composition, three as low. An examination of 22 cognitive variables (verbal and non-verbal) revealed that, although non-immigrant children from the three low immigrant density schools were on the average six months younger than the immigrants from the high immigrant density schools, their average scores in reading, listening, two non-verbal tests, a patterns task and a language elaboration task, were significantly higher. On the mathematics performance and the digit span test, however, there were no major group differences. Interestingly, the migrant children obtained higher average scores on the sentence completion tests, a result which may signify higher task motivation and a desire to please the experimenter, or which may merit further research.

A study of the educational achievement profiles of immigrant children was undertaken by de Lemos (1975) who compared 100 immigrant children from non-English-speaking backgrounds with 50 Australian and 50 immigrant children from English-speaking backgrounds, in each of years two, four and six. A consistent and marked pattern of differences emerged in the performance of English-speaking and non-English-speaking children at all three grade levels. Differences were more marked on the language tests, less marked on the non-verbal general ability test, the concept development test, and the arithmetic tests (differences in the latter tended to decrease with length of residence in Australia). The results of the de Lemos study were complicated by a cluster of SES status variables (father's occupation, ranking of residential area, geographic location of suburb, length of schooling of parents). The report concluded that there were no differences in the potential achievement of Australian and non-English origin immigrant children, but urged the development of more effective teaching programmes for immigrant children.

An earlier study by Pickering (1970) of year three children of differing ethnic background (Greek and Australian), with SES controlled, showed no significant group differences on the Illinois Test of Psycholinguistic Abilities (ITPA). In a further study, Pickering (1971) compared year two children from Greek backgrounds with a matched SES group of Australian children at both high and low SES levels. The tests comprised ITPA, reading and general ability tests and significantly discriminated between high and low SES Greek immigrants and between Greek and Australian children. The Greek children scored lower on the auditory-vocal tests and the Neale Analysis of Reading test. The pattern of results was basically similar for low SES Australians. In reconciling the results from both his studies, Pickering concluded that immigrant children overcame their initial language disadvantage once peer language models became available at school (ie once children began to speak more like their peers than like their parents). A later study by Walker (1973) did in fact find an association between exposure to English and an increase in verbal comprehension scores.

A most sophisticated analysis of the cognitive profiles of children from six ethclasses (Anglo-Australian middle class [MC] and lower class [LC], English, Yugoslav, Greek and southern Italian) was reported by Marjoribanks (1980). A number of major group differences emerged: in mathematics, Anglo-Australian MC scored higher than southern Italian and Greek, and Anglo-Australian LC higher than southern Italians; for word and word comprehension knowledge, Anglo-Australian MC higher than all groups except the English, and Anglo-Australian LC higher than southern Italians and Greeks; in mean IQ, Anglo-Australian MC higher than southern Italian and Yugoslav, and Anglo-Australian LC higher than southern Italian. Children from the various ethclasses did not differ significantly in their mean affective commitment or academic adjustment to school. Marjoribanks (1979) sees his data as supporting the proposition that families from different ethclasses create differential learning environments for their children (cultural capital) which influences their cognitive orientations and achievements. He goes on to warn that programmes devised to assist families and their children from one ethclass cannot easily be adopted for families in other groups. He argues that the significant dimensions along which ethnic family learning environments differ need to be understood before educators can have any impact on reconstructing the opportunity structures in formal schooling.

As to cognitive style, then, different strategies have been noted, different performance profiles delineated, and the potential of immigrant students acknowledged. The family process variables which influence cognitive style (its development and patterning) are only just beginning to be considered. The relationship of such dimensions to school achievement and orientation remain to be investigated at a psychosocial level although they have been seen elsewhere in terms of cultural reproduction.

Identity and self-concept

> Between school and home, tensions and misunderstandings have been due to the clash of different attitudes and cultures; to the lack of understanding by parents, on the one hand, of the ways and customs of Australian life, and by teachers, on the other, of family attitudes and relationships which prohibit, for example, the participation of the students, especially of daughters, in ordinary activities of the school such as camps and excursions. (Blakers, 1978: 68)

How different are the immigrant and host cultures? Is there evidence of major cultural clashes through different identity patterns? If so, how do these impinge on the educational process, especially in terms of equality of opportunity?

Martin (1978: 24) defines identity as the 'set of self-images held by an individual or groups' and argues that the self is constructed partly through interactions with others who affirm or deny our self-image. It can be shown that the major ethnic groups in Australia differ in the degree to which they exhibit a communal identity. The Greeks, with their distinct language, religious and welfare institutions, Saturday schools, social clubs and organizations, possess a fairly strong feeling of ethnic identity. In comparison, the Dutch and the British exhibit comparatively weak ethnic identity.

Ethnic membership, Taft (1978) argues, may determine people's feelings about their individual identity, about who they are, how they feel about their place in society and about their behaviour (social identity). These processes refer to adults and to children but in differing degrees. Taft (1978), reporting on a series of his studies, indicated that ethnic identity is lower in persons who have been in Australia longer, who are satisfied with life in Australia, and who have Australian friends. For Polish and Jewish adolescents he found that there was a definite but fairly low correlation between the ethnic identification of children and their parents.

The research on ethnic identity and education in Australia was recently reviewed by Holenbergh Young (1979). In her review, she suggests that ethnic identity and identification with the Anglo-Australian group have mainly been examined as part of the process of immigration, within models of assimilation or adaptation. She cites Harris (1976) as making a distinction between 'feeling ethnic' (in the sense of identification) and 'being ethnic' (in the sense of accepting and activating the cultural values of a particular group). The state of 'being ethnic' is said to be likely to lead to identification as ethnic by others and hence to 'feeling ethnic' (Young, 1978: 345). However, Young does not cite any Australian literature linking identity to school-related research or equality of educational opportunity.

One study on children by Isaacs (1976) reported that of 107 Greek children in inner-city schools in Sydney, 90 per cent were proud to be Greek, while some 10 per cent were unhappy at being so identified. In a study of 29 Russian children aged nine to ten years, and living in an outer suburb of Melbourne, Bodi (1976) assessed identity in relation to a process of future choices and expectations, and a friendship preference scale (Russian or Australian). Strong Russian ethnic identification was apparent for over half the sample, but friends were drawn from both groups.

The processes of 'construction of reality' and of 'construction of identity' among immigrants have been explored recently by Burns and Goodnow (1979) and Martin (1978) respectively. Their approaches focus on the meanings one event may hold for different individuals, and on perceptions of interactions, particularly those that affirm or deny one's own constructions.

In assessing the significance of identity and self-concept within a framework of inequality and disadvantage, Burns and Goodnow (1979) consider differences in goals, resources or ideologies. Disadvantage is perceived as more than the usual share of obstacles in reaching a goal (eg 'lack of English', 'old customs', 'lack of interest in schooling', 'prejudice of the host groups' etc). Such conceptions locate the problems within the disadvantaged individuals rather than the social context. Generalizing from this, immigrant youngsters in schools may suffer psychosocial consequences if their identity is not affirmed. Whether this influences their academic performance and vocational aspirations, however, is unknown.

A study on the social integration of Polish, Dutch and Italian students into Australian society was conducted by Wiseman (1971). The Italian sample was found to be involved extensively in informal ethnic group affiliations; the Polish sample showed only a small minority participating in informal associations, though a significant number of girls (but not boys) were involved in formally organized ethnic youth associations; and the Dutch were rarely involved in any type of ethnic association. Students with Italian parents tended to identify strongly with ethnic referents, the Poles and Dutch much less so. A large majority of the Italians and large minorities of the other two samples maintained ethnic language competence, a symbol of ethnic identity.

The role of language maintenance as part of the process of ethnic identity is contentious. Some argue that lack of ability to communicate in one's ethnic language precludes one from ethnic group membership. Kwong Wing Yee (1980), however, in her analysis of ethnic identity and language use among the Chinese community in Sydney, argues that the bonds between language and culture have yet to be demonstrated as well as discriminated. Her own analysis revealed three speech patterns between mother and child (Chinese predominant, English predominant, flexible use of both Chinese and English), although a shift towards English was evident. The importance of language as a symbol of ethnic identity was recognized but, as Kwong argues, symbolism alone cannot sustain a language — a useful function beyond the home is critical.

How these identity-formation processes affect educational opportunity structures of ethnic children largely remains to be investigated. Several studies highlight the psychosocial difficulties encountered by ethnic children as they move from their home cultures to Anglo-based school systems, but no direct links with equality of opportunity are drawn. Several 'problems' have been associated with immigrant origin, for example: initial adjustment to schooling (Taft and Cahill, 1978); uneasy transitions (Taylor, 1978; Greco, Vasta and Smith, 1977; Cox *et al*, 1978); identity conflicts (Bullivant, 1974; Johnston, 1965); culture-conflict or ambivalence (Connell *et al*, 1975; Buckland, 1972; Bottomley, 1974, 1975; Isaacs, 1976); feelings of alienation (Doczy, 1968; Johnston, 1965; Kovacs and Cropley, 1975); isolation and marginality (Cox, 1975; Taft, 1965, 1972, 1974); loss of self-esteem (Connell *et al*, 1975); and sense of loss (Jupp, 1966).

Some studies do, however, take a more positive approach. For example, de Lacey and Rich (1979) identified various behavioural resources of immigrant children. Doczy (1968) reports no evidence of culture conflicts as a result of differences between the norms of first and second generation boys and their parents. Likewise, Taft (1973) in a study of Jewish males and females found little conflict with parents, and Medding (1974) found evidence of a positive ethnic revival amoung Melbourne Jews. Burns and Goodnow (1979) highlight the shared goals of immigrants and Australians — interest in equality, financial achievement, academic success and appropriate social behaviour.

The diversity within Australia is great, but ethnicity is being increasingly perceived as producing not identity crises, but the possible enrichment of individuals and culture through the sharing of new patterns of social interaction.

Taft (1978) reports that little is known of whether teachers in Australian schools treat immigrants in their classes differently from Australian children, beyond the obvious differences arising from lack of proficiency in English. Doenau and Duncan (1980) analysed the behaviour of teachers in mixed Australian and ethnic classrooms and found different attitudes to Anglos and non-Anglos (mainly Greek). Non-Anglo males received the greatest amount of interaction with teachers, while non-Anglo females received the least. The authors query whether this pattern reflects a sensitivity to cultural expectations, particularly as the Greek girls' performance levels were high. In an earlier study, Taft (1978) found, for sixth-grade teachers in 15 Catholic schools, that there were fewer inter- actions of the teacher with the immigrant pupils than with the non-immi- grant, despite an apparent need for more. In addition, immigrant children were found to be less assertive or attention-seeking in their dealings with teachers. Such children, however, did not perceive Australian children as being favoured in class. Immigrants' self-esteem is thus probably not adversely affected by classroom treatment.

Concepts of self and academic achievement have been linked in overseas and local studies. The relationship between identity, self-concept and performance is complex, however, and not clearly articulated in the literature. A person is said to develop a concept of self partly through a process of socialization, internalization of stereotypes, feedback through interaction with others, introspection and action. Some studies have revealed minority group members in Australia as manifesting more negative and self-deprecating self-concepts than do their Anglo-Australian counterparts. However, the significance of such findings for the attainment of equality of opportunity is not clear.

Connell *et al* (1975), for example, in their survey of city youth in Sydney (12- to 20-year-olds) found that of all the groups sampled, the southern Italians reported the least satisfactory self-concept. The British group obtained higher self-concept scores than the Australians, but the overall trend was for immigrants to score lower. The Sydney survey indicated that the groups having the least satisfactory self-concept scores were the ones who spoke least English at home. The authors speculate as to whether culture conflict may induce some of the problems of personal adjustment experienced during adolescence by immigrants, but show no direct link with achievement or other school-related factors. A study by Wiseman (1977) reported no negative effects on self-esteem resulting from streaming in schools.

In analysing the relationship between the family and self-concept, Connell *et al* (1975) reported that ethnic groups already identified as more alienated from their parents' generation were among those who scored high on a lack of parental interest scale. The Yugoslavs and Asians reported a significantly greater lack of parental interest than did the Australians, and immigrant teenagers differed from their Australian counterparts in relations with their parents. Some groups were 'more under the parental thumb' than others, and were resentful of the restraint. At the extremes, southern Italians experienced the least satisfactory relationships with their parents, Germans the most. The Asians and Greeks were nearer the Italians than the Maltese, Yugoslavs, and Poles, all of whom show a greater degree of alienation from their parents than the Australians, British and Dutch. In terms of potential conflict between school and family values, only the Asians placed great importance upon being good at school work as a basis for forming friendship with Australians.

The question, then, of ethnic identity and self-concept and how these impinge on the opportunity structures of minority groups in Australia is unclear. During the period of assimilation, psychosocial problems were beginning to be articulated, and indeed became visible during the 'problem' phase. Today, however, given the emergence of ethnic identity as a perceived positive social force, underpinned by official policy at state and federal level, the likelihood of such self-construction processes militating against equality of educational opportunity is not high. Whether the reality will match the rhetoric, however, particularly during a period of high youth unemployment and general economic and educational cutbacks, remains to be seen.

Aspirations: children and their parents

A number of recent studies suggest that children from non-English-speaking ethnic backgrounds have high educational and occupational aspirations, and stay on at school longer than their Australian counterparts (eg Connell *et al*, 1975; Taft, 1975; Rosier, 1978; Martin and Meade, 1979). Such prolonged schooling does not, however, necessarily result in high academic achievement (see, for example, Marjoribanks, 1979a, 1979b, for an explanation related to environment and attitudinal factors; Rosenthal and Morrison, 1979 for a social and psychological analysis of related factors; and Connell *et al*, 1975 for an analysis of cultural disadvantage in family terms).

Throughout this period of extended schooling, parental aspirations are also generally found to be high and congruent with those of their children, although levels differ depending on specific ethnic groups (eg Browning, 1979 notes that Greeks and Turks rank higher than British, Yugoslavs, Australians and Italians). My recent study (Poole, 1981) reported that both immigrant and Australian parents held high educational and aspirational expectations for their adolescent children. Furthermore, Anglo and ethnic adolescents shared the values of their parents in these areas, rated their life-chances optimistically, and attributed success to their own ability and effort. An earlier review by Smolicz and Wiseman (1971) reported that immigrant parents, in general, had higher ambitions for, and offered more encouragement to their children than did Australians. Such parents, however, were less likely than their Australian counterparts to be able to offer assistance with school tasks.

Taft (1975) has argued that the aspirations of ethnic groups partly reflect their intellectual and scholastic ability, but also involve associated factors such as social class, motivation for emigrating, parental education, commitment to their children's educational success, and size of family of origin. However, despite Taft's data showing that education is seen as a means of upward social and occupational mobility by immigrants, and that this reflects high levels of aspiration, he concluded that:

> Children of non-English immigrants are not as successful academically (based on competitive scholarships, the matriculation examinations and the students' progress in tertiary institutions) as are students with an Australian or English-speaking immigrant background. (Taft, 1974: 64)

On the question of equality of opportunity for girls of ethnic background, Taft states:

> The Schools Commission Report, *Girls, School and Society* (1975) tried to establish whether aspirations and performance were the same for boys and girls among major migrant groups of non-English speaking origin and whether girls were more affected by the cultural differences between home and school. Their analysis of data and materials indicated that: 'The generally higher aspirations of non-English speaking migrant families do not extend as strongly to females as to males, and there are some indications that Italian girls fall considerably below other groups including Australians, in their aspirations. There is no evidence that the daughters of migrant parents perform any less well than the sons, but at both 16 and 18 year old levels in 1971 girls born in Greece, Italy and Yugoslavia were markedly more likely to have left the education system than were girls or boys of similar background.' (Taft, 1975: 140)

Questions of sex differences aside, Isaacs (1979) reported discrepancies between parents' and children's goals for the vocational future of Greek children. The higher goals of the parents for their children were attributed to parents' belief in the rewards following longer schooling, ie higher occupational status and prestige.

Parental attitudes to and aspirations for their children's education were studied by Browning (1979) among several major ethnic groups — British, Greek, Italian, Yugoslav, Turk — and Australians. Major differences in expressed attitudes to education were between English-speaking and non-English-speaking groups, in terms of the type, depth and breadth of education provided. Differences between parents and students were most frequent among Greeks and Italians, but Greeks and Italians differed from Turks and Yugoslavs. On the question of parents' hopes for their children's futures — level of schooling, type of further training, and occupational aspiration — major group differences emerged, with the Turks and Greeks registering high aspirations, the Australians and Italians being consistently lower on the three indices.

The most sophisticated examination of ethnic families and children's academic aspirations was undertaken by Marjoribanks (1979). By analysing children's achievements on an interactionist paradigm, Marjoribanks explored the relationships between family environments, school-related attitudes and cognitive performance of children from different Australian ethclasses. Learning environments of families from different ethclasses were analysed in relation to family type (academic orientation). Analyses of inequalities in children's educational attainment were explored in terms of differences between the learning environments of families from the mainstream culture and those from minority groups. Marjoribanks proposed that learning contexts should involve interactions between classroom, neighbourhood and family environments, and that they should assist children in acquiring those skills that are necessary in order to negotiate with mainstream social groups. He attempted to highlight the perspective that 'because of the realities of the distribution of power within society, certain ethclasses are disadvantaged in relation to the creation of learning environments associated with those achievements rewarded in society' (Marjoribanks, 1979: 20).

Major ethclass differences in learning environments emerged in Marjoribanks' data. English-speaking groups were characterized by relatively

strong pressure for English, weak pressure for dependence, individualistic value orientations, moderate to low aspirations, and moderate to high achievement orientations. In contrast, the Greek and Southern Italian families exhibit lower pressure for English, stronger pressure for dependence, more collectivistic value orientations, higher educational-occupational aspirations, and have moderate to lower achievement orientations, while the Yugoslavian profile represents, in general, an intermediate position between the Anglo and non-Anglo groups. (Marjoribanks, 1979: 61-2)

Results on children's cognitive performances highlighted the greater influence of ethclass on the scores of girls than of boys. Overall, it was found that different home learning environments relate to ethclass differences in children's academic performance, orientations, and aspirations.

A survey to determine what school meant to Australian-born and Greek-born parents of grade three children in seven inner-city urban schools was designed by Noble and Ryan (1976). The results highlighted the Australian parents' concern for the individual child's development and the Greek parents' concern with teacher control. Greek parents held more traditional views concerning the purposes of education, favouring an academic curriculum and stressing the school's responsibility in teaching good manners, discipline and respect.

In assessing possible influences on the relative academic performance of Dutch, Italian and Polish students, Wiseman (1971) found differences in study conditions at the social level ('undisturbed by things such as television, talking, people going in and out and so on'). Parental encouragement and assistance was available to all groups, but there were differences in parental involvement in school activities. Aspirational patterns, however, need to be viewed in association with performance patterns since these are more likely to be accurate reflections of equality of opportunity.

Performance

In 1977, Hewitt wrote:

> In the last decade there has been growing concern over the educational difficulties faced by migrant children, particularly those from non-English speaking backgrounds, yet there are surprisingly few detailed objective studies on the comparative performance of migrant and Australian children in our schools. (Hewitt, 1977: 157)

Be that as it may, there has been a spate of studies over the past few decades concerned with the comparative performance of immigrant and Australian youngsters. However, the results are not by any means consistent and the degree to which immigrant children are disadvantaged remains uncertain.

The Dovey Report (1960), for example, presented a fairly optimistic account of the successful performance and assimilation of immigrant children in Australia. Other sources emerged, however, indicating that under-achievement, early leaving, low grade placement, and language difficulties were cause for concern (see studies in Matsdorf, 1963 and later surveys of the Department of Education, NSW, 1971).

The first comprehensive review of the school attainment of immigrant children in Australian schools was undertaken by Smolicz and Wiseman (1971). Their findings were, however, somewhat equivocal, partly because of the failure of researchers to distinguish between first and second generation immigrants, between rural and urban settlers, and to account for social class and its influence on schooling. This lack of clarity is reflected in more recent studies. However, a consistently emerging trend is for immigrant children to stay on at school longer and to display high levels of vocational aspiration. Indeed, the general level of achievement by immigrants reflects an interesting phenomenon — difficulty in achievement at school but a high expectation of successful achievement. Taft (1975, 1977) attributes this to motivation and staying-power — voluntary immigrants need to succeed to justify their emigration, and their children stay on in secondary schools even if their grades are low. Other factors identified include: immigrant 'resources for achievement' (Burns and Goodnow, 1979), immigrant negotiation skills in penetrating bureaucracies (Martin, 1975) and in processing the plethora of information given to newcomers (Bullivant, 1976) before they can participate in existing opportunity structures.

Using a primary school sample, de Lemos (1975) investigated the performance of students from different ethnic backgrounds. Her results indicated that, once account had been taken of home-background variables (SES, parental education, etc), there were no significant differences in the potential achievement of immigrants.

In a recent longitudinal survey of Sydney High School students, Martin and Meade (1979) traced the progress of immigrant high school children (1974-77). The study was not concerned solely with educational opportunity and performance. Consideration was given to the institutional ideology of schools (participants' knowledge and definitions of the functions of schooling and concomitant practices) and to the immigration experience (eg whether immigration was a stunting or liberating experience). Staying-on rates were found to be higher for immigrant adolescents of non-English-speaking origin. In addition, immigrant children obtained a higher proportion of medium or high grades in an external examination (the Higher School Certificate). There were marked variations among the ethnic sub-groups, however (eg Greeks achieved more highly than Lebanese). The Italians, Lebanese and Maltese tended to be over-represented among those who left school early or who obtained low results. IQ and SES related strongly to accreditation (the attainment of entrance standard to higher education). Aspirational patterns were higher for immigrants and tended to be maintained despite 'mismatches' with IQ and grade levels. Overall, the accreditation comparisons between the total samples of children of non-English speaking and of Australian origin very much favoured the immigrant adolescents.

Not all studies show immigrant children achieving successfully. In a study of the academic achievement of Dutch, Italian and Polish students, Wiseman (1971) found that the ethnic samples contained higher proportions of repeaters of a school grade than the average for the state. General IQ, English and Arithmetic Standardized Test scores revealed greater differences on verbal performance, while relatively little difference was found on non-verbal IQ tests. This pattern of cognitive results is somewhat similar to that reported by Evans and Poole (1975).

Disadvantages incurred by immigrant children were also highlighted in the national literacy and numeracy studies in school performance undertaken by the Australian Council for Educational Research (ACER).

Keeves and Bourke (1977) found that, at age 14, there were some consistent differences in the performances of students with different language backgrounds. Students from English-speaking backgrounds or both English and a north European language combination achieved the highest level of performance while students from homes where no English was spoken obtained the lowest scores. Keeves and Bourke (1977) found that there was less consistency in the performance patterns of students from homes where English and south European or other languages were spoken. The levels of their performance tended, overall, to fall between the two extremes with the 'other language' group below the south European language group in performance.

Hewitt (1977), reviewing the performance of ten- and 14-year-old students from ethnic backgrounds in the final report of the National Literacy and Numeracy Study, found that many immigrant students encountered educational difficulties and that these were manifested in a number of ways:

> Teacher ratings indicated that 10 per cent of migrant students were not capable of understanding English sufficiently well to cope with normal classroom lessons and that 35 per cent of migrant students needed remedial assistance with reading or number work. Whilst half of these students needed assistance in both areas, just over half were receiving remedial help with reading whilst only about one third were being assisted with number work. These findings suggest the need for more assistance in the development of English language skills of migrant students. Migrant students were also less likely to be well accepted socially at school and tended to fall behind in their progression through school grades, probably due to poor school performance occurring as a result of lack of English language skills. (Hewitt, 1977: 177)

Williams *et al* (1980) in their recent national ACER analysis of achievement as defined by three basic skills (word knowledge, literacy and numeracy) found that a degree of disadvantage existed for students of non-English-speaking origin. Other things being equal (eg school type, SES, etc), immigrants performed at a consistently lower level on all three achievement measures. However, immigrant children were not disadvantaged in their probability of staying on at school. The researchers argued that:

> ethnic disadvantage in schools is a function of language and not of the status 'migrant'; and . . . that the parents of those disadvantaged by language encourage adaptation to the demands of the dominant culture probably as a path toward social mobility. (p 113)

In evaluating educational opportunity, although performance outcomes may be major indices, job placement and access to the economic structure is probably a more powerful social indicator of equality of opportunity. Regardless of performance patterns, is there a consistent pattern of immigrant disadvantage for school-leavers (early leavers and matriculants)?

In an analysis of 17-year-olds in Australia in relation to school, work and career, Williams *et al* (1980) found little evidence of disadvantage in occupational attainments for non-English-born early leavers. Indeed, other things being equal, immigrants left school later than other groups, took longer to find their first job, but were less likely to have been unemployed. In addition, they held marginally higher-status jobs than either the Australian-born or the English-born groups, and were more likely to have planned on or to have attempted further education.

The Williams *et al* (1980) survey, contrary to expectations, found that:

> Overall, ethnic disadvantage seems to be concentrated where we would least expect it, among migrant families whose mother-tongue is that of their adopted country. Early school leavers among the migrants from English-speaking nations, while showing negligible disadvantage within the schools, show a degree of disadvantage in the labour market. On the other hand, their counterparts from non-English-speaking nations are not significantly disadvantaged, on the whole, within the schools except for their literacy skill and, apart from taking longer to find a job, are not significantly different from Australian-born respondents in their occupational attainments. In fact, tests of significance aside, they do somewhat better. (p 91)

The possible explanations, Williams *et al* speculate, for this finding are that the ethnic job market has a greater availability of less competitive jobs, that the groups differ in achievement values, or that parental occupational and educational attainments of non-English-speaking groups may have been underestimated. Perhaps also ethnic minority employers favour applicants of their own ethnic group.

The pattern of immigrant aspiration and performance, then, cannot, apart from language-related aspects, be associated with lack of success or opportunity. Indeed, overall, immigrant students seem to out-perform and to aspire more highly than their Australian counterparts. Given this set of factors, the question of equality of opportunity seems to be answered.

Bilingual education

There is little doubt that the dominant language used in education in Australia is English. Indeed, one of the distinguishing features of Australian society is its monolingualism (Bostock, 1973), even though bilingual education was pioneered in Australia in the 1850s by German settlers who set up their own private Lutheran schools. The language of instruction was German, although a partial switch to English occurred in the late nineteenth century, apparently because parents considered English to be the key to their children establishing themselves in the wider Australian community (Taft and Cahill, 1978: 2; Clyne, 1977). Most of the German language schools, however, continued to use German as the language of instruction until World War I. Only then was discriminatory legislation against bilingual education introduced (see Clyne, 1977). After the war, a 'patriotic' law was passed making the use of English for instruction mandatory. This law still stands in the legislation of two states (Victoria and Western Australia), 'but today it is dormant and unlikely to be used to interfere with any bilingual or non-English instructional programs in schools' (Taft and Cahill, 1978: 2).

It was not until the 1970s that strong support for bilingual education began to emerge in Australia. This impetus emerged from both federal and state initiatives aimed at meeting the needs of minorities. For example, the report of the Australian Government Committee on the teaching of migrant languages in schools (Commonwealth Department of Education, 1976) identified the unsatisfied demands for the teaching of and in immigrant languages. In Victoria and South Australia, there were attempts to introduce multilingual facilities in government schools. Among the range of possibilities explored were: bilingual classes in inner-city schools (see Jaggs, 1975); multilingual learning material devised so that pupils with little or no English could continue their education in their own language while acquiring basic skills in the second language (Rado, 1974, 1977); and the Ten Schools Project in South Australia for the institution and evaluation of bilingual programmes, initially intended for children in six schools from Italian backgrounds, but expanded to include other ethnic languages. Other experiments in bilingualism have been conducted at the Adass Israel School, Victoria (English and Yiddish); St Peter's Lutheran School, Brisbane (English and German); Maronite Primary School, Sydney (Lebanese); a bilingual school in Darwin (English/ Portuguese and English/Chinese – see Clyne, 1977); a Japanese School, Terry Hills; and a Dutch School, Western Australia, and many others (see Smolicz, 1975).

The influential report mentioned above (Commonwealth Department of Education, 1976), urging education authorities to create widespread opportunities for children to study immigrant languages and cultures in schools, was tabled in Parliament in 1976. Here, the emphasis was on providing programmes for community language learning rather than espousing bilingual education *per se*. Such programmes are not without their problems as even within one ethnic group there can be noticeable language, social class and religious differences (see Hill, 1979 and the 1977 Report on *Our Multicultural Future and the School* for examples relating to Italians and Indians); and a tendency for ethnic language to become the 'language of age and local ethnic parochialism' (Smolicz and Harris, 1977: 105).

There is little or no disagreement in Australian education circles on the need for all students to become proficient in English, as a cultural goal and as a key to equality of opportunity. Questions concerning the provision of bilingual education and the creation of opportunities for community language learning are, however, more contentious. The debate centres on the desirability of and a rationale for the maintenance of the home language:

> On the one hand, we have the argument that the language of the home interferes with the learning of English: the solution often proposed is a conversion to the constant and monolingual use of English – at home, in the play-yard and in the classroom. This promotion of monolingualism has been objected to by many immigrants, Poles and Greeks in particular. Among Poles and Greeks, the national language is a symbol of identity and survival . . . (Burns and Goodnow, 1979: 139)

Views on this differ. Rado (Claydon, Knight and Rado, 1977), for example, stresses the importance of achieving balanced bilingualism through bilingual education, while de Lemos and di Leo (1977) show more concern with English proficiency within the old 'sink or swim' tradition of teaching immigrant children in Australian primary schools. Clyne (1980) sifts through the overseas research on primary school language and bilingual education to explode myths, to argue for a concern with the context of research data, and for an Australian approach to the issues:

> In fact, there is a need for a total revaluation of the role of languages in Australian education and curriculum development, especially for the progression from primary to secondary level. We must make our own decisions, since a curriculum can be developed only in a social and education context, but we must learn from the experiments of other countries, their achievements and their mistakes. (Clyne, 1980: 32)

Since many teachers have tried to persuade immigrant parents for years that their children will not succeed at school unless they speak and hear only English, Clyne (1977) argues that it may be necessary to re-educate parents, pupils and teachers in the value of bilingual education programmes.

Increasingly, however, there is an evolving set of propositions which suggest that being bilingual is not necessarily a handicap and that indeed it may even be an advantage (see Rado, 1974, 1977; Tenezakis, 1979; Keats and Keats, 1973; Horvath, 1979). The shift towards greater acceptance of bilingual alternatives has led, as Burns and Goodnow indicate, to a great deal of open debate about optimal timing and appropriate curricula for the twin goals of an effective bridge to English and maintenance of the mother tongue:

> The debate is not limited to specialists in education. Migrant parents, migrant spokesmen and migrant children also differ among themselves . . . . The differences occur in the degree of attachment to the survival of the language of the country of origin: [this is] different . . . from an attachment to being bilingual. They occur also with regard to whether the means to the achievement of linguistic survival are seen to lie within the family . . . within 'ethnic' schools outside the regular school system (eg Saturday schools), or within the regular school day (the language concerned is not only accepted as a matriculation subject but is taught in the schools as an elective within the regular school programme, beyond the first years of school). (Burns and Goodnow, 1979: 140)

Questions of access (by immigrants and Anglo-Australians), of structures and provisions (school-based v community based), of funding and resources (public v private), of additional time commitments by students in community language settings (extra-curricular v regular school day), of teacher competence and territoriality, and of the risks of social divisiveness, are being debated and will doubtless continue to be debated throughout the 1980s.

In their appraisal of ethnic languages in Australia, Smolicz and Harris (1977) argue that the prevailing cultural climate of Australian society inculcates in young ethnics, and often in their parents as well, a belief that: 'the two linguistic tendencies, one to develop English and the other to maintain the ethnic language, are mutually exclusive and not parallel and compatible' (p 88). On the basis of their research with Polish tertiary students, Smolicz and Harris (1977) present a viewpoint affirming that both processes may be activated simultaneously. Using an 'assimilation index' and an 'ethnicity index', Smolicz and Harris identified four idealized types — 'High ethnic', a group activating a dual system of linguistic values (good command of Polish and of English, high ethnicity, low assimilation); 'Ethnic-Australian', involving high scores on both indices and displaying balanced bilingualism and ease in both cultural milieus; 'Anglo-assimilate', high degree of assimilation, non-use of Polish language; alienated individuals low on both indices. The first two types do indicate that the bilingual and bicultural processes need not be mutually exclusive, but since the majority of students fell into the 'Anglo-assimilate' category their argument is a little romantic.

Smolicz and Harris do, however, present an interesting analysis of strategies needed to activate bilingualism:

> To achieve a self-reproducing pool of ethnic linguistic values, it will, therefore, be necessary to structure the system of education so as to ensure that individuals are given the opportunity to construct dual systems of linguistic values at approximately equal levels of sophistication. It is our view that, in the long run, the home domain can be preserved for the mother-tongue only if the young ethnics can converse in their ethnic language upon topics appropriate to their education and interests. (Smolicz and Harris, 1977: 91)

The debate on bilingualism, then, proceeds in Australia, especially alongside the residue of problems still encountered in devising materials and strategies for teaching English as a second language (ESL) (see Vander Touw, 1979; Dingwell, 1979; Horvath, 1979). The key questions concern ethnic motivation for language maintenance, the provision of resources for bilingual education, the functional uses of the two languages, the capacity of teachers to redirect their approaches and the evolving pattern of Australian society.

Conclusion

This chapter reviewed a selection of the major literature in Australia on the question of educational opportunity for ethnic minority groups. Special consideration was given to specified dimensions — cognitive style, identity, self-concept, aspirations, performance, parental attitude and bilingual education. These disparate dimensions were discussed within the broad and changing context of Australian society. A shift in social and political policy from assimilation, to problem-orientation, to a more pluralistic and participatory society was outlined. Schooling in Australia has tended to reflect such official policy phases and, given current policy, it is difficult to argue that there is a differential pattern of educational opportunity for immigrants and Australians. Access to educational systems and outcomes do not show major areas of immigrant disadvantage, except in areas of language-related performance.

Some reference has been made to reproduction theory. To the extent that obstacles to educational opportunity exist in Australia, the causes are more likely to be found in the class structure than in ethnic origin *per se*. Immigrants appear to be over-represented in the lower socioeconomic strata.

The emerging pattern is such that immigrant groups are not largely perceived as homogeneous, even within the same designated group (eg Italian), nor are the patterns of performance and aspiration similar for different ethnic groups. Some groups quite clearly see schooling as an avenue for social mobility; other groups place their values elsewhere. Some ethnic groups perform better than their Australian counterparts, others lack the motivation and/or cultural and family resources to take advantage of existing educational provisions. At this stage, there is no backlash in society against multicultural and bilingual educational programmes. Whether Australia will eventually follow the North American pattern of halting such programmes remains to be seen. Given that eventuality, minority groups may fall back into the less advantageous positions they held during the assimilationist and problem-oriented phases.

References

Ashenden, D J, Connell, R W, Dowsett, G and Kessler, S (1980) Class and secondary schooling: some proposals for an approach stressing situations and practices *Discourse* 1: 1-19

Australian Capital Territory Schools Authority (1979) *Multicultural Education* Working Party, Schools Office

Australian Commonwealth Education Portfolio (1979) *Education in a Multicultural Australia* Australian Government Publishing Service: Canberra

Bedford, E L (1979) *Multicultural Education* Ministerial statement, Ministry of Education: New South Wales

Blakers, C (1978) *School and Work* Australian National University Press: Canberra

Bodi, M (1976) *The effect of language acculturation on the attitudes of pre-adolescent immigrant children* Unpublished master's thesis, Monash University: Monash

Bostock, W W (1973) Monolingualism in Australia *Australian Quarterly* 45: 39-52

Bottomley, G (1974) Some Greek sex roles, ideals, expectation and action in Australia and Greece *Australian and New Zealand Journal of Sociology* 10: 8-16

Bottomley, G (1975) Community and network in a city *in* Price (1975)

Bottomley, G (1979) The study of social processes: some problems of theory and method *in* de Lacey and Poole (1979)

Browning, K (1979) Parental attitudes to and aspirations to their children's education *in* de Lacey and Poole (1979)

Buckland, D (1972) *The Greek family in Australia and the process of migration* Paper presented to the sociology section, 44th Congress of the Australian and New Zealand Association for the Advancement of Science: Sydney

Bull, J (1976) *The Ten School Project in Multicultural Education: Report of a Forum* State College of Victoria, Toorak: Melbourne

Bullivant, B M (1976) Social control and migrant education *Australian and New Zealand Journal of Sociology* 12: 174-83

Bullivant, B M (1980) Multiculturalism: no *Education News* 17: 17-20

Burns, A and Goodnow, J (1979) *Children and Families in Australia: Contemporary Issues and Problems* Allen and Unwin: Sydney

Claydon, L, Knight, T and Rado, M (1977) *Curriculum and Culture: Schooling in a Pluralist Society* Allen and Unwin: Sydney

Clyne, M (1977) Some experiences with primary school German in Melbourne: a first report *Babel* 13: 2

Clyne, M (1980) Primary school languages and bilingual education: some overseas research and legends *Australian Review of Applied Linguistics* 3: 29-38

Coleman, J S (1966) *Equality of Educational Opportunity* United States Government Printing Office: Washington DC

Commonwealth Department of Education (1976) *Report of the Committee on the Teaching of Migrant Languages in Schools* Australian Government Publishing Service: Canberra

Commonwealth Immigration Advisory Council (1960) *The Progress and Assimilation of Migrant Children* The Dovey Report, Australian Government Publishing Service: Canberra

Connell, W F, Stroobant, R, Sinclair, K, Connell, R and Rogers, K (1975) *12 to 20: Studies of City Youth* Hicks Smith: Sydney

Cox, D (1975) The adaptation of Greek youth in Melbourne *in* Price (1975)

Cox, D ed (1978) *An Uneasy Transition: Migrant Children in Australia* Commissioned by the International Association of Child Psychiatry and Allied Professions, Congress Organizing Committee

Davis, M and Goodnow, J J (1977) Problem solving strategies: use by Australian children with Australian and Greek parentage *Journal of Cross-Cultural Psychology* 8: 33-47

de Lacey, P R and Poole, M E eds (1979) *Mosaic or Melting Pot in Cultural Evolution in Australia* Harcourt Brace Jovanovich: Sydney

de Lacey, P R and Rich, P (1979) Young Australian newcomers: a study of some behavioural resources of immigrant children in Wollongong *in* de Lacey and Poole (1979)

de Lemos, M M (1975) *Study of the educational achievement of migrant children: Final Report* ACER: Hawthorn, Victoria

de Lemos, M M and di Leo, P (1978) Literacy in Italian and English of Italian high school students *Ethnic Studies* 2: 1-12

Department of Education, NSW (1971) *Migrant Education in NSW* Research Bulletin No 34, Division of Research and Planning, Department of Education: Sydney

Department of Education, NSW (1972) *Aims and Objectives of Secondary Education in NSW* Interim statement, Directorate of Studies, Department of Education: Sydney

Dingwell, S (1979) *Past and present trends in teaching English as a second language: a review and assessment of future needs* Commissioned working paper for Education Research and Development Committee (ERDC) Australian Government Publishing Service: Canberra

Doczy, A G (1968) *The social assimilation of adolescent boys of European parentage in the metropolitan area of Western Australia* PhD thesis, University of Western Australia: Nedlands

Doenau, S J and Duncan, M J (1980) *Classroom interaction, ethnicity and student achievement* Unpublished paper

Edgar, D L ed (1974) *Social Change in Australia* Cheshire: Melbourne

Edgar, D L ed (1975) *Education in Australian Society: A Book of Readings* McGraw-Hill: Sydney

Evans, G, Georgeff, M and Poole, M E (1980) Training in information selection for communication *Australian Journal of Education* 24: 137-54

Evans, G T and Poole, M E (1975) Relationships between verbal and non-verbal abilities for migrant children and Australian children of low socio-economic status: similarities and contrasts *Australian Journal of Education* 19: 209-30

Georgeff, M, Poole, M E and Evans, G T (1979) Information selection in language use and its relation to socio-economic status and ethnicity *in* de Lacey and Poole (1979)

Greco, T, Vasta, E and Smith, R (1977) I get these freaky feelings like I'm splitting into a million pieces: cultural differences in Brisbane, Australia *Ethnic Studies* 1: 17-29

Harris, R McL (1976) *Poles apart?: an intergenerational study of selected samples of postwar Polish immigrants in South Australia* PhD thesis, Adelaide University: Adelaide

Hewitt, R D (1977) Characteristics of students from other ethnic backgrounds *in* Keeves and Bourke (1977)

Hill, B V (1979) Exploring multicultural education *Education News* 16: 24-8

Holenbergh Young, R M (1979) Ethnic identity and education *in* de Lacey and Poole (1979)

Horby, P A ed (1976) *Bilingualism: Psychological, Social and Educational Implications* Proceedings of a Canadian-American conference on bilingualism, March 1976, State University of New York: New York

Horvath, B (1979) *The education of migrant children: a language planning perspective* Report to Education Research and Development Committee (ERDC): Sydney

Hunt, F J ed (1972) *Socialization in Australia* Angus and Robertson: Sydney

Isaacs, E (1976) *Greek Children in Sydney* Australian National University Press: Canberra

Isaacs, E (1979) Social control and ethnicity: the socialization and repression of a Greek child at school *in* de Lacey and Poole (1979)

Jaggs, B (1975) English is not enough *Education News* 15: 42-4

Jencks, C, Smith, M, Acland, H, Bane, M J, Cohen, D, Gintis, H, Heyns, B and Michelson, S (1972) *Inequality — A Reassessment of the Effect of Family and Schooling in America* Basic Books: New York

Johnston, R (1965) *Immigrant Assimilation: A Study of Polish People in Western Australia* Paterson Brokensha: Perth

Jupp, C (1966) *Arrivals and Departures* Cheshire-Landsdowne: Melbourne

Karmel, P H (1973) *Australia Interim Committee for the Australian Schools Commission. Schools in Australia: Report* Australian Government Publishing Service: Canberra

Keats, D M and Keats, J A (1973) *The Effect of Language on Concept Acquisition in Bilingual Children* Report to Education Research and Development Committee (ERDC) Australian Government Publishing Service: Canberra

Keeves, J P and Bourke, S E eds (1977) *Australian Studies in School Performance, Vol III: The Mastery of Literacy and Numeracy: Final Report* Education Research and Development Committee (ERDC) Australian Government Publishing Service: Canberra

Kovacs, M L and Cropley, A J (1975) *Immigrants and Society: Alienation and Assimilation* McGraw-Hill: Sydney

Kwong Wing Yee (1980) *Ethnic identity and language: a look at language use among the Chinese community in Sydney* Unpublished paper

Lenski, G E (1966) *Power and Privilege: A Theory of Social Stratification* McGraw-Hill: New York

Mackie, F (1974) Some suggestions on Greek diversity *in* Edgar (1974)

Marjoribanks, K (1979a) Ethnicity, family environment, school attitudes and academic achievement *in* de Lacey and Poole (1979)

Marjoribanks, K (1979b) *Ethnic Families and Children's Achievement* Allen and Unwin: Sydney

Martin, J I (1971) *Migration and social pluralism* Paper delivered at 37th Annual Summer School of the Australian Institute of Political Science

Martin, J I (1975) Family and bureaucracy *in* Price (1975)

Martin, J I (1978) *The Migrant Presence* Allen and Unwin: Sydney

Martin, J I and Meade, P (1979) *The Educational Experience of Sydney High School Students: A Comparative Study of Migrant Students of Non-English Speaking*

Origin and Students Whose Parents were Born in an English Speaking Country Australian Government Publishing Service: Canberra

Matsdorf, W S ed (1963) *Migrant Youth: Australian Citizens of Tomorrow* NSW Association for Mental Health: Sydney

Medding, P Y ed (1973) *Jews in Australian Society* Macmillan: Melbourne

Medding, P Y (1974) Jews in Australia *in* Stevens (1974)

Noble, T and Ryan, M (1976) What does school mean to the Greek immigrant parent and his child? *Australian Journal of Education* 20: 38-45

Novak, M (1972) *The Rise of the Unmeltable Ethnics: Politics and Culture in the Seventies* Macmillan: New York

Olson, D R (1970) Language and thought: aspects of a cognitive theory of semantics *Psychological Review* 77: 257-73

Organization for Economic Co-operation and Development *Educational Policy and Planning: Transition from School to Work or Further Study in Australia* OECD: Paris

Paulston, C B (1979) Bilingual/bicultural education *Review of Research in Education* 6: 186-228

Paulston, R (1976) *Conflicting Theories of Social and Educational Change: A Typological Review* University Centre for International Studies: Pittsburgh, Pa

Philp, H W and Kelly, M R (1974) Product and process in cognitive development: some comparative data on the performance of school age children in different cultures *British Journal of Educational Psychology* 3: 248-65

Pickering, D (1970) *An Examination of the Psycholinguistic Abilities and Disabilities of Grade 2 Children of Differing Socio-economic Status and Ethnic Background — Greek and Australian* Research Report 5/70, Curriculum and Research Branch, Victoria Education Department: Melbourne

Pickering, D (1971) *An Examination of the Psycholinguistic Abilities of some Greek Children* Research Report 10/71, Curriculum and Research Branch, Victoria Education Department: Melbourne

Poole, M E (1975) Understanding cognitive style as a basis for curricula provision in inner suburban schools *in* Edgar (1975)

Poole, M E (1979) Sex differences in the La Trobe 15 to 18 year old study *Bulletin, Victorian Institute for Educational Research* 1-18

Poole, M E (1980) *School Leavers in Australia* Australian Government Publishing Service: Canberra

Poole, M E (1981) Life chances: some comparisons of migrant and non-migrant Melbourne adolescents *Education Research and Perspectives* 8: 2

Price, C A ed (1975) *Greeks in Australia* Australian National University Press: Canberra

Rado, M (1974) *The implications of bilingualism* Paper presented at the Third Language Teaching Conference on Bilingual Education, La Trobe University, May 1974

Rado, M (1977) *Community languages, for whom?* Paper presented at the Eighteenth Annual Conference of the Australian College of Education, Adelaide, May 1977

Report on the Public Conference, Fremantle City Hall and Mount Lawley College of Advanced Education (1977) *Our Multicultural Future and the Schools*

Rosenthal, D and Morrison, S (1979) On being a minority in the classroom: a study of the influence of ethnic mix on cognitive functioning and attitudes in working class children *in* de Lacey and Poole (1979)

Rosier, M J (1978) *Early school leavers in Australia* International Association for the Evaluation of Educational Achievement, IEA Monograph Studies No 7, Almquist and Wiksell International: Stockholm and Australian Council for Educational Research: Hawthorn, Victoria

Schools Commission Report (1975) *Girls, School and Society* Report by a study group to the Schools Commission

Smolicz, J J (1975) Migrant cultures versus Australian school *Education News* 15: 17-21

Smolicz, J J and Harris, R McL (1977) Ethnic languages in Australia *The International Journal of the Sociology of Language* 14: 89-108

Smolicz, J J and Wiseman, R (1971) European migrants and their children: integration, assimilation, education *Quarterly Review of Australian Education* 4 (June): 1-44; 4 (September): 1-42

South Australia, Department of Education (1979) *Multicultural Education* Curriculum Directorate information brochure, Department of Education: Adelaide

Stevens, F S ed (1974) *Racism, the Australian Experience, Vol I: Prejudice and Xenophobia* (2nd edition) Australian and New Zealand Book Company: Sydney

Taft, R (1965) *From Stranger to Citizen* University of Western Australia Press: Nedlands

Taft, R (1972) Ethnic groups *in* Hunt (1972)

Taft, R (1973) The ethnic identification of Jewish youth *in* Medding (1973)

Taft, R (1975) *The career aspirations of immigrant school children in Victoria* Paper No 12, Department of Sociology, La Trobe University: Melbourne

Taft, R (1977) The study of immigrant adjustment: science or just common sense *Ethnic Studies* 1: 14-19

Taft, R (1978) *Australian attitudes to immigrants in Australia's multicultural society* La Trobe University Meredith Memorial Lectures, La Trobe University: Melbourne

Taft, R and Cahill, D (1978) *Initial adjustment to schooling of immigrant families* Commonwealth Department of Education and Academy of the Social Sciences in Australia: Canberra

Taylor, D A (1976) Bilingualism and intergroup relations *in* Horby (1976)

Tenezakis, M D (1979) Language and cognitive development in bilingual and monolingual children *in* de Lacey and Poole (1979)

Vander Touw, C (1979) *English: Second Language, First Priority?* Directorate of Research and Planning, Education Department, South Australia: Sydney

Walker, V J (1973) *Language ability of non-British migrant children in Melbourne and Hobart* Unpublished BAHons thesis, University of Tasmania: Hobart

Williams, T, Clancy, J, Batten, M and Girling-Butcher, S (1980) *School, Work and Career: Seventeen-year Olds in Australia* Australian Council for Educational Research, Research Monograph No 6

Wiseman, R (1971) Integration and attainment of immigrant secondary school students in Adelaide *Australian Journal of Education* 15: 253-9

Young, R E (1978) Childhood, adolescence and socialization *in* Hunt (1978)

Part 5:
Innovations in minority group education

17. Cross-cultural education in Alaska

James Orvik

Summary: This chapter outlines the cross-cultural nature of public education in Alaska. The state's vast size and sparse population, scattered widely in remote centres, pose unusual education problems, especially for its indigenous minorities. These minorities, speaking 20 distinct languages, are in various stages of transition — from traditional subsistence living to modern urbanization. The history of government treatment of these groups is outlined, with special emphasis given to the most recent educational developments, such as bilingual education and the pressure to create small secondary schools. The problems associated with these developments are discussed in detail. Finally, the current rapid rate of economic development, resulting from the discovery of enormous oil fields under Alaska's North Slope and from revenues derived from the Alaska Native Claims Settlement Act, is discussed in the light of new commitments from the state's institution of higher education to meet the needs of Alaska's indigenous population.

The size of the problem

Alaska became the forty-ninth of the United States of America in 1959. It was purchased from Russia in 1867 during the expansionist-minded administration of Abraham Lincoln, and at today's prices $7,200,000 for a land mass roughly the size of western Europe (exclusive of Scandinavia and the British Isles) may seem like a bargain. It took vigorous lobbying efforts, however, to convince the US Congress that the price of removing one more 'foreign influence' from North America was worth paying.

Those who worked for approving the purchase might now be termed 'accidental visionaries'. Not only has Alaska become a strategic link in the post-World War II defensive chain across the non-Soviet circumpolar north, but also the state's seemingly boundless wealth of natural resources is causing the rest of the nation to glance northward with increasing regularity.

However, the more attention that is paid to Alaska as an object of national interest, the more difficult it becomes not to notice that for centuries the land was already occupied. Alaska's indigenous societies, with interests in survival as valid as those of any nation state, have tolerated with exceptional politeness decades of Western exploitation, development, and modernization. Alaska's indigenous societies have also witnessed decades of Western-style public education designed primarily to assimilate them into the modern world.

But designs and their successful execution are not one and the same, particularly in colonial relationships. Public education in Alaska now reflects the cross-cultural conflicts inherent in this kind of relationship. The main purpose of this chapter is to outline the cross-cultural nature of public education in Alaska, particularly in its relationship to the state's indigenous minorities.

It would be impossible to understand the need for cross-cultural education in Alaska without having an image of the cultural diversity there. The population of Alaska is barely 500,000, most of whom live in the state's three largest cities: Anchorage, Juneau, and Fairbanks. Those of native descent, that is, the indigenous population, are in the minority, numbering about 60,000, one-seventh of the state's total population. In contrast to the non-native majority, however, most of the native population prefer to live in small villages which are scattered widely throughout the state.

The cultural diversity of Alaska is represented in the variety of its indigenous languages. According to Krauss (1979) there are 20 distinct languages native to Alaska. In fact, Alaska is the linguistic birthplace of North America's two great language families, the Eskimo-Aleut and the Athabaskan-Eyak-Tlingit family. Members of two additional language groups, the Haida and the Tsimpshian, migrated to Alaska from Canada in the last century. Table 1 shows the numbers representing each language group.

An important feature of Alaska's language groups is that they vary not only with respect to the language spoken, but also in the degree of viability each language enjoys. Table 2 shows the number of villages of each language group. These patterns of differential viability affect the language policy and, by extension, cultural policy implicit and explicit throughout the history of Alaskan education.

Educational developments: 1885—1976

For 17 years following the US purchase of Alaska, virtually no attention was paid by the US government to local education other than passively to allow the continued operation of a few Russian Orthodox church schools. It was not until 1885, after the passage of the Organic Act by Congress, that systematic attempts were made to provide public education in the territory. By contracting with various domestic mission groups, the US government was able to set up a few schools. By the turn of the century, the majority of schools in Alaska were operated for the education of native children. Even so, it is estimated that fewer than 10 per cent of the school age population were being served at that time (Dafoe, 1978).

Provision for public education in Alaska has always had to respond to

Language family	Language name	Population	Speakers	%
Eskimo-Aleut:				
Aleut:	Aleut	2000	700	35
Eskimo:	Sugpiaq	3000	1000	33
	Central Yupik	17,000	15,000	88
	Siberian Yupik	1000	1000	100
	Inupiaq	11,000	6000	55
Athabaskan-Eyak-Tlingit:				
Tlingit:	Tlingit	9000	2000	22
Eyak:	Eyak	20	3	15
Athabaskan:	Ahtna	500	200	40
	Tanaina	900	250	27
	Ingalik	300	100	33
	Holikachuk	150	25	17
	Koyukon	2100	700	33
	Upper Kuskokwim	150	100	67
	Tanana	360	100	28
	Tanacross	175	120	69
	Upper Tanana	300	250	83
	Han	65	20	31
	Kutchin	1100	700	64
Tsimshian:	Tsimshian	1000	150	15
Haida:	Haida	500	100	20

Source: Map of Alaska native languages, Alaska Native Language Center, University of Alaska

Table 1 *Alaska native languages and populations*

Language use	Eskimo-Aleut	Athabaskan-Eyak-Tlingit	Tsimshian	Haida	Total
Type A	31	5	0	0	36
Type B	40	7	0	0	47
Type C	54	52	1	2	109
Total	125	64	1	2	192

A — All people speak the native language including children.
B — Some children speak the native language.
C — No children speak the native language.

Table 2 *Numbers of Alaskan native communities by language group and language use*

the state's extreme cultural diversity under difficult geographical conditions. Partly because of the expense but mainly because of ethnocentric attitudes prevailing at the time, the earliest educational intentions of the government towards Alaska natives was to 'civilize' them into what has been termed the 'great American melting pot'.

From these intentions evolved a dual system of federal and territorial schools. The education of Alaska natives was considered the responsibility of the federal system, while the education of children representing the rapid influx which began in the 1890s of miners, fishermen, and tradesmen coming north to exploit the abundance of Alaska's natural resources, was considered a matter for local and territorial government.

Concise accounts of the subsequent developments in Alaskan education systems can be found in Darnell (1970, 1979), Dafoe (1978), and Barnhardt (1980). These accounts outline the major legislative and administrative provisions for public education in Alaska which, as summarized by Barnhardt (1980), appear in Table 3.

The most consistent evolutionary theme to be derived from this summary is that administrative control over education has become increasingly decentralized from federal to state to local levels. This trend reflects not only the increased social and political pressure for the initially dual system to become more responsive to cultural diversity throughout the state, but also the increased pressure to create the single unified system of public education as later called for in Alaska's State Constitution.

Bilingual education: 1976 to date

What the summary does not show, however, are a number of developments in the last decade especially relevant to cross-cultural education in Alaska. The first of these important developments was the proliferation of bilingual education programmes, beginning in 1970 with Yupik-speaking Eskimo children in Alaska (Orvik, 1975). These programmes were important for three reasons. First, they represented a total reversal of the explicit policies of many decades' standing, that native language and culture should be eradicated in the schools. Prior to 1970, the use of native languages in school was routinely discouraged, even punished, on the assumption that it interfered with the child's educational prospects. Secondly, the new programmes acknowledged the growing pressure by natives to assume a greater measure of control over the education of their children. Bilingual education exemplifies the kind of curriculum changes possible under local educational control. Thirdly, though it is too soon to tell for certain, these programmes have given some measure of hope that at least some of the native languages, Yupik for example, can be preserved against further erosion.

The demand for bilingual education has expanded markedly in the last decade partly for the reasons listed above and partly because of vigorous legislative and judicial activity on behalf of linguistic minorities throughout

1867 US purchase of Alaska from Russia.

1884 Organic Act: US Congress delegates responsibility of providing education for children of all races in the Territory, to the Bureau of Education in the Department of the Interior.

1900 US Congress grants legal authority to communities in Alaska to incorporate and establish schools and maintain them through taxation.

1905 Nelson Act: US Congress provides for the establishment of schools outside incorporated towns, and the governor of the Territory is made the *ex officio* superintendent of public instruction.

1917 Uniform School Act: US Congress creates a Territorial Board of Education and establishes the position of Commissioner of Education.

1931 US Congress transfers responsibility for education of Alaska natives from the Bureau of Education to the Office of Indian Affairs (both within the Department of the Interior).

1934 Johnson-O'Malley Act: US Congress provides financial assistance to states in providing public school programmes for natives, and authorizes contractual arrangements for the delivery of health, education and social services.

1951 Johnson-O'Malley Act extension: US Congress extends provisions of Johnson-O'Malley Act (JOM) to Alaska by clarifying its intent.

1951 PL 815-874: US Congress provides federal funding for territorial operation of schools on military bases.

1959 US Congress passes Alaska Statehood Act.

1963 Borough Act: Alaska State Legislature creates nine boroughs and all local school districts within the new boroughs are merged.

1965 Division of State-Operated Schools (SOS): Alaska State Department of Education reorganizes and establishes a new Division (SOS) which is given responsibility for rural and on-base schools.

1971 Alaska State-Operated School System: Alaska State Legislature establishes new system as an independent agency and transfers operational responsibilities for rural and on-base schools from the Department of Education to this new entity.

1975 Alaska Unorganized Borough School District: Alaska State Legislature abolishes the Alaska State-Operated School System and establishes the Unorganized Borough School District.

1976 Regional Educational Attendance Areas (REAAs): Alaska State Legislature abolishes the Unorganized Borough School District and establishes 21 REAAs. On-base schools contracted to nearby borough districts or continue as part of the new REAAs.

Table 3 *Chronological summary of majory educational legislation in Alaska*

the United States in general. The passage and expansion of Title VII of the Elementary and Secondary Education Act, the expanded application of the Johnson-O'Malley and Indian Education Acts to include bilingual education, and the far-reaching bilingual education mandates precipitated by the *Lau vs Nichols* Supreme Court decision* in 1974, are all benchmarks of the federal presence in bilingual education.

Alaska state legislation has further reinforced the local expansion of bilingual education. In 1972, a statute was passed requiring a state-operated school attended by 15 or more pupils whose first language is other than English to have at least one teacher fluent in the other language. Subsequent amendments expanded that statute to include all Alaskan districts (other than the 43 Bureau of Indian Affairs schools operated by the federal government[†]) and, under pressure from the US Office for Civil Rights, regulations have been adopted by the state by which the widest variety of language conditions can be responded to by the schools (Coon, 1979). More importantly, in 1978 the state Public School Foundation Program was amended to provide a primary source of Alaska state general funds with which to conduct bilingual education according to each district's weighted average daily membership.

It would be a mistake to conclude from the above that an expanding demand for bilingual education is consistently being matched by an equally expanding developmental effort. Even after a decade of intense federal and state legislative effort and fiscal support, the gap between the best intentions and their most modest execution seems to some to be wider than ever.

Problems of implementation

Of all the components of bilingual education programmes, the one most fraught with problems is that of staff development. This is a more difficult task in Alaska than it is elsewhere. First, there is the linguistic complexity referred to earlier. In addition to the complex distribution of indigenous languages there is an increasingly large complement of foreign languages

---

* In *Lau vs Nichols*, the US Supreme Court held that a child whose first language is other than English must be given special language instruction of some kind in order to benefit from the school's regular instructional programme. This decision precipitated a number of lower court rulings specifically designating bilingual education as the appropriate form of relief. Even more significantly, the *Lau vs Nichols* decision held that regulations promulgated by a federal agency, in this case the US Office for Civil Rights, have the 'force of law'. Thus, any district receiving federal funds (and virtually all do) must abide by these regulations or be subject to proceedings of noncompliance, proceedings the Office for Civil Rights seems quite willing to pursue. (*See also Chapter 18 — Ed.*)

† Bureau of Indian Affairs (BIA) schools are not subject to state laws. By memorandum of general agreement, the state and BIA have sought to turn BIA schools over to the state as expeditiously as possible, subject to community approval. Execution of the agreement has been slow but steady.

spoken among Alaska's non-indigenous urban populations, who are also covered by state and federal language regulations.

Secondly, the populations comprising each language are small. An Alaskan urban district may have as many as 14 different languages for which legally it must cater. Rural districts have fewer languages but their schools are typically small with multigrade classrooms scattered over a wide geographical region, sometimes separated by hundreds of miles without roads.

Next, most of Alaska's 20 indigenous languages have new, still evolving orthographies. In addition to the problems associated with materials development in languages with virtually no literacy traditions, the amount of staff development time taken in literacy training and grass-roots materials development is universally out of proportion to the time available to develop teaching competence or administrative know-how relevant to bilingual methods.

Furthermore, there are few certificated teachers fluent in the languages spoken by school children eligible for bilingual programmes. This problem exists both among native language speakers and non-native foreign language speakers. However, among the former the problem is compounded by the relatively low level of education among Alaska's natives in general. There are very few natives with undergraduate degrees of any kind.

Moreover, the majority sentiment, especially among the native communities, favours bilingual maintenance programmes as opposed to transitional programmes. The desire to maintain local languages and cultures has been the main motivating force behind the bilingual education movement in Alaska from its beginning in the early 1970s and will remain so for the foreseeable future. The effect of this popular mandate on staff development needs is obvious. In programmes designed to maintain minority languages and culture, linguistic skills, community sensitivity, and cultural background are more difficult to conceptualize, select and design training for, than in programmes which aim merely to develop English proficiency in the pupil. To some extent the question is unfortunately academic in so far as staff resources spread over very small language groups render transitional programmes the only feasible alternative.

Finally, logistical problems also impinge on the state's ability to deliver secondary education services to native students in small isolated communities. Until 1976, in order for high-school age students in small villages to continue their education beyond the elementary level, they had to be transported either to boarding schools, or boarding-home programmes. These programmes were usually hundreds, often thousands, of miles from home and family. The psychological and social effects, as may well be imagined, were often destructive both for the students and the communities from which they were sent (Kleinfeld, 1973).

The Consent Decree of 1976

In September 1976, the Governor of Alaska signed a Consent Decree to settle out of court a suit (Tobeluk vs Lind) brought against the state on behalf of all native pupils of secondary school age, claiming that the state's failure to provide high schools in native villages was a form of racial discrimination (State of Alaska, 1976). With the Consent Decree came the promulgation of regulations by the state board of education to provide a high school in any village with at least one student of secondary school age. In this settlement the state agreed that:

(a) Every child of school age has the right to a public education in the local community in which he resides.
(b) Neither the department (of education) nor a district may require a child to live away from the local community in which he resides to obtain an education (4 AAC 05.030).

Therefore,

(a) The governing body of a district shall provide an elementary school in each community in which eight or more children are available to attend elementary school.
(b) Unless the local school committee of the community requests that no secondary school be provided in that community, . . . *the governing body of the school district shall provide a secondary school* or, if so requested by the local school committee, a partial secondary school program in each community in the district in which:
   1) there is one or more children available to attend a secondary school; and
   2) there is . . . an elementary school operated by the district, or there is an elementary school operated by the Bureau of Indian Affairs (4 AAC 05.040, emphasis added).

As might be expected, the funding necessary to carry out such regulations is enormous. To date, more than $84,000,000 have been raised through bond issues and direct state appropriations for rural high school construction in 95 villages for about 2000 eligible students. However, these events provide an example of the intimate relationship between 'colonial' economics and internal Alaskan affairs, this time with a reversal favouring minority students.

It is interesting to note that such a large monetary 'settlement' did not come about simply because of overt generosity by members of the state legislature, generally not so inclined, or even as a salve on a raw social conscience because of previous shortcomings in appropriations for rural programmes. The money was appropriated because astute rural legislators (the 'bush caucus') teamed up with urban liberal legislators to increase the state tax on North Slope oil production, a tax increase that had met stiff opposition due in part to an effective oil lobby. The tax, which will generate hundreds of millions of dollars from the oil industry, probably would not have passed without the backing of 'bush' legislators acting as a block. Reward for the rural protagonists was, of course, the appropriation for small secondary school construction in the villages. It must seem to the oil producers in retrospect that it would have been less expensive to have donated a new school building to every village in Alaska than to have lost their case for lower taxes on oil. (Darnell, 1979: 441)

But the construction of buildings alone is not the answer to a problem of increasingly complex dimensions. Barnhardt *et al* (1979) point out that evidence for the educational superiority of small high schools was not the basis of the Consent Decree. Rather, the legal basis was that some communities (mostly Caucasian) had high schools, whereas others (mostly native) had none. There is no indication that any thought was given to the kinds of secondary programmes to be implemented. There is thus a serious gap between the intentions of the agencies acting out the need to solve a legal problem and the reality of creating workable programmes. Moreover, the construction of facilities prior to the design of operational concepts is making the problem even more difficult. The solution resides in provision of high school experience in a manner appropriate to the small numbers of pupils, their cultural differences and their geographical isolation.

An unforeseen paradox results from the small high school mandate. Villages which children have been leaving during their high school years over a period of several decades have made sociological adaptations appropriate to the extended absence of this particular age group from the community. Now these communities and their families must readjust to the presence of this age group, which is likely to strain the best designed facilities anywhere.

The foregoing is not intended to paint a completely negative picture of the rural secondary setting in Alaska. There are many indications that individual efforts are leading to promising solutions to a complex problem. But as Darnell commented recently:

> School buildings and dollars are tangible evidence that attention is being given to the problem. Not until answers are found to questions concerned with what goes on inside the facility and how that process relates to the community will the education authorities be able to provide rural secondary schools that may prove to be a superior option to conditions in current boarding schools. And since secondary programmes in village settings can by regulation be required where enrollment is as few as one, any solution will have to have an extreme range of alternative forms. Developing them, testing their effectiveness and training teachers in their use will require undertakings of the same magnitude as the effort going into the construction of school buildings. (Darnell, 1979: 441)

Even considering the many prior decades of policy implicitly constructed to eliminate cultural differences, the prospects of working out a more humane pluralistic system are not hopeless. Change in practice, whether in bilingual education or in secondary programme development, necessarily lags behind easily changed legislative and judicial theory; with time, funding, and concerted effort, educational practice could eventually catch up with current intentions.

An economic basis for future progress

The foundation for some of the necessary changes has already been established. Perhaps the most important area in which changes are taking place is in the state's economic status. Alaska has always been viewed, at least for the past two centuries, as an area for exploitation by the outside world. Armstrong, Rogers and Rowley (1978) describe northern economies in general as colonial in nature. That is, the natural resources of all the circumpolar nations are developed by southern capital for southern interests. Recent events in Alaska, namely the 1971 Alaska Native Claims Settlement Act and the discovery and development of the extensive oil fields on the north slope of Alaska's Brooks Range referred to earlier, have begun to change radically the 'colonial' nature of Alaska's economy.

The Alaska Native Claims Settlement Act was passed by the US Congress in 1971. This Act recognized that habitation and use prior to contact with outsiders is a valid basis for aboriginal claims to the land and its wealth. The ensuing settlement was designed not only to redress the above claim but also to establish a permanent economic base for overcoming the endemic poverty and powerlessness of rural Alaskan minorities.

The Act conveyed selection and title to 40,000,000 acres of land and $462,500,000 from the federal treasury to the natives of Alaska, by establishing 12 native regional corporations and over 200 village corporations. An additional $500,000,000 will eventually come from a 2 per cent royalty on Arctic Slope oil development. Alaska natives are profit-sharing shareholders in these corporations.

It would be inaccurate to say that this Act resulted entirely from recognition of the inherent justice of the claim. Perhaps the most important factor was the need to clarify title to extensive tracts of oil-rich land so that development could proceed unencumbered by questions of who had rights to what.

As to the development of oil in Alaska, estimates of recoverable reserves from the North Slope region alone have ranged from 50 billion barrels to 150 billion barrels (Armstrong, Rogers and Rowley, 1978). Additionally, there are potentially 300 trillion cubic feet of recoverable natural gas from these same fields. Since the announcement of their discovery in 1968, and their subsequent development beginning in the mid-1970s, the state royalties from these fields have given Alaska a 1980 general fund surplus in excess of $5 billion. This resource alone promises to change the economic prospects of Alaska so radically that the question of how to fund social and educational programmes for the state's cultural minorities is no longer at serious issue. What remain to be developed are the concepts whereby these financial resources can be transformed into effective action.

Providing native teachers

Coincidentally with its growing financial base, the state's institutions of higher education have responded to the needs of cultural minorities in a number of significant ways. Most notable is a concerted effort to infuse the educational system with fully qualified native teachers.

Until recently a pattern prevailed in which higher education in general, and teacher training in particular, was available only to those natives willing to move to an urban campus. This cycle unwittingly presupposed a high degree of Western enculturation, thus defeating the aim of developing rural native teachers. In order to break this cycle, a programme was designed to bring the 'campus' to the potential students, assuming that their reluctance to leave their home communities was in itself an indication of their strong identity with the life and culture of the local environment.

The resulting Cross-Cultural Education Development Program (X-CED), has three distinguishing characteristics. First, it is *cross-cultural* — it sees schooling and teaching as intimately related to the cultural patterns of the community in which they exist. Secondly, the programme has an *interdisciplinary* academic orientation. Education is seen as an applied field which draws heavily upon the concepts of anthropology, linguistics, sociology, economics, and English for its subject matter. Thirdly, and most important, the programme is *field-based*. It assumes that the desired cross-cultural perspective of its graduates is best developed through extensive involvement in real-life field experiences.

From these features follow the general objectives of the X-CED programme:

1. to improve the quality of education for Alaska's multicultural population by assisting educators in developing a cross-cultural understanding of educational issues;
2. to provide a programme of cross-cultural studies to students on site in rural Alaska communities;
3. to prepare educators uniquely suited to live and work in cross-cultural educational settings; and
4. to provide alternative approaches to educational problem-solving and programme development.

In its first ten years of operation this programme has graduated some 60 Alaska native certificated teachers. While this figure may seem small by global standards, it is worth noting that it represents about ten times as many native teachers working in Alaskan school systems as in all the years prior to the programme's inception in 1970.

A system that can cope with change

Implicit in this approach to teacher training is the necessity for co-operative responses to culture change, especially when it is rapid. The institutions that follow on the heels of colonial economics must realistically be regarded as permanent, public education being perhaps the main such institution. But permanency does not necessarily imply appropriateness. It is when educational institutions fail to seek ways to become more sensitive to the facts of existence regarding encompassed minority cultures that permanence becomes oppressive and minorities become marginal, economically as well as socially.

The X-CED programme has been described here not as being a definitive answer but as an example of the potential benefit of co-operative change, such as that envisioned by Goodenough (1963). Teacher training has sought a degree of self-transformation in order to extend a measure of co-operation to previously neglected constituents. This constituency in turn is responding with increasing acceptance, perceiving that this new approach is useful and appropriate to local educational needs. The co-operative aspect of this approach is best viewed as an assumption that neither the local minority constituency, nor the untransformed public education system, is capable of successfully defining the problem, much less solving it. Thus, a literally cross-cultural system, which transcends the currently limited capabilities of either the minority constituency or the education system, is evolving to 'repackage' Western education in a synthesis of ideologies and cultures more appropriate to the complex future all Alaskans seem destined to face.

References

Armstrong, T, Rogers, G and Rowley, G (1978) *The Circumpolar North* Methuen: London

Barnhardt, C (1980) *Historical Status of Elementary Schools in Rural Alaskan Communities, 1867-1979* Center for Cross-Cultural Studies, University of Alaska: Fairbanks, Alas

Barnhardt, R, Van Ness, H, Bacon, J, Cochran, T, Dolan, L, Harrison, B, Juettner, B, Madsen, E, Nabielski, K R, Sipe, M and Wagner, T (1979) *Small High School Programs for Rural Alaska, Vol I* Center for Cross-Cultural Studies, University of Alaska: Fairbanks, Alas

Bjarne, B and Jensen, K eds (1979) *Eskimo Languages: Their Present-day Conditions* Scientific symposium held at the Department of Greenlandic on the occasion of the 50th anniversary of the University of Aarhus: Denmark

Coon, E D (1980) *Bilingual-Bicultural Education in Alaska: Guidelines for Conducting Programs in Elementary and Secondary Schools* Alaska State Department of Education: Juneau, Alas

Dafoe, D M (1978) *The Governance, Organization, and Financing of Education for Alaska Natives* Center for Northern Educational Research, University of Alaska: Fairbanks, Alas

Darnell, F (1970) *Alaska's Dual Federal-State School System* Unpublished doctoral dissertation: Wayne State University: Detroit, Mich

Darnell, F (1979) Education among the native peoples of Alaska *Polar Record* 19: 431-46

Goodenough, W H (1963) *Cooperation in Change* Russell Sage Foundation: New York

Kleinfeld, J S (1973) *A Long Way from Home* Center for Northern Educational Research, Institute for Social and Economic Research, University of Alaska: Fairbanks, Alas

Krauss, M E (1979) The Eskimo languages in Alaska, yesterday and today *in* Bjarne and Jensen (1979)

Orvik, J M (1975) An overview of Alaska native bilingual education *Topics in Culture Learning* 3: 109-24

State of Alaska (1976) *Tobeluk vs Lind Consent Decree* Alaska State Department of Education: Juneau, Alas

United States Supreme Court (1974) *Lau vs Nichols, No 72-6520*

18. The American Indian's language and culture in US education

Carol M Eastman

Summary: In this chapter some experiments to improve the education of American Indians are described. Many of these insist that funding be given directly to local Indian communities to run their own schools, while others seek to ensure that teachers are drawn from widely divergent cultures. *Contract schooling* has also been tried as a means of improvement by including Indian culture in the curriculum and encouraging parent, teacher, child and school board member interest in community schools.

Since the 1970s, US education policy has encouraged economic *and* educational development of American Indians by increasing self-determination. This policy hopes to open up possibilities for Indians to participate in the modern world while retaining their Indian identity. Many of the problems American Indians have in the US education system come from disharmony between their culture and that of the dominant society. Complicating this are differences in English language ability and a concomitant separation between school and community culture.

Following this account of directions in American Indian education policies, the chapter looks at specific suggestions derived from the author's research on the NW Coast of North America into the reintroduction as 'cultures' of Indian languages no longer widely used for practical purposes. This concept of a 'culture language' which may be taught in the schools within a curriculum in the dominant language will be seen as a way to achieve both the aims of US education policy and those of the Indian groups, and to bridge the school/ community gap.

Introduction

In describing approaches to language planning in the US, Rubin (1978: 4) touched upon the overall plight of American Indians and other minorities from a public education standpoint. It appears that:

> Throughout the history of American public education, the public has been concerned with the failure to acquire basic skills (reading, writing) but this concern has often been muted by the efforts to prevent the psychological impact of failure, hence students were passed without much concern for performance.

Lately, though, the view has developed that if students fail to acquire basic skills, they are victims of educational malpractice. It is also being recognized that American Indians and other minorities are victims of *language variety stereotyping.* That is, Indians are classed socially and economically as 'inferior' because their linguistic characteristics separate them from the dominant society; they speak 'Indian English' or just 'Indian'. This, coupled with a lack of basic skills, leads to '. . . unequal treatment in the public domain, especially education . . . and the courts' (Rubin, 1978) and it prohibits access to satisfactory employment.

In the US, the only agency that tries to influence public education in the various states with regard to language inadequacies is the Office of Bilingual Education, set up in 1969 as part of the US Office of Education with the following purposes:

1. nationally to assess the educational needs of children and other persons with limited English-speaking ability and the extent to which their needs are being met from federal, state or local efforts;
2. to plan bilingual education programme extensions and to report on and evaluate preceding bilingual education activities (Rubin, 1978: 5).

Stemming from a 1974 court decision (*Lau vs Nichols*), the US Office of Civil Rights was asked to implement a plan to give special attention in school to children with limited English. The Lau vs Nichols case (414 US 563, 1974) resulted in the US Supreme Court upholding a guideline under Title VI of the 1964 Civil Rights Act requiring a public school district to provide special language assistance to non-Engish speaking students of Chinese descent. This court decision set the precedent that non-English speaking students in general are entitled to special language assistance. The Office of Bilingual Education responded to this decision by supporting bilingual education programmes, by training bilingual teachers, and by developing and distributing bilingual education/teaching materials.

To meet the needs of children with limited English, the Office of Civil Rights enunciated the so-called *Lau Remedy* (1975) as a way of responding to the Lau vs Nichols decision. This asserted that children whose home language is not English should receive bilingual education. Though scholars are now investigating alternative solutions to the problems of limited English, language stereotyping, and the lack of basic skills that plague American minorities, at present bilingual education is *the* primary method being developed for teaching American Indians in the US and generous funding is being provided for the development of curriculum and teaching materials to this end.

The American Indian as a minority

In view of general enlightenment with regard to minority education in America, efforts are being made by government educators to see that the education of American Indians is effective, particularly where Indians have limited English. Of course, the nature of limited English needs to be made explicit and the kinds of efforts likely to solve the problem need to be analysed.

> . . . the problem of learning school material not only relates to language knowledge but also to an individual student's ability to take advantage of school as well as to teachers' attitudes toward and training for dealing with children of limited English. (Rubin, 1979: 1)

In this chapter, we will look at what has been and is being done in American Indian education, in particular bearing in mind that 'the new interest in bilingual education is a matter of the recognition of the coincidence of the linguistic barrier to education with other kinds of social disadvantage' (Spolsky, 1974: 2032).

Attention to the problems of Indians and other minorities who 'do poorer than average in the educational system' in the US is a result of political pressure 'built up for minority groups' (*op cit*). As late as 1964, some educators were not aware that there were a substantial number of non-English speakers attending US schools. As a result, such children were either put into remedial reading classes or classes for the retarded or else they dropped out. Schools, unprepared for non-English students, taught them as if they knew English.

Now, schools are beginning to see that the varieties of English used by students who are English-speaking may also affect teacher attitude toward the students. Sociolinguists suggest that there are similar marks of social and stylistic variation and they are attempting to communicate to teachers 'the nature of the language of their students' and to describe the way teachers may address the complex language issue in their classrooms (*op cit*).

The main educational problem confronting Indians in the US is that their failure to control adequate English is keeping them out of jobs and holding them back in school. This problem is due to the fact that students either know no English, know only 'limited English', or know only a 'socially unacceptable' English dialect.

Recognition of this problem should be accompanied by a recognition that, due to a shift in American values away from the 'melting pot idea', it is now felt that everyone has a right to ethnic and linguistic identity. Up to now, most bilingual programmes in the US have aimed at assimilation. For the 1970s and 1980s, then, it can be considered as axiomatic 'that a bilingual education policy is desirable in the US . . .' (Drake, 1979: 2). Yet, caution is required because, despite a move away from an assimilation goal,

> Values have shifted toward tolerance of ethnics but not necessarily in favor of pluralism. Attitudes favoring ethnic inclusion do not necessarily favor the maintenance or even the acknowledgement of ethnic difference. (*op cit*: 3)

We will first see how this paradox is being addressed by educators, government officials and linguists and then we will offer some suggestions as to what might be done in the future — how, perhaps, both American Indian ethnic identity and advancement within the US socioeconomic system might be facilitated through education. It may be possible to accommodate both assimilationists (who seek to erase ethnic differences) and pluralists (who want to maintain ethnic differences).

American Indian education in the 1970s

American Indians in the US represent a rapidly growing population. As a 'minority' they are unique in that:

> They are descendents of the first Americans. They neither arrived voluntarily in search of a new nationality nor were they forcibly brought to these shores; they have a multitude of languages and cultures developed entirely in the New World — thus they do not necessarily share the values of European civilization; and, most important, many hold special treaty relationships with the United States Government. (Fuchs and Havighurst, 1973: 31)

While American Indian communities have provided rich data in the growth of American linguistics (Kari and Spolski, 1978), until recently few scholars have looked outside the structure of these languages to see how they are used and who uses them. Sociolinguists who specialize in studying language use are now beginning to focus on Amerindian bilingualism in response to the need to develop bilingual education techniques and materials. In 1962 it was estimated that 'only 40 per cent of the 300 American Indian languages still extant had more than 100 speakers and that more than half of these had speakers of very advanced ages only' (*op cit*: 654). Many American Indian languages are rapidly being eroded. Educators, linguists, and government officials are beginning to show 'an increasing sense of responsibility towards the speakers of the language' as well as a greater interest 'in studies of language in use; studies of context, of diversity, and of the sociological aspects of language which are no longer considered uninteresting' (*op cit*: 658-9). Notably, there is a growing emphasis on training remaining native speakers as linguists or to be teachers of the language. Yet it is also common for Indians to have no Indian language at all, and many are monolingual in 'limited English'.

The national study of American Indian education

From 1967 to 1971, material was gathered on American Indian education to determine the status of the teaching of Indians and to document the existing policy toward their language and culture (Fuchs and Havighurst, 1973). In the US, the presence of large numbers of Indians in public schools is a relatively recent phenomenon. The national study was inspired by the recognition of a move of Indians from BIA (Bureau of Indian Affairs) schools to public schools as well as by the growing interest in the 1960s in US minority groups in general. American Indians attend either public, BIA boarding, BIA day, or mission schools. A major new policy direction in the 1970s has been towards placing the responsibility for Indian education in the hands of the Indians themselves. The then President, Richard M Nixon's 1970 Message on Indian Policy asserted:

that the Indians will get better programs and that public monies will be more effectively expended if the people who are most affected by these programs are responsible for operating them. (*op cit*: 18)

At the same time as self-determination is being advised, there is also a trend away from BIA and mission schools, toward public education. This is producing a situation where, in some cases, there are Indians running their own federally funded schools and developing their own curricula. Let us now look briefly at the types of schools in which Indians are currently enrolled. Regardless of type of school attended, up to the present time many Indians:

> live in the relatively more isolated and traditional Indian communities. Children in these communities come from homes where a native language is spoken and attend school with close to 100 per cent Indian enrollment. They are often the first generation to complete high school. (*op cit*: 38)

Indians generally attend either contract, BIA (day or boarding) public (Indian majority), consolidated public, or public (non-Indian majority) schools. However, currently, we are seeing a tendency for increased Indian attendance in urban non-Indian public schools that is likely to continue in the 1980s.

Contract schools

In 1970 only one-third of the Indian children for whose education the government was responsible were still in BIA schools and only one in 20 was in a mission school (*op cit*: 35). Some of the BIA schools have recently been 'contracted', ie the federal government pays public school districts to absorb students from the Indian school. Whereas original contract schools were assimilationist in intent, a new approach is to 'contract' schools to Indian groups instead of to public school districts in the interest of self-determination. Examples of this may be seen in, for example, the Rough Rock Demonstration School in Arizona and a government-financed school run by local Navajo in New Mexico called the Ramah School.

This 'new' contract schooling is seen as a way to achieve 'superior pedagogy and improved academic achievement' (*op cit*: 259) by including local (Indian) culture in the curriculum and by the:

> infusion of excitement and interest as well as the encouragement of formal, active involvement of parents, teachers, children, and school board members in the development of their own community school which makes it possible for students to continue to live at home. (*op cit*: 258)

The Rough Rock Demonstration School at Chinle, Arizona, on the Navajo reservation (begun in 1966) uses Navajo as 'the main language of instruction for the younger children', supplemented by a continuous programme in Navajo culture and language for all grades' (*op cit*: 209). The setting up of this school established the legal precedent of giving funds directly to local communities to run their own schools. Both Rough Rock and the Ramah School employ teachers from the local area who have the expertise to teach traditional language, culture, and history.

Because of the long history of a US educational policy geared to eradicating Indian languages and cultures in the interest of assimilation, it is now required that curricular materials be developed 'from scratch' if bilingual/bicultural programmes are to 'work'. An example may be seen in this quote from the Fuchs and Havighurst study:

> Much of the materials for the Navajo curriculum at Rough Rock are being developed at the Navajo Curriculum center associated with the school. Books and classroom materials; recording of oral histories by Navajo elders and medicine men; *Coyote Stories, Black Mountain Boy* and *Grandfather Stories* have been translated into English. Dr Oswald Werner of Northwestern University has developed an orthography which is the basis for the written language. Craftsmen and Artists give talks and demonstrations. (1973: 211)

As the Indians themselves take on more responsibility for their own education, we shall see increased support for Indian language and culture programmes. Rough Rock is unique in that the school's goal is to transmit traditional Indian culture. Most schools, even with bilingual/bicultural programmes, still emphasize the transmission of non-Indian culture to Indians to enable them to cope with society at large.

The Ramah School (begun in 1970) is a Navajo-run high school in New Mexico which includes Navajo culture in its curriculum and is run by an all-Indian school board with staff from a wide range of backgrounds. That such contract schools are experimental may be seen in the words of anthropologist and former Commissioner of Indian Affairs Phileo Nash, who summarizes the school situation of the Indian as follows:

> The public schools tend to treat the Indian child like any other rural American, which often places the Indian child at a disadvantage. The BIA schools tend to have curricula which ignore those who have no desire to enter the middle class. The contract school has many social advantages. Its educational performance is as yet undemonstrated. (Nash, 1970: 107-8)

BIA elementary boarding schools

Generally, these are area-based; where there are few non-Indians they are often on reservations, and students usually live within 25 miles of the school. No provisions are made for them to live at home. The teachers live within the school compound: there is usually a high turnover and they have little contact with the Indian community. Curriculum is BIA-prescribed and the educational goal is assimilation despite the teacher/student/community gap. In general the curriculum apes that of the public schools except for English language drill. In the case of the Shanto (Navajo) Boarding School in Arizona, Fuchs and Havighurst found that:

> culturally sensitive curriculum materials were not evident in classroom use, nor was any interest apparent in the direction of training Navajo teachers or of promoting education as a career among Navajo youth. No Navajo teachers existed as role models for student aspirations. (1973: 49)

The 'distance' between the boarding school and the community, particularly with regard to communication with parents, is especially great given low parent literacy and the common absence of mass media (*op cit*: 53).

BIA and public day schools

These, in general, are state or federally (BIA) run schools that happen to be in communities where few non-Indians live. Teachers are certificated and hired by the state and work nine months of the year or are BIA appointed. Often, when posted to such communities, teachers are reluctant to stay for more than their contracted two years. The state of Alaska, for example, hires many teachers from the 'lower 48' who are not prepared for the comparatively high cost of living there and who have 'minimal cross-cultural sensitivity' (*op cit*: 60). All instruction is in English and the curriculum is prescribed either by the state or the BIA. Often 'hands-on' technical training is emphasized and occasionally community people may be called in to tell stories about their culture or sing songs and relate oral traditions (in English) in language arts.

Consolidated public day schools

There are also a number of rural and small city areas where a large proportion of the students in the public schools are Indian. In one school there may be both BIA and state-hired teachers and many of them may live in or near the community, resulting in a lower turnover rate than in the two types of schools discussed above. There are even some Indian teachers in these schools but little teacher/community interaction. Most children in the schools no longer know the Indian languages but there is no overt stricture against using them. These schools are starting to incorporate schools from outlying areas and are becoming 'central' schools; as this happens, more Indians from outside are increasing the Indian/non-Indian ratio.

Schools with Indian minorities

Here we find Indians to be 'invisible' and officials espousing 'apparent egalitarianism' may fail to heed 'the needs and problems of the minority groups' (*op cit*: 94). These are the schools in which, as we enter the 1980s, rumblings of 'red power' are heard. Such schools are modern non-segregated 'regular' schools; the Indian students speak no Indian language and live in 'European'-style houses in neighbourhoods along with everyone else. For the most part, these schools as yet provide no special programmes for Indian children although most have plans to do so.

Urban Indians who form minorities in public schools tend to be either (a) assimilating into the general middle class, (b) interested in their tribal culture and maintaining contacts with the reservation, or (c) transient and anonymous. Fuchs and Havighurst found group (c) to be the largest

(1973: 113). In general, non-assimilated urban Indians have 'a belief that a high school education can be useful and is sometimes necessary' (*op cit*: 115); but poverty, family obligations, and frequent moves militate against educational attainment. Thus, many Indians, in urban schools particularly, drop out. Those that stay 'tend to be merged into the ranks of the "disadvantaged", attend predominantly lower class schools in the inner city, and little attention [is] paid to their unique characteristics as Indians' (*op cit*: 117).

There is a growing feeling that teachers need to know:

> a good deal about the local tribal culture and history, not only to be able to teach about them, but also to know and respect their unique elements, to understand the tribe's system of rewards and problems of culture change. And in schools where several different tribes are represented, it is important for teachers to have in addition a general knowledge of the Indian peoples, their histories, and conditions. (*op cit*: 199)

In summary, parents and students in the isolated all-Indian communities favour their schools while in the urban areas with White majorities there is more dissatisfaction. In the 1980s the problems which have to be addressed are those of Indians in integrated urban schools, those concerning educational self-determination and those related to 'limited English' as a barrier to economic development for all Indians.

Curriculum

The education of Amerindians is based on the US public education curriculum with the goal of preparing 'Indian students for employment in the dominant economy and for successful lives in modern society' (Fuchs and Havighurst, 1973: 205). Few today quarrel with this as a desirable goal, but there are questions about materials and methods that need to be addressed, eg:

1. Should tribal history and culture be taught?
2. What is the place of language instruction?
3. Should the emphasis be vocational or academic?
4. How should Indian ethnic identity be catered for?

Most people feel that history, culture and language should be taught, that *both* vocational and academic courses are necessary, and that all children are entitled to learn about their own group culture. The problems arise in deciding *how* to do this. The advocates of bilingual/bicultural education programmes disagree with teachers of English as a second language that school failure is due to 'limited English'. They feel instead that:

> the teaching of literacy in English to those who do not have adequate command of the language is a major part of the educational problem faced by Indian youths. They therefore urge that instruction in reading be given in the home language of the child first. (*op cit*: 209)

The new contract schools mentioned above are in the bilingual/bicultural camp and, as such, go further to argue that bilingual instruction is a 'humane approach to instruction, avoiding the frightening, frustrating experiences of the non-English speaking child in an all-English environment' (*op cit*).

The future: the American Indian's language and culture in US education in the 1980s

While experiments in contract schooling using bilingual teaching and materials may be useful where there are bilingual Amerindian students, it is increasingly the case that 'limited English' monolingual Indians are migrating to cities and being schooled there while their parents have come to find better jobs and living conditions. We will increasingly see the burden of Indian education placed on urban public schools with a decrease in Indian attendance at mission or BIA day or boarding schools. Perhaps the contracting of schools to Indians in the interest of self-determination may be adapted to an urban multi-ethnic context. At the least, Indian community participation in educational programme planning would be desirable. The National Study of American Indian Education urged that during the 1970s:

> the federal and state governments devote monies to a special program in all cities with one hundred or more Indian children and youth of school age to improve the educational environment for Indian children. (*op cit*: 292)

It is likely that despite the tendency to move to city schools, all types of Indian education described here will continue to serve some Indians for another 20 years. Thus, methods and materials developed for use in special programmes should be made to apply, as far as possible, to Indian children in general.

Where it is the case that children come to school speaking no English, bilingual education is clearly called for. Again from the Fuchs and Havighurst study we learn that:

> At present, at least half of Indian and Eskimo children are in this situation. They are fluent in speaking their native language and they have great difficulty in learning to speak and read in English. The other half — those Indian children who live in the cities and those in the more acculturated tribes — generally have English as their basic language and can follow the normal school curriculum. (*op cit*: 311)

Below, I offer a suggestion as to how it might be possible to solve the educational problems of this other half — ie those Indians who are native speakers of English yet retain, and wish to retain, Indian ethnicity.

A suggestion for the 1980s

Where American Indian languages are no longer used by people to communicate with each other but where they are important symbols of the group's identity, it may be possible to devise a curriculum using such languages as 'culture'. A 'culture language' allows various groups to communicate their uniqueness. Where English is the major language of instruction, American Indian and other students would be taught the history and culture of their area using the indigenous vocabulary and categories by which the concepts are traditionally conveyed. This idea has been referred to as *language resurrection* (Eastman, 1979c) and the language resurrected consists mainly of what may be referred to as *culture-loaded vocabulary* (Eastman, 1979a). Such a vocabulary consists of items pertaining to what is 'special' in the Indian community rather than what is common to all languages, ie to the 'culture-specific' rather than to 'culture-free'.

A culture language, so conceived, does not involve using the Indian languages to speak or communicate in general. Rather, it consists of a stock of vocabulary reflecting Indian cultural concepts (eg unique cosmology, counting systems, mythology, fishing and hunting techniques, oral tradition). Where language resurrection is feasible, there must be people available who still know the language so that the vocabulary can be collected. On the Northwest Coast of North America there are elderly Indians who are fluent in their languages while their grandchildren know only English. Fuchs and Havighurst noted that:

> the desire to revive a language nearly lost has stimulated the local school board on the Yakima reservation in Washington state to add to the school curriculum Sahaptin, a language spoken by the Yakima, Umatilla, and Warm Spring Indians. (*op cit*: 214)

The Tahola public school, also in the state of Washington, has developed curricular material and instruction in the local Quineault language, culture, and history. In such programmes, the choice of language and culture to be resurrected, revived, or reintroduced may be determined by the history of the locale of the school. Then, as Civics is taught in US schools, study of the area's 'culture language' may be required of *all* students in the school — not just those who are of the 'relevant' ethnic group.

Such a basis of choice, of course, is in America unique to Indians since other minorities are immigrant rather than indigenous. Items of culture-loaded vocabulary are those that do not translate well into English and for which there is usually no equivalent English term. In the process of compiling a culture language, it is sometimes necessary to develop (eg where the language has never previously been written down or described) a practical spelling system. Materials on the history, literature, and culture of the area are then prepared, using the culture language, not English. Existing materials in the language are collected, preserved, translated and generally made usable and accessible (Eastman, 1979b). The skills required of students of culture language:

> are precisely those lauded by most government education policies (ie literacy, history, literature, social studies, and so forth) [and] the sense of group heritage achieved is both ethnic and regional. (Eastman, 1979b: 14)

How to implement an Amerindian language and culture policy

Currently, bilingual programmes for American Indians are either set up at the instigation of the group desiring the programme or initiated by state, local, or federal government education organizations. Most programmes include the collection of oral traditions, the teaching of regional cultural values, and the training of teachers to be sensitive to the linguistic and cultural complexity of their students.

It is not uncommon to find that, regardless of the type of school attended by Indians, Indian language maintenance is not possible; English tends to become dominant. Even Indians who want to continue to 'possess' their language do not always want to be taught in it. Since there are rarely adequate materials or trained teachers, bilingual education commonly consists of rough translations of the English curriculum rather than cultural enrichment and equal education.

The American Indian situation today is one in which the grandparent generation knows the languages and the grandchildren want to learn them. The middle generation, the parents of today's schoolchildren, were educated for assimilation — kept from the language in many cases by their parents who were discouraged from 'talking Indian' in *their* schools. With the shift to cultural pluralism, we find many Indians cut off from access to their language and culture as a result of this experience. The phenomenon of 'third generation return' when 'what the son wishes to forget, the grandson wishes to remember', does not actually result in a cultural (or language) revival but, instead, in 'a vague nostalgia and an undefined ideology [which] . . is primarily a reaction to the conditions of life in the twentieth century' (Drake, 1978: 9).

A programme of reintroducing language as culture in such situations would foster both a new modern cultural pluralism *and* help to lend reality to the ideal by helping to eradicate limited English in the process. This may be accomplished by teaching the culture language within the existing common language (English) and curriculum of the schools.

> Let it be admitted that the language-as-culture program need not be imposed on rural schools whose children do not speak English and whose program of bilingual education and language maintenance (whether government- or group-inspired) is already operating successfully. (Eastman, 1979b: 16)

In such cases linguists are hired to describe the language, produce a grammar (lesson and dictionary) and develop an orthography, and from these tools curricular materials are produced for teaching 'regular' subjects in the language. In practice, however, the scope of such programmes is limited, since so few American Indian languages have been analysed linguistically, let alone made usable in these ways.

Using the idea of languages-as-culture would allow more realistic materials to be developed. Sociolinguistic (rather than 'pure' linguistic) analysts might then be the people to call on, since:

> their interests, in language research and application, relate to cultural as well as to linguistic variables. They are concerned with the relation of language to

ethnicity, to political, social and cultural change, to education and the like. Sociolinguistic training has also provided them with the necessary skills to produce the requisite materials to be used . . . . As linguists they are able to assist groups to devise orthographies and achieve literacy. (*op cit*: 16)

By introducing an Indian culture language into the curriculum of schools where American Indians (as well as others) go, it is possible to foster the development of educational skills in English *and* to revive aspects of the Indian language and culture at the same time. In this way *all* segments of the school's community are involved and benefit — from the monolingual assimilated urban Indian to the non-English-speaking rural one.

Conclusion

In this chapter we have seen that many of the problems American Indians have in the US educational system arise from disharmony between their culture and that of the dominant society. Complicating this are deficiencies in the ability of Indians to read, write and speak school English, a problem exacerbated by the gulf between the culture of the school (rural, urban, mission, BIA, day, boarding, contract) and that of the community.

United States educational policy with regard to Indian education in the 1980s aims to solve the problem of limited English and simultaneously to sanction a new cultural pluralism. This reversal of the previous assimilationist policy causes particular problems for Indian education since assimilation was quite successful in its efforts to erode Indian languages and cultures in many cases.

I have tried to show how complex and diverse is the American Indian situation in the US and to see what materials and methods have been used to address Indian education problems so far. More responsibility for their education is being placed in the hands of Indians themselves, and the controversial idea of self-determined Indian bilingual contract schools has been tried in Arizona and New Mexico. Part of the controversy surrounding self-determined contract schools opting for bilingual education results from what Drake calls 'a growing national debate about bilingual education which signals a crisis in bilingual education policy' (1978: 4). It may be that 'the growing opposition to bilingual education represents a strong continuity of American values that has been ignored in the general euphoria of the bilingual education movement in the last several years' (*op cit*).

Given the likelihood that Indian education will increasingly be the responsibility of urban public schools and that pupils will increasingly be monolingual in 'limited English' (rather than monolingual in Indian languages, bilingual, or fluently monolingual in English), I suggest that programmes to teach what I call 'culture languages' might be tried as a way to achieve the educational goals of the 1980s. In order to teach American Indians effectively it is commonly thought to be necessary to (a) eliminate 'limited English', (b) foster Indian self-determination of education policy, and (c) facilitate cultural pluralism. A programme of language and culture reintroduction, roughly along the lines suggested here, would employ local Indians as 'resources', would require students to use general study skills in English, and would actively involve teachers in the community. The idea of 'culture language' which may be taught in the schools within a general curriculum in English is one way to achieve the aims both of US educational policy and of the Indian groups whose language and culture is involved. It is also a likely way to bridge the continuing school/community gap.

References

Bergman, R, Muskrat, J, Tax, S, Werner, O and Witherspoon, G (1969) Problems of cross-cultural educational research and evaluation (mimeo) cited in *School Review* **79** 1: 107-8

Chafe, W L (1962) Estimates regarding the present speakers of North American Indian languages *International Journal of American Linguistics* **28**: 162-71

Drake, G (1979) Ethnicity, values and language policy in the United States *in* Giles and Saint-Jacques (1979)

Eastman, C M (1979a) 'Culture-loaded' vocabularies and language resurrection (research note) *Current Anthropology* **20** 2: 401-2

Eastman, C M (1979b) Language re-introduction: activity and outcome language planning *General Linguistics* **19** 3: 99-111

Eastman, C M (1979c) Language resurrection: a language plan for ethnic interaction *in* Giles and Saint-Jacques (1979)

Eastman, C M (1980) *Language planning, identity planning and world view* (manuscript)

Fishman, J A *ed* (1978) *Advances in the Study of Societal Multilingualism* Mouton: The Hague

Fuchs, E and Havighurst, R J (1973) *To Live On This Earth: American Indian Education* Doubleday (Anchor Books): New York

Giles, H and Saint-Jacques, B *eds* (1979) *Language and Ethnic Interaction (Selected Papers from the 9th World Congress of Sociology)* Pergamon: Oxford

Kari, J and Spolski, B (1978) Trends in the study of Athapaskan language maintenance and bilingualism *in* Fishman (1978)

Nash, Phileo (1976) quoted *in* Bergman *et al* (1969)

Rubin, J (1978) The approach to language planning within the United States 1 *Language Planning Newsletter* **4** 4: 1, 3-6

Rubin, J (1979) The approach to language planning within the United States 2 *Language Planning Newsletter* **5** 1: 1, 3-6

Sebeok, T A *ed* (1974) Linguistics and adjacent arts and sciences *Current Trends in Linguistics* **12** Mouton: The Hague

Spolsky, B (1974) Linguistics and the language barrier to education *in* Sebeok (1974)

Webber, R D (1979) An overview of language attitude studies with special reference to teachers' language attitudes *Educational Review* **31** 3: 217-32

19. Materials and methods for teaching Aboriginal children in Australia

Doug White

Summary: Materials and methods of teaching embody a particular relationship between some of the members of a given culture and society and its young people. Educators may not be aware of the process in which they are engaged, and may believe that they are carrying out only particular activities such as teaching maths, reading, science and the like. In Australian schools, Aboriginal children are usually taught by European Australians, and ordinary problems are magnified by social inequality and cultural difference. The materials and methods of teaching in use sometimes assume this relationship to be one of disadvantage/advantage, and then the methods used resemble those for slow learners and other disadvantaged students; in other cases, these attitudes are mixed with a recognition of cultural difference as a variable to be considered; others — and these are few — derive from Aboriginal assertiveness, and attempts are made to teach within a framework of assumptions about cultural equality and independence. The picture is further complicated by the situations in which Black-White relationships arise: in particular the long-occupied areas where language and the original culture have been deeply transformed, areas where language and recognizably traditional ways exist but the land has been alienated, and areas where the land is held and language and religious life flourish.

The methods of teaching and the materials used express various forms of the relationship between Blacks and Whites, and hence are likely to undergo rapid transformation when these relationships change.

The history of the development of methods for teaching Aboriginal children is a record of failure. Schemes and methods which have had promising beginnings and which have been enthusiastically advocated have disappeared a few years later. One of the most sympathetic and thoughtful of Australian educators, Max Hart, included in his book *Kulila* an account of a promising development of a community school at Hermannsburg, a long established Lutheran missionary outpost in Central Australia (Hart, 1974). The Aboriginal community, the Western Aranda people, were taking responsibility for the school. Nohasson Ungwanaka, secretary to the community council, was quoted by Hart as saying:

> Already many of our people feel that the school is not just the Mission's business but all the people's or community's business. The school is not outside any more like before, but is already a little bit inside the community. (Hart, 1974: 86)

By the time the book was published, the school was no more. Family groups were leaving the settlement, and the school became empty of students. Within four years 16 small settlements based on Aboriginal social units had been established throughout that part of the country of the Western Aranda to which people still had access.

Thus this particular failure brought with it a success, for it appears that the new form of social organization is one preferred by and appropriate to the people. The community council was acceptable, compared with what had existed before; but given the possibility of an Aboriginal form of social organization the council evaporated. Not all failures and misunderstandings are of this kind. Sometimes people have been driven from their land, or the inroads of miners, disease and alcohol have destroyed the communities and the people. But all cases illustrate the difficulty that European-originating Australians have in determining the proper character of Black-White relations, and the difficulty of interpreting the usefulness of the various methods of teaching Aboriginal children in Australia.

The Aboriginal people of Australia live in all parts of the country, including Tasmania. (At least 2000 people of Aboriginal descent living in Tasmania face a difficulty over and above that of others in Australia, for their actual existence is scarcely recognized, owing to the official belief that Truganini, the last of her people, died in 1876.) The Aborigines — and in using this term I shall follow the practice that those who call themselves Aborigines shall be so described — vary in their circumstances. Those in parts of the country which have been longest occupied by Europeans have had their lands taken away, their old tribal structures broken up, and often their languages destroyed by the practice of removing children from their parents and the breaking up of the communities which re-formed after the holocaust of the nineteenth century. In the centre and north of the country, although the alienation of the land by mining companies continues and the cultures are still under attack, the languages are in use, the old kinship structures remain, and the ancient religion still has meaning. Here the people have some control over cultural change. While for educational purposes a rough distinction can be made between the Aboriginal people of the south and east and those of the north and centre, not too much should be made of this. In recent years, with a loss of confidence and character by the traditional culture of European Australia and the rise to influence of the Third World countries, a pan-Aboriginality has developed and is allied with some sections of White Australia. Awareness of common oppression has become conscious.

In these circumstances the education of Aboriginal children includes a number of varied elements. They all have schooling, but in the tribal regions, they receive another education from adult Aborigines which has nothing to do with the world of school. Children are told stories of the making of the country and the people, and young men and women are, as part of their transition to adulthood, taught the stories which it will be their responsibility to maintain and transmit, and are instructed on their other duties. In all parts of the country, the education which is conducted by the official apparatus of schooling, although it is not fully available to all Aboriginal children, is concerned with the teaching and learning of the English language and with access to the modes of relationship characteristic of the main society. It is this schooling which will be discussed in this chapter.

In the parts of the nation in which Aborigines have not yet reclaimed any part of the country for themselves, the official schooling is of greater significance. Even here, this is not the only form of schooling. A conference on Aboriginal education in south-eastern Australia (held in Melbourne in 1978 and attended by 80 Aboriginal people) made recommendations which indicate that the Aboriginal view is that distinctive schooling is required. The two cultures, even where English is a common language and their economic bases appear similar, are quite different. A report on the conference says:

> While Aboriginal culture does not value materialism, it does espouse such social values as responsibility for the well-being of others, sharing, and non-destructive competition. The general Australian society seems to worship material values and strongly favours individualism and competition. (Bourke, 1980)

The conference recommended that:

> The promotion of a common feeling of Aboriginality or kinship among all descendants of the indigenous people of this land, including the Tasmanians and the Torres Strait Islanders, is necessary because we constitute only 1 per cent of the total population. This will demand that programs be devised which will strengthen Aboriginal culture and identity.

In addition, and alongside these assertions of a cultural framework for Aboriginal education, there was also a demand for schooling to help improve the position of the Aboriginal population on the socioeconomic scale. At present, unemployment and the proportion employed in unskilled and semi-skilled occupations indicate the relatively worse economic situation for Aborigines as against other inhabitants of Australia.

The problem is to find and develop materials and methods of teaching which can improve the access and opportunity of Aborigines, within a context which preserves and enhances their cultural autonomy and independence. This is partly a problem for official schooling, at least while schooling is in the hands of non-Aborigines; but education must remain partly in the hands of Aborigines, for the maintenance and transmission of a culture cannot be conducted by those outside it. In attempting to achieve a common feeling of Aboriginality, craftsmen, dancers and story-tellers from the north sometimes visit the people of the south.

To complete the educational picture, although it is formally outside the scope of this chapter, mention should be made of the materials and methods by which non-Aboriginal Australian children are informed about Aboriginal society. To quote Bourke again:

> The intrinsic factors [affecting educational programs] . . . would include low self-esteem, racism, Aboriginal identity, teacher expectations, cultural

differences, depiction of Aborigines in the media, in textbooks, and in literature, and training of teachers. Many of these intrinsic factors can, in part at least, be attributed to the low esteem in which Aborigines are held by other Australians. (Bourke, 1980)

To be effective, a policy and programme for teaching Aboriginal children must include, exemplify, and transform the relationships between Blacks and Whites in Australia. It is in this light that the materials and methods used within official schooling will be examined. In Australia, multiculturalism is often mentioned in educational discussion; as a result of migration, other minorities exist apart from Aborigines. But there has been little discussion about whether multiculturalism is (and perhaps, given the present character of Australian society, must be) a form of management of a varied population, a programme for assimilation which avoids identity crises; or whether it is to be part of a process of social transformation towards an association of relatively autonomous and independent cultural and social groups.

The first group of materials and associated teaching programmes will be that developed under the name of bilingualism. Bilingual education has been most developed in the Northern Territory, which at the time of its introduction was administered by the Australian Government. (Education is now a function of the elected government of the Northern Territory.) A report on bilingual education for Aboriginal children was prepared for the Australian parliament in 1973 (Australian Department of Education, 1974). The report indicated that 138 languages and dialects were spoken in the Territory, and that the largest number of children in any language group was a little over 400 (the Tiwi and Walpiri languages).

Not all of these languages had been studied by linguists, and hence the relationships between them were not in all cases formally known. Many had not been written down. No Australian languages had a written form beyond pictographs before European occupation. In many communities where people had been displaced from their original country, more than one language is spoken. The report indicated the following arguments for bilingualism:

1. the propagation of respect for language and culture of the community, self-concept and pride in ethnic identity;
2. the child's first language should be the language in which initial literacy is developed. The order of educational development considered appropriate was oral fluency in the local language to literacy in the local language to oral fluency in English followed by the transfer of literacy to English.

The first of these reasons for the advocacy of bilingualism is couched in terms of identity, a somewhat different concept from cultural autonomy. The culture of the people does not depend on the establishment of a literary form of the language: the cultures are oral, the mode of relationship that of direct contact, the source of understandings based on oral transmission. The second reason is clearly instrumental — literacy in

English is more effectively achieved, it was believed, by its introduction in the local language. The inquiries of the reporters led them to believe that bilingualism was supported by the Aboriginal communities, and that Aborigines and educationists agreed on the need for literacy in English.

Since that initial report, a large amount of work has been done in the analysis of languages, the development of materials in the languages, and in teaching. The three have been inter-related, as linguists have worked with teachers, and Aboriginal and English language teachers worked together to produce materials. The materials are sometimes traditional stories told to children, more often accounts of events in the lives of the older people, and reports of current happenings. As the languages are local, these materials are produced locally.

It is difficult to ascertain the success of the bilingual programme in the Northern Territory. The 1973 report said that there were 56 communities with schools in the Territory, and that these were attended by 4223 children. A report made in 1977 indicated that there were 19 schools included in the formal bilingual programme; 1354 children were taught in these formal programmes, and a further 338 in informal programmes. In quantitative terms, this is a remarkable achievement; in qualitative terms, evidence is less clear. The purposes of the bilingual programme, as originally stated, are rather different from those which might be expressed by an oppressed national minority with a literary culture around which the school curriculum might develop. The bilingual programme for Aboriginal schools is a creation of sympathetic Whites, although it usually has the support of the communities, and aims to maintain Aboriginal identity while providing Aborigines with the use of English. However, some doubts have been expressed about the efficiency of such a programme. A teacher at the 1978 conference of bilingual teachers commented:

> One personal criticism of the bilingual programme in use is that the children are not learning English well enough to enable them to communicate confidently outside their own language group. The adults of the community have a much better command of English than the children coming through the school. In the past, English was used for school, shop, work (European bosses) etc. But now all these English experiences are gone. The store is self-service and speech is not necessary; Aboriginal men are bosses and instructions are given in Maung. (Australian Department of Education, 1978)

It appears that 'identity' may turn into independence, and with independence or autonomy, the schooling programme loses its significance.

It is difficult to see into the future. Since the early 1970s, the 'outstation' or 'homeland' movement has affected communities everywhere where tribal lands are open to the people, and small groups have established small settlements based on kinship associations. For example, the large established Hermannsburg mission settlement, a township of the Aranda people near Alice Springs, has fragmented into 16 separate outstations. These make problems for organized schooling and are usually serviced by visiting teachers, with local aides.

A bilingual programme long preceding that in the Northern Territory exists at Ernabella, in the school of the mission established by the Presbyterian church to the Pitjantjatjara people in 1940. Since then, the early years of teaching have been conducted in Pitjantjatjara; again, local materials have been developed. Visiting the village now, one of the advantages of these years of teaching is evident; the notices for excursions, visiting folk singers, prohibiting dogs in the shops, and the like are in the Pitjantjatjara language. Outside this, it seems that literacy is of little significance; very few books have been translated into Pitjantjatjara, and reading in either Pitjantjatjara or English is not of great significance for most people. Some exceptions are Christian pastors (Christianity seems to be an addition to the traditional religion, rather than an alternative by conversion) and those who handle the political negotiations with the state and mining companies seeking prospecting rights. Teachers at Ernabella with whom I briefly discussed the languages used in the school programme said that the first three years were in Pitjantjatjara, but not exclusively so. Children learned English at the same time. Those who became particularly good at English were sometimes criticized or became concerned at becoming 'turned into whitefellas'.

Language teaching to Aboriginal children is thus a complex problem. Much seems to hinge on the 'identity'/'autonomy' dimension; as autonomy is asserted, identity ceases to be a problem. People speak their own languages, but continue to need English for formal relations with European authorities. But they have less contact with just those authorities — the schoolteachers — who can best teach them the written form of English. Further moves to autonomy might lead to a resolution in that the handling of relations with other Australians will become a problem for the people, and the need to learn English will then be a matter for their determination.

The establishment of three independent Aboriginal schools was reported by Willmot (1975). One of these, at Strelley near Port Hedland in Western Australia, is perhaps characteristic of new developments in the method and context of teaching. The people of Strelley came into prominence within White Australia when they took part in a strike of Aboriginal stockmen in 1946. Since that time, the group have maintained themselves by mineral prospecting, with the help of the White man Don McLeod who assisted in the strike of 1946. In 1970 they purchased Strelley Station. For a long time, the people refused a school, until the federal government agreed to fund a school independent of the state system. The Strelley Community School was established in 1976. As an educational adviser to the people has said:

> Education for the Nomads [the name the group give themselves] represents a concern by the total community for the maintenance and further growth of a life style and economic system which will provide further depth and meaning to their cultural heritage. For a number of years therefore, the leaders of the group have been determined that education as a life long process should be retained within the framework of the value systems and social organization of their own society. (Bucknall, 1976)

A similar school opened at Noonkanbah, an Aboriginal station to the north, in 1978. Education in these schools is bilingual. Material is produced by the White teachers and community members and is part of the move-ment to develop Aboriginal culture and the relation of Aboriginal people to White Australian society on a basis of Aboriginal autonomy.

This bilingual approach is different from the 'maintenance of identity' approach, and perhaps this shows in subtle ways in the materials. A page from a school book published at Strelley in the Nyangamurta language reads, under a picture of two children and a goanna looking from the beach to a steamer at sea:

> Palaja palanga yirrirnipulu rtima katukarnapulu. Maruntulu mungkangalu yirrirninyi pala rtima munumpalulu. Jipi.

In translation, 'Then they saw the steamer and they both got out. The goanna stayed put, looking around, not seeing anything. The End' (Plater, 1979). The goanna, a large lizard, is an important food item for those Aborigines whose food is still partly obtained from local sources. It is also significant in representing an association between people, land, and nature. The bilingual approach at Strelley is part of a move towards reshaping the relationship between Aborigines and Whites in Australia. It represents an active assertiveness by the people, not the bestowal of a foreign way of life on to a passive people whose concepts are to be remade for them, nor the finding of a place for them within these imposed structures. Remaking, we might say following Paulo Freire, is included in the educative process instead of one form or another of domestication.

A basis for English learning and teaching within the context of an asserted independence and cultural equality may develop out of such schools. The movement for independent schools, which are oriented around a core of Aboriginality, is growing, and includes people of the south and east, illustrating 'the tendency of mixed race and urban Aborigines to identify more strongly with their Aboriginal heritage rather than with European culture [which] has become more evident' (Willmot, 1975).

Bilingualism, as a method of teaching and management is the policy of the South Australian Education Department and remains the policy in the Northern Territory. Communities which have successfully achieved a degree of control over their affairs, as at Strelley and elsewhere, also favour bilingual education with a somewhat different emphasis. In most cases, materials are developed locally, although in South Australia where there is a clear majority Aboriginal language (Pitjantjatjara) some materials are developed centrally. Not all states favour bilingualism. Queensland education is strictly monolingual and monocultural, and provides examples of different methods of teaching.

In the Queensland school system, from the beginning, the attempt is made to teach English. This does not imply that Aboriginal languages, or the non-standard English used by many Aborigines, are to be regarded as inferior. A guide to teachers of Aboriginal/Islander students in Queensland secondary schools says:

> The people most intimately concerned with our students are their parents.

Recent research in Queensland suggests that, at present, parents consider the mastery of standard English to be a major task of the school. This view overlaps that of educators who stress that in a multi-cultural society it is important to give all students the opportunity to master English to the extent that they can operate effectively in the mainstream society if and when they wish. (Murray, 1977)

Primary schools with a predominantly Aboriginal population take account of this situation by using locally produced materials. The materials may be prepared by Aboriginal teacher aides, and draw upon local history and natural features, but they are written in English.

Finally, something should be said about the problems of materials and methods in teaching mathematics. Language, experience, identity and culture have been given most curriculum attention. Mathematics is not usually treated as 'cultural', and yet it provides intractable problems because of its cultural character. Aboriginal society is not based on trading relations, in which the object traded has a value measured by its abstract qualities. Exchange occurs more as part of the pattern of communal relationships. The functional arithmetic which seems the most useful to teach is the arithmetic of buying and selling. Arithmetic tends therefore to cut across the assumptions of everyday communal life. Some attempts have been made to study the arithmetic of the gambling card games frequently played (Holm and Japanangka, 1976) but this has not led to much success. The possibility that the mathematics of spatial or social relations could be taught more readily has been put forward, but no programme has been constructed.

Greater success in the education of Aboriginal children requires the further advance of the independence movement, which requires the formulation of Black-White relations on a more equal basis. Schooling is part of this movement and will develop a different character when teachers and curriculum-makers re-shape their practice to accord with such new relations. The first signs of this development are now apparent.

References

Australian Department of Education (1974) *Bilingual Education in Schools in Aboriginal Communities in the Northern Territory* Australian Government Publishing Service: Canberra

Australian Department of Education (Northern Territory Division) (1978) *Report on the Seventh Meeting of the Bilingual Education Consultative Committee* Darwin

Bourke, C (1980) The future of aboriginal education in south-eastern Australia *The Educational Magazine* 37 2: 31-4

Bucknall, J R (1976) Strelley: An alternative in aboriginal education *The Aboriginal Child at School* 4 2: 30-3

Hart, M (1974) *Kulila* Australia and New Zealand Book Co: Sydney

Holm, N and Japanangka, L (1976) The mathematics of card playing in an aboriginal community *The Aboriginal Child at School* 4 5: 19-22

Murray, E E (1977) *Teaching Aboriginal/Islander Students English in Secondary Schools* Queensland Education Department: Brisbane

Plater, D (1979) School, tribal style *The Age* 14.6.79

Willmot, E (1975) Aboriginal education in Australia *Education News* 15 1: 6-15

20. In-service education for the teaching of minority groups in England and Wales

David Dunn, John Eggleston and Anjali Purewal

Summary: In recent years an increasing number of in-service courses relevant to the special needs of teachers of minority groups has been made available in England. The establishment of these courses has been inconsistent, disparate and slow, owing to the decentralization of decision-making about in-service provision, the contentious status of minority groups, and an uncertainty as to what such courses should entail.

Courses providing skills for teaching English as a Second Language are relatively well-established. A current trend is the provision of courses offering more general coverage of issues confronting teachers in a multiracial society and attended mainly by teachers of minority groups. A wide range of such courses has arisen in a variety of institutions, including short and long courses with full-time or part-time attendance that lead to an equally wide range of achievement and qualification.

A detailed study of a selection of these courses is being undertaken by the authors. Preliminary indications are given of the characteristics and circumstances of teachers involved, and their motives for attending. The content of the courses is outlined, and consideration given to the potential consequences arising for teachers of minority groups and their pupils.

Introduction

The advent of substantial and visible ethnic minorities in England and Wales is seen as a novel phenomenon by many. Even the most well-meaning of older indigenous teachers sometimes appear to have a nostalgic longing for the days when a headline 'race dispute' was likely to signify a photo-finish in the Derby. This has resulted in a lack of attention to the needs and aspirations of minority group children in initial teacher education courses.

Young teachers often find themselves employed to teach children whose ethnic backgrounds may be largely unfamiliar, alongside older staff who have watched the racial composition of their classrooms change around them. The need for in-service education appears paramount not only for teachers in inner-city communities, the areas of immediate concern, but also for all teachers if the implications of our increasingly mobile and changing society are to be understood and accepted in all parts of the country.

Yet the response of the English educational system to this need has been inconsistent, disparate and slow. Three major factors account for this response. First, educational decision-making is decentralized. Secondly, the climate of political and public opinion has given no clear lead as to the direction of educational policy in this area (except in identifying the presence of coloured minorities as a problem). Thirdly, it has been unclear to those responsible for provision what kinds of courses would be suitable to meet the perceived needs.

Decision-making and in-service education in England and Wales

The Department of Education and Science (DES) is the ministry responsible for education throughout England and Wales. On matters of curriculum it generally seeks to influence rather than to direct policy, acting through intermediaries like the Schools Council and Her Majesty's Inspectorate.

However, its influence is rarely brought to bear upon issues where no apparent consensus exists, and consequently there have been few clear-cut recommendations as to the nature of provision desirable for in-service education for teachers of minority groups. Recommendations have been implicit only in the small number of general publications on the education of minority groups, of which one might cite *English for Immigrants* (Ministry of Education, 1963) and *The Continuing Needs of Immigrants* (Department of Education and Science, 1972). The DES also seeks to influence by example and organizes a small number of national in-service courses available to key decision-makers. Such courses have included study visits to some of the original homelands of minority groups.

The most trenchant statements about education and minority groups emanating from the DES occurred in a recent Green Paper (Williams and Morris, 1977). This paper stated that 'Our society is a multicultural multiracial one and the curriculum should reflect the different cultures and races that now make up our society' (10.11) and that 'the education appropriate to our Imperial past cannot meet the requirements of modern Britain' (1, 11-12). However, according to the then Prime Minister, under whose aegis the concept was developed, 'a Green Paper represents the best that the government can propose on a given issue, but, remaining uncommitted, it is able without loss of face to leave its final decision open until it has been able to consider the public reaction to it' (Wilson, 1971). For the education of minority groups the decisions remain wide open.

In consequence, most decisions to mount in-service courses devolve on to other institutions. Most institutions active in mounting in-service courses for teachers of minority groups are controlled by local education authorities (LEAs). LEAs themselves are subject to locally elected councils, whose political independence is moderated by the fact that a major proportion of their budget is gained from central rather than local taxation.

Local authorities control most tertiary education institutions active in providing in-service education for teachers of minority groups. These institutions have a great deal of autonomy at the level of individual course provision, and within many the tradition of apparent autonomy for individual teaching staff is also closely guarded. Local authorities also directly control their teachers' centres — institutions having a local role in the provision of short courses for teachers employed by the authority. These courses are often run under the aegis of local authority advisers or inspectors, who have a general innovative, advisory and monitoring capacity throughout their authority. Advisers may also have a personal involvement in course initiation.

This diffusion of responsibility gives individuals a critical role in initiating and designing in-service courses. Developments in particular colleges and authorities in England and Wales appear to be ascribable to the efforts of key individuals who for various reasons have been highly motivated to innovate. Such individuals often have biographical characteristics such as overseas teaching experience which have given them insight into the needs of minorities within Britain.

The effectiveness of innovating lecturers or advisers is dependent upon the institutional context in which they operate as individuals, and on their ability to manipulate that context. This helps to explain many disparities in provision. Concerned individuals are more likely to be employed and effective within structures which are supportive, or at least not antagonistic. Such structures are often in authorities with a high proportion of minority group children, or institutions with particular ethnic traditions. However, if key figures are ineffectual or antagonistic, little or no provision will develop. Other factors extrinsic to the needs of minority groups are also often relevant. Special mention could be made here of the pressures on education caused by the declining birth-rate within Britain; falling student numbers may encourage lecturers to design new courses to preserve their jobs and status.

Other institutions also play some part in providing in-service education for teachers of minority groups. Voluntary colleges, usually controlled by religious foundations, and universities are the most noteworthy. These bodies are subject to much the same processes as LEA institutions, but their apparent autonomy is greater. However, autonomy does not necessarily indicate that their academic freedom to mount such courses is exploited; provision in the university sector is particularly deficient in this field. Explanations for this may be sought in the recruitment of university staff with experience in private and highly selective sectors of secondary education and the frequent remoteness of their personal classroom experience. Such factors have limited the exposure of lecturers to multi-racial classrooms.

Other bodies also influence decision-making in the field of in-service provision. First, award-bearing courses require validation by external organizations, such as universities, the Council for National Academic Awards (CNAA) and the Royal Society of Arts (RSA). These bodies are able to exert both positive and negative influence on the provision of courses. Secondly, national research and development organizations also exert influence, not least by legitimizing existing trends. The Schools Council, for example, has funded or co-funded several research projects into the education of minority groups which have left their mark on in-service provision in one way or another.

Lastly, but by no means least, the influence of the classroom teacher cannot be ignored. Developments in the education of minority groups have in general originated in individual classrooms or schools. Pressure for the dissemination and refinement of these developments has been made by classroom teachers, as individuals, through community relations councils and many teacher organizations. Special mention should be made of the Association for the Teaching of English to Pupils from Overseas which became the National Association for Multiracial Education in 1973. Its change of name recognized 'the concern of its members that it was focusing on only one element of the wider educational needs of multi-racial schools' (NAME, no date).

Political and public opinion on minorities in England and Wales

It has been claimed that the provision of in-service education for teachers of minority groups in England and Wales is critically dependent upon the innovating role of individuals operating in complex and fluid institutional and political contexts. Public opinion, whether antagonistic or supportive to minority aspirations, affects these innovators in their relationships with colleagues and superiors. These relationships are vital for the hierarchical advancement of innovators, and for their ability to pursue desired educational objectives. Political opinion has an evident inter-relationship with public opinion, and can also serve to provide additional and crucial forms of legitimation which can support or counter the aspirations of individuals and local authorities.

'Minority group' has not so far been defined in an English context. In fact it is not a term in common use, though there are a few in-service courses entitled 'The education of minority groups'. The general term is 'minority ethnic group' or 'ethnic minority', where 'ethnic' often appears to be synonymous with non-White. The term does not usually refer to indigenous linguistic and cultural minorities such as the Welsh or gypsies, and certainly not to minorities within the indigenous mainstream culture. It is almost never applied to by far the largest non-indigenous group in England — the Irish, nor to the large numbers of English-speaking residents from North America, the Antipodes, and Southern Africa.

Ethnic minorities in England and Wales are typically regarded as comprising non-White persons and their descendants, primarily from the Indian sub-continent and East Africa, the Caribbean, and Hong Kong. The term is also used for other communities formed during predominantly post-war immigration, if these have in places become identifiable linguistic communities, eg Italians and Cypriots. However, the central reference remains to the communities from residual colonies, Pakistan and what is now called the New Commonwealth. We have referred to these people as substantial and visible minorities.

There have been Black communities in England and Wales for centuries, but their oppression has not been sufficiently visible to disturb the liberal illusion of British tolerance. However, 'the settlement of coloured colonials in Britain has brought to the surface the submerged historical prejudices of the British' (Hiro, 1971). This settlement served to supply a demand for migrant labour common throughout western Europe, but when the demand ceased new settlement was almost entirely terminated by a series of Immigration Acts which were and are racist in many of their effects (Sivanandan, 1976).

Most public and political debate about minority groups in England and Wales has focused on immigration control and fear that the numbers of immigrants are 'swamping' indigenous culture. In-service provision which might be interpreted as giving favourable treatment to minority groups must be seen in this context. It must also be stressed that this background generated a mentality, shared by many educators, in which immigrants were seen as 'a problem'. The introduction of special in-service provision post-dated heightened immigration — indeed in 1963 no courses existed. However, when provision was initiated, a prime aim was to equip teachers to cope with the problems that immigrant children represented in school. The minority group child, not schooling or society, was viewed as problematic. Many educators persist in holding this viewpoint.

It was initially expected that immigrants would be assimilated into the fabric of the 'British way of life', and consequently little special educational provision was made available. On the basis that all children should be treated similarly, immigrants were expected to adapt to the indigenous community, and not vice versa. The increasing influx of native speakers of South Asian languages forced a realization that assimilation could not proceed without some provision of facilities for teaching English as a Second Language (ESL). This led to the first major area of in-service education for teachers of minority groups in England.

Meanwhile the viability of assimilation as a policy was gradually being diminished by the course of events. Settlers from the West Indies, mostly speaking varieties of English and with colonial experience of British culture, found that they faced experiences in housing, employment and personal relationships that reinforced their ethnicity. Most South Asian settlers had never wished to become assimilated in the sense expected by the indigenous population, and they too faced discrimination and racism.

Public opinion adapted to changing circumstances. An important opinion leader was a former Home Secretary who advocated integration: 'not [as] a flattering process of assimilation but as equal opportunity, accompanied by cultural diversity, in an atmosphere of mutual tolerance' (Jenkins, 1966). The term integration has now been replaced in some circles by the currently fashionable 'cultural pluralism', as integration and assimilation are often equated in popular usage.

An important element in the partial revision of public attitudes towards minority groups was their increasingly native status. Reliable figures for minority groups in Britain do not exist, for technical and political reasons, but nearly half the ethnic minority population is now British-born. In 1976 the Registrar General's quarterly returns showed that one child in eight is born to a mother whose place of birth was outside the UK, including the one child in 14 whose mother was born in the New Commonwealth and Pakistan (Kohler, 1976). These children will be entering compulsory education in 1981, and many will come from distinctive ethnic communities. Furthermore their slightly older peers have begun to develop ethnically distinctive patterns of adaptation or resistance to indigenous institutions. These patterns also entail teacher education for needs which would not still exist had assimilation occurred.

However, the support for minority group aspirations implicit in terms like 'integration' and 'cultural pluralism' is not necessarily apparent in public practice. In education most special resources allocated to teachers of minority groups continue to support provision which could be interpreted as assimilatory. In-service provision grounded in currently fashionable notions of multiculturalism runs contrary to the predilections of many educational practitioners and policy-makers who preserve the image of minority groups predominant a decade or more ago. Cultural pluralism is, in any case, a concept with certain inherent difficulties when applied in a class-based society with established mechanisms of social reproduction and educational selection.

What kind of in-service provision?

The predicament of course providers should now be clearer. Neither the educational establishment nor the political climate provides adequate guidelines for the establishment of courses for teachers of minority groups. While the assimilatory ideology prevailed, decisions appeared simple. The aim was to provide teachers with the skills to equip children with technical expertise in the English language — this alone could perhaps be sufficient to provide equal opportunity to excel or fail as demanded by the English educational consensus. All that remained was the battle for resources against the competing demands for other types of provision not specifically devoted to the supposed special needs of 'immigrants'.

However, concentration solely on English language teaching soon proved insufficient. Practical issues facing teachers in schools with a high proportion of minority group children, and a more idealistic concern to form relationships with those children, soon forced the provision of at least some information on the 'background of immigrants' even in courses on language teaching. This was legitimized by a major Schools Council project which developed teaching materials for ESL and included among its publications *The Social Background of Immigrant Children from India, Pakistan and Cyprus* (Butterworth and Kinnibrugh, 1970).

The deficiencies of a purely 'technicist' approach (Williams, 1979) were particularly apparent in another project attempting similar developments for children of West Indian origin (Schools Council, 1972). While some of the teaching materials produced by this project have proved valuable, some educationists were critical of what they believed to be an underlying assumption that 'dialect interference' was the prime cause of underachievement among children of Caribbean origin. This criticism was expressed by Coard (1971) who maintained that English schooling tells the West Indian child that 'his language . . . and his entire family and culture is second-rate' and that 'all the great men in history were White'. Such notions supported the view among some innovators that teachers of minority groups needed to re-examine the whole process, context and content of education. Lack of attention to the languages and cultures of other minority groups was also prevalent.

Coard's work was also interpreted as supporting the provision of Black Studies in schools, and publications such as *Black Makers of History* (Morris, 1974) sought to fill a perceived need. But Black Studies, influenced by American models, was not widely endorsed by inclusion in in-service provision. For official bodies concerned to legitimize educational trends its appeal seemed too nakedly separatist, while it was also criticized for providing a low-status curriculum for ethnic minority pupils.

What has emerged as the dominant influence for change among most teachers of minority groups is a movement known variously as multiracial education, multicultural education or multi-ethnic education. The three terms emerged at different dates and reflect differing underlying analyses, but their meanings are interchangeable. This chapter will henceforth employ the term multicultural.

Teachers concerned with multicultural education have attempted to re-examine the processes, context and content of education appropriate for minority group children and for the wider society in which they live. In-service courses have attempted to encourage this re-analysis, yet such a holistic endeavour is closely linked to the ideological preconceptions of course providers, who may subscribe to differing perspectives on both education and social change. Despite this diversity, course organizers have many objectives in common. One set of objectives in multicultural education regarded sympathetically by many organizers emphasizes cognitive and affective aspects of self-respect and respect for others, and suggests that learning experiences should be selected so as to avoid ethnocentrism (Jeffcoate, 1976).

We are at present engaged in research on a selection of courses in multicultural education, in a project funded by the DES and entitled 'In-service teacher education in a multi-racial society'. Preliminary findings from this research will be reported later in this chapter, but it is first necessary to give a brief overview of courses still aiming to provide mainly technical assistance to teachers of minority groups in the field of English as a Second Language.

In-service education for teachers of English as a Second Language

This type of provision still takes up most of the in-service contact-hours provided for teachers of minority groups. It is also the most institutionalized, in that the predominant qualification is widely available, taught to standardized national requirements, and is a necessary qualification for many advertised posts. The nature of this qualification deserves analysis.

The Certificate in Teaching English as a Second Language in Multi-cultural Schools is validated by the Royal Society of Arts, a respected institution, but one often associated with low-status qualifications in other sectors of education. The Certificate is gained, subject to success in examinations and teaching practice, after a course of one term's full-time study or after one year in its 90-hour part-time equivalent. Twenty-three approved centres in England provide courses leading to the Certificate, and these centres are predominantly institutions of further and higher education, excluding universities (RSA, 1980).

The syllabus for the RSA Certificate has evolved, both locally and nationally, from the syllabus for the similar Certificate in Teaching English as a Foreign Language. It was claimed that the tradition of teaching EFL through age-graded, textbook-oriented courses was inappropriate for settlers, and more context-dependent methods were developed. A demarcation of interest thus occurred in English language teaching, and separate career and course structures are now prevalent.

The new specialism of ESL has continued to develop, increasingly providing teachers with information about and analysis of the cultural backgrounds of their pupils. This has inevitably shown the limitations of the narrow linguistic and technically pedagogic content of most courses.

Other in-service courses in ESL exist: local centres provide a wide range of two- or three-day courses, and there are ESL components in other more general courses; but with the exception of a Diploma validated by the University of London and not widely available, the RSA Certificate is the highest qualification obtainable. No taught in-service courses leading either to degree or higher-degree level qualifications exist. Furthermore, the majority of ESL teachers have actually received no in-service education even below the level of the RSA Certificate, and the majority will also have received little education about the technicalities of English in their prior studies. Many teachers seem to have been appointed on the dubious argument that if they can speak English and can also teach, they can therefore teach English.

The ESL field also includes the only in-service education intended for teachers of adult minority groups, excluding the occasional *ad hoc* seminar. A special RSA Certificate was introduced in 1976, and courses now occur at eight centres, though only around 200 teachers have qualified to date (Arora, 1980). Less formal provision lasting some four-eight sessions occurs for home tutors, and certain authorities provide other short courses: one runs a one-term three-hours-per-week course for retraining EFL lecturers for ESL. The Manpower Services Commission's Industrial Language Training units have, in the past, been noteworthy in providing thorough induction and on-the-job training for their lecturers. The adult ESL field has provided the only broadcast series for in-service education of teachers of minority groups in England (Nicholls, 1979), although the Open University includes some relevant material in more general courses.

In-service provision in multicultural education

The range available (1979-80)

Courses in multicultural education are available in a variety of modes. The longest course leading to the highest qualification is a Bachelor of Education degree course. This three-year part-time course, available at one polytechnic, is validated by the Council for National Academic Awards (CNAA). There are options of varying length not exceeding one term full-time equivalent in a number of courses leading to more general BEd degrees elsewhere. The BEd, as a qualification, arose during the gradual move towards an all-graduate teaching profession. Until recently, many initial training courses led to the Certificate in Education, typically gained after a three-year full-time course. A BEd, typically achieved after a one-year full-time course, enables a teacher with a Certificate to gain graduate status. However, specialist BEds, such as the one in multicultural education, are also taken by teachers who have already graduated in another discipline.

Courses leading to a postgraduate diploma in multicultural education are available at seven centres in England. They are more commonly part-time but are equivalent to a one-year full-time course. One is validated by CNAA, the remainder by local universities. Most courses are held in non-university colleges, and not all recruit a new intake yearly.

Short courses lasting one term part-time or less are available at a variety of institutions, mainly non-university colleges and local authority teachers' centres. These do not lead to any form of award, although attendance certificates may be provided. Full-time attendance does occur, typically of a few days only, but much provision is available only outside teachers' working hours and with no remuneration for attendance. A very few other courses are available lasting more than one term part-time, but these do not lead to formal academic qualifications.

In-school in-service education in multicultural education occurs in a few schools in a few authorities. One authority has a team of *animateurs* working intensively on school development in several schools on a four-year programme; in one typically in-school in-service education consists of *ad hoc* course provision of a few hours organized by heads or local advisory staff.

No teacher in England has access to the full range of provision. The major full-time award-bearing course recruits only about 20 teachers, almost entirely from one metropolitan authority generous with second-ment. Access to part-time courses is dependent on travelling distance, while local authority short courses are generally limited to teachers in the providing authority, who will also need consent from their head teachers to attend any such full-time provision.

Who attends?

Teachers participating in in-service courses in multicultural education come from a diversity of schools and posts with a range of attitudes and expectations. Predominantly they teach in schools with a significant number of ethnic minority pupils. Some do attend from other schools for a variety of reasons which often stem from particular personal experience.

Only a small proportion of teachers from multiracial schools see themselves as likely to benefit from courses in multicultural education. As attendance is mainly voluntary, personal commitment is crucial. Teachers of pupils aged under 11 seem more likely to participate than those of older children, while specialists in maths and sciences are infrequent participants.

Many participants are relatively inarticulate about their motives for attending courses. Some feel that the ethnic composition of their school is sufficient explanation for their presence. Others feel that they need to know more about the children they teach, either from general interest, or to assist their practical classroom management, or to achieve better relationships with pupils. This demand for knowledge is often phrased in terms of the children's 'background' or 'culture'. A few will articulate specific demands, either seeking to understand particular cultural traits they find puzzling, or seeking help with certain aspects of curriculum. A number of participants will already possess coherent ideologically-based strategies for change, and seek further knowledge or qualifications in order to enhance their ability to implement educational change.

A similar range of opinion exists among participants about minority group children, although this does not correlate precisely with the ability to articulate motives for attendance. Some appear to be ignorant of their pupils' backgrounds, and unable to distinguish between different cultural groupings such as Moslems and Sikhs. These participants are more likely to have an assimilationist view of education, and are also likely to call children born in England 'immigrants'. Others will refer to 'ethnic minorities', and will have greater but varying knowledge of their pupils. Some participants are themselves from a minority group: such teachers are frequently assigned to or seek a responsibility for minority group pupils, which does not help their advancement in other areas of responsibility and salary.

Course content

A number of topics recur in courses in multicultural education. The boundaries between the topics mentioned below are in some cases rather arbitrary, and the topics are not exclusive: the concerns of individual course organizers may result in unusual and specialized elements. Short courses will often concentrate solely on one or two topics or aspects within them and may also occasionally be directed at teachers of a specific minority group.

Teaching English as a Second Language is often included in general courses on multicultural education as a relevant field rather than as the central issue. Coverage can include linguistic and cultural issues relevant to teaching, and practical advice on recommended techniques and materials. A particular emphasis may be placed on aspects relevant to classroom teachers of other subjects.

Attention will often be paid to bidialectism among pupils of West Indian origin, frequently emphasizing the linguistic parity of creoles with other languages, the syntax of creole forms of English, and the use and development of patois among adolescents in England. Some attention may be paid to other mother tongues spoken in England, such as Punjabi, Gujarati, Urdu, Hindi and Chinese, emphasizing their lack of recognition in the English educational system.

Aspects of school organization may be covered, including the relationship between parents from minority groups and the school; the potential offensiveness of some types of school meals, uniform and religious assemblies for some pupils; and external and internal selection processes including banding, setting and streaming.

Possible changes in curriculum to enhance the opportunities of minority group pupils are usually explored. Suggestions include the provision of additional topics within the curriculum, such as additional languages or aspects of minority group cultures, and an emphasis on language across the curriculum. A current tendency is to advocate enriching existing syllabuses and resources with aspects perceived as recognizing or celebrating ethnic diversity, in all disciplines, particularly literature in English, history, religious education, home economics, social studies and geography. The search for stereotyping, inaccuracy and cultural bias in existing materials is an important activity.

The religion and family organization of ethnic minority cultures are often considered, sometimes in historical and sociological depth. The processes of migration to and settlement within Britain and the resulting community patterns and resources may be discussed. Aspects of Britain's history, such as economic developments since World War II and colonialism are sometimes considered, together with their social and political concomitants. Courses often pay particular attention to manifestations of racism in Britain, at both the institutional and individual levels.

The attitudes of teachers to ethnic minority pupils are often explored, though sometimes only indirectly through discussion or exploration of the sociological and psychological backgrounds of pupils in general. Labelling, stereotyping, selection, motivation and intelligence are among the issues discussed. Many courses involve participants in individual or group activities in syllabus or resource design related to the perceived needs of their own pupils.

The consequences of courses

Participants' perceptions of the consequences of their attendance vary widely. Some feel little or no personal gain, beyond the awareness of a few resources or minor items of information. Others report a fundamental transformation of their approach to teaching, their pupils, and life in general. The impact of the course depends upon the initial viewpoint of the participant, the quality and length of the course, and the extent to which it bears directly upon individual circumstances.

The extent to which personal consequences are transformed into potential consequences for pupils and institutions also varies. Even participants who report a transformation of attitude may be prevented from implementing changes in teaching by structural or interpersonal constraints. The ethos of the participant's institution and the participant's status are relevant here.

A number of participants claim a greater understanding of and respect for the diversity of needs and aspirations of minority group pupils. Many, including some ethnic minority participants, claim a greater awareness of the nature and processes of racism within their institutions. Some introduce fresh resources or modify existing syllabuses, and a few introduce entirely new courses. Some participants alter the organization of their classrooms or schools in ways designed to benefit minority group pupils, while a few teachers report changes in marking strategies. A number of participants claim enhanced relationships with pupils, and some with pupils' parents; this is variously ascribed to increased empathy stemming from greater awareness, increased reference to matters pertaining to pupils' interests during curricular and extra-curricular activities, and changes in curriculum resources and organization.

Many participants spread the ideas gained on courses, either informally or in structured ways through the existing hierarchy or through innovatory activities involving other teachers. Some report enhanced promotion prospects, and a few ascribe recent promotions to their attendance on courses. A few comment on enhanced self-confidence within their institutions, either through skills acquired or solidarity achieved during courses.

Few participants are prepared to claim that their pupils do better as a direct result of in-service courses. More are prepared to say that innovations of the nature they have introduced will generally enhance attainment, but that it would be difficult to prove. A similar ambiguity exists over claims for enhanced inter-ethnic respect and pupil self-respect, although some participants have anecdotal evidence to support their beliefs.

In terms of participants' overall satisfaction it seems to be important that the course should be 'practical' and relate directly to their own role. Given the diversity of participants, this is not easy to achieve. Participants seem likely to value the contributions of those who have themselves taught minority groups, particularly ethnic minority lecturers themselves, unless these contributions are dramatically at variance with the perceptions of participants.

While longer courses have the more intensive consequences, this does not diminish the necessity for a broad range of provision. The vast majority of course attendance is voluntary, and a longer course can require a high degree of commitment and attendance which may conflict with domestic life. School-based in-service courses are often proposed to resolve this and other dilemmas. These courses can and do fulfil a valuable role, but some participants on other courses report a welcome release from in-school constraints and hierarchy. It would be unwise to emphasize the importance of in-school programmes to the detriment of alternative provision.

The only existing document of any substance on in-service education for teachers of minority groups in England was published some years ago (Community Relations Commission, 1974). As a programmatic document this is still worthy of attention, for provision in many local authorities by no means matches past ideals.

Conclusion

In-service education in teaching of English as a Second Language is not extensive. Provision in multicultural education is even less so, although the potentially valuable consequences of such courses have been reported.

There remains the question of how far multicultural education has become an island isolated from the rest of in-service provision. A few local authorities make attempts to ensure that specific attention is paid to the education of minority groups in other in-service courses on specific disciplines or educational management. However, the suspicion exists that, outside the token areas described in this chapter, attention paid to minority groups in in-service education is grossly disproportionate to their numerical importance in English schools.

References

Arora, R K (1980) *Report on English as a Second Language for Adults* Mimeographed paper for Advisory Committee for Adult and Continuing Education Enquiry into Ethnic Minorities: London

Butterworth, E and Kinnibrugh, D (1970) *Scope. Handbook 1: The Social Background of Immigrant Children from India, Pakistan and Cyprus* (Schools Council Project on English for Immigrant Children) Books for Schools: London

Coard, B (1971) *How the West Indian Child is made Educationally Subnormal in the English School System* New Beacon Books: London

Community Relations Commission (1974) *In-Service Education of Teachers in Multi-Racial Areas* CRC: London

Department of Education and Science (1972) *The Continuing Needs of Immigrants* Education Survey 14, HMSO: London

Hiro, D (1971) *Black British, White British* Eyre and Spottiswoode: London

Jeffcoate, R (1976) Curriculum planning in multiracial education *Educational Research* **18** 3: 192-200

Jenkins, R (1976) Address given to a meeting of Voluntary Liaison Committees. Reprinted by National Committee for Commonwealth Immigrants: London

Kohler, D F (1976) *Ethnic Minorities in Britain: Statistical Data* Community Relations Commission: London

Ministry of Education (1963) *English for Immigrants* HMSO: London

Morris, S (1974) *Black Makers of History* The COBS: London

National Association for Multiracial Education (no date) Publicity material NAME: Burton-on-Trent

Nicholls, S (1979) Mimeographed notes for the radio programme *Teaching English as a Second Language* BBC: London

Royal Society of Arts (1980) *Certificates in the Teaching of English as a Second or Foreign Language* RSA: London

Schools Council (1972) *Schools Council Project on Teaching English to West Indian Children: Concept 7-9* Schools Council: London

Sivanandan, A (1976) *Race, Class and the State: The Black Experience in Britain* Institute of Race Relations: London

Williams, J (1979) Perspectives on the multi-cultural curriculum *The Social Science Teacher* **8** 4: 126-33

Williams, S and Morris, J (1977) *Education in Schools: A Consultative Document* (Cmnd 6869) HMSO: London

Wilson, H (1971) *The Labour Government 1964-70* Weidenfeld and Nicholson/ Michael Joseph: London

21. Teacher education for a multicultural society: courses at Bradford College

Peter Chambers

Summary: Bradford College is a comprehensive community college, providing a range of courses to meet the needs of its urban, industrial, multicultural community. The College's academic policy and its teacher education programme are shaped by three aims: (a) to be responsive to community needs; (b) to ensure the interaction of community values with those of wider social organizations; (c) to equip all ethnic groups with the ability both to play a full role in their own community and to be successful within the majority culture.

To implement these, the College encourages ethnic minority students, places teacher education in the context of community, and involves members of ethnic minority groups in planning and teaching. Using its inner-city location, it centres all school experience on predominantly multiracial schools to which its staff are systematically attached. Professional preparation focuses on the specific needs of these schools, and is based on the interaction between school experience and college teaching. Curriculum materials emphasize the mastery of teaching skills in language and mathematics and the inter-relation of school and community in the educative process. Undergraduate students come to this after a Diploma in Higher Education which has sensitized them to the nature of urban, multicultural society, whilst postgraduate students are oriented through the Education Studies course. All programmes place great stress on giving students credibility in the eyes of schools. The College believes that its achievement is distinctive but recognizes that it can be improved.

Response to a multicultural community

The city of Bradford has a long established reputation for hosting immigrants. Even now that the town planners and developers have finished knocking its city centre about, the signs are still there. Little Germany keeps its listed buildings, the Polish clubs flaunt their bold signs and a Lithuanian School of Dance offers Saturday morning instruction. These immigrant communities made such an impact on the young J B Priestley that he saw it as a matter of regret that Bradford would never again enjoy such a diversity of cultures (Priestley, 1934: 161). How wrong his prophecy was: in the city's streets today Sikh temples proudly fly their flags, Asian greengrocers display their wares, Muslim butchers offer halal poultry, West Indian youngsters congregate in the main shopping centre and Hindu mothers wait outside the schools. Bradford College is set in the very heart of this urban industrial multicultural city and it is perhaps symbolic that its immediate neighbours on the short road down to the town centre are an Italian pizzeria, a Chinese restaurant, a French creperie, a curry house, a fish and chip shop and a Greek eating house. Across the road, the Deutsche Evangelische Kirche faces the Students Union Building, and round the corner is a succession of banks whose head offices are all in the Indian Sub-Continent. The College thus inhabits its own 'Latin Quarter' (Clough, 1979), and given its commitment to community education it is hardly surprising to find the curriculum geared to meeting the needs of a great many ethnic minorities, or to meet students of every colour, class or creed in the corridors. It is in the context of a community college that its teacher education courses must be viewed.

A comprehensive community college

Bradford College was formed in 1975 when the Bradford College of Art and Technology (itself a recent merger of the former Regional College of Art and the Technical College) was merged with the Margaret McMillan Memorial College of Education under the Principalship of Eric Robinson, whose vision of the new polytechnics as the 'comprehensive people's universities' was already widely known (Robinson, 1968: 219). He was able to capitalize on the entrepreneurial responsiveness of the further education system (Cantor and Roberts, 1979: 195), the regional roots of the College of Art, which had made its community arts programme a major focus of its work, and the tradition of teacher education, symbolized by the name of Margaret McMillan and implemented in a range of teacher education courses responsive to the disadvantaged and which, as early as 1966, offered a special certificate in education course for Asian teachers.

It was not, therefore, difficult to get the new College to accept an academic policy with two principal commitments: namely to establish itself as a comprehensive college of further and higher education, and to provide a range of courses that would meet the needs of the urban, industrial multicultural community of Bradford (Bradford College, 1977). There are, however, difficulties in implementing such a policy. Any attempt to respond to the challenge of a multi-ethnic society through education has to acknowledge the enormous social and political complexity of the problems as well as the sheer range of educational provision necessary.

To publicize such commitment is to raise issues of scale, ideologies and priorities. Thus, although the College is proud of the way it provides programmes in response to the needs of ethnic minority groups, it is uneasy about whether its response is sufficient and whether its priorities are right and ideologically justifiable. If it tries to meet the needs of one particular ethnic group, say through a policy of positive discrimination, it runs the risk of stigmatizing the 'beneficiaries' and of causing resentment among other groups. Nevertheless, the College does see itself as having to provide courses which allow students from minority groups to compete on similar terms with those in the mainstream. Society at large is unsure whether it seeks the assimilation of minority groups or their accommodation within a pluralist system (Saunders, 1980); the College therefore has to make agonizing decisions about its priorities. Whatever else the College seeks to do, however, it does not intend to create outsiders: its multi-ethnic policy requires its programmes to demonstrate the interaction between the different community values and those of the wider culture (Chambers, 1979a).

A multi-ethnic education policy

The implementation of this policy takes a variety of forms. First, it affects the main thrust of the total College programme and permeates all its courses. College courses have to satisfy the requirement that they help to prepare people to live and work in an urban, industrial multicultural society. This has led to the provision of support courses, for example in language and communication skills, for many of its conventional further education courses to help students whose difficulties may arise from their ethnic backgrounds. These are intended to make traditional courses more accessible and acceptable to students from ethnic minority groups; alternative forms of access are thus provided to mainstream courses, which in turn help to fund less formal opportunities for multi-ethnic education.

Secondly, the College has developed specific courses in multi-ethnic education. These include courses designed to help students cope more easily with living and working in the United Kingdom; courses to foster the cultural values of the communities with which the students identify; and courses which aim to enable all students, regardless of origin, to appreciate the pluralist nature of British society and to understand the salient elements of its diverse culture. This 'accommodationist' stance is probably the most characteristic value pursued, and permeates all the courses on offer, including those in teacher education.

The College, therefore, tries to ensure that the large number of students who hail from diverse cultural backgrounds do meet, in the main, a body of staff and a set of opportunities within the College which are sympathetic to their different cultural values. This policy is manifest in the College's catering policy, the counselling support given by its student services organization, its staffing policy and its social arrangements. It is further supported by its development of an 'open access policy', which in time will make it truly community-responsive, and by the direction of its research policy, which has identified multi-ethnic education as the main area of its research activities.

Teacher education: the preparation of students to teach in a multiracial society

The ethos described has high significance for the College's teacher education programmes, which are restricted to students wishing to teach children between the ages of three and 13. These courses must not only reflect that ethos, but they must also provide a lead in implementing it and in capitalizing on the extensive expertise that has been accumulated. Inevitably, the problems are complex. As an example, the decision to merge the School of Education with the School of Adult and Community Education, although given impetus by the cutback in teacher training numbers and the need to provide an adequate administrative and logistical base for its courses, was also used as a means of opening up teacher education to the community context. In this way it related courses for teachers in urban, multicultural schools to a major commitment to meeting the social and community needs of ethnic minorities and of certain disadvantaged groups in ways designed to generate greater community autonomy and individual independence.

The snag was that one group derived its academic justification from a generalized professional standpoint, the other from immediate response to community needs. The first group, committed to preparing students 'for schools as they really are' (UCET, 1979), saw its primary task as establishing professional credibility; the second, responsive to the community 'as it really is', aimed to dissolve 'artificial barriers that tend to fragment certain experiences' (Newman and Oliver, 1967). The two groups thus tended to pull in opposing directions, for even though the schools used for teaching experience were in areas of high-density ethnic minority populations, there was often less responsiveness to community needs than the community activists would have liked. Conversely, the community education tutors were unconvinced of the value of developing some of the skills, for example in the basic tool subjects of the curriculum, that were believed by the schools to be indispensable.

Establishing policy

The dialogue that followed led the College to attempt to formulate a policy for teacher education that kept the exploration of this dilemma in the forefront of its thinking. It recognized that the academic policy of a community college must create a bridge between the immediate and local concerns of community groups and the wider political, social and educational perspectives of society. In so doing, the College acknowledged that genuine community education does not start in the educational institution; the initiative lies within the community. Despite the fact that a particular community might be hard to identify and that its constituent sub-groups might have different values and conflicting interests, the nature of that community should shape the College's curriculum so that the latter can be seen to reflect the key values of the community. Implementing a curriculum of this kind, responsive to the diversity of community needs, is no easy task for the teacher and doubly difficult for the teacher trainer. The teacher will have to respond to contradictions and conflicts as well as to his or her own ideas of what constitutes the community's needs. Further, if those in authority over the teacher pursue policies informed by professional and educational values different from those held by community leaders, the difficulties for teachers are certain to be intensified and the problems for teacher educators gain proportionate magnitude. While community activists persuasively focus their energies on the immediate and the local, the 'officials', epitomized by teacher educators, persistently try to place the immediate and local into wider political, social and educational contexts. In so doing, the one group acknowledges the strength of community education to lie in its 'ghetto' characteristics, while the other values the wider educational perspective as a source of new values or comparative activities that can be of help to the community. Both groups, in turn, identify the weaknesses of the alternative perspective: introspectiveness on the community side, lack of engagement on the 'official' side.

The development of an appropriate policy in the face of these cultural dilemmas comes up against institutionalized values. The values of the training institution may not only differ from those held in the community but also from those held in the schools. School value systems have traditionally been 'closed'. Some have even seen community ties as dysfunctional, for example, those who justify the selection system as a means of providing upward social mobility for working-class children. Whereas current approaches to schooling have seen an opening up of these closed systems, the concept of 'total institution' (Goffman, 1968) is not quite a parody of many schools (or colleges or university departments of education for that matter). The reality of curriculum decision-making is that it is initiated from the professional standpoint and thus community values tend to be used as a context rather than a justification.

Community responsiveness, a vocational orientation and an emphasis on the practical value of educational theory, were already firmly established within the College's teacher education curriculum. They were there as a result of a professional judgement that the College's courses should be designed in response to its location. The pluralism that shaped its values was the main impetus behind the design of its Diploma of Higher Education/Bachelor of Education degree programme, but there was increasing awareness that its implementation was neither sufficiently open to community values in itself nor was it succeeding in broadening education in schools.

There are good reasons for this. It is not easy for a teacher to make organized learning responsive to the community in ways consistent with mainstream achievement and that do not challenge the very community origins in which the pupils have their roots (Keddie, 1971). Furthermore, the demands of the classroom are as immediate to the teacher as community priorities are to the community activist. Ideas take second place to institutional imperatives for teachers — such as issues of control, the value of certain forms of knowledge and the need for certain kinds of organization. There is no doubt that in meeting such requirements teachers can come into conflict with community values not only in the obvious ways but in a variety of subtle responses to pupils that scarcely trouble the teacher's conscious classroom decision-making.

This is well-illustrated by reference to language usage. The logic of non-standard English (Labov, 1970) illustrates the complexity of language exchange between classroom and community. A teacher's use of language can fundamentally affect human relationships in the classroom. Habit and unthinking reactions are involved as well as deliberate responses. Moreover, since these interactions are the major ways in which community and educational values are brought together, it is important that teachers are trained to realize that the way they see their roles and habitual activities actually influences their interaction with the community. Yet it is likely that such awareness does not have high priority in schools 'as they are', particularly if they are not open to their communities. Schools tend to emphasize the enormous demands of the classroom, but community education has to go beyond the school and the process of schooling into the community so that teachers will need to come into contact with parents, with other adults and with other children.

Consequently, the teacher education programme at Bradford College had to be designed to raise students' consciousness of social interaction so that community awareness became incorporated into their thinking about the nature of teaching. Since, however, that awareness had then to be translated into action, it became necessary to arrange for student teachers to be allowed to practise in situations that enabled them to apply such awareness. If the institutional imperatives are as significant as has been argued, then practice in schools lacking in community orientation would create similar communication blocks to those already described between school and community. In order to equip teachers to operate in situations that were more responsive to community needs, the College decided that its teacher education programme had to reflect a community commitment in its selection of knowledge, in its structure and practices, in its relationships with its practice schools and in its philosophy.

The problems were heightened by the existence of a multi-ethnic community. Several issues emerged. The value of pluralism was not necessarily shared by all the sub-groups within the community that the College served, whether they were dominant or minority. The schools did not always accept the same philosophies and indeed, in some instances, racist attitudes were found in schools which otherwise would have been ideal partners in the training process. In turn, the College did not always succeed in demonstrating what its ideological position on pluralism actually meant to students on teaching practice or to the schools who received them. Nor were all its staff convinced that such a philosophy would be in the best interests of the students or the schools. Nevertheless, while accepting that these difficulties and dilemmas remained, the College determined to articulate a policy for teacher education that was genuinely responsive to the needs of the multi-ethnic communities with which it interacted so closely. As a result, its policy laid down three criteria that the teacher education programme should satisfy. It should:

1. be community informed and responsive to community-defined needs;
2. ensure the interaction of community values with those of wider social organizations;
3. equip all members of the community, including those from sub-groups, both to play a full role in their own community and to achieve fully within the majority culture. (Bradford College, 1980)

Implementing policy

To implement this policy, the College has identified five major areas of action. These are admissions policy, administrative structures, school liaison, course content, and staffing policy.

1. Admissions policy

The College encourages students from ethnic minority backgrounds; it aims to maintain a comprehensive provision of further and higher education based on principles that deny no student access to qualifications for entry to further and higher education. The objectives for the DipHE programme which leads on to the BEd (Honours) degree course state that:

> the College will pursue an affirmative policy towards students from ethnic minority backgrounds and endeavour to ensure a balanced and varied mix of students within permitted admission procedures.

It elaborates this by focusing study on areas of particular interest to such students, within the context of an accepted route to professional qualifications, as with Asian Studies in the DipHE programme, or the proposal to allow competent students on the PGCE course to follow part of their course in their mother tongue.

2. Administrative structures

The College had already placed its teacher education programme in the context of Community Studies when it merged the School of Education with the School of Adult and Community Education. It began by rejecting the principle of exclusivity: it was agreed that no member of staff should devote his or her time solely to teacher education courses, but would undertake some teaching elsewhere in the College. Staff engaged in teacher education and those in other community-related areas of work were allowed to change places, so as to give community experience to teacher educators and to enable those directly concerned with community provision to contribute to courses in teacher education.

3. School liaison

A regular and systematic attachment to a school was included within the required duties of teacher educators, so as to help prepare students for teaching in these schools. It was recognized that successful students would have to teach children in ways that would fulfil the expectations of their immediate superiors and employers, and that it was not sufficient to identify relevant skills and competencies, and present them as generalized statements in a College-based programme. They had to be implemented in response to the needs of a specific group of children in a particular school serving a particular community.

To reduce the dangers of institutional conflict, a close partnership was developed between teachers from the school and tutors from the College. The attachment was designed to foster collaboration and to help the tutor to become not only well-versed in theory and good practice but also familiar with their specific implementation in a particular school. It would help staff members to practise their own teaching skills in an appropriate context, and to make the sort of contacts with the local community that would increase the openness of education and would help the students to develop their skills and sensitivities. The partnership was also developed as a way of increasing the interchange between staff in schools and colleges by freeing some teachers to contribute to or participate in College courses.

Given the relatively small number of staff available for this work and the requirement to identify good practice, it was necessary to limit the number of schools. The process of relating theory to practice was assisted by providing the necessary arena for students to develop both the skills and knowledge to achieve professional credibility and an appropriate commitment to multi-ethnic community education. Its inner city location allows the College to provide school experience in predominantly multi-racial schools and staff are attached to them on a systematic basis. Students bring a high level of motivation to those parts of the course that directly relate to the acquisition of classroom skills; this provides the base upon which students can ultimately ground their theories of education. Both the teacher and tutor can help the student to reconcile the conflicting requirements of having to conform to professional expectations and to develop judgemental capacities of what is and what is not appropriate. Close co-operation has helped the student to see where practical prescriptions are needed and where theory may be critical and exploratory; the delicate relationship between theory and practice can best be strengthened if the differences and similarities are made explicit in as many common situations as possible. Any separation of theory and practice according to the places where it is taught or learned can only be harmful.

4. Course content

The course content derives from the specific needs of the schools, and the professional preparation of students has increasingly become a negotiated pattern of teaching studies implemented by professional studies in a curriculum workshop. The workshop is both the place with resources where students, tutors, co-operating teachers and visiting schoolchildren can work and also the dominant strategy used in tutor-student interaction. The student is encouraged to judge the relevance of his perceptions of curriculum issues against a continuing examination of his experiences in school (Proctor, 1979), with the aid of a much closer relationship between placements, school experience, formal college courses and workshops.

Nevertheless, certain key aspects of course content are identified as having particular relevance for students intending to teach in a multiracial school. The selection of material for curriculum courses reveals a heavy emphasis on the mastery of teaching skills in language and mathematics, while creative and environmental studies provide vehicles for learning about integrated approaches to the curriculum which are seen as essential for students preparing for work in urban first and middle schools.

Theoretical study concentrates on the teaching/learning processes and on the inter-relation of school and community in the educative process, although only so far as they can be illustrated in practice. Students also elect to follow a specific option in 'Developing Linguistic Competence' or 'Community Multicultural Studies'. The course culminates in the selection of an individual curriculum study which allows the student the opportunity to bring together the previous and current academic experiences in a project focused on the curriculum. Students are encouraged to study topics which relate directly to multicultural education. Some attempt is also made to expose students to differing cultural values, for example as revealed in religious practices; but the primary task is seen as developing professional competence, because of the need for professional credibility and specific preparation for multiracial schools. This priority exemplifies the College's approach to professional studies as the starting point for coherent theories of education (Chambers, 1979b).

This programme acknowledges that students following the College's courses are preoccupied with the demands made upon them by their actual experience in school and it is designed to fulfil their expectations. The College is, however, fully aware that such an approach can lead to a simplistic acceptance of the *status quo* and an obsession with coping skills or mere survival.

It remains therefore to justify the apparently limited curriculum. With regard to the BEd students, there is no case to answer. The 'professional year' is an integral and cumulative part of a three-year programme in which the first two years are devoted to a detailed and exploratory study of the problems of living in urban multicultural society. The students are thus sensitized to the nature of the multicultural society within which the schools operate without the pressures of having to perform to predetermined criteria of professional competence. They follow an extensive course of study which includes obligatory core units in human studies, industrial society and professional studies, which respectively offer students insights into the nature of human development in an urban society; into the ways in which people in societies have responded to the challenges of industrialization, urbanization and institutionalization; and into the ways in which professional practice has been organized to meet the developing needs of urban society. They also elect to follow a major course in language, literature and society; history and politics; urban geography; or Asian studies, together with minor options which are designed either to reinforce their understanding of social processes or to equip them to offer other curriculum subjects, such as music or art, if they decide to become teachers.

In the case of the PGCE students, the College, like most others, recognizes the problems of the one-year course and the necessity to compromise. It does, however, build its educational theory component entirely on the ways in which schools can respond to the multi-ethnic society. By exposing students both to the extremist views held by specific community activists and to 'good practice' in 'accommodationist' community education, it endeavours to provide a non-directive framework in which students can make up their own minds about the theoretical positions they wish to take. Further, by incorporating this element into the same curriculum workshops as those in which they develop professional studies, the links between theory and practice are slowly established. One example will suffice. Creative studies is used as an induction component. This year the task was the building of dens. The co-operative aspects soon surfaced with the requirement to get materials, work out constructive skills and determine the form of presentation. The finished products were of high quality and the process simulated much of the experience of organizing creative studies. More significantly, the two tutors adopted contrasting roles: one dispensed materials lavishly while the other guarded stock with jealous care. This power struggle has already prompted the students to analyse the relationship between dominant and minority groups in the distribution of resources. Without the structural changes that placed teacher education in the community context that particular combination of staff would never have been established.

5. Staffing policy

The College principle of racial mingling not only means that students will rub shoulders with peers from diverse ethnic backgrounds but should also imply that the staff will reflect the same diversity. Regrettably, this is not yet so. Nevertheless, members of ethnic minority groups already on the staff of the College are involved in planning and teaching all the main courses of teacher education and every effort is being made to increase that involvement. Racial discrimination laws clearly work both ways to hinder this process, but the College's staffing policy has been organized to ensure that each course team includes at least one member of staff who comes from an ethnic minority background. Extending the same principle, staff have been recruited to the teacher education programme whose experience has been in multicultural education either in this country or overseas.

Almost there

The philosophy and implementation of this multi-ethnic education policy represent a conscious and determined effort to respond to the needs of the Bradford community in ways that do justice to the needs of sub-groups without denying the values of society at large. Questions of priority and scale have already been raised and it is equally clear that the conceptual issues under consideration will require further thought. The ways in which 'permeation' and preparation for schools as they are at present may mean that many teacher education programmes may not appear to be multi-cultural on the surface in either content or processes, but may nevertheless be significant because students of ethnic minority backgrounds have privileged access to them. The challenge to the College is to allow this access in ways that do not debase the ultimate qualification and which do not prevent it from reaching out into the community groups, who are at present perceived as disadvantaged. It will only succeed in doing this if its planning remains coherent (Polk, 1979). To assist co-ordination there is a multicultural education unit, whose objectives include the development of a comprehensive action policy throughout the College; the monitoring and teaching of courses; recommending innovative action; the formulation and implementation of research policy in multicultural education; and the promotion of staff development. One of its major tasks at present is to live up to these objectives. Additionally, a number of research projects, including the joint inquiry into mother tongue teaching, are building up the College's knowledge of how to respond to the needs of the ethnic communities.

Conclusion

The College's programme for teacher education aims to stress multicultural community responsiveness. This policy requires its teacher education programme to be open, community-informed and capable of making its students sensitive to the interaction between the local community and wider social groupings in a multicultural context. The College believes that to succeed in this, it must not only make use of schools as they are, but must also prepare students to command credibility in them as a prerequisite of being able to do anything about reforming them. Adopting Hirst's model (Hirst, 1979), these requirements mean that:

1. students must know how communities are composed, how to relate to society at large, and how contemporary schools and the present educational and social services respond to these communities;
2. the practical judgements that students make must arise from that knowledge, from what they recognize as feasible in terms of present practice and future changes, and from what they know of the organization of social power;

3. students must master skills which will give them credibility in contemporary schools and enable them to act as a resource for community needs;

4. students need the motivation to master what is necessary at present, without losing sight of the need to prepare for a better tomorrow, which will depend upon them becoming open-minded and receptive to the possibilities of change (Bradford College, 1980).

The multi-ethnic community education approach at Bradford College illustrates how ideologies of education can become embodied in institutional values even though they may cause conflicts between training institutions and schools. Only a subtle analysis of this relationship and its potential for conflict will allow effective preparation of teachers for schools as they are. The diversity of schools makes necessary the selection of those which combine good practice with an interest in curriculum development; and where students can gain the necessary knowledge to judge what values to hold, what methods to use and what criteria to develop to evaluate their effectiveness. The complexity of the teaching process will require students to master the basic skills necessary to gain credibility not only in 'good' schools but also in 'difficult' ones. Without such credibility they will be unable both to develop personally as teachers and to extend their range of techniques and skills to meet the enormous complexity of teaching in a multicultural setting.

The variety of individual student needs, capabilities and aspirations requires the College to put varying emphases upon the four elements of the Hirst model for different students. Whereas all will need to master skills, those who can achieve competence quickly are encouraged to extend their knowledge, judgements and dispositions so they can take professional initiatives more rapidly. It is difficult to reconcile these competing demands in a crammed training course unless the programme allows for individuality. The diversity of cultures which is such a marked feature of Bradford and its College population serves as a vivid reminder of this individuality. The attempt to respond to it and to prepare teachers to work in a multiracial society represents a starting-point. I believe that the contribution we are making is distinctive and that our students are approaching the multicultural school with confidence and maturity. The more we succeed, the more conscious we are of falling short of the totality of need. We hope to continue to make improvements and to disprove Priestley's prophecy.

References

Alexander, R and Wormald, E eds (1979) *Professional Studies for Teaching* Society for Research into Higher Education (SRHE): Guildford

Bradford College (1977) *Academic Policy* 11.2.77

Bradford College (1980) *A Policy for Teacher Education* Margaret McMillan School of Community and Teaching Studies: Bradford

Cantor, L M and Roberts, I F (1979) *Further Education Today: A Critical Review* Routledge and Kegan Paul: London

Chambers, P (1979a) The meaning of community education in college: a comparative discussion *Journal of Further and Higher Education* 3 3: 75-86

Chambers, P (1979b) The scope and direction of professional studies since James *in* Alexander and Wormald (1979)

Clough, H D (1979) Bradford College: Eric's Latin Quarter *Learn* March: 22-5

Goffman, E (1968) *Asylums* Penguin: Harmondsworth

Hirst, P H (1979) Professional studies in initial teacher education: some conceptual issues *in* Alexander and Wormald (1979)

Keddie, N (1971) Classroom knowledge *in* Young (1971)

Labov, W (1970) The logic of non-standard English *in* Williams (1970)

Newman, F M and Oliver, D W (1967) A proposal for education in community *in* Raynor and Harden (1973)

Polk, K (1979) *Multicultural Education Programmes at Bradford College (UK)* International Management Training for Educational Change (IMTEC): Manchester/ Oslo

Priestley, J B (1934) *English Journey* Heinemann: London

Proctor, J (1979) Professional Studies in the BEd (CNAA) at Bradford College *in* Alexander and Wormald (1979)

Raynor, J and Harden, J eds (1973) *Equality and City Schools* Routledge and Kegan Paul: London

Robinson, E E (1968) *The New Polytechnics* Penguin: Harmondsworth

Saunders, M (1980) Towards a curriculum for ethnic minority pupils *New Community* 8 1-2: 76-83

Universities Council for the Education of Teachers (1979) *The PGCE Course and the Training of Specialist Teachers for Secondary Schools* UCET: London

Williams, F ed (1970) *Language and Poverty: Perspectives on a Theme* Markham: New York

Young, M F D ed (1971) *Knowledge and Control* Collier-Macmillan: London

22. Immigrant workers (Gastarbeiter) in West Germany: teaching programmes for adults and children

Ingeborg Gutfleisch and Bert-Olaf Rieck

Summary: By the end of 1979 over 4,100,000 foreign workers were living in West Germany — more than ever before, in spite of the formal ban on new recruitment imposed in 1973. Three-quarters of these are 'guest workers' with their families, ie they come from countries with which Germany had agreements on the recruitment of labour. After 1973, the structure of the foreign population changed considerably. The formerly high proportion of workers whose families were still living in their home countries has rapidly decreased; nearly all of those who remained after the ban on recruitment have brought their families to the Federal Republic.

German education policy for foreigners is full of contradictions. At present, it is expected that while the so-called first generation will return to their homelands, the so-called second generation — about 1,000,000 foreign children and adolescents at present — are subject to a policy of integration. For the different target groups, three kinds of educational measures can be distinguished: (1) language courses for adults (first generation), which are not obligatory and depend mainly on local initiative; (2) schooling programmes for foreign children in ordinary German classes, preparatory classes, special classes for foreign pupils, or bilingual classes; and (3) training programmes (including language tuition) for the high percentage of adolescents and young adults without school-leaving certificates, apprenticeships, jobs, or sufficient knowledge of German. This chapter describes the background, present situation, and projects in this field.*

Employment of immigrant workers in West Germany

In the immediate post-war period the employment of foreign labour played only a marginal role in West Germany. By the end of the 1950s, however, the unemployment rate had fallen sharply and even the influx from the eastern parts of Germany could not compensate sufficiently for the growing labour shortage. This led the German economy to begin recruiting immigrant workers from Mediterranean countries. The German government entered into bilateral agreements with the following countries, among others: Italy (1955), Spain (1960), Greece (1960), Turkey (1961), Yugoslavia (1968), and established recruitment agencies in these. In 1965, in accordance with the EEC agreement, Italians were assured free movement of labour within the EEC. The number of foreign workers

* The terminology used in this chapter is explained on page 355.

increased steadily to 1,300,000 in 1966. Because of the economic crisis it declined by about 30 per cent in 1966-67, but it resumed its climb up to its maximum of about 2,600,000 in 1973. The start of the worldwide economic crisis in the same year put a complete stop to recruiting activities.

The West German government and economists always claimed that the employment of foreign labour was a temporary measure related to the economic situation, and that consequently the permanent settlement of foreigners in West Germany was not desirable. The Employers' Association commented on this:

> The great advantage in employing foreign workers is that it puts at our disposal mobile manpower. It would be dangerous to restrict this mobility by a policy of settlement. (Katsoulis, 1978: 19)

For this reason, economists in particular used to call for obligatory 'rotation' of foreign workers to keep social costs to a minimum level — ie recruitment of trained labour, employment for a fixed period (a maximum of five years as a rule), and subsequent return home. The 'recruitment stop' of 1973, however, finally put an end to such models.

The ending of recruitment, the relatively high rate of unemployment among foreigners, and restrictive measures in the employment laws for foreigners (the work permit being the central instrument in the control of foreign labour) led after 1973 first to a rapid, then to a slower decline in the number of foreign workers employed in West Germany. In 1978, only about 1,900,000 immigrant workers were still employed in the Federal Republic. Yet the total foreign population of about 4,000,000 — three-quarters coming from 'recruitment countries' — has remained more or less constant; and in addition there has been a clear upward tendency during the last few years.

This means that the return home of some has been more than balanced by the bringing in of the families of others, which is permitted for residents of at least one year's standing in West Germany. As a result the structure of the foreign population has undergone significant changes. For example, nine out of ten Italians in Germany were working in 1961, but only five out of ten in 1978. While formerly the single male immigrant worker was typical of the foreign population, today the focus has shifted towards the family. At least one member of most immigrant families has been living in the Federal Republic for ten or more years; and 80-90 per cent of all immigrants have no immediate intention of returning home (Kühn, 1979; Forschungsverbund, 1979). In view of these facts, it should be indisputable that West Germany is *de facto* 'an immigration country' with a growing minority from the Mediterranean countries. But this is a fact which the government refuses to accept even now.

The body of laws regarding aliens in West Germany is formulated in such a way that 'not even the illusion of a right of residence can be maintained' (Franz, 1974: 41). Foreigners living in West Germany for more than three months, and/or wishing to work, need a residence permit. It can be given if 'the foreigner's presence does not impair the interests of the Federal

Republic'; its granting is at the discretion of the government office concerned with foreigners. Furthermore, foreigners (except citizens of the EEC) who want to be employed need a work permit. Its granting is strictly dependent on 'the employment situation and the demand for labour'. German workers enjoy preference. Residence and work permits are usually issued for a limited period and often with a number of restrictions. Even after a stay of many years, expulsion is possible as a result of minor violations of the law.

In 1978, the legal foundation was laid for the granting to immigrant workers of a gradual stabilization of their legal status, after a stay of five to eight years, and under certain conditions. In practice, these conditions are so demanding that up to now, only a small proportion of those legally entitled have been given the benefit of an improvement in their residential status (Kühn, 1979).

In addition, all legal rights cease to exist for those who emigrate again and, finding that they cannot re-establish themselves in their home country, want to come back to West Germany: they will not be given a renewal of their work permit. The preconditions for naturalization are so restrictively applied that virtually only immigrants married to a German succeed.

Recently, the first signs of a long-term reorientation of immigration policy have begun to appear, but they have not yet had any effect on practice. The trend for the future seems to be that immigrant workers and their spouses (the so-called 'first generation'), and their children born or raised here (the so-called 'second generation') are to be treated in quite different ways. Whereas the first generation remains at the mercy of the former policy more or less unchanged but with a stronger demand for emigration included, measures on the integration of the second generation are being strongly intensified and should result eventually in an 'optional right of naturalization'.

This solution would take into account the fact that there is a discrepancy between the views and value systems of parents and children which far exceeds the normal generation gap. Whereas the parents hold on to their national culture and identity, most of the children are encultured or primarily socialized in a different sub-culture and identify with certain aspects of the German culture (Schrader, Nikles and Griese, 1976). Those immigrant workers of the first generation who want to stay permanently in West Germany and want to be integrated are not properly catered for by this solution.

As well as political and legal conditions, the social context plays an important part. In this respect, the situation of foreign workers in West Germany is largely comparable to their position in other European countries. Immigrant workers represent a 'new' social class — below all existing social classes: ie the immigrants have gone into jobs with low status which are no longer or very seldom accepted by German workers (Schrader, Nikles and Griese, 1976; BSfA, 1979).

More than 90 per cent of the immigrants coming from the 'recruitment countries' are employed as manual workers, compared with about 50 per cent of Germans. Half of the immigrants are in semi-skilled jobs, a third in unskilled, and a fifth in skilled (1972). They are concentrated in certain industries where there is heavy or dirty work, or which have poor safety records. They are also in jobs with unsocial working hours and below-average rates of pay. Foundries, service industries, textiles, mechanical engineering, and chemicals have the highest proportions of foreigners (BSfA, 1979). The average income of immigrant workers remains significantly less than that of their German counterparts. Their housing conditions too are often below standard: there is a strong tendency in the large towns to concentrate the immigrants in slum clearance areas in poor housing (Forschungsverbund, 1979).

A considerable cultural and social distance exists between Germans and immigrants. As a rule, contact with Germans is restricted to the workplace; private contact seldom amounts to more than the exchange of greetings. Closer contacts involving family or leisure time activities are found only within the small group of immigrant workers whose knowledge of German is very good (Schrader, Nikles and Griese, 1976; Forschungsverbund, 1979; Heidelberger Forschungsprojekt, 1977).

We have discussed the background fully, because it is only by examining the context of the history of immigrant workers in the Federal Republic, and the legal and social situation of foreigners, that the kind of educational measures and initiatives taken and not taken by West Germany can be understood. Furthermore, the background information may make it evident why many things offered in one place or another were not accepted by the target group as had been expected.

The most striking feature of the immigrants' existence is a fundamental insecurity, which seriously affects the way they live in West Germany and which makes any long-term planning more or less impossible. This situation naturally has an effect on the immigrants' motivation to learn German or to take part in any teaching programme. 'The foreign workers' motivation as well as their consciousness vacillates between adaptation to the foreign society and commitment to the familiar form of life' (Barkowski, Harnisch and Kumm, 1979: 4). Such a state of permanent suspense has a particularly negative effect on the education of the second generation; for here decisions, which have to be made by the parents as well as by the German government, are of essential importance to the development of the children's national and cultural identity.

In what follows, educational measures for foreign workers and their families in West Germany will be dealt with in three sections: 1. Language tuition and advanced training for adults; 2. Teaching programmes for foreign children, including preparatory classes and programmes outside school training; 3. Special measures for foreign adolescents without training or jobs, and programmes for young adults for the belated acquisition of the German school-leaving certificate.

Language tuition and advanced training for adults

German language courses for adults

As a rule the foreign workers recruited — with the exception of some of the Yugoslavs — did not have any knowledge of German when they arrived. The German recruiting agencies in the countries of origin did not pre-train the workers (for example, by means of language instruction or by giving information about society and culture in Germany). In West Germany, the initiative of the recruiting firm largely determined whether and to what extent workers were given help after their arrival. Normally, this aid was restricted to instruction by compatriots who had immigrated earlier or by company interpreters; very rarely, the firms themselves organized language courses and if they did, they were usually designed according to the immediate needs of the particular employment.

One such course offered in the workplace was the audio-visual language programme: 'German in the Workplace' (*Deutsch am Arbeitsplatz*) from the Eschweiler Bergwerksverein AG (about 20,000 workers, 25 per cent of whom were immigrants). Until the recruitment stop in 1973, all foreigners newly joining the firm were given linguistic and vocational pre-training in a factory-owned education centre for four weeks before they started work, during which time they received their regular wages. The teaching materials — oriented towards employment — were provided by the firm itself (Bendit, 1979).

However, it must be stressed that the provision of an obligatory intensive preparatory course like this was a rare exception; for there was and is no legal requirement, of the kind existing in Sweden for example, obliging employers to release without loss of pay workers who are not proficient in German. Normally, the acquisition of German is left to the private initiative and motivation of each immigrant who, after working hours or at weekends, has to take the trouble to attend one of the outside language courses. The provision of such courses is in any case not universal, and those available are often very expensive — especially those in private colleges, but sometimes also those in further and adult education (*Volkshochschulen*).

During the early years of massive immigration, language courses meeting the interests of this target group were more or less completely lacking. In theory, the general courses in 'German for foreigners' of the *Volkshochschulen* were open to foreign workers, but the *Volkshochschulen* are oriented towards the middle class, and are rarely attended even by German workers. Moreover, the concepts and methods used in the general German language classes offered there are adapted to target groups with different demands and, what is more, with different educational backgrounds. This is true in particular for those courses which prepare for the certificate in German as a Foreign Language (*Zertifikat 'Deutsch als Fremdsprache'*; DVV, 1977).

This mismatch is plainly reflected in the following figures: in a sociological study done by the Bundesanstalt für Arbeit 1973, less than 6 per cent of the interviewees claimed to have acquired their knowledge of German in language classes. According to another study (Mehrländer, 1974) only 10 per cent had ever attended German courses. Thus more than 90 per cent of all immigrant workers acquired their German solely through contact (usually very restricted) with fellow workers, neighbours, and friends. These restricted learning opportunities are linked to the social and cultural distance from the German-speaking majority on the one hand, and to the lack of opportunity to acquire the language in courses on the other hand; as a result, the language used by immigrant workers among themselves has tended to stabilize at an early level and thus there developed pidginized varieties of German, for instance 'tarzanca' (Tarzan-talk), as it is known by the Turks concerned (Heidelberger Forschungs-projekt, 1978; Klein and Dittmar, 1979). In terms of their degree of deviation from standard German, these pidginized varieties acquired in a natural setting can be quite distinct; they are in any case a severe handicap in the subsequent acquisition of the standard language or even of a colloquial localized form of German.

Language courses specifically designed for immigrant workers have been offered only for a few years. That such programmes came into existence at long last was mainly due to the initiative of groups engaged in work with immigrants, and people who — at least partially — tried to fill the existing gap by organizing language courses for foreigners in special centres and at charity and trade union institutions. It was only in 1974 that the Ministry of Labour established a central institution to co-ordinate and promote language courses for foreign workers.

The *Sprachverband Deutsch für ausländische Arbeitnehmer eV* in Mainz brings together the main organizations with an interest in language training. These include the *Volkshochschulen* charity organizations, trade union educational institutions, and the Goethe-Institute. As a purely co-ordinating agency the *Sprachverband* does not put on courses itself: it takes charge of financing the courses given by its members, and also, more recently, those courses resulting from independent initiatives. The language training must comply with its guidelines: for instance, the teaching material must be chosen in accordance with the recommendations of the *Sprachverband*, and teachers are obliged to complete a two-week training course.

In 1979, about 1800 courses with about 25,000 participants were supported in the Federal Republic and West Berlin. This means that a little under 1 per cent of the adult foreign population was attending a course.

The *Sprachverband* publishes a list of teaching programmes rec-ommended for teaching immigrants German. The first of these lists was issued in 1977 and contained five textbooks and two instructional films for adults; the (current) 1978 list contains only two textbooks, one of them recently added to the list, and no films. This could be taken as a comment on the quality of the teaching materials available at present. Of the two instructional films, one (*Guten Tag*) was in any case intended for another purpose (television abroad). The second film (*Viel Glück in Deutschland*) was indeed produced for the target group of immigrant workers and was lavishly financed by the public authorities, but — as it turned out — it has only been of limited use.

The textbooks are all published by commercial publishers and focus only partly on immigrant workers. Of those recommended, only one is neutral as far as the learners' mother tongue is concerned (Demetz and Puente, 1973); the other is presented in two languages, Turkish and German (Augustin and Liebe-Harkort, 1977). Another textbook for immigrant workers was published after the issuing of the list (Neuner *et al*, 1979). A syllabus now being produced — 'Threshold Level "German for foreign workers"' (*Grundbaustein 'Deutsch für ausländische Arbeiter'*) — has been compiled by the Pedagogical Research Board of the Association of German Adult Education Institutions (*Pädagogische Arbeitsstelle des Deutschen Volkshochschulverbands*) in collaboration with the *Sprachverband* and the Council for Cultural Co-operation of the Council of Europe (1978; von der Handt, 1979). Two of the three textbooks mentioned above have emerged from the project 'Advanced training for teachers of German as a foreign language' (*Lehrerfortbildung Deutsch für ausländische Arbeiter*). However, the title of the project is misleading, for until a few years ago there was *no* special training to teach German as a foreign language in the Federal Republic.

To date, only a few universities (Bielefeld, Bochum, and Munich) have arranged special courses in teaching German as a foreign language: these are also open to German nationals and include the field of adult education (for a survey see Ehnert, 1980). At present, therefore, teaching of German as a foreign language to foreign workers is almost exclusively done by tutors with no special experience of adult education or even of teaching, eg social workers, educationists, students and teachers from other specializations. They are prepared for their task in a two-week course by the *Lehrerfortbildung* project, and there are also one- to two-week continuation courses; but even so, almost all teachers in this field are amateurs.

Conventionally designed language classes have often not been very successful. The number of participants in comparison with the total number of foreigners is small; women and shiftworkers are hardly reached; the drop-out rate is relatively high; and, in terms of educational background and occupation, the average participant belongs to the upper stratum of the foreign population. This situation has led to the development of alternative language training programmes whose general features are: 1) that they are conducted not in institutions of adult education but in places where the people concerned work and live — on company premises and in residential accommodation; 2) that language learning in these courses is not treated in isolation from everyday life. The following are some examples of these programmes.

Lernstatt. This model of industrial language training is provided by an independent project, *Cooperative Arbeitsdidaktik* ('Co-operative for Learning at Work') in Berlin. They offer it to interested firms which then have to pay the cost. *Lernstatt* courses have been put on in several large-scale enterprises with a high percentage of foreign workers (such as BMW, Hoechst, and Kraftwerk Union). They are tied closely to the needs of the workplace and the training sessions are held there during work time or immediately afterwards. Before the *Lernstatt* courses (the neologism is coined from '*lernen*' [learn] and '*Werkstatt*' [workshop]) are started, there is a research phase during which the project group observes workplaces and work-processes and takes photographs of them. With this material as a basis, 'language catalogues' are worked out. A special feature of the *Lernstatt* is that the instruction itself is not given by professional teachers, but by German foremen and supervisors who have been prepared for their task by the project members (Kasprzik, 1974).

Theory and Practice of Foreign Language Acquisition: German for Foreign Workers. This Berlin project aims to develop a language teaching theory and model, and to study directed language acquisition processes. It has been developing a programme called *Industrial Language Training for Shiftworkers after Working Hours.* Unlike the *Lernstatt* which deliberately eschews methodology in the strict sense, this project stresses the necessity of specially adapted methodological concepts and of the employment of specially trained teachers. The results of the project are documented in a teacher's manual *Deutsch für ausländische Arbeiter* (Barkowski, Harnisch and Kumm, 1980). As stated by Barkowski, Harnisch and Kumm, however, industrial language training has severe limitations:

1. of the total numbers of foreigners employed in a firm, only a small number of the better qualified and more highly motivated people are reached;
2. those who attend the courses are mostly men;
3. members of the workers' families are excluded (Barkowski, Harnisch and Kumm, 1979b).

As a result, the project has developed a model which is oriented to the foreign family:

German for Foreign Workers: Project-related and Project-oriented Learning in the Community. This model came into existence in connection with a citizens' action project at Kreuzberg (a Berlin district with a very high proportion of foreigners), where it is planned that the foreign population should participate in reconstruction measures and in the construction of a centre for foreigners. The learning objective in this model is not the acquisition of school knowledge but the realization of a concrete aim: 'collectively planned changes in the living conditions and the environment around us'. The project includes information for tenants, and guidance by social workers; the teaching, carried out with tenants' groups in a 'contact shop' (*Kontaktladen*) continues the advisory work (Barkowski, Harnisch and Kumm, 1979b).

A similar project was developed by the group already mentioned, *Cooperative Arbeitsdidaktik*, viz 'Learning in the Community' (*Lernstatt im Wohnbezirk*). It is presented in detail in CAD (1978).

Language Training for Unemployed Women. These women (10 per cent of adults) who, as a result of their isolation, have the least language proficiency, have hardly ever been persuaded until now to take part in any of the conventional language courses. Thanks to local initiatives, however, several training programmes have recently been worked out which take into consideration the special problems and needs of this minority within the foreign population. Particularly successful in this connection was the incorporation of language teaching units into home economics courses (Gürkan, Laqueur and Szablewski, 1979; Weische-Alexa, 1979).

Advanced training

Since in the economy of the Federal Republic foreign workers have the function of temporarily filling occupational categories needing low skills, government and industry have only a limited interest in promoting the advanced training of immigrants.

Vocational training in the workplace is normally restricted to the initial period of employment. There are a limited number of places in external continuation courses (mostly run by the *Internationaler Bund für Sozialarbeit*), and under certain conditions these courses are financed as 'retraining' by the Department of Employment. In some places, where a legal right to paid educational leave exists, special training for immigrants is offered (Langenohl-Weyer and Vink, 1979; Braun and Fröhlich, 1979). (Paid educational leave in France is discussed by Pierre Caspar in the *WYBE 1979* — Ed.)

Taken overall, the range and effectiveness of these measures is small. Sixty per cent of immigrants have never taken part in any kind of advanced training; and according to regional research in Cologne only 1 per cent can complete a vocational training as skilled workers in this way.

Linked vocational education and language training courses are offered to Italian immigrants by educational institutions of the Italian trade unions. These include courses for the late acquisition of the Italian school-leaving certificate (*scuola media*), for training as skilled workers, and for improving proficiency in German. This model was first tried out in Switzerland where the Italian trade unions have been active for a long time, and where a special German language programme for Italians was developed (Ghionda and Rovere, 1977).

Foreign children in schools

It is difficult to generalize in this field since cultural and educational policies are matters for each individual state within the Federal Republic (*Kulturhoheit der Länder*); thus the decrees issued and the actual situation inside the schools are quite different in each of the states. An outline agreement which has existed since 1964 — the 'Recommendations of the Standing Conference of State Ministers of Education' (revised in 1971 and 1976; see Vink and Dederichs, 1976) — leaves almost full powers to the individual states. The following sketch confines itself to describing the main types of educational models for foreign children, giving an account of the present situation in schools in some states and outlining some proposals for alternative models.

Pre-school programmes

About 400,000 foreign children are of pre-school age, ie under six years (Seidel, 1979). Of all foreign children of kindergarten age, less than half attend a public institution for pre-school education, eg 30 per cent in Bavaria and 49 per cent in Baden-Württemberg, compared with about 70 per cent of German children (BSfA, 1979; Jung, 1980). This is significant in the light of general agreement that attending such an institution is very important for learning German.

Besides a general distrust of public education for infants and fears of conflict within the family, the principal reason for this relatively low rate of attendance is that in the Federal Republic the standard form of public education for infants is the kindergarten — an institution which is open only for a limited number of hours distributed between mornings and afternoons. Since in most foreign families both parents work, they are not in a position to bring their children to the kindergarten and pick them up again twice a day.

The real need is for places in day nurseries (*Kindertagesstätten*) whose opening hours coincide with working hours. Legitimate fears of cultural and family alienation could also be counteracted by the employment of foreign staff in bilingual and multilingual nursery schools and day nurseries. This has been done in several projects, in Bavaria (BSfA, 1979), Hamburg, Berlin, Lower Saxony, North Rhine-Westphalia, and Hesse (López-Blasco, 1979).

A model of language development for foreign children of pre-school age was adopted by Baden-Württemberg in 1979. The plan is for the development of special playgroups for five-year-old children open for from two to five hours per week. However, legitimate suspicions have been voiced that separate 'pre-schools for foreign children' (*Ausländervorschulen*) might be established in the future alongside the German kindergarten, which would hinder rather than encourage the integration of foreign children into the German educational system (Baden-Württembergisches Arbeitsministerium, 1979).

School programmes

In 1978, there were about 500,000 foreign school-age children in the Federal Republic. As a basic principle, foreign children and adolescents in West Germany are subject to compulsory education in German schools; the recommendations of the Standing Conference of State Ministers of Education in 1976, however, do not explicitly exclude the establishment of national schools.

These 'recommendations' propose the following regulations:

Ordinary German classes: Foreign children and adolescents who are able to follow the teaching in a German class without significant language difficulties are integrated into 'regular classes' (*Regelklassen*) according to their age or school achievement. The proportion of foreign pupils in regular classes should, however, not exceed 20 per cent.

Special classes for foreign pupils: If the proportion of foreign pupils who have to be integrated is significantly higher than 20 per cent, special classes for foreign pupils can be established. In terms of their curriculum these are modelled on the ordinary German classes, and use German as the language of instruction. For foreign pupils without sufficient knowledge of German there are preparatory classes using both mother tongue and German as mediums of instruction, intensive courses, and language development in supplementary classes.

Preparatory classes: These can be either multinational or nationally homogeneous. In nationally homogeneous preparatory classes, mother tongue lessons can be given by a foreign teacher. The curriculum has to match that of the ordinary German classes, and the instruction concentrates on the teaching of German. After a maximum of two years in a preparatory class the pupils are supposed to transfer into an ordinary German class.

Classes using both mother tongue and German as medium of instruction (bilingual classes): In these classes pupils with the same mother tongue are taught by German and foreign teachers following a special curriculum, whereby German is taught at first using 'German as a foreign language' methods. In contrast to the preparatory classes, the transfer to regular classes is not governed by regulations.

Intensive training and language development in additional lessons: Where the number of foreign pupils without sufficient knowledge of German is not high enough to establish separate classes, intensive courses and/or additional language development in German as a second language have to be provided.

Supplementary mother tongue teaching: Pupils attending regular or preparatory classes without mother tongue teaching are supposed to have the opportunity of taking part in voluntary supplementary training in the mother tongue up to a maximum of five hours per week. In some of the states (Baden-Württemberg, Bavaria, Berlin) the supervision of this training is not the responsibility of the German authorities but of those of the countries of origin (see Vink and Dederichs, 1976; Friberg and Hohmann, 1976; Akpinar, 1979).

This rough outline must be filled out with details of how particular school models have developed and which models are preferred within the different states. With the growing number of foreign children, there seems to be a general tendency towards segregation and special training programmes, in place of the original aim of complete integration into the German school system. This is the case both where foreign children remain in preparatory classes much longer than scheduled, and where special classes for foreigners are the main form of organization.

This is particularly true in Bavaria, where preparatory classes have virtually ceased to exist, and where 'bilingual classes', especially for Turkish children, are instead the rule. In other states too, with the exception of Berlin and Hesse, bilingual classes are used more and more; such as the so-called 'prolonged preparatory classes' (*Vorbereitungsklassen in Langform*) in North Rhine-Westphalia. There is another peculiarity in Bavaria, in that about 60 per cent of Greek children living there attend Greek national private schools (BSfA, 1979).

A common argument advanced for the establishment of bilingual classes and national schools is by reference to parent's wishes (eg Savvidis, 1974). This argument must be examined very critically for a number of different reasons. First, as we have pointed out above, many parents are not at all sure of their position in the Federal Republic, whether for legal or related reasons or because they have no real chance to re-integrate themselves into their countries of origin. Secondly, the generation gap arising from the differences in socialization makes it at least uncertain whether the second generation is willing to 'go back' to a country which they often know only from holiday trips. Thirdly, it is still the case that foreign parents have only a very partial understanding of the German school system (see Neumann, 1980; Zografou, 1978).

Teaching in 'bilingual classes' and 'prolonged preparatory classes' has been strongly attacked on pedagogical grounds as well. They are seen as 'national schools' (Vink and Dederichs, 1976: 73), 'national one-room schools' (Jung, 1980: 14), 'ghetto-classes' or 'ghetto-schools' (Müller, 1974: 158). Separated from the culture of the host country as well as from that of the country of origin, they are unable to prepare pupils adequately for life in either country.

> The children are not given sufficient language proficiency either in their mother tongue or in German, so that their capacity to act remains limited, and their German language proficiency is not good enough to allow transfer into an ordinary German class. (Akpinar, 1979: 111)

Overall, then, the schooling of foreign children is unsatisfactory. Foreign children from the major emigration countries are over-represented in non-selective schools and schools for educationally subnormal children; they are correspondingly under-represented in continuation schools (ie schools going beyond the minimum leaving age — the *Gymnasien* and *Realschulen*). In Baden-Württemberg, for example, of all foreign pupils from the major sources of immigration only 8 per cent attend continuation schools. The equivalent figure for Bavaria is 6 per cent. Half, according to official statistics in Bavaria, or two-thirds, according to unofficial estimates, do not achieve any form of educational certification; the corresponding figure for German pupils is no more than 10 per cent (Boos-Nünning, 1976; Jung, 1980).

Proposals to improve the schooling of foreign children. Proposals of two very different kinds can be distinguished. The first type aims to realize in German schools the multiculturalism of German society by the establishment of 'integration classes' (*Integrationsklassen*) (see Forschungsgruppe ALFA, 1976), or 'encounter classes and encounter schools' (*Begegnungs-klassen und -schulen*) (Weinrich, 1980). In those classes or schools both foreign and German children would be instructed by foreign and German teachers. The mother tongues of both groups would be subjects on the curriculum. For some subjects, the mother tongue of the foreign children would be the medium of instruction for both groups.

The second type of proposal aims at an extension of the present preparatory classes and bilingual classes to bilingual schools for nationally homogeneous groups, within which only foreign pupils would be offered a bicultural teaching programme by foreign and German teachers under the supervision of the German school authorities. The arguments given in support of this system are that learning opportunities for children are better when they are taught in their mother tongue, that ethnic or national groups should have the right to preserve their mother tongue, and finally, that positive experience has been gained from this model in other bilingual communities (eg the UK, USA, and USSR) (Menk and Stölting, 1973). In a recent paper, Stölting (1977) also considered the possibility of including German children in bilingual/bicultural instruction, thus coming closer to the type of proposal first mentioned. However, both models separate the foreign children according to nationality and are therefore not designed for a genuinely multicultural education.

Initial and in-service teacher training. Great strides have been made in this field in recent years. Whereas a few years ago special training opportunities virtually did not exist, several colleges of education (*Päda-gogische Hochschulen*) and universities have now established special courses or options (*Studiengänge/Teilstudiengänge*) dealing with the teaching of foreign children. Some universities offer further qualifications for trained teachers who follow special courses in this field (Reich, 1979). A TV/correspondence course for in-service teacher training has been developed by the Deutches Institut für Fernstudien an der Universität Tübingen (1980).

Out-of-school programmes

To counteract social and educational discrimination against foreign children, several community action groups in the Federal Republic have started to offer out-of-school programmes. Their members are mostly students, older pupils, housewives, and teachers. They organize playgroups for pre-school children, homework supervision, groups for language development, and leisure time activities for adolescents. Vink (1976) estimates that at least 450 of these action groups exist; some of them are linked together in a parent organization, the *Verband der Initiativgruppen in der Ausländerarbeit VIA eV* in Bonn. Grants are sometimes given by the states for the out-of-school and other aids to socialization for children of immigrant workers (see Akpinar, López-Blasco and Vink, 1979).

Special measures for foreign adolescents and young adults without school-leaving certificates, apprenticeships or jobs

Within the last few years, the number of foreign adolescents in West Germany has been rapidly increasing, partly from the ranks of those who were brought up and went to school in that country and partly from those who came to be with their families after leaving school.

Among the first group, there is a high percentage without a German school-leaving certificate; members of the second group as a rule are equipped with only a very limited proficiency in German. However, both groups do have one thing in common: they have extreme difficulty in finding training or even a job. The exact number of adolescents concerned is not known; official statistics unfortunately are not very reliable about this, as — for various reasons — not all foreign adolescents are registered. It is estimated that in 1975-76 there were 50,000 to 100,000 living in the Federal Republic (Vink, 1979).

The fact that this problem has often been labelled a 'social time bomb' may explain why, in this field, an extensive training programme has been established with the help of a large amount of money and within a very short period of time. The programme is known as 'Preparatory Vocational Training and Social Integration' (*Massnahmen zur Berufsvorbereitung und sozialen Eingliederung — MBSE*). In terms of measures for young foreigners the most important courses are these financed by the federal authorities (*Bundesanstalt für Arbeit*) and co-ordinated by the *Sprachverband*. They were initiated in 1976, and since then have changed several times. In their present form they are one-year full-time courses of 40 hours a week which cover preparatory vocational training, language courses, and counselling. Two-thirds of the total training time of 1850 hours is reserved for preparatory vocational training, one-third for language training and general education. The lessons take place in groups of 12-15. Three groups at a time have at their disposal three instructors (foremen), two teachers and one counsellor, all employed on a full-time basis. School-leavers who participate in such courses have the right to a work permit. In the 1978-79 school year 187 courses for about 3500 (mostly Turkish) adolescents were completed.

As in adult education, the teachers come from various educational backgrounds, and have not been specially trained. They are prepared for their task in a two-week introductory course, supplemented by one or two weeks of advanced training per year (see Sprachverband, 1980).

A special and very helpful teaching programme has been developed for German classes and classes in elementary science in vocational schools and preparatory courses (Eckes and Wilms, 1975; Jirsa and Wilms, nd).

Intensive language training. For those adolescents who, as a result of their limited language proficiency, are not able to attend an *MBSE* course, it was decided late in 1979 to establish an intensive language teaching programme (10-20 hours per week for a period of three to four months).

Courses to attain a school-leaving certificate (Hauptschulabschluss-lehrgänge). Far more than half of all foreign adolescents leave school without a certificate. This is taken into account by several institutes for adult education which offer special teaching programmes for foreigners to enable them to acquire a school-leaving certificate. To co-ordinate and further develop these local activities, a project was initiated in 1979 by the Pedagogical Research Board of the Association of Adult Education Institutions with the support of the (Federal) Ministry of Education and Science, viz the Development and Piloting of Teaching Programmes for the Late Acquisition of the School Leaving Certificate by Young Foreign Adults (PAS/DVV, nd).

All the projects mentioned concerning foreign adolescents are too recent for us safely to evaluate their quality and effect. Nevertheless, they represent important initiatives in the attempt to match teaching provision to the needs of minority groups.

Acknowledgement

We wish to thank Euan Reid (Linguistic Minorities Project) who carefully corrected a first draft of this article and made a number of valuable suggestions.

Note on terminology

In West Germany several terms are in use for the members of these minorities. Mainly they reflect the ideological viewpoint of the user. *Gastarbeiter* is euphemistic or colloquial; *ausländische Arbeitnehmer* is the official usage of the government and employers, implying the employers' perspective on the relation between capital and labour; *ausländische Arbeiter* stresses the class-membership of immigrants; and *Ausländer* does not differentiate between immigrant workers and other foreigners generally. In sociological literature one finds the more precise terms *Arbeitsimmigrant* and *Arbeitsemigrant*. Officially taboo in West Germany is the expression *Fremdarbeiter*, since it was used during Fascist times, although it is still quite common in Switzerland today. We have used 'foreign worker' as a translation of the official *ausländische Arbeitnehmer* as well as of *ausländische Arbeiter*, the term we normally use; 'foreigner' for *Ausländer*; and 'immigrant worker' for *Arbeitsimmigrant* and *Arbeitsemigrant*.

References

Akpinar, U (1979) Zur Schulsituation der Kinder ausländischer Arbeitnehmer *in* Langenohl-Weyer (1979)

Akpinar, U, López-Blasco, A and Vink, J (1979) *Pädogogische Arbeit mit ausländischen Kindern und Jugendlichen: Bestandsaufnahme und Praxishilfen* (2nd ed) Juventa: Munich

Ansay, T and Gessner, V eds (1974) *Gastarbeiter in Gesellschaft und Recht* C H Beck: Munich

Augustin, V and Liebe-Harkort, K (1977) *Feridun. Ein Lesebuch und Sprachpro-gramm, nicht nur für Türken* Abado: Munich

Baden-Württembergisches Arbeitsministerium (1979) Vorläufige Richtlinien des Ministeriums für Arbeit, Gesundheit und Sozialordnung für die Bezuschussung von Massnahmen der Sprachförderung für ausländische Kinder im Vorschulalter mit Mitteln des Landes vom 24.1.79 *Materialien zum Projektbereich 'Ausländische Arbeiter'* 26: 26-9

Barkowski, H, Harnisch, U and Kumm, S (1979a) Kriterien zur Beurteilung von Lehrwerken für den Deutschunterricht mit ausländischen Arbeitern *Deutsch lernen* 4: 3-10

Barkowski, H, Harnisch, U and Kumm, S (1979b) Sprachlernen mit Arbeitsemigranten im Wohnbezirk *Deutsch lernen* 1: 5-16

Barkowski, H, Harnisch, U and Kumm, S (1980) *Lehrerhandbuch. Deutsch für ausländische Arbeiter* 2 vols Scriptor: Königstein/Ts

Bayrisches Staatsministerium für Arbeit und Sozialordnung (1979) *Ausländische Arbeitnehmer in Bayern. Bericht '79. Uber Entwicklung, Situation und Probleme der Ausländerbeschäftigung* Munich

Bendit, R (1979) Kommunikations und Sprachproblematik bei ausländischen Kindern, Jugendlichen und Erwachsenen *in* Langenohl-Weyer (1979)

BMA (1977) *Vorschläge der Bund-Länder-Kommission zur Fortentwicklung einer umfassenden Konzeption der Ausländerbeschäftigungspolitik* Der Bundesminister für Arbeit und Sozialordnung IIa 5-24: 200/22, 28.2.77

BMA (1979) *Rahmenvorstellungen für Massnahmen zur Berufsvorbereitung und sozialen Eingliederung junger Ausländer* (MBSE) *MSBE-Info* 15: 7-11

Boos-Nünning, U (1976) Lernprobleme und Schulerfolg *in* Hohmann (1976)

Boos-Nünning, U, Hohmann, M and Reich, H H (1976) *Integration ausländischer Arbeitnehmer: Schulbildung ausländischer Kinder* Studien zur Kommunalpolitik 14: Bonn

Braun, G and Fröhlich, C (1979) Bildungsurlaub 'Deutsch für ausländische Arbeiter': Ein Erfahrungsbericht aus der VHS-Praxis *Deutsch lernen* 1: 17-30

CAD (1978) Institut für Zukunftsforschung/Cooperative Arbeitsdidaktik *Lernstatt im Wohnbezirk. Kommunikationsprojekt mit Ausländern in Berlin-Wedding* Campus: Frankfurt/New York

Council for Cultural Cooperation (1978) A European unit/credit system for modern language learning by adults *Threshold Level in German for Foreign Workers* Meeting of experts on the definition of language learning objectives for migrants, Strasbourg 4-5.4.78 DECS-EES 16

Demetz, H-J and Puente, J M (1973) *Deutsch — Ihre neue Sprache Grundbuch* Falken: Niedernhausen

Deutscher Volkshochschulverband eV and Goethe-Institut (1977) *Das Zertifikat Deutsch als Fremdsprache* (2nd ed) Bonn-Bad Godesberg/Munich

Deutsches Institut für Fernstudien an der Universität Tübingen (1980) *Fernstudium Erziehungswissenschaft: Pilotprojekt 'Ausländerkinder in der Schule'* Fernstudien-materialien für die Lehrerfortbildung, Einheiten A-D: Tübingen (mimeo)

Eckes, H and Wilms, H (1975) *Deutsch für Jugendliche anderer Muttersprache* Institut für Film und Bild: Grünwald

Ehnert, R (1980) Uberblick über die derzeitig vorhandenen und geplanten Ausbildungsgänge Deutsch als Fremdsprache *Informationen Deutsch als Fremd-sprache* 3

Forschungsgruppe ALFA (1976) Empfehlungen zu einer Weiterentwicklung des schulischen Angebots für ausländische Kinder *in* Boos-Nünning, Hohmann and Reich (1976)

Forschungsverbund (1979) *Gastarbeiter in der Bundesrepublik Deutschland.* Ergebnisse des Forschungsverbundes 'Probleme der Ausländerbeschäftigung', Bundesministerium für Forschung und Technologie: Bonn (mimeo)

Franz, F (1974) Die aufenthaltsrechtliche Stellung der ausländischen Arbeiter *in* Ansay and Gessner (1974)

Friberg, D and Hohmann, M (1976) Schulpflicht und Schulrecht: Die Situation in den einzelnen Bundesländern *in* Hohmann (1976)

Ghionda, C and Rovere, G (1977) *Manuale di Tedesco per i lavoratori italiani emigrati* ME/DI SVILUPPO: Milan

Gürkan, U, Laqueur, K and Szablewski, P (1979) Unterricht mit nichterwerbstätigen ausländischen Frauen *Deutsch lernen* 1: 31-42

Heidelberger Forschungsprojekt 'Pidgin-Deutsch' (1977) *Die ungesteuerte Erlernung des Deutschen durch spanische und italienische Arbeiter. Eine soziolinguistische Untersuchung* Osnabrücker Beiträge zur Sprachtheorie, Beiheft 2: Osnabrück

Heidelberger Forschungsprojekt 'Pidgin-Deutsch' (1978) The acquisition of German syntax by foreign migrant workers *in* Sankoff (1978)

Hohmann, M ed (1976) *Unterricht mit ausländischen Kindern* Schwann: Düsseldorf

Jirsa, W and Wilms, H (no date) *Deutsch für Jugendliche anderer Muttersprache* Institut für Film und Bild: Grünwald

Jung, W (1980) Ausländerkinder in Baden-Württemberg: Eine Bestandsaufnahme *Ausländerkinder — Forum für Schule und Sozialpädagogik* 1: 4-20

Kasprzik, W (1974) *Lernstatt: Erfahrungen und Folgerungen aus einem Modellversuch in der Automobilindustrie* Cooperative Arbeitsdidaktik: Berlin

Katsoulis, H (1978) *Bürger zweiter Klasse: Ausländer in der Bundesrepublik* Campus: Frankfurt/New York

Klein, W and Dittmar, N (1979) *Developing Grammars: The Acquisition of German Syntax by Foreign Migrant Workers* Springer: Berlin/Heidelberg/New York

Kühn, H (1979) *Stand und Weiterentwicklung der Integration der ausländischen Arbeitnehmer und ihrer Familien in der Bundesrepublik Deutschland* Memorandum des Beauftragten der Bundesregierung: Bonn

Langenohl-Weyer, A and Vink, J (1979) Weiterbildung mit Ausländern *in* Langenohl-Weyer (1979)

Langenohl-Weyer, A et al (1979) *Zur Integration der Ausländer im Bildungsbereich: Probleme und Lösungsversuche* Juventa: Munich

López-Blasco, A (1979) Ausländische Kinder im Kleinkindalter *in* Langenohl-Weyer (1979)

Mehrländer, U (1974) *Soziale Aspekte der Ausländerbeschäftigung* Neue Gesellschaft: Bonn-Bad Godesberg

Menk, A-K and Stölting, W (1973) Bilinguale Schulen für Kinder ausländischer Arbeiter *Materialien Deutsch als Fremdsprache* 1: 149-55

Müller, H ed (1974) *Ausländerkinder in deutschen Schulen* Klett: Stuttgart

Neumann, U (1980) *Erziehung ausländischer Kinder: Erziehungsziele und Bildungsvorstellungen in türkischen Arbeiterfamilien* Schwann: Düsseldorf

Neuner, G et al (1979) *Deutsch aktiv: Ein Lehrwerk für Erwachsene* Langenscheidt: Berlin/Munich

PAS/DVV (no date) Pädogogische Arbeitsstelle des Deutschen Volkshochschulverbands *Projektbeschreibung: Hauptschulabschluss-Lehrgänge für Ausländer* Frankfurt (mimeo)

Reich, H H (1979) Deutschlehrer für Gastarbeiterkinder: Eine Übersicht über Ausbildungsmöglichkeiten in der Bundesrepublik *Deutsch lernen* 3: 3-14

Sankoff, D ed (1978) *Linguistic Variation: Models and Methods* Academic Press: New York

Savvidis, G (1974) *Zum Problem der Gastarbeiterkinder in der Bundesrepublik Deutschland* University of Munich dissertation: Munich

Schrader, A, Nikles, B W and Griese, H M (1976) *Die zweite Generation. Sozialisation und Akkulturation ausländischer Kinder in der Bundesrepublik* Athenäum: Kronberg/Ts

Seidel, H (1979) Ausländische Arbeitnehmer in der Bundesrepublik Deutschland: Ein statistischer Überblick *Deutsch lernen* 1: 52-76

Sprachverband (1980) *Massnahmen zur sozialen und beruflichen Eingliederung ausländischer Jugendlicher* (MSBE) Bericht über das Kursjahr 1978-79: Mainz (mimeo)

Stölting, W (1976) Zur Diskussion über die sprachliche Situation und die Schulbildung der Gastarbeiterkinder *Studium Linguistik* 2: 73-7

Vink, J (1976) Ausserschulische Sozialisationshilfen *in* Hohmann (1976)

Vink, J (1979) Berufliche Bildung ausländischer Jugendlicher *in* Langenohl-Weyer (1979)

Vink, J and Dederichs, E (1976) Empfehlung der Kultusministerkonferenz vom 8.4.76: Synopse zur KMK-Empfehlung 1971 und Kommentar *Materialien zum Projektbereich 'Ausländische Arbeiter'* 14: 67-81

von der Handt, G (1979) Projekt 'Deutsch für ausländische Arbeitnehmer' *Informationsdienst Bildungsarbeit mit ausländischen Arbeitern* 2: 49-50

Weinrich, H (1980) *Bilinguale Erziehung in der Begegnung mit Kindern ausländischer Arbeitnehmer* Paper given at the Symposium 'Bilinguale Erziehung in der Begegnung mit Kindern ausländischer Arbeitnehmer', University of Munich 20-22.2.80 (mimeo)

Weische-Alexa, P (1979) Deutschunterricht mit türkischen Hausfrauen: Ein Bericht aus der Unterrichtspraxis *Deutsch lernen* 1: 43-51

Zografou, A (1978) *Die Ursachen für die Konfliktsituation der griechischen Schulkinder in der Bundesrepublik und ihre Beschulung aus der Sicht der Griechen* Diakonisches Werk in Hessen und Nassau: Frankfurt (mimeo)

Part 6:
Bibliography and biographical notes

Bibliography

Agnes McMahon and Rosamond Mitchell

The bibliography is divided into four sections. The first covers published books and pamphlets by individual authors, the second lists publications (books and documents) issued by official bodies, and the third includes articles, periodicals and working papers. These three sections include nearly all of the references cited in individual chapters; unpublished manuscripts and a few specialized references have been omitted.

In section IV a number of key references from sections I, II and III listed in the various chapters have been annotated. An asterisk (*) beside a particular entry in the main part of the bibliography indicates that it has been annotated in section IV.

Section I: Books and pamphlets

Abdulaziz, M M (1971) Tanzania's National Language policy and the rise of Swahili political culture *in* Whiteley (1971)

Abernethy, D (1969) *The Political Dilemma of Popular Education* Stanford University Press: Stanford, Cal

Abrahams, R and Troike, R *eds* (1972) *Language and Cultural Diversity in American Education* Prentice-Hall: Englewood Cliffs, NJ

Afolayan, A (1976) The six-year primary project in Nigeria *in* Bamgbose (1976)

Akpinar, U (1979) Zur Schulsituation der Kinder ausländischer Arbeitnehmer *in* Langenohl-Weyer *et al* (1979)

Akpinar, U, López-Blasco, A and Vink, J (1979) *Pädagogische Arbeit mit ausländischen Kindern und Jugendlichen: Bestandsaufnahme und Praxishilfen* (2nd ed) Juventa: Munich

Alatis, J E *ed* (1978) *Georgetown University Round Table on Languages and Linguistics* University of Georgetown Press: Washington DC

Alexander, R and Wormald, E *eds* (1979) *Professional Studies for Teaching* Society for Research into Higher Education (SRHE): Guildford, Surrey

Anderson, W W and Grant, R W (1975) *The Newcomers* York University: Toronto

*Andersson, T and Boyer, M (1978) *Bilingual Schooling in the United States* (2nd ed) National Educational Library Publishers: Austin, Tex

Ansay, T and Gessner, V *eds* (1974) *Gastarbeiter in Gesellschaft und Recht* C H Beck: Munich

Armstrong, T, Rogers, G and Rowley, G (1978) *The Circumpolar North* Methuen: London

Arora, R K (1980) *Report on English as a Second Language for Adults* Mimeographed paper for Advisory Committee for Adult and Continuing Education enquiry into ethnic minorities: London

*Ashworth, M (1975) *Immigrant Children and Canadian Schools* McClelland and Stewart: Toronto

Ashworth, M (1976) *The Settlement of Immigrants: The Need for a Policy* University of British Columbia: Vancouver

Asmah, H O (1979) Languages of Malaysia *in* Llamzon (1979)

Aspira (1968) *Hemos Trabajado Bien* Aspira: New York

Augustin, V and Liebe-Harkort, K (1977) *Feridun. Ein Lese-buch und Sprachprogramm, nicht nur für Turken* Abado: Munich

Baetens Beardsmore, H (1977) Anomie in bicultural education *in* de Grève and Rosseel (1977)

Baetens Beardsmore, H and Van de Craen, P (1979) The development of triglossia in Flemish Belgium *in* Van der Velde and Vandeweghe (1979)

Bagley, C and Verma, G K (1979) *Racial Prejudice, the Individual and Society* Saxon House: Farnborough, Hants

Bagley, C, Verma, G K, Mallick, K and Young, L (1979) *Personality, Self-esteem and Prejudice* Saxon House: Farnborough, Hants

Bagley, C and Young, L (1979) The identity, adjustment and achievement of trans-racially adopted children *in* Verma and Bagley (1979)

Baker, D G ed (1975) *Politics of Race* Saxon House/D C Heath: London

Baldwin, J (1971) *Nobody Knows My Name* Penguin: Harmondsworth

Ballin, R, Bleach, J and Levine, J (1980) *A Wider Heritage: A Selection of Books for Children and Young People in Multi-cultural Britain* National Book League: London

*Bamgbose, A ed (1976) *Mother Tongue Education: The West African Experience* Unesco/Hodder and Stoughton: Paris and London

Banks, J A (1973) *Teaching Ethnic Studies: Concepts and Strategies* Council for the Social Studies: Washington DC

Barkowski, H, Harnisch, U and Kumm, S (1980) *Lehrerhandbuch. Deutsch für ausländische Arbeiter* (2 vols) Scriptor: Königstein/Ts

Barnhardt, C (1980) *Historical Status of Elementary Schools in Rural Alaskan Communities, 1867-1979* Center for Cross-Cultural Studies, University of Alaska: Fairbanks, Alas

Barnhardt, R, Van Ness, H, Bacon, J, Cochran, T, Dolan, L, Harrison, B, Juettner, B, Madsen, E, Nabielski, K R, Sipe, M and Wagner, T (1979) *Small High School Programs for Rural Alaska, Vol 1* Center for Cross-Cultural Studies, University of Alaska: Fairbanks, Alas

Beeby, C (1966) *The Quality of Education in Developing Countries* Harvard University Press: Cambridge, Mass

Beethan, D (1967) *Immigrant School-leavers and the Youth Employment Service in Birmingham* Institute of Race Relations/Oxford University Press: London

Belloncle, G (1979) *Jeunes Ruraux du Sahel* Harmattan: Paris

Bendit, R (1979) Kommunikations und Sprachproblematik bei ausländischen Kindern, Jugendlichen und Erwachsenen *in* Langenohl-Weyer *et al* (1979)

Bereiter, C and Engelmann, S (1966) *Teaching Disadvantaged Children in the Pre-school* Prentice-Hall: Englewood Cliffs, NJ

Bernstein, B (1972) Social class, language and socialization *in* Giglioli (1972)

Bernstein, B (1973) A brief account of the theory of codes *in* Lee (1973)

Berry, J W, Kalin, R and Taylor, D M (1976) *Multiculturalism and Ethnic Attitudes in Canada* Government of Canada: Ottawa

Birnie and Ansre eds (1968) *Proceedings of the Conference on the study of Ghanaian Languages at the University of Ghana* Ghana Publishing Corporation: Accra

Bjarne, B and Jensen, K eds (1979) *Eskimo Languages: Their Present-day Conditions* Scientific symposium held at the Department of Greenlandic on the occasion of the 50th anniversary of the University of Aarhus: Denmark

Blackwell, J (1851) *Ceinion Alun* (Works) In Welsh: London

Blakers, C (1978) *School and Work* Australian National University Press: Canberra

Boos-Nünning, U (1976) Lernprobleme und Schulerfolg *in* Hohmann (1976)

Boos-Nünning, U, Hohmann, M and Reich, H H (1976) *Integration ausländischer Arbeitnehmer: Schulbildung ausländischer Kinder* (Studien zur Kommunal politik 14): Bonn

Bottomley, G (1975) Community and network in a city *in* Price (1975)

Bottomley, G (1979) The study of social processes: some problems of theory and method *in* De Lacey and Poole (1979)

Brody, E *ed* (1969) *Behaviour in New Environments* Sage Publications: Beverly Hills, Cal

Brody, E (1969) Migration and adaptation *in* Brody (1969)

Brooks, I R (1976) *Native Education in Canada and the United States: A Bibliography* Office of Educational Development, University of Calgary: Calgary, Alberta

*Brown, D M (1979) *Mother Tongue to English: The Young Child in the Multicultural School* Cambridge University Press: Cambridge

Browning, K (1979) Parental attitudes to and aspirations to their children's education *in* De Lacey and Poole (1979)

Brunnerk, H S and Hagelstrom, V V (1912) *Present Day Political Organizations of China* Kelly and Walsh: Shanghai

Bull, J (1976) *The Ten School Project in Multicultural Education: A Report of a Forum* State College of Victoria, Toorak: Melbourne

Burchett, W and Alley, R (1976) *China: The Quality of Life* Penguin: Harmondsworth

Burns, A and Goodnow, J (1979) *Children and Families in Australia: Contemporary Issues and Problems* Allen and Unwin: Sydney

Butcher, H *ed* (1968) *Educational Research in Britain* University of London Press: London

Butterworth, E and Kinnibrugh, D (1970) *Scope Handbook 1: The Social Background of Immigrant Children from India, Pakistan and Cyprus* (Schools Council Project on English for Immigrant Children) Books for Schools: London

Cantor, L M and Roberts, I F (1979) *Further Education Today: A Critical Review* Routledge and Kegan Paul: London

Chambers, P (1979) The scope and direction of professional studies since James *in* Alexander and Wormald (1979)

Chandra, U K (1973) *Racial Discrimination in Canada* B and B Research Associates: San Francisco, Cal

Chenault, L R (1938) *The Puerto Rican Migrant in New York City* Columbia University Press: New York

Clammer, J R (1976) *Sociological Approaches to the Study of Language and Literacy in South East Asia* (Sociology Working paper 56) Department of Sociology: University of Singapore

*Claydon, L, Knight, T and Rado, M (1977) *Curriculum and Culture: Schooling in a Pluralist Society* Allen and Unwin: Hornsby, New South Wales

Clement, W (1975) *The Canadian Corporate Elite* Macmillan Carleton Series: Toronto

Clignet, R and Foster, P (1966) *The Fortunate Few* Northwestern University Press: Evanston, Ill

Clyne, M (1972) *Perspectives on Language Contact* Hawthorn: Melbourne

Clyne, M *ed* (1976) *Australia Talks: Essays on the Sociology of European and Aboriginal Languages in Australia* Pacific Linguistics, Series D23, Department of Linguistics, Research School of Pacific Studies, Australian National University: Canberra

Coard, B (1971) *How the West Indian Child is made Educationally Subnormal in the English School System* New Beacon Books: London

Coleman, J S (1966) *Equality of Educational Opportunity* United States Government Printing Office: Washington DC

Collins, D (1979) *Immigration: The Destruction of English Canada* B M G Publishing: Richmond Hill, Ontario

Connell, W F, Stroobant, R, Sinclair, K, Connell, R and Rogers, K (1975) *12 to 20: Studies of City Youth* Hicks Smith and Sons: Sydney

Connor, W (1979) An overview of the ethnic composition and problems of non-Arab Asia *in* Kang (1979)

Coon, E D (1980) *Bilingual-Bicultural Education in Alaska: Guidelines for Conducting Programs in Elementary and Secondary Schools* Alaska State Department of Education: Juneau, Alas

Coopersmith, S (1967) *The Antecedents of Self-Esteem* Freeman: San Francisco, Cal

Cordasco, F (1973) Teaching: the Puerto Rican experience *in* Banks (1973)

*Cordasco, F (1976) *Bilingual Schooling in the United States: A Sourcebook for Educational Personnel* McGraw-Hill: New York

Cordasco, F and Bernstein, G (1979) *Bilingual Education in American Schools: A Guide to Information Sources* Gale Research Company: Detroit, Mich

Cordasco, F and Bucchioni, E eds (1972) *The Puerto Rican Community and Its Children on the Mainland* Scarecrow Press: Metuchen, NJ

Cordasco, R and Covello, L (1968) *Studies of Puerto Rican Children in American Schools: A Preliminary Bibliography* Migration Division, Commonwealth of Puerto Rico: New York

Corner, T C ed (1978) *Education in Multicultural Societies* Conference Proceedings of the Comparative Education Society in Europe (British Section): Edinburgh

Coughlin, R J (1960) *Double Identity: the Chinese in Modern Thailand* Hong Kong University Press: Hong Kong

Court, D and Ghai, D P eds (1974) *Education Society and Development* Oxford University Press: Nairobi

Covello, F (1953) *Recommendations Concerning Puerto Rican Pupils in our Public Schools* Benjamin Franklin High School: New York

Covello, L (1967) *The Social Background of the Italo-American School Child* E J Brill: Leiden

Covington, A (1976) Black people and Black English: attitudes and de-education in a biased macroculture *in* Harrison and Trabasso (1976)

Cox, D (1975) The adaptation of Greek youth in Melbourne *in* Price (1975)

Cremin, L A (1961) *The Transformation of the School* Alfred Knopf: New York

Criper, C and Ladefoged, P (1971) Linguistic complexity in Uganda *in* Whiteley (1971)

Cubberley, E P (1909) *Changing Conceptions of Education* Houghton Mifflin: Boston, Mass

Dafoe, D M (1978) *The Governance, Organization, and Financing of Education for Alaska Natives* Center for Northern Educational Research: University of Alaska, Fairbanks, Alas

Deal, D M (1979) Policy towards ethnic minorities in South West China, 1927-1965 *in* Kang (1979)

*de Grève, M and Rosseel, E eds (1977) *Problèmes Linguistiques des Enfants de Travailleurs Migrants* AIMAV-Didier: Brussels

De Lacey, P R and Poole, M E eds (1979) *Mosaic or Melting Pot: Cultural Evolution in Australia* Harcourt Brace Jovanovich: Sydney

De Lacey, P R and Rich, P (1979) Young Australian newcomers: a study of some behavioural resources of immigrant children in Wollongong *in* De Lacey and Poole (1979)

De Lemos, M M (1975) Study of the educational achievement of migrant children: Final Report of the Australian Council for Educational Research (ACER): Hawthorn, Victoria

Demetz, H J and Puente, J M (1973) *Deutsch — Ihre neue Sprache Grundbuch* Falken: Niedernhausen

Deosaran, R and Gersham, J (1976) *An Evaluation of the 1975-76 Chinese-Canadian Bi-cultural Program* Research Department, Toronto Board of Education: Toronto

Deutsch, M ed (1967) *The Disadvantaged Child* Basic Books: New York

Dingwell, S (1979) *Past and present trends in teaching English as a second language: a review and assessment of future needs* Commissioned working paper for ERDC (Education Research and Development Committee) Australian Government Publishing Service: Canberra

Dorsey, B J (1975) The African secondary school leaver *in* Murphree (1975)

D'Oyley, W ed (1978) *Black Presence in Multi-ethnic Canada* Ontario Institute for Studies in Education: Toronto

Drake, G (1979) Ethnicity, values and language policy in the United States *in* Giles and Saint-Jacques (1979)

Dressler, W U and Meid, W eds (1978) *Proceedings of the XIIth International Congress of Linguists* Innsbrucker Beiträge zur Sprachwissenschaft

Dreyer, J T (1976) *China's Forty Millions* Harvard East Asian Series No 87, Harvard University Press: Cambridge, Mass

Dubow, F (1976) Language, law and change: problems in the development of a national legal system in Tanzania *in* O'Barr and O'Barr (1976)

Eastman, C M (1979) Language resurrection: a language plan for ethnic interaction *in* Giles and Saint Jacques (1979)

Eckes, H and Wilms, H (1975) *Deutsch für Jungendliche anderer Muttersprache* Institut für Film und Bild: Grunwald

Edgar, D L ed (1974) *Social Change in Australia* Cheshire: Melbourne

Edwards, J R (1977) Ethnic identity and bilingual education *in* Giles (1977)

Edwards, J R (1977) Reading, language and disadvantage *in* Greaney (1977)

*Edwards, J R (1979) *Language and Disadvantage* Edward Arnold: London

Edwards, J R (1979) Judgements and confidence in reactions to disadvantaged speech *in* Giles and St Clair (1979)

*Edwards, V K (1979) *The West Indian Language Issue in British Schools: Challenges and Responses* Routledge and Kegan Paul: London

Ehnert, R (1980) Uberblick über die derzeitig vorhandenen und geplanten Ausbildungsgänge Deutsch als Fremdsprache *Informationen Deutsch als Fremdsprache* 3

Ekvall, R (1965) Nomads of Tibet, a Chinese dilemma *in* Harper (1965)

Epronti, E O and Denteh, A C (1968) 'Minority' languages *in* Birnie and Ansre (1968)

*Epstein, N (1977) *Language, Ethnicity and the Schools: Policy Alternatives for Bilingual-Bicultural Education* Institute for Educational Leadership, George Washington University: Washington DC

Fishman, J A ed (1966) *Language Loyalty in the United States* Mouton: The Hague

Fishman, J A (1968) Nationality — nationalism and nation — nationism *in* Fishman, Ferguson and Das Gupta (1968)

Fishman, J A ed (1978) *Advances in the Study of Societal Multi-lingualism* Mouton: The Hague

Fishman, J A, Ferguson and Das Gupta, Y P eds (1968) *Language Problems of Developing Nations* Wiley: New York

Fitzpatrick, J (1971) *Puerto Rican Americans: The Meaning of Migration to the Mainland* Prentice-Hall: Englewood Cliffs, NJ

Forschungsgruppe ALFA (1976) Empfehlungen zu einer weiterentwicklung des schulischen Angebots für ausländische kinder *in* Boos-Nünning, Hohmann and Reich (1976)

Franz, F (1974) Die aufenthaltsrechtliche Stellung der ausländischen Arbeiter *in* Ansay and Gessner (1974)

Friberg, D and Hohmann, M (1976) Schulpflicht und Schulrecht. Die Situation in den einzelnen Budesländern *in* Hohmann (1976)

*Fuchs, E and Havighurst, R J (1972) *To Live On This Earth* Doubleday (Anchor Books): New York

*Gaarder, A B (1977) *Bilingual Schooling and the Survival of Spanish in the United States* Newbury House: Rowley, Mass

Gachukia, E (1970) The teaching of vernacular languages in Kenyan primary schools *in* Gorman (1970)

Gaucher, J (1968) *Les Debuts de l'Enseignement en Afrique Francophone* Le Livre Africain: Paris

Genesee, F (1980) *A Comparison of Early and Late Immersion Programs* Department of Psychology, McGill University: Montreal

Georgeff, M, Poole, M E and Evans, G T (1979) Information selection in language use and its relation to socio-economic status and ethnicity *in* De Lacey and Poole (1979)

Ghionda, C and Rovere, G (1977) *Manuale di Tedesco per i lavoratori italiani emigrati* ME/DI SVILUPPO: Milan

Giglioli, P ed (1972) *Language and Social Context* Penguin: Harmondsworth

*Giles, H ed (1977) *Language, Ethnicity and Intergroup Relations* Academic Press: London

Giles, H, Bourhis, R and Davies, A (1975) Prestige speech styles: The imposed norm and inherent value hypotheses *in* McCormack and Wurm (1975)

Giles, H and Powesland, P (1975) *Speech Style and Social Evaluation* Academic Press: London

Giles, H and St Clair, R eds (1979) *Language and Social Psychology* Blackwell: Oxford

*Giles, H and Saint-Jacques, B eds (1979) *Language and Ethnic Relations* Pergamon: Oxford

Gilmour, P and Lansbury, R (1978) *Ticket to Nowhere* Penguin: Harmondsworth

Glazer, N (1976) *Affirmative Discrimination: Ethnic Inequality and Social Policy* Basic Books: New York

*Glazer, N and Moynihan, D P eds (1975) *Ethnicity: Theory and Experience* Harvard University Press: Cambridge, Mass

Gleitman, L and Gleitman, H (1970) *Phrase and Paraphrase* Norton: New York

Goffman, E (1968) *Asylums* Penguin: Harmondsworth

Goodenough, W H (1963) *Cooperation in Change* Russell Sage Foundation: New York

Gordon, M M (1978) *Human Nature, Class and Ethnicity* Oxford University Press: New York

Gorman, T P ed (1970) *Language in Education in Eastern Africa* Oxford University Press: Nairobi

Gorman, T P (1973) Language allocation and language planning *in* Rubin and Shuy (1973)

Gorman, T P (1974) The development of language policy in Kenya with particular reference to the educational system *in* Whiteley (1974)

Grant, G (1978) The provision of social services in rural areas *in* Williams (1978)

Grant, N (1977) Language and education *in* Lowe *et al* (1977)

Grant, N (1978) Education for multi-cultural society *in* Corner (1978)

Gray, R (1960) *The Two Nations* Oxford University Press: London

Greaney, V ed (1977) *Studies in Reading* Educational Company: Dublin

Green, A (1976) *Immigration and Post-War Canadian Economy* Macmillan: Toronto

Greenfield, T B (1976) Bilingualism, multiculturalism and the crisis of purpose in Canadian culture *in* Swain (1976)

Halsey, A H and Goldthorpe, D (1980) *Origins and Destinations: Family, Class and Education in Modern Britain* Oxford University Press: Oxford

Harper, F ed (1965) *This is China* Dragonfly Press: Hong Kong

Harrison, D and Trabasso, T eds (1976) *Black English: A Seminar* Erlbaum: Hillsdale, NJ

Hart, M (1974) *Kulila* Australia and New Zealand Book Co: Sydney

Harvey, E B and Masemann, V L (1975) *Occupational Graduates and Labour Force* Ontario Ministry of Education: Toronto

Haugen, E (1966) *Language Conflict and Language Planning: The Case of Modern Norwegian* Harvard University Press: Cambridge, Mass

*Hawes, H (1979) *Curriculum and Reality in African Primary Schools* Longman: London

Head, W A (1975) *The Black Presence in Canadian Mosaic* Ontario Human Rights Commission: Toronto

Heidelberger Forschungsprojekt 'Pidgin-Deutsch' (1978) The acquisition of German syntax by foreign migrant workers *in* Sankoff (1978)

Hemphill, R J (1974) Language use and language teaching in the primary schools of Kenya *in* Whiteley (1974)

Henry, F (1978) *The Dynamics of Racism in Toronto* York University: Toronto

Hess, R and Bear, R eds (1968) *Early Education* Aldine: Chicago, Ill

Hess, R and Shipman, V (1968) Maternal influences upon early learning: the cognitive environments of urban pre-school children *in* Hess and Bear (1968)

Hewitt, R D (1977) Characteristics of students from other ethnic backgrounds *in* Bourke and Keeves (1977)

Hidalgo, H (1971) *The Puerto Ricans of Newark, New Jersey* Aspira: Newark, NJ

Higham, J (1975) *Send These to Me* Atheneum: New York

Hill, C P (1981) Some developments in language and education in Tanzania since 1969 *in* Polomé (forthcoming)

Hiro, D (1971) *Black British, White British* Eyre and Spottiswoode: London

Hirst, P H (1979) Professional studies in initial teacher education: some conceptual issues *in* Alexander and Wormald (1979)

Hodgkin, R (1976) *Born Curious* Wiley: London

Hohmann, M ed (1976) *Unterricht mit ausländischen Kindern* Schwann: Düsseldorf

Holenbergh Young, R M (1979) Ethnic identity and education *in* De Lacey and Poole (1979)

Holmes, M (1978) Multiculturalism and the school *in* D'Oyley (1978)

Hopkins, T (1977) The development and implementation of the national language policy in Kenya *in* Kotey and Der-Houssikian (1977)

*Hornby, P A ed (1977) *Bilingualism: Psychological, Social and Educational Implications* Academic Press: New York

Horvath, B (1979) *The education of migrant children: a language planning perspective* Report to Education Research and Development Committee (ERDC): Sydney

Hughes, D R and Kallen, E (1974) *The Anatomy of Racism: Canadian Dimensions* Harvest House: Montreal

Hunt, F J ed (1972) *Socialization in Australia* Angus and Robertson: Sydney

Isaacs, E (1976) *Greek Children in Sydney* Australian National University Press: Canberra

Isaacs, E (1979) Social control and ethnicity: the socialization and repression of a Greek child at school *in* De Lacey and Poole (1979)

Isayev, M K (1977) *National Languages in the USSR: Problems and Solutions* Progress Publishers: Moscow

Itebete, P (1974) Language standardisation in Western Kenya — the Luluyia experiment *in* Whiteley (1974)

Jean-Baptiste, J (1979) *Les Haitiens au Canada* Ministry of Supplies and Services: Ottawa

Jeffcoate, R (1979) *Positive Image Towards a Multi-racial Curriculum* Chameleon Books: London

Jeffrey, P (1976) *Migrants and Refugees: Muslim and Christian Pakistani Families in Bristol* Cambridge University Press: London

Jencks, C, Smith, M, Acland, H, Bane, M J, Cohen, D, Gintis, H, Heyns, B and Michelson, S (1972) *Inequality: A Reassessment of the Effect of Family and Schooling in America* Basic Books: New York

Jensen, A (1973) *Educability and Group Differences* Harper and Row: New York

Jirsa, W and Wilms, H (no date) *Deutsch für Jugendliche anderer Muttersprache* Institut für Film und Bild: Grünwald

Johnston, R (1965) *Immigrant Assimilation: A Study of Polish People in Western Australia* Paterson Brokensha: Perth

Jupp, C (1966) *Arrivals and Departures* Cheshire-Landsdowne: Melbourne

*Kang, T S ed (1979) *Nationalism and the Crises of Ethnic Minorities in Asia* Greenwood Press: Westport, Conn

Kari, J and Spolski, B (1978) Trends in study of Athapaskan language maintenance and bilingualism *in* Fishman (1978)

Karmel, P H (1973) *Interim Committee for the Australian Schools Commission. Schools in Australia: Report* Australian Government Publishing Service: Canberra

Kasprzik, W (1974) *Lernstatt: Erfahrungen und Folgerungen aus einem Modellversuch in der Automobilindustrie* Cooperative Arbeitsdidaktik: Berlin

Katsoulis, H (1978) *Bürger zweiter Klasse. Ausländer in der Bundesrepublik* Campus: Frankfurt/New York

Kay, G (1972) *Distribution and Density of the African Population in Rhodesia* Miscellaneous Series 12, University of Hull: Hull, Yorks

Keats, D M and Keats, J A (1973) *The Effect of Language on Concept Acquisition in Bilingual Children* Report to Education Research and Development Committee (ERDC), Australian Government Publishing Service: Canberra

Keddie, N (1971) Classroom knowledge *in* Young (9171)

Keddie, N ed (1973) *Tinker, Tailor . . . The Myth of Cultural Deprivation* Penguin: Harmondsworth

Keeves, J P and Bourke, S F eds (1977) *Australian Studies in School Performance, Vol III: The Mastery of Literacy and Numeracy: Final Report* Education Research and Development Committee (ERDC): Australian Government Publishing Service: Canberra

Kenske, G E (1966) *Power and Privilege: A Theory of Social Stratification* McGraw-Hill: New York

King, K (1974) Primary schools in Kenya — some critical constraints *in* Court and Ghai (1974)

Klein, W and Dittmar, N (1979) *Developing Grammars: The Acquisition of German Syntax by Foreign Migrant Workers* Springer: Berlin/Heidelberg/New York

Kleinfeld, J S (1973) *A Long Way from Home* Center for Northern Educational Research, Institute for Social and Economic Research, University of Alaska: Fairbanks, Alas

*Kloss, H (1977) *The American Bilingual Tradition* Newbury House: Rowley, Mass

Kohler, D F (1976) *Ethnic Minorities in Britain: Statistical Data* Community Relations Commission: London

*Kotey, P F A and Der-Houssikian, H eds (1977) *Language and Linguistic Problems in Africa* Hornbeam Press: Columbia, SC

Kovacs, M L and Cropley, A J (1975) *Immigrants and Society: Alienation and Assimilation* McGraw-Hill: Sydney

Krauss, M E (1979) The Eskimo languages in Alaska, yesterday and today *in* Bjarne and Jensen (1979)

Labov, W (1970) The logic of non standard English *in* Williams (1970)

Ladefoged, P, Glick, R and Criper, C (1972) *Language in Uganda* Oxford University Press: London

Lambert, W E (1977) The effects of bilingualism on the individual: cognitive and sociocultural consequences *in* Hornby (1977)

*Lambert, W E and Tucker, G R (1972) *Bilingual Education of Children: The St Lambert Experiment* Newbury House: Rowley, Mass

Langenohl-Weyer, A and Vink, J (1979) Weiterbildung mit Ausländern *in* Langenohl-Weyer *et al* (1979)

Langenohl-Weyer, A *et al* (1979) *Zur Integration der Ausländer im Bildungsbereich. Probleme und Lösungsversuche* Juventa: Munich

Lattimore, O (1950) *Pivot of Asia* Little, Brown: Boston, Mass

Lattimore, O (1962) *Inner Asian Frontiers of China* Beacon Press: Boston, Mass

Laxer, R M ed (1979) *Bilingual Tensions in Canada* Ontario Institute for Studies in Education: Toronto

Leacock, E ed (1971) *The Culture of Poverty: A Critique* Simon and Schuster: New York

Lee, D J ed (1979) *Emerging Ethnic Boundaries* University of Ottawa Press: Ottawa

Lee, V ed (1973) *Social Relationships and Language* Open University Press: Bletchley

Lenin, V I (1916) The significance of the right to self determination and its relation to federation *Collected Works XXII* Progress Publishers: Moscow (1964 edition)

Lenin, V I (1921) *Selected Works* International Publishers: New York

Lenneberg, E (1967) *Biological Foundations of Language* Wiley: New York

Lenski, G E (1966) *Power and Privilege: A Theory of Social Stratification* McGraw-Hill: New York

Lewis, E G (1978) Bilingualism in education in Wales *in* Spolsky (1978)

Lewis, L J (1962) *Phelps-Stokes Commission on Education in Africa* (abridged version) Oxford University Press: London

Lim Kiat Boey ed (1980) *Bilingual Education* Anthropology Series 7, South East Asian Ministers Education Organization (SEAMEO), Singapore University Press: Singapore

Lind, L (1974) New Canadianism: melting the ethnics in Toronto schools *in* Martell (1974)

Linton, R ed (1945) *The Science of Man in the World Crisis* Columbia University Press: New York

*Little, A and Willey, R (1981) *Multi-ethnic Education: The Way Forward* Schools Council Pamphlet 18, Schools Council: London

Llamzon, T A (1979) *Education in a Multicultural Australia* Australian Government Publishing Service: Canberra

Loh, P F-S (1975) *Seeds of Separatism: Educational Policy in Malaya 1874-1940* Oxford University Press: Kuala Lumpur

López-Blasco, A (1979) Ausländische Kinder im Kleinkindalter *in* Langenohl-Weyer et al (1979)

Lowe, J, Grant, N and Williams, T D eds (1977) *Education and Nation-Building in the Third World* Scottish Academic Press: Edinburgh

Lupul, M R (1976) Bilingual education and the Ukrainians in Western Canada: possibilities and problems *in* Swain (1976)

Mackie, F (1974) Some suggestions on Greek diversity *in* Edgar (1974)

Mallick, K and Verma, G K (1981) Teaching in the multi-ethnic, multicultural school *in* Verma and Bagley (1981)

Maloney, C, Zobl, H and Stölting, W (1977) *Deutsch im Kontakt mit anderen sprachen* Scripton Verlag: Kronberg

Margolis, R J (1968) *The Losers: A Report on Puerto Ricans and the Public Schools* Aspira: New York

Marjoribanks, K (1979) Ethnicity, family environment, school attitudes and academic achievement *in* De Lacey and Poole (1979)

*Marjoribanks, K (1980) *Ethnic Families and Children's Achievements* Allen and Unwin: Sydney

Martell, G (1974) *The Politics of the Canadian Public Schools* James Lewis and Samuel: Toronto

Martin, J I (1971) Family and bureaucracy *in* Price (1971)

*Martin, J I (1978) *The Migrant Presence: Australian Responses 1947-1977* Allen and Unwin: Sydney

Martin, J I and Meade, P (1979) *The Educational Experience of Sydney High School Students: A Comparative Study of Migrant Students of Non-English Speaking Origin and Students Whose Parents were Born in an English Speaking Country* Australian Government Publishing Service: Canberra

Marx, G (1971) *Racial Conflict: Tension and Change in American Society* Little, Brown: Boston, Mass

Masemann, V (1975) Immigrant student's perceptions of occupational programmes *in* Wolfgang (1975)

Matsdorf, W S ed (1963) *Migrant Youth: Australian Citizens of Tomorrow* New South Wales Association for Mental Health: Sydney

McCormack, W and Wurm, S eds (1975) *Language in Many Ways* Mouton: The Hague

McDiarmid, G and Pratt, D (1971) *Teaching Prejudice* Ontario Institute for Studies in Education: Toronto

McKinney, D W, Connor, L and Hull, E (1978) A note on socio-economic position of 1971 census enumerated Black employed males in Canada *in* D'Oyley (1978)

Medding, P Y (1974) Jews in Australia *in* Stevens (1974)

Mehrlander, U (1974) *Soziale Aspekte der Ausländerbeschaftigung* Neue Gesellschaft: Bonn-Bad Godesberg

Milner, D (1975) *Education and Race* Penguin: Harmondsworth

Monserrat, J (1961) Community planning for Puerto Rican integration in the United States *in* Cordasco and Bucchioni (1972)

Morris, S (1974) *Black Makers of History* COBS: London

Müller, H ed (1974) *Ausländerkinder in deutschen Schulen* Klett: Stuttgart

Murphree, M W (1975) Race and power in Rhodesia *in* Baker (1975)

*Murphree, M W, Cheater, G, Dorsey, B J and Mothobi, B D (1975) *Education, Race and Employment in Rhodesia* ARTCA: Salisbury

Murphy, R and Denis, A B (1979) Schools and the conservation of the vertical mosaic *in* Lee (1979)

Murray, E E (1977) *Teaching Aboriginal/Islander Students English in Secondary Schools* Queensland Education Department: Brisbane

Musaev, K M (1965) *Alfavity Yazykov Narodov SSSR* Nauka: Moscow

Myerhoff, B G and Simić, A eds (1978) *Life's Career-Aging: Cultural Variations on Growing Old* Sage Publications: Beverly Hills, Cal

Neumann, U (1980) *Erziehung ausländischer Kinder: Erziehungsziele und Bildungsvorstellungen in türkischen Arbeiterfamilien* Schwann: Düsseldorf

Neuner, G et al (1979) *Deutsch aktiv. Ein Lehrwerk für Erwachsene* Langenscheidt: Berlin/Munich

Newman, F M and Oliver, D W (1967) A proposal for education in community *in* Raynor and Harden (1973)

Nicholls, S (1979) Mimeographed notes for the radio programme *Teaching English as a Second Language* BBC: London

Novak, M (1972) *The Rise of the Unmeltable Ethnics: Politics and Culture in the Seventies* Macmillan: New York

O'Barr, J F (1976) Language and politics in Tanzanian government institutions *in* O'Barr and O'Barr (1976)

O'Barr, W M and O'Barr, J F eds (1976) *Language and Politics* Mouton: The Hague

O'Bryan, K G, Reitz, J G and Kuplowska, O (1975) *Non-official Languages: A Study in Canadian Multiculturalism* Government of Canada: Ottawa

Ohannessian, S, Ferguson and Polomé, E eds (1975) *Language Surveys in Developing Nations* Centre for Applied Linguistics: Ottawa

Osuna, J J (1948) Report on visits to New York City schools *in* Cordasco and Buccioni (1972)

Palante (1971) *Young Lords' Party* McGraw-Hill: New York

Parai, L (1974) *The Economic Impact of Immigration* Manpower and Immigration Canada: Ottawa

Passow, A (1970) *Deprivation and Disadvantage* Unesco Institute for Education: Hamburg

Patterson, G N (1960) *Tibet in Revolt* Methuen: London

Paulston, R (1976) *Conflicting Theories of Social and Educational Change: A Typological Review* University Centre for International Studies: Pittsburgh, Pa

Perez, D (1971) The chains that have been taken off slaves' bodies are put back on their minds *in* Palante (1971)

*Perren, G E ed (1976) *Bilingualism and British Education: The Dimensions of Diversity* Centre for Information on Language Teaching, Reports and Papers 14, CILT: London

Philips, S (1972) Acquisition of roles for appropriate speech usage *in* Abrahams and Troike (1972)

Pickering, D (1970) *An Examination of the Psycholinguistic Abilities and Disabilities of Grade 2 Children of Differing Socio-economic Status and Ethnic Background, Greek and Australian* Research Report 5/70, Curriculum and Research Branch, Victoria Education Department: Melbourne

Pickering, D (1971) *An Examination of the Psycholinguistic Abilities of Some Greek Children* Research Report 10/71, Curriculum and Research Branch, Victoria Education Department: Melbourne

Pipes, R (1957) *Formation of the Soviet Union: Communism and Nationalism 1917-1923* Harvard University Press: Cambridge, Mass

Platt, J T (1978) Aspects of polyglossia and multilingualism in Malaysia and Singapore *in* Dressler and Meid (1978)

Platt, J T and Weber, H (1980) *English in Singapore and Malaysia: Status — Features — Function* Oxford University Press: Kuala Lumpur

Polk, K (1979) *Multicultural Education Programmes at Bradford College (UK)* International Management Training for Education Change: Manchester/Oslo

Pollak, M (1972) *Today's Three-year Olds in London* Heinemann: London

Polomé, E (1975) Problems and techniques of a sociolinguistically-oriented survey: the case of Tanzanian survey *in* Ohannessian, Ferguson and Polomé (1975)

Polomé, E ed (1981) *Language in Tanzania* International African Institute: London

Poole, M E (1975) Understanding cognitive style as a basis for curricula provision in inner suburban schools *in* Edgar (1975)

Poole, M E (1980) *School Leavers in Australia* Australian Government Publishing Service: Canberra

Porter, J (1965) *The Vertical Mosaic* University of Toronto Press: Toronto

Prator, C M (1975) The survey of language use and teaching in Eastern Africa in retrospect *in* Ohannessian, Ferguson and Polomé (1975)

Prewitt, K ed (1971) *Education and Political Values* East African Publishing House: Nairobi

Price, C A ed (1975) *Greeks in Australia* Australian National University Press: Canberra

Priestley, J B (1934) *English Journey* Heinemann: London

Proctor, J (1979) Professional studies in the BEd (CNAA) at Bradford College *in* Alexander and Wormald (1979)

Purcell, V (1966) *The Chinese in South East Asia* Royal Institute of International Affairs, Oxford University Press: London

Pye, L W (1975) China: ethnic minorities and national security *in* Glazer and Moynihan (1975)

Rawkins, P M (1979) *The Implementation of Language Policy in the Schools of Wales* Centre for the Study of Public Policy: University of Strathclyde

Raynor, J and Harden, J eds (1973) *Equality and City Schools* Routledge and Kegan Paul: London

Richmond, A H (1967) *Post-War Immigrants in Canada* University of Toronto Press: Toronto

Robinson, E E (1968) *The New Polytechnics* Penguin: Harmondsworth

Rose, A (1972) Minorities *in* Sills (1972)

Rosenthal, D and Morrison, S (1979) On being a minority in the classroom: a study of the influence of ethnic mix on cognitive functioning and attitudes in working class children *in* De Lacey and Poole (1979)

Rosenthal, R and Jacobson, L (1968) *Pygmalion in the Classroom* Holt, Rinehart and Winston: New York

Rosier, M J (1978) *Early School Leavers in Australia* International Association for the Evaluation of Educational Achievement, IEA Monograph Studies No 7, Almquist and Wiksell International: Stockholm and Australian Council for Educational Research: Hawthorn, Victoria

Rubin, J and Jernudd, B eds (1971) *Can Language be Planned?* University Press: Hawaii

Rubin, J and Shuy eds (1973) *Language Planning: Current Issues and Research* Georgetown University Press: Washington DC

Sankoff, D ed (1978) *Linguistic Variation: Models and Methods* Academic Press: New York

Schneider, S G (1976) *Revolution, Reaction or Reform: The 1974 Bilingual Education Act* Las Americas: New York

Schrader, A, Nikles, B W and Griese, H M (1976) *Die zweite Generation. Sozialisation und Akkulturation ausländischer Kinder in der Bundesrepublik* Athanäum: Kronberg/Ts

Sebeok, T A ed (1974) *Linguistics and Adjacent Arts and Sciences* Current Trends in Linguistics 12, Mouton: The Hague

Shaheen, S (1956) *The Communist (Bolshevik) Theory of National Self-Determination* 'S-Gravenhage: The Hague

Sharma, P G and Kumar, S eds (1977) *Indian Bilingualism* Kendriya Hindi Sansthan: Agra

*Sharp, D (1973) *Language in Bilingual Communities* Explorations in Language Study, Edward Arnold: London

Sharp, D, Bennett, G and Treharne, C (1977) *English in Wales: A Practical Guide for Teachers* Schools Council: London

*Sharp, D, Thomas, B, Price, E, Francis, G and Davies, I (1973) *Attitudes to Welsh and English in the Schools of Wales* Schools Council Research Studies, Macmillan Education: London

Shibutani, T and Kwan, K (1971) Changes in life conditions conducive to inter-racial conflict *in* Marx (1971)

Silén, J A (1971) *The Puerto Rican People: A Story of Oppression and Resistance* Monthly Review Press: New York

Sills, D ed (1972) *International Encyclopedia of the Social Sciences* (Vol 9/10) Collier-Macmillan: New York

Simić, A (1979) White ethnic and Chicano families: continuity and adaptation in the New World *in* Tufte and Myerhoff (1979)

Sivanandan, A (1976) *Race, Class and the State: The Black Experience in Britain* Institute of Race Relations: London

Skinner, G W (1958) *Leadership and Power in the Chinese Community in Thailand* Cornell University Press: Ithaca, NY

*Skutnabb-Kangas, T and Toukomaa, P (1976) *Teaching Migrant Children's Mother Tongue and Learning the Language of the Host Country in the Context of the Socio-cultural Situation of the Migrant Family* Tutkimuksia Research Reports 15, Department of Sociology and Social Psychology, University of Tampere: Finland

Smith, D (1976) *The Facts of Racial Disadvantage* Penguin: Harmondsworth

Smith, F (1973) *Psycholinguistics and Reading* Holt, Rinehart and Winston: New York

*Smolicz, J J (1979) *Culture and Education in a Plural Society* Curriculum Development Centre: Canberra

Smolicz, J J and Lean, R (1980) Australian languages other than English — a sociological study of attitudes *in* Lim Kiat Boey (1980)

Smolicz, J J and Lean, R (1980) Parental and student attitudes to the teaching of ethnic languages in Australia *ITL (Instituut voor Toegepaste Linguistiek) — A Review of Applied Linguistics* 35

Smolicz, J J and Secombe, M J (1981) *The Australian School through Polish Eyes* Melbourne University Press: Melbourne

Snow, E (1937) *Red Star over China* Random House: New York

Spolsky, B (1974) Linguistics and the language barrier to education *in* Sebeok (1974)

*Spolsky, B and Cooper, R L eds (1978) *Case Studies in Bilingual Education* Newbury House: Rowley, Mass

Stevens, F S ed (1974) *Racism, the Australian Experience, Vol I: Prejudice and Xenophobia* (2nd edition) Australian and New Zealand Book Company: Sydney

Stölting, W (1977) Die sprachpolitik an deutschen schulen für ausländische kinder *in* Malony, Zobl and Stölting (1977)

Sumner, R (1972) *Motivation Attitude Intensity Scale* National Foundation for Educational Research: Slough

Sun Yat Sen (1953) *Memoirs of a Chinese Revolutionary* China Cultural Service: Taipei

Swain, M and Barik, H C (1976) *Five years of primary French immersion: Annual reports of the bilingual education project to the Carleton Board of Education and the Ottawa Board of Education 1972-75* Ministry of Education, Ontario: Toronto

Swinerton, E, Kuepper, W and Lackey, G (1975) *Ugandan Asians in Britain* Croom Helm: London

Taft, R (1965) *From Stranger to Citizen* University of Western Australia Press: Nedlands, Western Australia

Taft, R (1972) Ethnic groups *in* Hunt (1972)

Taft, R (1973) The ethnic identification of Jewish youth *in* Medding (1973)

Taft, R (1975) *The Career Aspirations of Immigrant School Children in Victoria* Paper No 12, Department of Sociology, La Trobe University: Melbourne

Taft, R and Cahill, D (1978) *Initial Adjustment to Schooling of Immigrant Families* Commonwealth Department of Education and Academy of the Social Sciences in Australia: Canberra

Tajfel, H *ed* (1978) *Differentiation Between Social Groups* Academic Press: London

Tan, D E (1975) *A Portrait of Malaysia and Singapore* Oxford University Press: Singapore

Tan, T-S (1978) *Language Policies in Insular Southeast Asia: A Comparative Study* Southeast Asia Studies Programme, Nanyang University: Singapore

Taylor, J (1976) *The Halfway Generation: A Study of Asian Youths in Newcastle upon Tyne* National Foundation for Educational Research: Slough

Teitlebaum, H and Hiller, R J (1977) *The Legal Perspective in Bilingual Perspectives: Law* Centre for Applied Linguistics: Arlington, Va

Tenezakis, M D (1979) Language and cognitive development in bilingual and monolingual children *in* De Lacey and Poole (1979)

Tomkins, C and Lovering, J (1973) *Location, Size, Ownership and Control Tables for Welsh Industry* Cyngor Cymru: Cardiff

Toukomaa, P and Skutnabb-Kangas, T (1977) *The Intensive Teaching of the Mother Tongue to Migrant Children at Pre-School Age: Tutkimuksia Research Reports 26* Department of Sociology and Social Psychology, University of Tampere: Finland

Touraine, A (1977) *The Self Production of Society* University of Chicago Press: Chicago, Ill

Townsend, H E R (1971) *Immigrant pupils in England: The LEA Response* National Foundation for Educational Research: Slough

Townsend, H E R and Brittain, E M (1972) *Organisation in Multi-Racial Schools* National Foundation for Educational Research: Slough

Tremenheere, S (1840) *Report of the Committee of the Council on Education on the State of Elementary Education* HMSO: London

Tsend, Yu-hao (1930) *Modern Chinese Political and Legal Philosophy* Commercial Press: Shanghai

Tucker, G R and Cziko, G A *eds* (1978) The role of evaluation in bilingual education *in* Alatis (1978)

Tufte, V and Myerhoff, B *eds* (1979) *Changing Images of the Family* Yale University Press: New Haven, Conn

Turnbull, C M (1977) *A History of Singapore 1819-1975* Oxford University Press: Kuala Lumpur

Ubale, B (1977) *Equal Opportunities and Public Policy* Ontario Human Rights Commission: Toronto

Vander Touw, C (1979) *English: Second Language, First Priority?* Directorate of Research and Planning, Education Department, South Australia: Sydney

Van de Velde, M and Vandeweghe, W eds (1979) *Sprachstrucker, Individium und Gesellschaft* Akten des 13 Linguistischen Kolloquiums, Gent, 1978 1: 191-200, Max Niemeyer Verlag: Tübingen

Vazquez Calzada, J (1979) Demographic aspects of migration *in* Centro de Estudios Puertorriquenos (1979)

Veenhoven, W A ed (1976) *Case Studies on Human Rights and Fundamental Freedoms: A World Survey* 3 Martinus Nijhoff: The Hague

Veness, T (1962) *School Leavers* Methuen: London

Verma, G K and Bagley, C (1979) *Race, Education and Identity* Macmillan: London

Verma, G K and Bagley, C eds (1981) *Self-Concept, Achievement and Multi-Cultural Education* Macmillan: London

Verma, G K, Bagley, C and Mallick, K (1980) *Illusion and Reality in Indian Secondary Education* Gower Publishing: Farnborough, Hants

Vink, J (1976) Ausserschulische Sozialisationshilfen *in* Hohmann (1976)

Vink, J (1979) Berufliche Bildung ausländischer Jugendlicher *in* Langenohl-Weyer *et al* (1979)

Von der Muhll, G (1971) Education, citizenship and social revolution in Tanzania *in* Prewitt (1971)

Wagenheim, F (1975) *A Survey of Puerto Ricans on the US Mainland in the 1970s* Praeger: New York

Wales, N (1939) *Inside Red China* Doubleday, Doran: New York

Wanjala Welime, J D (1970) Some problems of teaching Swahili at advanced level in Kenya *in* Gorman (1970)

Wax, M and Wax, R (1971) Cultural deprivation as an educational ideology *in* Leacock (1971)

Weinreich, U (1974) *Languages in Contact* Mouton: The Hague

Wenger, C (1981) *Rural Industrialisation: Development and Deprivation* University of Wales Press: Cardiff

Whiteley, W H (1968) Ideal and reality in national language policy: Tanzania *in* Fishman, Ferguson and Das Gupta (1968)

Whiteley, W H (1969) *Swahili: The Rise of a National Language* Methuen: London

Whiteley, W H (1971) Some factors influencing language policies in Eastern Africa *in* Rubin and Jernudd (1971)

Whiteley, W H ed (1971) *Language Use and Social Change: Problems of Multilingualism with special reference to Eastern Africa* International African Institute/Oxford University Press: London

*Whiteley, W H ed (1974) *Language in Kenya* Oxford University Press: Nairobi

Williams, F ed (1970) *Language and Poverty: Perspectives on a Theme* Markham: New York

Williams, F (1976) *Explorations of the Linguistic Attitudes of Teachers* Newbury: Rowley, Mass

Williams, Glyn ed (1978) *Social and Cultural Change in Contemporary Wales* Routledge and Kegan Paul: London

Williams, Gwyn A (1978) *The Merthyr Rising* Croom Helm: London

Williams, S and Morris, J (1977) *Education in Schools: A Consultative Document* (Cmnd 6869) HMSO: London

Williams, T, Clancy, J, Batten, M and Girling-Butcher, S (1980) *School, Work and Career: Seventeen-year olds in Australia* Australian Council for Educational Research, Research Monograph No 6

Willis, P (1977) *Learning to Labour* Saxon House: Farnborough, Hants

Wilson, H (1971) *The Labour Government 1964-70* Weidenfeld and Nicholson/ Michael Joseph: London

Winters, C A (1979) *Mao or Muhammed: Islam in the People's Republic of China* Asian Research Service: Hong Kong

Wirth, L (1945) Problems of minority groups *in* Linton (1945)

Wiseman, S (1968) Educational deprivation and disadvantage *in* Butcher (1968)

Wolfgang, A ed (1975) *Education of Immigrant Students: Issues and Answers* Ontario Institute for Studies in Education: Toronto

Wright, E N (1970) *Student's Background and its Relationship to Class and Programme in School* Research Report 91, Toronto Board of Education: Toronto

Yong Yap and Cotterell, A (1977) *Chinese Civilization from the Ming Republic to Chairman Mao* Book Club Associates: London

Young, M F D ed (1971) *Knowledge and Control* Collier Macmillan: London

Young, R E (1978) Childhood, adolescence and socialization *in* Hunt (1978)

Zubrzycki, J (1976) Cultural pluralism and discrimination in Australia, with special reference to white minority groups *in* Veenhoven (1976)

Section II: Official publications

Association Canadienne d'Education de Langue Française (1978) Pour un plan de développement de l'éducation française au Canada *Revue de l'Association Canadienne d'Education de Langue Française* 7: 1-29

Australian Capital Territory Schools Authority (1979) *Multicultural Education* Working Party, Schools Office

Australian Commonwealth Education Portfolio (1979) *Education in a Multicultural Australia* Australian Government Publishing Service: Canberra

Australian Schools Commission Committee on Multicultural Education (1979) *Education for a Multicultural Society* Australian Government Publishing Service: Canberra

Baden-Württembergisches Arbeitsministerium (1979) Vorläufige Richtlinien des Ministeriums für Arbeit, Gesundheit und Sozialardnung für die Bezuschussung von Massnahmen der Sprachforderung für ausländische Kinder im Vorschulalter mit Mitteln des Landes vom 24.1.79 *Materialien zum Projektbereich 'Ausländische Arbeiter'* 26: 26-9

BMA (1977) *Vorschläge der Bund-Länder-Kommission zur Fortentwicklung einer umfassenden Konzeption der Ausländerbeschaftigungspolitik* Der Bundesminister für Arbeit und Sozialordnung IIa 5-24, 200/22, 28.2.77

BMA (1979) Rahmenvorstellungen für Massnahmen zur Berufsvorbereitung und sozialen Eingliederung junger Ausländer (MBSE) *MSBE-Info* 15: 7-11

BSfA (1979) Bayrisches Staatsministerium für Arbeit und Sozialordnung *Ausländische Arbeitnehmer in Bayern. Bericht 1979 Uber Entwicklung, Situation und Probleme der Ausländerbeschäftingung* Munich

CAD (1978) Institut für Zukunftsforschung/Cooperative Arbeitsdidaktik *Lernstatt im Wohnbezirk. Kommunikationsprojekt mit Ausländern in Berlin-Wedding* Campus: Frankfurt/Main/New York

Canadian Association in Support of the Native Peoples (1976) *And What About Canada's Native Peoples?* Canadian Association in Support of the Native Peoples: Ottawa

Central Statistical Office (1976) *Census of Population 1969* Government Printer: Salisbury, Zimbabwe

Centro de Estudios Puertorriqueños (1979) *Labor Migration under Capitalism: The Puerto Rican Experience* Monthly Review Press: New York

CILT (1976) *Bilingualism and British Education: The Dimensions of Diversity* CILT Reports and Papers 14: 31-47: London

Commission for Racial Equality (1978) *Looking for Work: Black and White School Leavers in Lewisham* HMSO: London

Commonwealth Department of Education (1976) *Report of the Committee on the Teaching of Migrant Languages in Schools* Australian Government Publishing Service: Canberra

Commonwealth Immigration Advisory Council (1960) *The Progress and Assimilation of Migrant Children* The Dovey Report, Australian Government Publishing Service: Canberra

Community Relations Commission (1974) *In-Service Education of Teachers in Multi-Racial Areas* CRC: London

Community Relations Commission (1975) *Participation of Ethnic Minorities in the General Election, October 1974* HMSO: London

Community Relations Commission (1977) *Urban Deprivation, Racial Inequality and Social Policy: A Report by the Community Relations Commission* HMSO: London

Community Relations Council (1978) *Performance of West Indian Children: Cause for Concern: West Indian Pupils in Redbridge* CRC: London

Council of Ministers of Education (1978) *The State of Minority Language Education in the Ten Provinces of Canada* Council of Ministers of Education: Toronto

Department of Education and Science (1972) *The Continuing Needs of Immigrants* Education Survey 14, HMSO: London

Department of Education and Science (1974) *Educational Disadvantage and the Educational Needs of Immigrants* DES: London

Department of Education and Science (1975) *Circular 7/65: The Education of Immigrants* DES: London

Department of Education and Science (1975) *Educational Priority, Volume 3: Curriculum Innovation in London's Educational Priority Areas* (Barnes, J ed) HMSO: London

Department of Education, Australia (1974) *Bilingual Education in Schools in Aboriginal Communities in the Northern Territory* Australian Government Publishing Service: Canberra

Department of Education, Australia (Northern Territory Division) (1978) *Report on the Seventh Meeting of the Bilingual Education Consultative Committee* Darwin

Department of Education, New South Wales (1971) *Migrant Education in New South Wales* Research Bulletin No 34, Division of Research and Planning, Department of Education: Sydney

Department of Education, New South Wales (1972) *Aims and Objectives of Secondary Education in New South Wales* Interim Statement, Directorate of Studies, Department of Education: Sydney

Deutscher Volkshochschulverband eV and Goethe-Institut (1977) *Das Zertifikat Deutsch als Fremdsprache* (2nd ed) Bonn-Bad Godesberg/Munich

Deutsches Institut für Fernstudien an der Universität Tübingen (1980) *Fernstudium Erziehungswissenschaft: Pilot-projekt 'Ausländerkinder in der Schule'* Fernstudienmaterialien für die Lehrerfortbildung, Einheiten A-D: Tübingen (mimeo)

Fédération des francophones hors Québec (1977) *Les héritiers de Lord Durham* Vols 1 and 2 Ottawa

Forschungsverbund (1979) *Gastarbeiter in der Bundesrepublik Deutschland* Ergebnisse des Forschungsverbundes 'Probleme der Ausländerbeschäftigung', Bundesministerium für Forschung und Technologie: Bonn (mimeo)

Gouvernement du Québec (1974) *La Langue Officielle* (Loi 22) Editeur Officiel du Québec: Québec

Gouvernement du Québec (1977) *Charte de la Langue Française* (Loi 101) Editeur Officiel du Québec: Québec

Government of Canada (1969) *Official Languages Act* Queen's Printer: Ottawa

Inner London Education Committee (1977) *Multi-Ethnic Education: Joint Report of the Schools Sub-Committee and Further Education Sub-Committee* Inner London Education Authority: London

International Council for Educational Development (1979) The world educational crisis revisited: interim report on educational inequalities *Newsletter* December

IPAR-Buea (1977) *Report on the Reform of Primary Education* Institute for the Report of Primary Education (IPAR): Buea, Cameroon

Mayor's Committee on Puerto Rican Affairs in New York City (1951) *Puerto Rican Pupils in American Schools* Office of the Mayor: New York

Ministry of Education (1963) *English for Immigrants* HMSO: London

Ministry of Education — Welsh Department (1927) *Welsh in Education and Life: Report of the Departmental Committee* HMSO: London

National Indian Brotherhood (1972) *Indian Control of Indian Education* National Indian Brotherhood: Ottawa

New China News Agency (1969) The educational revolution in the minority areas of China *Hsinhua News Agency* Nov 9

New China News Agency (1970) Central China national minorities build new socialist mountain region through self-reliance *Hsinhua News Agency* April 21

New York City Board of Education (1947) *A Program of Education for Puerto Ricans in New York City* Board of Education: New York

New York City Board of Education (1953) *Teaching Children of Puerto Rican Background in New York City Schools* Board of Education: New York

New York City Board of Education (1959) *The Puerto Rican Study: A Report on the Education and Adjustment of Puerto Rican Pupils in the Public Schools of the City of New York* Board of Education: New York

New York City Board of Education (1965) *Educating Students for whom English is a Second Language: Programs, Activities, and Services* Board of Education: New York

New York City Office of the Mayor (1968) *Puerto Ricans Confront Problems of the Complex Urban Society* Office of the Mayor: New York

Ontario Human Rights Commission (1977) *Life Together: A Report on Human Rights in Ontario* Queen's Printer: Toronto

Organization for Economic Co-operation and Development (1975) *Educational Policy in Canada: External Examiners Report* Canadian Association for Adult Education and the Students Administrative Council, University of Toronto: Toronto

Organization for Economic Co-operation and Development (1976) *Educational Policy and Planning: Transition from School to Work or Further Study in Australia* OECD: Paris

Rhodesian Government (1964, 1974, 1975) *Annual Reports of the Secretary for African Education* Government Printer: Salisbury

Rhodesian Government (1976) *Report on Education* Government Printer: Salisbury

Rhodesian Government (1979) *Annual Report of the Secretary for Education* Government Printer: Salisbury

Rhodesian Government (1979) *Act No 8* Government Printer: Salisbury

Royal Commission on Bilingualism and Biculturalism (1967) Vol 1 General Introduction: *The Official Languages* Queen's Printer: Ottawa

Royal Commission on Bilingualism and Biculturalism (1970) Vol 4 *The Cultural Contribution of the Other Ethnic Groups* Queen's Printer: Ottawa

Royal Institute of International Affairs (1963) *Nationalism* Frank Cass: London

Royal Society of Arts (1980) *Certificates in the Teaching of English as a Second or Foreign Language* Royal Society of Arts: London

Schools Commission Report (1975) *Girls, Schools and Society* Report by a study group to the Schools Commission: London

Schools Council (1972) *Schools Council Project on Teaching English to West Indian Children: Concept 7-9* Schools Council: London

South Australia Department of Education (1979) *Multicultural Education* Curriculum Directorate Information Brochure, Department of Education, Adelaide

Sprachverband (1980) *Massnahmen zur sozialen und beruflichen Eingliederung ausländischer Jugendlicher* (MSBE) Bericht über das Kursjahr 1978-79: Mainz (mimeo)

Statistics Canada (1980) *International and Interprovincial Migration in Canada* Statistics Canada: Ottawa

Toronto Board of Education (1975) *Draft Report of Workgroup on Multicultural Programs* Toronto Board of Education: Toronto

Toronto Board of Education (1976) *The First Report of the Workgroup on Multicultural Programs* Toronto Board of Education: Toronto

Toronto Board of Education (1976) *We are All Immigrants to this Place* Toronto Board of Education: Toronto

Toronto Board of Education (1979) *Report of the Sub-Committee on Race Relations* Publications Department, Toronto Board of Education: Toronto

Unesco (1975) *Intergovernmental Conference on Cultural Policies in Africa. Problems and Prospects. Accra 27 October—6 November 1975* Unesco with the co-operation of the Organization of African Unity (OAU): Paris

Unesco Staff Association (1976) *Cultural Identity* Staff Association Committee on Life-long Education: Paris

Unesco (1977) *Education in Africa in the Light of the Lagos Conference* Educational Studies and Documents 25 Unesco: Paris

United States Immigration Commission (1911) *Report of the Immigration Commission* (41 vols) Government Printing Office: Washington DC

Universities Council for the Education of Teachers (1979) *The PGCE Course and the Training of Specialist Teachers for Secondary Schools* UCET: London

Vink, J and Dederichs, E (1976) Empfehlung der Kultusministerkonferenz vom 8.4.76: Synopse zur KMK-Empfehlung 1971 und Kommentar *Materialien zum Projektbereich 'Ausländische Arbeiter'* 14: 67-81

World Bank (1980) *Education Sector Policy Paper* World Bank: Washington DC

Section III: Articles, periodicals and working papers

Abudarham, S (1980) The role of the speech therapist in the assessment of language-learning potential and proficiency of children with dual language systems or backgrounds *Journal of Multilingual and Multicultural Development* 1 3: 187-206

Anderson, E (1969) The social factors have been ignored *Harvard Educational Review* 39: 581-5

Arens, W (1975) The Waswahili: The social history of an ethnic group *Africa* 45 4: 426-37

Arrighi, G (1970) Labour supplies in historical perspective: a study of the proletarianization of the African peasantry in Rhodesia *Journal of Development Studies* 6

Ashenden, D J, Connell, R W, Dowsett, G and Kessler, S (1980) Class and secondary schooling: some proposals for an approach stressing situations and practices *Discourse* 1: 1-19

Atkinson, J W (1957) Motivational determinants of risk-taking behaviour *Psychological Review* 64: 359-73

Baker, A (1978) Asians are not all alike *New Society* 2.11.78

Ballard, R and Holden, B (1975) The employment of coloured graduates in Britain *New Community* 4: 325-36

Bancroft, G (1979) A place to stand *Multiculturalism* 2: 17-21

Barkowski, H, Harnisch, U and Kumm, S (1979) Kriterian zur Beurteilung von Lahrwerken für den Deutschunterricht mit ausländischen Arbeitern *Deutsch lernen* 4: 3-10

Barkowski, H, Harnisch, U and Kumm, S (1979) Sprachlernen mit Arbeitsemigranten im Wohnbezirk *Deutsch lernen* 1: 5-16

Beeby, C (1980) The thesis of stages fourteen years later *International Review of Education* 26: 4

Bernstein, B (1959) A public language: some sociological implications of a linguistic form *British Journal of Sociology* 10: 311-26

Bloom, B (1969) The Jensen article *Harvard Educational Review* 39: 419-21

Bonacich, E (1972) A theory of ethnic antagonisms: the split labour market *American Sociological Review* 37: 547-59

Bostock, W W (1973) Monolingualism in Australia *Australian Quarterly* 45: 39-52

Bottomley, G (1974) Some Greek sex roles: ideals, expectation and action in Australia and Greece *Australian and New Zealand Journal of Sociology* 10: 8-16

Bourke, C (1980) The future of Aboriginal education in South-eastern Australia *The Educational Magazine* (Victorian Education Department, Melbourne) 37 2: 31-4

Brann, C M B (1975) Standardisation des langues et éducation au Nigeria *African Languages/Langues Africaines* 1: 204-24

Braun, G and Fröhlich, C (1979) Bildungsurlaub 'Deutsch für ausländische Arbeiter': Ein Erfahrungsvericht aus der VHS-Praxis *Deutsch lernen* 1: 17-30

Brittain, E (1976) Multi racial education: teachers' opinions on aspects of school life, Part II *Educational Research* 18: 2

Brumfit, A (1971) The development of a language policy in German East Africa *Journal of the Language Association of Eastern Africa* 2 1: 1-9

Buchignani, N (1977) Bibliography: a review of historical and sociological literature on East Indians in Canada *Canadian Ethnic Studies* 9: 17-31

Bucknall, J R (1976) Strelley: an alternative in aboriginal education *The Aboriginal Child at School* 4 2: 30-3

Bullivant, B M (1976) Social control and migrant education *Australian and New Zealand Journal of Sociology* 12: 174-83

Bullivant, B M (1980) Multiculturalism: no *Education News* 17: 17-29

Chafe, W L (1962) Estimates regarding the present speakers of North American Indian languages *International Journal of American Linguistics* 28: 162-71

Chambers, P (1979) The meaning of community education in college: a comparative discussion *Journal of Further and Higher Education* 3 3: 75-86

Chikombah, C (1980) Education in transition: the educators' problem in Zimbabwe *The Bulletin of the Institute of Education* 16 2: 62-6

Clough, H D (1979) Bradford College: Eric's Latin Quarter *Learn* March 1979: 22-5

Clyne, M G (1977) Some experiences with primary school German in Melbourne: a first report *Babel* 13 2

Clyne, M (1980) Primary school languages and bilingual education: some overseas research and legends *Australian Review of Applied Linguistics* 3: 29-38

Coelho, E (1978) Curriculum change for a multicultural society *Teacher Education* 12: 82-91

Cordasco, F (1973) The children of immigrants in schools: historical analogues of educational deprivation *Journal of Negro Education* 42 3: 44-53

Cordasco, F (1975) Spanish-speaking children in American schools *International Migration Review* 9 3: 379-82

Cordasco, F (1978) Bilingual and bicultural education in American schools: a bibliography of selected references *Bulletin of Bibliography* 35 2: 53-72

Cronbach, L (1969) Heredity, environment and educational policy *Harvard Educational Review* 39: 338-47

Cummins, J (1978) Educational implications of mother-tongue maintenance *Canadian Modern Language Review* 34: 395-416

Cummins, J (1979) Cognitive/academic language proficiency, linguistic interdependence, the optimal age question and some other matters *Working Papers in Bilingualism* 19: 197-205

Cummins, J (1979) Immersion programmes: the Irish experience *International Review of Education* 49: 222-51

Cummins, J and Das, J P (1977) Cognitive processing and reading difficulties: a framework for research *The Alberta Journal of Educational Research* 23: 245-56

Darnell, F (1979) Education among the native peoples of Alaska *Polar Record* 19: 431-46

Davis, M and Goodnow, J J (1977) Problem solving strategies: use by Australian children with Australian and Greek parentage *Journal of Cross-Cultural Psychology* 8: 33-47

De Lemos, M M and Di Leo, P (1978) Literacy in Italian and English of Italian high school students *Ethnic Studies* 2: 1-12

Deosaran, R A (1977) Educational aspirations: individual freedom or social injustice *Interchange* 8: 72-87

Driver, G and Ballard, R (1979) Comparing performance in multi-racial schools *New Community* 11: 2

Eastman, C M (1979) 'Culture-loaded' vocabularies and language resurrection (research note) *Current Anthropology* 20 2: 401-2

Eastman, C M (1979) Language re-introduction: activity and outcome language planning *General Linguistics* 19 3: 99-111

Edwards, J (1981) Critics and criticisms of bilingual education *Modern Language Journal* (in press)

Edwards, J (1981) Bilingual education: facts and values *Canadian Modern Language Review* (in press)

Elliston, I (1978) Is racism increasing in schools? *Multiculturalism* 2: 27-8

Emerson, R (1975) The fate of human rights in the Third World *World Politics* 27 2: 201-26

Evans, G, Georgeff, M and Poole, M E (1980) Training in information selection for communication *Australian Journal of Education* 24: 137-54

Evans, G T and Poole, M E (1975) Relationships between verbal and non-verbal abilities for migrant children of low socio-economic status: similarities and contrasts *Australian Journal of Education* 19: 209-30

Ferguson, C A (1959) Diglossia *Word* 15: 325-40

Fishman, J A (1980) Bilingual education, language planning and English *English World-wide: A Journal of Varieties of English* 1: 11-24

Fishman, J A (1980) Bilingualism and biculturalism as individual and as societal phenomena *Journal of Multilingual and Multicultural Development* 1 1: 3-15

Fishman, J A (1980) Minority language maintenance and the ethnic mother tongue school *The Modern Language Journal* 64 2: 167-72

Fowler, B, Madigan, R and Littlewood, B (1977) Immigrant school-leavers and the search for work *Sociology* 1 Jan 77

Freedman, M (1958) Chinese communities in Southeast Asia: a review article *Pacific Affairs* 31: 300-4

Genesee, F (1978) A longitudinal evaluation of an early immersion school program *Canadian Journal of Education* 3: 31-50

Genesee, F (1979) Scholastic effects of French immersion: an overview after ten years *Interchange* 9: 20-9

Giles, H, Bourhis, R, Trudgill, P and Lewis, A (1974) The imposed norm hypothesis: a validation *Quarterly Journal of Speech* 60: 405-10

Ghosh, R (1978) Ethnic minorities in the school curriculum *Multiculturalism* 2: 24-6

Ghurkan, U, Laqueur, K and Szablewski, P (1979) Unterricht mit nichterwerbstatigen ausländischen Frauen *Deutsch lernen* 1: 31-42

Glazer, N (1979) Affirmative discrimination: where is it going? *International Journal of Comparative Sociology* 20 1-2: 14-30

Gollnick, D M (1980) Multicultural education *Viewpoints in Teaching and Learning* 56: 1

Grant, N (1974) Sexual equality in the Communist world *Compare* 4 1: 24-30

Greco, T, Vasta, E and Smith, R (1977) I get these freaky feelings like I'm splitting into a million pieces: cultural differences in Brisbane, Australia *Ethnic Studies* 1: 17-29

Greeley, A M (1971) The rediscovery of diversity *The Antioch Review* 31: 352-63

Greenland, J (1980) Western education in Burundi 1916-1973: the consequences of instrumentalism *Les Cahiers du CEDAF* (Brussels) 2-3

Guilavogui, G (1975) The basis of the educational reform in the Republic of Guinea *Prospects* 5 4: 435-44

Gupta, Y P (1977) The educational and vocational aspirations of Asian immigrant and English school leavers *British Journal of Sociology* 28: 185-98

Guthrie, (1980) Stages of educational development: Beeby revisited *International Review of Education* 26 4

Halevy, Z and Etsioni-Halevy, E (1974) The 'religious factor' and achievement in education *Comparative Education* 10 3: 193-200

Hamalian, A (1979) National integration in multi-ethnic societies: the differential role of schooling and non-formal educational agencies *Compare* 9: 33-44

Hanf, T *et al* (1975) Education: an obstacle to development? *Comparative Education Review* 19 1: 68-87

Hawkins, J (1978) National minority education in the People's Republic of China *Comparative Education Review* 22 1: 147-61

Head, W A and Lee, J (1978) The Black presence in the Canadian mosaic: discrimination in education *Interchange* 9: 85-92

Heckhausen, H (1977) Achievement motivation and its constructs: a cognitive model *Motivation and Emotion* 1: 283-329

Heidelberger Forschungsprojekt 'Pidgin-Deutsch' (1977) *Die ungesteuerte Erlernung des Deutschen durch spanische und italienische Arbeiter. Eine soziolinguistische Untersuchung* Osnabrück (Osnabrücker Beiträge zur Sprachtheorie, Beiheft 2)

Heyneman, S (1976) Influences on academic achievement: a comparison of results from Uganda and more industrialized societies *Sociology of Education* 49: 3

Heyneman, S (1979) Why impoverished children do well in Ugandan schools *Comparative Education* 15 2: 175-85

Hill, B V (1979) Exploring multicultural education *Education News* 16: 24-8

Holm, N and Japanangka, L (1976) The mathematics of card playing in an Aboriginal community *The Aboriginal Child at School* 4 5: 19-22

Inkeles, A (1960) Soviet nationality theory in perspective *Problems of Communism* 9 May/June 1960: 25-34

Jaggs, B (1975) English is not enough *Education News* 15: 42-4

Jeffcoate, R (1976) Curriculum planning in multi-racial education *Educational Research* 18 3: 192-200

Jensen, A (1969) How much can we boost IQ and scholastic achievement? *Harvard Educational Review* 39: 1-123

Jung, W (1980) Ausländerkinder in Baden-Württemberg: Eine Bestandsaufnahme *Ausländerkinder — Forum für Schule und Sozialpädagogik* 1: 4-20

Kagan, J (1969) Inadequate evidence and illogical conclusions *Harvard Educational Review* 39: 274-7

Khan, V S (1980) The 'mother tongue' of linguistic minorities in multicultural England *Journal of Multilingual and Multicultural Development* 1: 71-88

Kravetz, N (1980) Education of ethnic and national minorities in the USSR: a report on current developments *Comparative Education* 16 1: 13-24

Kuo, E C Y (1979) Measuring communicativity in multilingual societies: the cases of Singapore and West Malaysia *Anthropological Linguistics* 21 7: 328-40

Lal, A (1970) Sinification of ethnic minorities in China *Current Scene* 8 4: 1-25

Lasry, J (1980) Mobilité professionelle chez les immigrants juifs Nord-Africans à Montréal *International Review of Applied Psychology* 29: 17-30

Little, A N (1975) Performance of children from ethnic minority backgrounds in primary schools *Oxford Review of Education* 1: 2

Lupul, M R (1976) The portrayal of Canada's 'other' peoples in senior high school history and social studies text-books in Alberta 1905 to present *Alberta Journal of Educational Research* 22: 1-33

Mabey, C (1981) British literacy *Educational Research* 23: 2

Maijala, H M (1977) Experiences of an immigrant child in Toronto *TESL Talk* 8: 48-52

Markus, R L (1980) Difficulties encountered by Soviet immigrant children in adapting to secondary schools in their new homeland *TESL Talk* 11: 14-25

Mazrui, A (1979) Language policy after Amin *Africa Report* 24 5: 20-2

McQuillan, B (1977) A cross-section of cultures: education week at Harbourfront *Multiculturalism* 1: 13-15

Menk, A-K and Stölting, W (1973) Bilinguale Schulen für Kinder ausländischer Arbeiter *Materialien Deutsch als Fremdsprache* 1: 149-55

Mhina, G (1979) The Tanzanian experience in the use of an African language in education: a case for Swahili *African Affairs/Langues Africaines* 5 2: 63-71

Moulton, R W (1965) Effects of success and failure on level of aspiration as related to achievement motives *Journal of Personality and Social Psychology* 1: 399-406

Müller, H (1979) Ausländische arbeitkinder in der Bundesrepublik Kindheit 1: 169-84

Mulusa, T (1978) Adult Education and Kiswahili *Kenya Journal of Adult Education* 6 2: 18-22

Nagata, J A (1977) Ethnic differentiation within an urban mercantile community in Malaysia *Ethnicity* 4: 4

Noble, T and Ryan, M (1976) What does school mean to the Greek immigrant parent and his child? *Australian Journal of Education* 20: 38-45

Olson, D R (1970) Language and thought: aspects of a cognitive theory of semantics *Psychological Review* 77: 257-73

Orvik, J M (1975) An overview of Alaska native bilingual education *Topics in Culture Learning* 3: 109-24

Palmer, H and Tropper, H (1973) Canadian ethnic studies: historical perspectives and contemporary implications *Interchange* 4: 15-23

Paulston, C B (1979) Bilingual/bicultural education *Review of Research in Education* 6: 186-228

Philp, H W and Kelly, M R (1974) Product and process in cognitive development: some comparative data on the performance of school age children in different cultures *British Journal of Educational Psychology* 3: 248-65

Pike, K L (1979) Social linguistics and bilingual education *System* 7 2: 99-109

Pipes, R (1953) Bolshevik national theory before 1917 *Problems of Communism* 2 (May): 22-7

Platt, J T (1976) Some aspects of language planning in Malaysia *Kivung* 9 1: 3-17

Platt, J T (1976) Speech repertoires and societal domains of Malaysian Chinese *Speech Education* 4 1: 1-23

Platt, J T (1977) A model for polyglossia and multilingualism with special reference to Singapore and Malaysia *Language in Society* 6 3: 361-78

Platt, J T (1977) Code selection in a multilingual-polyglossic society *Talanya* 4: 64-75

Porter, J (1969) Bilingualism and the myths of culture *Canadian Review of Sociology and Anthropology* 6: 111-19

Porter, J (1972) Dilemmas and contradictions of multi-ethnic society *Royal Society of Canada: Transactions* 10: 193-205

Ramcharan, S (1979) East Indian immigration to Canada *Multiculturalism* 2: 14-16

Reich, H H (1979) Deutschlehrer für Gastarbeitkinder: Eine Ubersicht über Aus-bildungsmöglichkeiten in der Bundesrepublik *Deutsch lernen* 3: 3-14

Richman, J (1910) The social needs of the public schools *Forum* 43 2: 161-9

Richmond, A (1974) Language, ethnicity and the problem of identity in a Canadian metropolis *Ethnicity* 1 1: 175-206

Richmond, A H (1976) Black and Asian immigrants in Britain and Canada: some comparisons *Journal of Community Relations Commission* 4: 501-23

Rist, R (1970) Student social class and teacher expectations: the self-fulfilling prophecy in ghetto education *Harvard Educational Review* **40**: 411-51

Rosenthal, R (1973) The Pygmalion effect lives *Psychology Today* **7**: 56-63

Rubin, J (1978) The approach to language planning within the United States *Language Planning Newsletter* **4**: 1 and 3-6 (November)

Rubin, J (1979) The approach to language planning within the United States *Language Planning Newsletter* **5** 1: and 3-6 (February)

Rutter, M L *et al* (1974) Children of West Indian immigrants 1. Rates of behavioural deviance and of psychiatric disorder *Journal of Child Psychology and Psychiatry* **15**: 241-62

Rutter, M L *et al* (1975) Home circumstances and family patterns *Journal of Child Psychology and Psychiatry* **16**: 105-24

Samuda, R J (1980) How are the schools of Ontario coping with a new Canadian population: a report of recent research findings *TESL Talk* **11**: 44-51

Saunders, M (1980) Towards a curriculum for ethnic minority pupils *New Community* **8** 1-2: 76-83

Seidel, H (1979) Ausländische Arbeitnehmer in der Bundesrepublic Deutschland: Ein statistischer Uberblick *Deutsch lernen* **1**: 52-76

Seligman, C, Tucker, G and Lambert, W (1972) The effects of speech style and other attributes on teachers' attitudes towards pupils *Language in Society* **1**: 131-42

Shapson, S and Purbhoo, M (1977) A transition program for Italian children *The Canadian Modern Language Review* **33**: 486-97

Smolicz, J J (1975) Migrant cultures versus Australian school *Education News* **15**: 17-21

Smolicz, J J (1981) Language as core value of culture *RELC* (Regional English Language Centre) *Journal of Applied Linguistics* (Singapore)

Smolicz, J J and Harris, R McL (1977) Ethnic languages in Australia *International Journal of the Sociology of Language* **14**: 89-108

Smolicz, J J and Lean, R (1979) Parental attitudes to cultural and linguistic pluralism in Australia: a humanistic sociological approach *Australian Journal of Education* **23**: 3: 227-49

Smolicz, J J and Secombe, M J (1977) A study of attitudes to the introduction of ethnic languages and cultures in Australian schools *The Australian Journal of Education* **21** 1: 1-24

Smolicz, J J and Wiseman, R (1971) European migrants and their children: integration, assimilation, education *Quarterly Review of Australian Education* **4** (June): 1-44 4 (September): 1-42

Stölting, W (1976) Zur Diskussion über die sprachliche Situation und die Schulbildung der Gasterbeiterkinder *Studium Linguistik* **2**: 73-7

Sue, S (1977) Psychological theory and implications for Asian Americans *The Personnel and Guidance Journal* **55**: 381-9

Swain, M and Cummins, J (1979) Bilingualism, cognitive functioning and education *Language Teaching and Linguistics: Abstracts* **12** 1: 4-18

Swain, M, Lapkin, S and Andrew, C M (forthcoming) Early French immersion later on *Journal of Multilingual and Multicultural Development*

Taft, R (1977) The study of immigrant adjustment: science or just common sense *Ethnic Studies* **1**: 14-19

Thomas, A M (1954) American education and the immigrant *Teachers College Record* **55** 2: 253-67

Tien, Hung-Mao (1974) Sinification of national minorities in China *Current Scene* **12**: 11 (November)

Triandis, H (1974) Psychologists on culture and thought *Reviews in Anthropology* **1**: 484-92

Van Dyck, W C and Arkell, R N (1979) Stereotyping in the classroom *Multiculturalism* **3**: 22-5

Varlaam, A (1974) Educational attainment and behaviour at school *Greater London Intelligence Quarterly* 29 Dec 1974

Vecoli, R (1974) The Italian Americans *The Centre Magazine* 7.8.74: 36-40

Verma, G K (1977) Some effects of curriculum innovation on the racial attitudes of adolescents *International Journal of Intercultural Relations* 1: 67-78

von der Handt, G (1979) Projekt 'Deutsch für ausländische Arbeitnehmer' *Informationsdienst Bildungsarbeit mit ausländischen Arbeitern* 2: 49-50

Webber, R D (1979) An overview of language attitude studies with special reference to teachers' language attitudes *Educational Review* 31 3: 217-32

Weische-Alexa, P (1979) Deutschunterricht mit türkischen Hausfrauen: Ein Bericht aus der Unterrichtspraxis *Deutsch lernen* 1: 43-51

Widgren, J (1975) Recent trends in European migration policies *International Review of Education* 21: 275-85

Wiens, H J (1962) Some of China's thirty five million non-Chinese *Journal of Hong Kong Branch of the Royal Asiatic Society* 2: 54-74

Williams, J (1979) Perspectives on the multi-cultural curriculum *The Social Science Teacher* 8 4: 126-33

Willmot, E (1975) Aboriginal education in Australia *Education News* 15 1: 6-15

Wiseman, R (1971) Integration and attainment of immigrant secondary school students in Adelaide *Australian Journal of Education* 15: 253-9

Wiseman, S (1973) The educational obstacle race: factors that hinder pupil progress *Educational Research* 15: 87-93

Wright, M (1965) Swahili language policy 1890-1940 *Swahili* 25 1: 40-8

Yalden, J (1980) Current approaches to second language teaching in the UK *System* 8 2: 151-6

Zachariev, A (1978) Droits à l'éducation *International Review of Education* 24 3: 263-72

Section IV

Andersson, T and Boyer, M (1978) *Bilingual Schooling in the United States* (2nd ed) National Educational Library Publishers: Austin, Tex
The first edition of this book appeared in 1970, in response to the Bilingual Education Act of 1968. It was of central importance in providing guidance and information on bilingual schooling for educators and teachers involved in implementing the bilingual education projects which multiplied in the 1970s in the United States. The second edition draws on the developments and experience of the 1970s. Early chapters discuss the nature of bilingualism, the history of bilingual schooling in the United States and justifications for bilingual schooling. Two core chapters then deal with the planning and implementation of bilingual programmes. A dozen appendices bring together a range of important documents from different sources, including several influential legal decisions.

Ashworth, M (1975) *Immigrant Children and Canadian Schools* McClelland and Stewart: Toronto
Canada, with its heavy and sustained immigration from an increasingly varied range of countries, has currently in its schools a considerable proportion of immigrant children (perhaps 700,000 in all, though the precise numbers are not known) whose mother tongues are neither of the two 'official' languages, French or English. This book surveys provision for the integration of these minority group children into mainstream, English-medium education in English-speaking Canada. The main data-gathering technique used was a questionnaire administered to teachers of English as a Second Language working in the schools. The author concludes that ESL provision is insufficient; she also reveals a virtual absence of mother tongue teaching for these groups.

Bamgbose, A *ed* (1976) *Mother Tongue Education: The West African Experience*
Unesco/Hodder and Stoughton: Paris and London
This book was commissioned under a Unesco programme to provide a narrative
account of developments taking place in selected countries of West Africa for those
concerned with mother tongue education. Contributions from Sierra Leone and
Dahomey describe situations where preparations are being made for the first introduction of the mother tongue into the school system. One from Ghana describes a
long tradition of mother tongue education, and two from Nigeria describe special
projects, one introducing a major language as a medium of instruction throughout
primary education, and the other introducing several smaller languages into the
schools.

Brown, D M (1979) *Mother Tongue to English: The Young Child in the Multicultural*
School Cambridge University Press: Cambridge
This book, written by an experienced teacher in multicultural primary schools in
Britain, and illustrated with much anecdotal material, is in three parts. The first part
provides a general introduction to the problems and needs of young children from
ethnic minorities in such schools. The second part reports on detailed case studies of
two Bengali mother tongue children placed in normal infant school classes. The
children were observed throughout their first term of schooling; the case for the
placing of such children in specialized language groups is argued on the basis of these
studies. The third part of the book makes extensive practical recommendations for
teachers in multicultural primary schools.

Claydon, L, Knight, T, and Rado, M (1977) *Curriculum and Culture: Schooling in a*
Pluralistic Society Allen and Unwin: Hornsby, New South Wales
This book examines the phenomenon of cultural pluralism and the challenges it
presents to the institutions of schooling in Australian society. Several theoretical
chapters are complemented by data drawn from an experimental project, the Multilingual Project, which provided parallel social studies texts for use with the 10-14 age
group in English and in a range of minority languages of European origin. These texts
were used in multi-ethnic classrooms by minority mother tongue children, with
considerable success according to the authors. Examples of the material, and of
pupils' reactions, are given.

Cordasco, F (1976) *Bilingual Schooling in the United States: A Sourcebook for*
Educational Personnel McGraw-Hill: New York
This collection is intended primarily as a textbook for use in the pre- and in-service
training of teachers for bilingual education. It brings together two dozen articles
written in the past ten years or so, by a range of American authors, including some of
those most influential in the area. Part I deals with the historical background; Part II
provides a range of definitions of bilingualism and a typology of bilingual education;
Part III introduces a more general sociolinguistic analysis; and Part IV surveys current
programmes and practices in bilingual education in the United States, and sketches
the parameters of staff training. The appendices provide an overview of relevant court
decisions and legislation, and a corpus of abstracts describing representative projects.

de Grève, M and Rosseel, E *eds* (1977) *Problèmes Linguistiques des Enfants de*
Travailleurs Migrants AIMAV-Didier: Brussels
In 1976 a seminar was held by AIMAV, in collaboration with the Commission of the
EEC, to consider the 'linguistic problems' facing children of immigrant workers. This
book contains 15 papers presented at the seminar, in French, English and Italian.
They cover a diversity of areas, including questions of school organization, the
methodology of linguistic research, the process of language acquisition, the socio-
cultural situation of immigrant children, and various practical experiments. The
introduction outlines the general conclusions arising from seminar discussions: the
impossibility of dissociating the immigrants' language from the wider culture; the
need to provide specialist instruction in the language of the host country, as well as in
the mother tongue, within the school system; the need for specialist teacher training;
the need for continuing education for adult immigrants; and the need for multi-

cultural education to embrace the host majority as well as the immigrant minority.

Edwards, J R (1979) *Language and Disadvantage* Edward Arnold: London
This book deals with the central notion of 'disadvantage' in speech and language, principally as it affects school-age children. The author rejects theories of linguistic deficiency, and argues that the difficulties faced by speakers of non-standard language varieties derive essentially from social attitudes to speech. Any solution must lie in the moderation or eventual elimination of prejudicial attitudes towards certain speech styles. One chapter is devoted to a consideration of minority language or dialect groups, which the author considers to be special cases within this broader category of linguistic disadvantage.

Edwards, V K (1979) *The West Indian Language Issue in British Schools: Challenges and Responses* Routledge and Kegan Paul: London
The performance of West Indian children in British schools has become a matter of concern. It is widely believed that an important factor in these children's relative failure is the language they use, West Indian Creole. This book provides an account of this variety of English, stressing its adequacy as a linguistic system and emphasizing the importance, for teachers of West Indian children, of familiarity with Creole. A number of innovatory approaches to language are discussed, all based on the assumption that the soundest approach to teaching Standard English is to show that different dialects are accepted and appreciated by the school.

Epstein, N (1977) *Language Ethnicity and the Schools: Policy Alternatives for Bilingual-Bicultural Education* Institute for Educational Leadership, George Washington University: Washington DC
A sceptical examination of current bilingual education policies in the United States makes up the main part of this book. The author points out the relative stress on minority languages to the neglect of minority cultures in current American projects. He also points out the lack of clear evidence to date that bilingual education programmes have produced enhanced academic or English language attainment of minority children. He perceives a policy drift, with confusion between the contradictory goals of transitional bilingualism on the one hand, and minority language maintenance on the other, and calls for a clarification of the objectives for which federal funds are being spent. The book includes an equally polemical rejoinder from Jose Cardenas, an advocate of bilingual education, who stresses the limited character of current programmes.

Fuchs, E and Havighurst, R J (1972) *To Live on This Earth* Doubleday (Anchor Books): New York
This book reports understandings and conclusions about American Indian education which the authors have recorded over a considerable period of observation and study of Indian children and societies and of education in general. It draws upon the National Study of American Indian Education conducted in 1968-70. The book begins by describing contemporary Indian society, and considers in detail levels of ability and attainment of Indian children and young people. The schooling provided for them is described in terms of organization and curriculum, together with the perceptions of such schooling among Indian community members. Some innovatory schemes which involve Indians themselves in the control and administration of education are favourably discussed.

Gaarder, A B (1977) *Bilingual Schooling and the Survival of Spanish in the United States* Newbury House: Rowley, Mass
This book is a collection of essays written over a ten-year period. They relate to two broad themes: bilingual schooling, and the role and prospects of the Spanish language in the United States. Topics include, for bilingual schooling, the rationale, school organization, teaching methods, preparation of teachers and relationships with the community. For the Spanish language they include the relationship of dialects to the standard language, the self-destructive nature of collective bilingualism, cultural pluralism, and the possibilities of establishing a stable diglossic relationship between

Spanish and English. Throughout the writer raises the question of whether Spanish speakers in the US are sufficiently loyal to their language and culture to maintain them, or whether bilingual schooling is only a short-term expedient aimed at social justice and eventual cultural integration.

Giles, H ed (1977) *Language, Ethnicity and Intergroup Relations* Academic Press: London

The content of this book is concerned with the inter-relationships between the three topics of the title. A substantial proportion of the 13 papers report on experiments carried out within a social psychological framework, mapping the linguistic attitudes of a variety of ethnic groups. An article by J R Edwards looks at the relationship between ethnic identity and bilingual education. He argues that effective bilingual/ bicultural education should be restricted to those groups whose desires and needs it truly reflects; that most current bilingual education programmes are in effect compensatory programmes for the academically disadvantaged; and that cultural pluralism is likely to be better served by a new approach to bilingual education which would not be tied to ideas of compensation. Another article by Verdoodt argues the case for mother tongue teaching for the children of immigrant workers in a European context.

Giles, H and Saint-Jacques, B eds (1979) *Language and Ethnic Relations* Pergamon: Oxford

This book is a collection of 17 papers from a range of academic perspectives (social psychology, sociolinguistics, economics, politics and demography). One group of papers focuses on the different dynamic relationships that operate between language and ethnicity, and the ways in which members of an ethnic group are heterogeneous. Another group examines the nature of inter- and intra-ethnic linguistic interaction. The concluding paper, co-authored by Giles, proposes that language should be studied not only as a barometer of ethnic relations but also as a creator and definer of them.

Glazer, N and Moynihan, D P eds (1975) *Ethnicity: Theory and Experience* Harvard University Press: Cambridge, Mass

The joint editors of this book claim that ethnic identity has become more salient, ethnic self-assertion stronger, and ethnic conflict more marked, on an international scale, in the past 20 years. They argue that whereas ethnic groups were formerly seen as survivals from an earlier age, they are better understood as forms of social life capable of renewing and transforming themselves; and they therefore question the widely held assumption that such groups are destined eventually to disappear through assimilation into the majority social group. To support this argument the editors have assembled half a dozen theoretical essays on ethnicity, and 11 accounts of how the phenomenon currently expresses itself in a variety of nations and parts of the world, including China, India and the Soviet Union.

Hawes, H (1979) *Curriculum and Reality in African Primary Schools* Longman: London

This book provides a general survey of the primary school curriculum in ten English-speaking African countries. A mass of information is presented on the structure and content of the curriculum (official and actual), strategies used for curriculum development, and the implementation of innovations. The trend towards the use of African languages as the medium of instruction is documented. The focus of the book is on the educational problems faced by developing countries as national units; however, among his recommendations for change the author advocates greater flexibility in the primary school curriculum to suit regional or local contexts.

Hornby, P A ed (1977) *Bilingualism: Psychological, Social and Educational Implications* Academic Press: New York

The theoretical papers in this book (presented originally at an academic conference) can be fitted into three general themes: the cognitive and social consequences of bilingualism for the individual, bilingual communities, and the development and maintenance of language diversity in society. Important papers by Lambert and Ben-Zeev rehearse by now well-established criticisms of the early research tradition which claimed the existence of a universal negative relationship between bilingualism and intelligence. These papers reflect the contemporary emphasis on the importance of sociolinguistic factors in understanding bilingualism, and in particular that of the social standing of the languages in question. The editor Hornby consequently suggests different educational strategies for children from minority and majority language groups in bilingual settings. He sees the former benefiting most from mother tongue education, the latter from second (minority) language education.

Kang, T S ed (1979) *Nationalism and the Crises of Ethnic Minorities in Asia* Greenwood Press: Westport, Conn
This collection of articles by American sociologists consists in the main of a set of case studies of ethnic relations in Asia. Current theories of ethnic group relations are reviewed, with particular emphasis on the application of these theories to Asiatic settings. Existing ethnic group relations in Asian countries, and the life patterns of Asian ethnic groups, are described; discrimination and inter-group conflict are examined; and Asian ethnic relations are compared with Western experience. Most of the case studies contain references to educational policies and problems within the more general accounts of the present situation of particular ethnic groups.

Kloss, H (1977) *The American Bilingual Tradition* Newbury House: Rowley, Mass
This is an updated version of a history of American linguistic policy, first published in German in 1963. Early chapters outline the ethno-linguistic background, and describe the extent to which the central government has in the past made use of languages other than English. The main substance of the book consists in detailed accounts of the historical evolution of what the author calls 'toleration-oriented' minority rights, and 'promotive' minority rights. The last of these accounts takes in outlying American possessions as well as the mainland of the United States. A mass of statistical information is provided throughout.

Kotey, P F A and Der-Houssikian, H eds (1977) *Language and Linguistic Problems in Africa* Hornbeam Press: Columbia, SC
This volume contains the proceedings of the Seventh Conference on African Linguistics, 36 papers in all. Three sections of the book deal with general linguistic topics (phonology, syntax and historical linguistics). The fourth section deals with language policies and includes several articles referring to vernacular languages in education. That by Bokamba and Tlou argues that the democratization of educational access necessitates increased mother tongue education.

Lambert, W E and Tucker, G R (1972) *Bilingual Education of Children: The St Lambert Experiment* Newbury House: Rowley, Mass
This book, by now a 'classic' in the area, has been highly influential in the development of the more positive attitudes towards bilingual education which have been apparent in the 1970s. It describes a community-based Canadian project, aimed at developing native-like skills in a second language by having that language used as the main medium of instruction. The progress of two groups of children through a second-language-medium programme was monitored on many dimensions including linguistic, cognitive and attitudinal development. The results were generally favourable to the experiment; the authors conclude that in any community with a commitment to bilingualism priority for early schooling can and should be given to the language otherwise least likely to be developed.

Little, A and Willey, R (1981) *Multi-ethnic Education: The Way Forward* Schools Council Pamphlet 18, Schools Council: London
This pamphlet outlines the main findings of a research project set up in 1978 by the Schools Council. Its object was to survey current provision, and to assess priorities for action, in relation to education for the 11-16 age group in a multi-ethnic society. On the basis of a survey of local education authorities and a sample of secondary

schools in England and Wales, the researchers argue that the only large-scale response to the perceived special needs of minority ethnic groups has been the provision of basic ESL teaching. Continuation/advanced ESL, the particular needs of children of West Indian origin, and mother tongue teaching, are identified as special needs as yet inadequately provided for. The report also deals with the need for reappraisal of the school curriculum as a whole to make it relevant to all pupils in a multi-ethnic society, both in multiracial schools and in schools with few or no minority ethnic group pupils.

Marjoribanks, K (1980) *Ethnic Families and Children's Achievements* Allen and
    Unwin: Sydney
The inequality of academic achievement of children from different social status and ethnic groups is one of the most complex problems confronting educators. This book reports on a research study addressing this issue, carried out in an Australian setting. An examination was made of relations between the family learning environments, attitudes to school, and academic performance of 11-year-old children from the four largest Australian ethnic groups, differentiated by social class. Research evidence was collected by semi-structured interview, attitude questionnaire, and intelligence and academic attainment tests. The author concluded that major changes in family, neighbourhood and school environments were required for any significant reduction of differences in ethnic group achievement. He recommends ESL assistance for the parents of ethnic families, and increased provision of minority-language teaching in schools.

Martin, J I (1978) *The Migrant Presence: Australian Responses 1947-1977* Allen and
    Unwin: Sydney
This book reviews the responses of selected Australian institutions to changes in the population brought about by the immigration programme pursued since the end of the Second World War. Three areas are covered: education (two chapters), health services (two chapters), and trade unions. The author says that education is the only clearly identifiable area in which there has been a comprehensive nation-wide response to the presence of non-English-speaking immigrants in Australia. For adult immigrants education has always meant simply learning English. The thrust of child immigrant education has been and still is the same, although there is now an accumulation of challenges to English-dominated approaches. Several different (and to a degree incompatible) concepts of immigrant education now compete for legitimacy and resources. The author is sceptical about the 'cultural pluralist' model; she says that the thesis of cultural pluralism rests on the doubtful assumptions that ethnic culture can be sustained without ethnic communities and that a culturally diverse society is different from a structurally pluralist one.

Murphree, M W, Cheater, G, Dorsey, B J and Mothobi, B D (1975) *Education, Race
    and Employment in Rhodesia* ARTCA: Salisbury
This book reports on a large-scale research study carried out in Rhodesia in the early 1970s. The first part of the study was concerned with Black school-leavers at the Form IV and Form VI levels, their background, aspirations, expectations, academic achievement and subsequent employment experience. The second part of the study examined the occupational structure into which the school-leavers sought to move, with particular reference to the constraints imposed by general government policy and managerial practice on the efficient use of the human resource potential which they represented. The survey revealed uniformly high occupational aspirations among the Black secondary school students; in the post-school study, however, a large majority of the group were found to be unemployed or under-employed. In addition to documenting the situation in the early 1970s the book provides background historical information on the development of African education in Rhodesia.

Perren, G E *ed* (1976) *Bilingualism and British Education: The Dimensions of
    Diversity* CILT Reports and Papers 14, CILT: London
The papers collected in this volume originated from a conference organized by the

Centre for Information on Language Teaching and Research in 1976. A paper by Campbell-Platt attempts to estimate the current size of minority language communities in Britain, in the virtual absence of official statistics on this topic. One by Khan reviews these communities' own provision for language maintenance, through 'mother tongue schools' outside the state education system. Three papers review the position of Welsh, which by contrast with almost all other minority languages enjoys a secure place within the state schools; but taken as a whole the papers clearly reflect a continuing lack of commitment in British education to the general introduction of minority languages within the schools, with practical difficulties and lack of community support as the main stated obstacles.

Sharp, D (1973) *Language in Bilingual Communities* Edward Arnold: London
This book, from the series *Explorations in Language Study* edited by Doughty and Thornton, is intended for teachers and trainee teachers. The author aims to clarify some of the issues involved in language teaching and learning in bilingual communities, taking Wales as an example for detailed examination. After an introductory outline of the language situation in Wales, and consideration of the wide variety of linguistic options facing the individual in a bilingual community, the second half of the book is devoted to educational issues. Goals and techniques for first and second language teaching and learning are discussed, taking into account the differing social status of the dominant and minority languages. The book concludes with proposals for strengthening the language education of teachers for bilingual communities.

Sharp, D, Thomas, B, Price, E, Francis, G and Davies, I (1973) *Attitudes to Welsh and English in the Schools of Wales* Schools Council Research Studies, Macmillan Education: Basingstoke and London
This book reports on a large-scale research study carried out in Welsh schools in the late 1960s. Several thousand children at three different age levels, drawn from areas of Wales having different proportions of Welsh speakers, constituted the research sample. Specially-constructed attitude scales, and Welsh and English attainment tests, were administered to the children. The study found that linguistic background is the most important source of variation of attitude to both languages (eg a Welsh background making for favourable attitudes towards Welsh). Even in the strongest Welsh areas attainment in English equalled that in non-Welsh areas. The book also contains information on the extent of provision of Welsh-medium instruction, as well as the teaching of Welsh as the first and second language, in the schools of Wales.

Skutnabb-Kangas, T and Toukomaa, P (1976) *Teaching Migrant Children's Mother Tongue and Learning the Language of the Host Country in the Context of the Socio-cultural Situation of the Migrant Family* Tutkimuksia Research Reports 15, Department of Sociology and Social Psychology, University of Tampere: Finland
In this research report the authors claimed that children of Finnish immigrant workers in Sweden tended to be characterized by 'semi-lingualism', ie their skills in both Finnish and Swedish (as measured by standardized tests) were considerably below Finnish and Swedish norms. The extent to which the mother tongue had been developed prior to contact with Swedish was strongly related to how well Swedish was learned. Children who migrated at age ten maintained a level of Finnish close to Finnish students in Finland and achieved Swedish language skills comparable to those of Swedes. However, children who were seven to eight years of age when they moved to Sweden or who moved before starting school were most likely to achieve low levels of literacy skills in both languages. Skutnabb-Kangas and Toukomaa argue on the basis of these results that the minority child's first language has functional significance in the developmental process and should be reinforced by the school.

Smolicz, J J (1979) *Culture and Education in a Plural Society* Curriculum Development Centre: Canberra
The first part of this book makes a systematic examination of humanistic sociological theory and its societal and educational implications. It is argued that 'enculturation' takes place mainly in the family and the school. The child's rejection or acceptance

of his ethnic cultural heritage is seen as largely dependent on the role which the school assumes in a plural society, and whether it acts as an agency for the inculcation of the values of the dominant ethnic group alone or strives for a culturally pluralist solution. The author is an advocate of 'internal' cultural pluralism, ie a pluralism internalized within each member of society, rather than a form which encapsulates individuals within their own particular culture. This principle is applied in the concrete educational recommendations outlined in the final chapter, for the Australian context.

Spolsky, B and Cooper, R L *eds* (1978) *Case Studies in Bilingual Education* Newbury
   House: Rowley, Mass
This book is a collection of 15 papers, each providing a general introduction to the bilingual education policy of a particular nation or language group. The first eight papers review the national policies of Belgium, Canada, China, India, New Zealand and the countries of Oceania, South Africa, the Soviet Union, and Wales. The second part of the book includes accounts relating to several linguistic minorities within the USA, the Chinese outside China, Caribbean creoles, and Kiswahili. The book contains a great deal of information at a macrosociolinguistic level; while some of the situations described are relatively well-known, the article on China in particular opens up an area not generally familiar.

Whiteley, W H *ed* (1974) *Language in Kenya* Oxford University Press: Nairobi
This substantial book is one of a series arising from the Survey of Language Use and Language Teaching in East Africa. Each volume in the series deals with the linguistic situation in a single country; that on Kenya has been selected to represent the series as a whole, and the others provide similar information in relation to Uganda, Tanzania etc.

   The book is in three parts. The first deals with the present complex language situation, and the distribution and classification of Kenya's African and Asian languages. Part Two is devoted to a number of detailed studies of language use, and Part Three to language in education. The editor points to the striking fact that generations of educators have advocated the use of the vernacular in early education, only to discover that their recommendations were diluted by the practical difficulties of implementation.

Biographical notes
on contributors and editors

Brandon J Ashworth (Chapter 15) graduated from York University in 1979 with honours in psychology, and is currently a research assistant on the project concerned with the occupational adaptation of ethnic minority adolescents in Britain (under the direction of Dr G K Verma). His research interests include achievement motivation and inter-ethnic perception.

George Bernstein (Chapter 11) taught Hispanic students in New York City public schools from 1958 to 1966. During the years 1959 to 1962, he also directed a volunteer course, Basic English for Adults, in Spanish Harlem. In the years 1967 to 1969, he was active at Montclair State College (NJ) in programmes for preparing teachers for New Jersey schools with Hispanic and other minority groups, and helping such pupils when they arrived at the Montclair College campus. He has taught numerous courses which focused on Hispanic communities and their educational needs. He is presently a staff member of the Bilingual Education Program and School of Education Coordinator of the Latin American Area Studies Program at Montclair State College.

Joti Bhatnagar (Chapter 14) is Professor of Education at Concordia University, Montreal, Canada. After obtaining his BSc and LLB degrees from Agra University, India, he undertook his postgraduate studies at the Institute of Education, University of London where he obtained an MA and a PhD. He has taught at school and university levels in India, Britain, Canada and Australia. His main interests include the education of minorities and immigrants, cross-cultural education, part-time education and the social psychology of education. He has published a book *Immigrants at School*, edited another book *Educating Immigrants*, and has written chapters in several books published in England, the Netherlands and India. He has written numerous articles in professional journals, popular newspapers and magazines. He has organized symposia at major national and international conferences such as the International Congress of Psychology, the International Congress of Applied Psychology, the International Congress of Cross-Cultural Psychology, and the International Congress on Education. He is an active member of the Canadian Society for Study of Education. As an immigrant himself, the education of immigrants is an area of immense personal and professional interest to him. He has supervised several theses in this field, and is currently working on a book on the problems of minority group education in Canada.

Peter Chambers (Chapter 21) is the Vice-Principal and Director of Academic Planning at Bradford College. After teaching in the army and in Leicester, he was involved in teacher education in Birmingham and Walsall and in Adult Education in Northampton before taking up his present post. His experience with the Council for National Academic Awards and as Head of an Education Department led him to emphasize the grounding of educational theory in the educative process. This concern to develop professional forms of knowledge in response to actual practice in schools highlighted the need to develop a teacher education curriculum for a multi-ethnic society. The community commitment of Bradford was the logical focus of this work. His published writings include work on the nature of teacher training, educational theory, non-verbal communication, sensitivity training, professional studies, teacher motivation, research in education, pupils' rights and community education.

Francesco Cordasco (Chapter 11), a cultural historian and sociologist, is a professor of education at Montclair State College, and has taught at New York University, the City University of New York, Long Island University, and the University of Puerto Rico. He has served as a consultant to the Migration Division, Commonwealth of Puerto Rico, to the United States Office of Education, and to federal, state and community anti-poverty programmes. He is the author of books on ethnic communities in the United States, immigrant children, urban education, educational sociology, and bilingual schooling.

Alison d'Anglejan (Chapter 5), a Canadian, is Associate Professor in the Faculty of Education at the Université de Montréal. Her own childhood experience of being educated in a second language stimulated an interest in bilingualism which led to a PhD in psycholinguistics at McGill University. Her published work includes studies in the cognitive and social aspects of language learning and in language policy and language education.

Betty Jo Dorsey (Chapter 13) is a senior lecturer in the sociology of education at the University of Zimbabwe, where she has been on the staff since 1967. She has also been a research associate at St Antony's College, Oxford. She has conducted research on the education, aspirations and employment of school-leavers in Botswana, Britain and Zimbabwe, and has published numerous articles on this topic. Her study 'The African secondary school leaver' *in* Murphree, M W *ed* (1975) *Education, Race and Employment* (ARTCA: Salisbury) is the most extensive published sociological analysis of education in Zimbabwe. She is currently engaged in further research on this topic and in the development of distance teaching techniques for the in-service training of teachers in Zimbabwe.

David Dunn and Anjali Purewal (Chapter 20) are research fellows in the Department of Education, University of Keele, England. They are currently involved in a project funded by the Department of Education and Science on in-service teacher education in a multi-racial society.

Carol M Eastman (Chapter 18) is Professor of Anthropology and Adjunct Professor of Linguistics at the University of Washington, Seattle. Her special interests are in the Swahili language of East Africa (its dialects, literature, language policy) and in analysing the Haida language (an American Indian language of the North West Coast of North America), a linguistic isolate. Her work with Haida, a language which has undergone considerable linguistic erosion and which is no longer used for general communication, led to the idea of developing such languages as 'culture' languages rather than reviving them for general use. Professor Eastman is the author of *Aspects of Language and Culture* (Chandler and Sharp: San Francisco, 1975), *Linguistic Theory and Language Description* (J B Lippincott: Philadelphia, 1978) and is completing a book on language planning entitled *Language Sense: An Introduction to Language Policy, Planning and Choice* (Chandler and Sharp: San Francisco, forthcoming).

John Edwards (Chapter 2) is Associate Professor in the Department of Psychology at St Francis Xavier University, Antigonish, Nova Scotia. Born in Southampton, England, he is a graduate of McGill University, Montreal, and took his PhD in 1974.

Before taking up his present position he was a research fellow at the Educational Research Centre, St Patrick's College, Dublin. He is the author of *Language and Disadvantage* (Edward Arnold: London and Elsevier: New York, 1979), *The Irish Language: An Annotated Sociolinguistic Bibliography* (in press), and is the editor of *The Social Psychology of Reading* (in press). He is presently engaged upon two other books of a sociolinguistic nature. Dr Edwards' research interests include the problems of disadvantaged children, bilingual education, and ethnicity and ethnic group relations; he has published articles and chapters on these and other topics. He is currently investigating ethnic group relations among the White, Black and Acàdian populations of north-eastern Nova Scotia.

John Eggleston (Chapter 20) is Professor of Education and head of the Education Department at the University of Keele, England. He is Chairman of the Editorial Board of the *European Journal of Education*, and currently consultant to OECD projects on adolescence and basic education. He is also a member of the Council of Europe working party on the diversification of tertiary education in Southern Europe. He is director of the Department of Education and Science project on teacher training for multicultural education and is the author of many books and papers, including *The Ecology of the School, The Sociology of the School Curriculum, Teacher Decision Making* and *School-Based Curriculum Development*.

Nigel Grant (Chapter 4) was born in Glasgow in 1932, and was educated at Inverness Royal Academy and Glasgow University, where he studied English. After teacher training and military service, he taught in Glasgow schools, took the MEd degree, and was appointed lecturer at Jordanhill College of Education in 1960. In 1965 he moved to the University of Edinburgh, where he developed comparative education courses, pursued research (PhD 1969), and became Reader and Head of the Department of Educational Studies. He returned to the University of Glasgow in 1978 on appointment to the Chair of Education. Other commitments have included chairmanship of the British Section of the Comparative Education Society in Europe and the Scottish Educational Research Association, and four years as editor of *Comparative Education*. He has lectured in the USA, Canada, Denmark, Germany, Ireland and Egypt, and Poland, and has conducted field studies there and elsewhere in Western Europe, the USSR and Eastern Europe. Writings include various papers on comparative education, *Soviet Education* (Penguin, 1979), *Society, Schools and Progress in Eastern Europe* (Pergamon, 1969) and, with R E Bell, *A Mythology of British Education* and *Patterns of Education in the British Isles*. He is currently engaged in further study of the education of national minorities, including Britain and Ireland, and on an international study of the functioning of educational systems.

Jeremy Greenland (Chapter 7) is a research fellow at Bristol University School of Education, directing a survey of the in-service training of primary school teachers in Anglophone Africa. He was assistant editor of the *International Review of Education* 1978-79. Before that he developed curriculum for English language and principles of education courses at Buea in Cameroon, and taught at teacher training institutions in Burundi. His doctoral dissertation was on the evolution of western education in Burundi.

Ingeborg Gutfleisch and Bert-Olaf Rieck (Chapter 22) worked from 1974 to 1979 on a research project on the natural acquisition of German by Spanish and Italian immigrant workers in West Germany. In addition, they taught German courses for immigrant workers. At present, they are working on a longitudinal study of natural second language acquisition by adults. They have published extensively, both in English and in German.

Arpi Hamalian (Chapter 14) is Assistant Professor in Educational Studies and Chairman of the Department of Education at Concordia University, Montreal. After receiving her BBA degree in Business Administration and Economics and MA degrees in Sociology and Anthropology from the American University of Beirut, Lebanon, she pursued her doctoral studies at the University of Wisconsin, Madison, in Educational Policy Studies. Her main areas of interest in education are: education and multiculturalism, the education of immigrants and minorities, political socialization and literacy, and higher education. Areas of the world where she has studied, taught and conducted research are: the Middle East, the Near East, Europe, the United States and Canada. She has published articles on anthropology, social networks and informal education; the political education of economic élites; professoral subcultures; pupil control ideology; and educational policy in multi-ethnic societies. She is an active member of several anthropological and educational associations, a member of the editorial board of *Canadian and International Education* and editor of the *Newsletter of the Comparative and International Education Society of Canada.*

Eric Hoyle (Consultant Editor) has been Professor of Education at the University of Bristol since 1971. His previous posts included teaching in two secondary schools, a college of education and a university. His interests and published works are in the areas of educational administration, the process of innovation, the professional development of teachers and the relationship between research and policy.

He is also interested in the sociology of knowledge and the sociological study of organizations and of the professions. He was founding co-editor of *Research in Education* and is on the editorial boards of a number of other journals including the *British Journal of Teacher Education.* He was research consultant to the Donnison Commission on direct grant schools, vice-chairman of the Educational Research Board of the Social Science Research Council and is currently a member of the Executive Committee of the Universities Council for the Education of Teachers and a co-opted member of Avon Education Committee. He has lectured in various colleges and universities in Africa, Australia, North America and Malaysia.

Agnes McMahon (Bibliography) has been a research assistant in the University of Bristol School of Education since 1976 when she joined the evaluation team for the Teacher Induction Pilot Scheme (TIPS) Project. She is currently working on the dissemination phase of this project, one aspect of which involves the production of induction handbooks for use by school and LEA personnel. Prior to this she taught history in secondary schools in London and then moved to Dublin where she was a member of the Humanities team in the Curriculum Development Unit in Trinity College. During this period she was a member of various writing teams and edited a unit of materials on Celtic Ireland.

Jacquetta Megarry (Series Editor) is the Depute Director of the Scottish Microelectronics Development Programme, a government-funded agency which is encouraging the use of microcomputers in Scottish education. She was previously a lecturer at Jordanhill College of Education (1973-80) where she contributed to pre-service and in-service training of teachers for primary, secondary and further education in the departments of education and audio-visual media. In her last year at Jordanhill she held a small grant from the Equal Opportunities Commission to investigate gender-typing in Scottish education.

She has also held a variety of posts, both in teaching (mainly in secondary schools) and in research and development (on alternative approaches to science teaching in the Highlands and Islands and on computer-based learning in the north of England). She has published extensively in academic journals and has designed a range of distance learning materials. Her editing has included the establishment of the journal *Simulation/Games for Learning* and a number of related books (on behalf of the Society for Academic Gaming and Simulation in Education and Training) as well as the *World Yearbook of Education* (since 1978).

Her links with British minorities (Welsh and Irish by birth and Scots by association) contributed to an interest in the education of minorities which was enhanced by living in Glasgow and travelling extensively in Europe, North America and the Soviet Union, and further stimulated by regular visiting professorships at Concordia University in cosmopolitan Montreal.

Stanley Nisbet (Associate Editor) retired from the Chair of Education at the University of Glasgow in 1978. Starting his professional life as a classics teacher he was caught up in the vigorous psychometric activity at Moray House in Edinburgh under Godfrey Thomson, and his early work was in this field. After five years of wartime service in the RAF, partly spent in its Training Research Branch, and a short spell in the University of Manchester, he became Professor of Education at Queen's University, Belfast and was involved in some of the post-war educational developments in Northern Ireland. From 1951 to 1978 he was Professor of Education at the University of Glasgow, holding various administrative posts in the University (eg Dean of the Faculty of Arts, 1965-67) and serving on many bodies outside the University (eg the Scottish Council for Research in Education). His teaching was mainly on educational theory, curriculum study (in 1957 he wrote one of the earliest books in this field) and comparative education (with a special interest in Germany and the USSR). Much of his writing has consisted of contributions to official publications. Since his retirement he has participated in projects on a number of subjects, including home-school co-operation in the EEC countries and the monitoring of in-service courses for primary school teachers.

James Orvik (Chapter 17) is Associate Professor of Education at the Center for Cross-Cultural Studies, University of Alaska, Fairbanks. He received an MS in clinical psychology from San Diego State University in 1965, and a PhD in social-personality psychology from the University of Colorado in 1970. Since coming to the University of Alaska in 1969 he has developed research interests in bilingual education, teaching performance in rural schools, rural telecommunications, and the social psychology of language. In 1979, Dr Orvik studied at the Scott Polar Research Institute, Cambridge University, under an award from the Ford Foundation. While at Cambridge he pursued a variety of topics regarding the education of indigenous minorities in the circumpolar north.

John Platt (Chapter 10) was born in Singapore and, after a period in England, completed his secondary education at St Andrew's School. His tertiary education has been in Australia, firstly at the University of Adelaide and then at Monash University. His Monash University MA thesis, *An Outline Grammar of the Gugada Dialect* on an Australian Aboriginal speech variety, was published by the Australian Institute of Aboriginal Studies, and his PhD thesis *Grammatical Form and Grammatical Meaning* by North-Holland.

Since 1974, he has been teaching courses in sociolinguistics at Monash University where he is Associate Professor in the Department of Linguistics. In that year, too, he commenced research, with support from the Australian Research Grants Committee, on the English of Singapore and Malaysia and on various other aspects of language use and language policies in those two multilingual nations.

He is joint author of a textbook, *The Social Significance of Speech* (North-Holland: Amsterdam) and *English in Singapore and Malaysia: Status-Features-Functions* (Oxford University Press: Kuala Lumpur) as well as of numerous articles, including over 20 articles and reviews published since 1975 on variation in Singaporean English, speech variety choice in Singapore and Malaysia and language planning and policies in Malaysia.

Millicent Poole (Chapter 16) holds a BA and a BEd from Queensland University, an MA (Honours) from the University of New England and a PhD from La Trobe University, Melbourne. After a period of secondary school teaching in Queensland and New Zealand, she took up a position as research assistant at the University of New England. This was followed by a period as senior tutor, lecturer and senior lecturer at La Trobe University. She is currently Associate Professor in Education at Macquarie University. In 1975 she was a visiting research fellow at Berkeley University, California. From 1977-79 she was the national organizer of Research Training Workshop for the Australian Association of Research in Education (AARE) and was President of the Association in 1979. For the winter semester in 1978 she was a visiting research associate at the University of Oregon, Eugene. Throughout, she has been interested in the language usage and thinking patterns of children and adolescents. She participated in a longitudinal study of creative primary school students and their transition to secondary school; a longitudinal language curriculum programme, 'HOPEG'; and a major study of adolescents' values and attitudes to teachers, schools and curriculum. Her interest in multicultural and cross-cultural research developed through her interest in language, cognition and adolescent transitions. She is the author of over one hundred journal articles and book chapters. Among her major books are *Under 5 in Australia* (with P Edgar and others); *Before School Begins; Social Class and Language Utilization at the Tertiary Level; Mosaic or Melting Pot: Cultural Evolution in Australia* (with P de Lacey); and *Creativity Across the Curriculum.*

Catrin Roberts (Chapter 9) graduated in social and political sciences from the University of Cambridge. Subsequently she was involved in research projects within the Departments of Social Theory and Education at the University College of North Wales, Bangor, before moving to her present post lecturing in sociology at the Manchester University Education Department. Her research interests have focused upon the sociology of language and bilingual education in Wales.

Derrick Sharp (Chapter 3) is a senior lecturer in the Department of Education, University College of Swansea, where he has been since 1962. Previously he taught in secondary schools for some 14 years. Between 1967 and 1977 he directed two Schools Council research and development projects in Wales, the first on 'Attitudes to Welsh and English in the Schools of Wales', the second on 'The Teaching and Learning of English in Wales, 8 to 13'. He has been Chairman of the National Association for the Teaching of English (NATE) and active in the National Congress on Languages in Education (NCLE). His publications include *Language in Bilingual Communities* and *English at School: The Wood and the Trees.* He is Editor of the *Journal of Multilingual and Multicultural Development*, which first appeared in 1980.

J J Smolicz (Chapter 1) is widely recognized for his studies on cultural pluralism and multicultural education and for his development of humanistic sociology as a basis for research. He began his research on ethnic cultures in Australia soon after his appointment to Adelaide University in 1965, and was one of the first to undertake such studies in Australia.

His interest in plurality of cultures arises from his own background. Dr Smolicz was born in Poland and received his primary education in French in Lebanon and his secondary education in the Highlands of Scotland. He studied natural and social sciences, first at Edinburgh and later at Lincoln College, Oxford where he was a Carnegie Research Fellow. He was Chairman of the Department of Education at Adelaide University from 1975 to 1980 and has been Reader in Education since 1972. Dr Smolicz is a fellow of the Academy of the Social Sciences in Australia and of the Australian College of Education. He was a member of the Australian Government Committee on the Teaching of Migrant Languages in Schools from 1974 to 1976. The Curriculum Development Centre in Canberra has recently published his *Culture and Education in a Plural Society.*

Carew Treffgarne (Chapter 12) has been lecturing in the Department of Education in Developing Countries, University of London Institute of Education since January 1978. She is involved in postgraduate courses in educational development and planning, specializing in language policy and language planning and in issues raised by the implementation of language policy in formal and non-formal education.

She has taught English as a foreign language in the Ivory Coast and Britain and has conducted surveys of language teaching across the West African Region for the Africa Educational Trust and the Ford Foundation. Her current research interests are in comparative language policy, and in language use by selected African Governments in the conduct of national and international affairs.

Gajendra Verma (Chapter 15) is currently senior lecturer in the psychology of education at the Postgraduate School of Studies in Research in Education, University of Bradford. He is also director of a research project concerned with the occupational adaptation of ethnic minority adolescents in their early working life. Prior to this project he was responsible for directing three other research projects in the area of race and education.

Dr Verma is author/co-author/co-editor of the following books: *Race and Education Across Cultures* (Heinemann, 1975); *Race, Education and Identity* (Macmillan, 1979); *Personality, Self-esteem and Prejudice* (Saxon House, 1979); *Racial Prejudice, the Individual and Society* (Saxon House, 1979); *Illusion and Reality in Indian Secondary Education* (Gower Publishing, 1980); *The Impact of Innovation* (University of East Anglia Press, 1980); *What is Educational Research?* (Gower Publishing, 1981); *Self-concept, Achievement and Multicultural Education* (Macmillan, 1981); *Problems and Effects of Teaching About Race Relations* (Routledge and Kegan Paul, 1981, forthcoming).

His principal teaching areas are in the psychology of education, curriculum development and curriculum evaluation, and his main research interests include multicultural education, social psychology, educational evaluation and inter-ethnic perception.

Keith Watson (Chapter 6) holds degrees from Edinburgh, London and Reading universities, where he took his doctorate on education in South East Asia. He worked for ten years with the British Council in various countries, including Bangladesh and Thailand. His interest in Chinese education began when he first visited China at the time of the Cultural Revolution; his interest in the education of minority groups stems from his experiences in South East Asia. He has written numerous papers on minority education, community education and education in Asia, and is the author of *Educational Development in Thailand*. Since 1975 he has been a lecturer in comparative education at Reading University.

Doug White (Chapter 19) is a member of the Centre for the Study of Innovation of the School of Education, La Trobe University. He is a student and teacher of the theory and practice of the curriculum. In 1974 he spent six months living on a Central Australian Aboriginal settlement and has maintained contact with people in the area.

Glyn Williams (Chapter 9) was born in Llanberis, Wales. He studied at the University College of Wales, Aberystwyth and the University of California at Berkeley, and has conducted research on a variety of topics in Argentina, Mexico, the USA and Wales. He currently teaches sociology in the Department of Social Theory and Institutions at the University College of North Wales, Bangor, and previously taught in the Department of Sociology at the University of San Francisco. His main research interests at the moment are language reproduction and social reproduction.

Index